PUBLICATIONS OF
THE MANCHESTER CENTRE FOR ANGLO

Volume 8

Edgar, King of the English 959–975

New Interpretations

King Edgar ruled England for a short but significant period in the middle of the tenth century. Two of his four children succeeded him as king and two were to become canonized. He was known to later generations as 'the Pacific' or 'the Peaceable' because his reign was free from external attack and without internal dissension, yet he presided over a period of major social and economic change: early in his rule the growth of monastic power and wealth involved redistribution of much of the country's assets, while the end of his reign saw the creation of England's first national coinage, with firm fiscal control from the centre. He fulfilled King Alfred's dream of the West Saxon royal house ruling the whole of England, and, like his uncle King Æthelstan, he maintained overlordship of the whole of Britain.

Despite his considerable achievements, however, Edgar has been neglected by scholars, partly because his reign has been thought to have passed with little incident. A time for a full reassessment of his achievement is therefore long overdue, which the essays in this volume provide.

Saturday 27th MAY
2023 Ann
Domon
4, A-Mb
hopeped

27/05/2023 Ann Homon

London, British Library, Cotton Vespasian A.viii, fol. 2v

Edgar, King of the English 959–975

New Interpretations

edited by
DONALD SCRAGG

THE BOYDELL PRESS

First published 2008
The Boydell Press, Woodbridge

ISBN 978–1–84383–928–6

The Boydell Press is an imprint of Boydell & Brewer Ltd
PO Box 9, Woodbridge, Suffolk IP12 3DF, UK
and of Boydell & Brewer Inc,
668 Mt Hope Avenue, Rochester, NY 14620, USA
website: www.boydellandbrewer.com

A CIP catalogue record for this book is available
from the British Library

Contents

Part IV: Edgar and the Monastic Revival

Illustrations

Contributors

Lesley Abrams, University of Oxford

Julia Barrow, University of Nottingham

Frederick M. Biggs, University of Connecticut at Storrs

Julia Crick, University of Exeter

Mercedes Salvador-Bello, Universidad de Sevilla

Shashi Jayakumar, Singapore

Catherine E. Karkov, University of Leeds

Simon Keynes, University of Cambridge

C. P. Lewis, Institute of Historical Research, University of London

Hugh Pagan, London

Alexander R. Rumble, University of Manchester

Donald Scragg, University of Manchester

Barbara Yorke, University of Winchester

Preface

The reign of King Edgar is undoubtedly a crucial one in the history of tenth-century England, yet it remains an enigmatic one in many respects because of the paucity of reliable evidence for it. This book takes a fresh look at what evidence there is, and evaluates it in new and significant ways. The origin of the collection of essays that it contains was in presentations to an international conference organized by the Manchester Centre for Anglo-Saxon Studies in April 2005, the latest of an on-going series on Anglo-Saxon kings from Offa to Harthacnut. I am very grateful for help with the administration of this conference by Brian Schneider, and acknowledge a generous grant by the British Academy in its support.

At the Edgar conference, nine of the essays in this book were presented, although they have been extensively rewritten and enlarged for the present purpose. To them three new essays are added, those of Simon Keynes, Chris Lewis and Barbara Yorke, and in addition the valuable conspectus of charters prepared by Simon Keynes which will surely now become the foundation of study for the period. Keynes' wide-ranging essay which opens the book is based on the charter evidence, and is comparable with his seminal study of Edgar's son, *The Diplomas of King Æthelred* (Cambridge, 1980). It seems to me that his review of Edgar's reign will prove just as important and extensively quoted as the latter. The two Keynes pieces are followed by three studies relating to the short but politically obscure period when Edgar ruled north of the Thames while his brother Eadwig concentrated on the south, a full account of the major players of the two reigns by Shashi Jayakumar, a detailed examination of a single charter relating to Chester by Chris Lewis, and a controversial proposal that we view this period as a late example of joint kingship by Fred Biggs. These are followed by four studies of different aspects of Edgar's life and reign. Barbara Yorke's account of women has an important place in this volume for a variety of reasons, most significantly because the status of royal women seems to have changed under Edgar. Dominion over the whole of Britain is another issue of Edgar's reign, given his reported rowing down the Dee by tributary kings, and his style as ruler of 'Albion' in charters is here fully explored by Julia Crick. Because of his earlier rule of Mercia and Northumbria, his relationship with the Danelaw is important too, studied here in depth in a wide-ranging chapter by Lesley Abrams. Finally in this section, because the reform of the coinage in the last years of Edgar's reign has been well documented, Hugh Pagan's essay on monetary matters concentrates on the earlier coin issues. The last section of the book is devoted to what is, in many respects, the most significant development of the reign, the great monastic renewal, significant not least because one result of it is the survival in the reformed monasteries of such records as we have of

Edgar's reign and also those of his sons. Here are essays offering new interpretations of the date of the start of the movement (Barrow), the most famous icon of
the reform, the frontispiece of the New Minster charter (Karkov), reproduced as
the frontispiece to this book, the changing landscape of Winchester (Rumble),
and the *Chronicle* poems about Edgar seen as pro-reform propaganda (Salvador-
Bello). The very limited material available for study of the reign makes it inevi-
table that there is some overlap between chapters, although I hope that any
contradictory views that result will be considered healthy.

   I should like to thank all of the contributors for their work in making this the
most definitive account of the reign of Edgar that has appeared, and to congratu-
late them on the result. I would also like to record my very warm appreciation
to Caroline Palmer for her encouragement and support (especially in dark days
when I thought the book would never be finished), and for her enthusiasm for
the project.

Donald Scragg
Manchester, 2007

Abbreviations

Abing	*Charters of Abingdon Abbey*, ed. S. E. Kelly, 2 pts, AS Charters 7–8 (Oxford, 2000–1)
ANS	*Anglo-Norman Studies*
ASC	*Anglo-Saxon Chronicle* [followed by letters designating versions]
ASE	*Anglo-Saxon England*
Baker, *MS F*	*The Anglo-Saxon Chronicle. A Collaborative Edition. Volume 8, MS F*, ed. P. S. Baker (Cambridge, 2000)
BAR	British Archaeological Reports
Bately, *MS A*	*The Anglo-Saxon Chronicle. A Collaborative Edition. Volume 3, MS A*, ed. J. Bately (Cambridge 1986)
Bath	*Charters of Bath and Wells*, ed. S. E. Kelly, AS Charters 13 (Oxford, 2008)
BCS	W. de G. Birch, *Cartularium Saxonicum*, 3 vols. (London, 1885–93)
BIHR	*Bulletin of the Institute of Historical Research*
BL	London, British Library
Blackwell Encycl.	*The Blackwell Encyclopaedia of Anglo-Saxon England*, ed. Michael Lapidge, John Blair, Simon Keynes and Donald Scragg (Oxford, 1999)
Blair, *Church*	John Blair, *The Church in Anglo-Saxon Society* (Oxford, 2005)
BNJ	*British Numismatic Journal*
BT(S)	Joseph Bosworth and T. Northcote Toller, *An Anglo-Saxon Dictionary* (Oxford, 1882–98); *Supplement* by T. Northcote Toller (Oxford, 1921), *Enlarged Addenda and Corrigenda* by Alistair Campbell (Oxford, 1972).
Burt	*Charters of Burton Abbey*, ed. P. H. Sawyer, AS Charters 2 (Oxford, 1979)
Campbell, *Æthelweard*	*The Chronicle of Æthelweard*, ed. A. Campbell (London, 1962)
CantCC	*Charters of Christ Church, Canterbury*, ed. N. Brooks and S. E. Kelly, 3 pts, AS Charters (Oxford, forthcoming)
CantStA	*Charters of St Augustine's Abbey, Canterbury*, ed. S. E. Kelly, AS Charters 4 (Oxford, 1995)
CCSL	Corpus Christianorum, Series Latina (Turnhout, 1953–)
Councils & Synods	*Councils & Synods with Other Documents relating to the English Church*, I, *A.D. 871–1204*, ed. D. Whitelock, M. Brett, and C. N. L. Brooke (Oxford, 1981)

CSASE	Cambridge Studies in Anglo-Saxon England
CTCE	C. E. Blunt, B. H. I. H. Stewart and C. S. S. Lyon, *Coinage in Tenth-Century England from Edward the Elder to Edgar's Reform* (Oxford, 1989)
Cubbin, *MS D*	*The Anglo-Saxon Chronicle. A Collaborative Edition. Volume 6, MS D*, ed. G. P. Cubbin (Cambridge, 1996)
DOE	*Dictionary of Old English*, ed. A. Cameron *et al.* (Toronto, 1986–)
Earle and Plummer	*Two of the Saxon Chronicles Parallel*, ed. Charles Plummer on the basis of an edition by John Earle, 2 vols. (Oxford, 1892–9)
EEMF	Early English Manuscripts in Facsimile
EETS	Early English Text Society
	os original series
EHD	*English Historical Documents c. 500–1042*, ed. D. Whitelock, 2nd ed. (London, 1996)
EME	*Early Medieval Europe*
EPNS	English Place-Name Society
EPNSJ	*English Place-Name Society Journal*
FS	*Frühmittelalterliche Studien*
Hamilton, *Gesta*	*Gesta Pontificum Anglorum*, ed. N. E. S. A. Hamilton, RS (London, 1870)
HBS	Henry Bradshaw Society
HSJ	*Haskins Society Journal*
Irvine, *MS E*	*The Anglo-Saxon Chronicle. A Collaborative Edition. Volume 7, MS E*, ed. S. Irvine (Cambridge, 2004)
JEGP	*Journal of English and Germanic Philology*
Jnl Brit. Stud.	*Journal of British Studies*
JW, *Chronicon*	*The Chronicle of John of Worcester*, ed. R. R. Darlington and Patrick McGurk, 2 vols. to date (Oxford, 1995–8)
KCD	J. M. Kemble, *Codex Diplomaticus Ævi Saxonici*, 6 vols. (London, 1839–48)
Keynes, *Attestations*	Simon Keynes, *An Atlas of Attestations in Anglo-Saxon Charters c. 670–1066*, ASNC Guides, Texts, and Studies 5 (Cambridge, 2002)
Keynes, *Diplomas*	S. Keynes, *The Diplomas of King Æthelred "the Unready", 978–1016: A Study in their Use as Historical Evidence* (Cambridge, 1980)
Lapidge and Winterbottom, *WulfstW*	*Wulfstan of Winchester, The Life of St Æthelwold*, ed. Michael Lapidge and Michael Winterbottom, OMT (Oxford, 1991)
LE	*Liber Eliensis*, ed. E. O. Blake, Camden Society 3rd ser. 92 (London, 1962)
LS	*Ælfric's Lives of Saints*, ed. Walter W. Skeat, EETS os 76, 82, 94, 114 (London, 1881–1900, repr. in 2 vols. (London, 1966)

Malm	*Charters of Malmesbury Abbey*, ed. S. E. Kelly, AS Charters 11 (Oxford, 2005)
MScand	*Mediaeval Scandinavia*
ODNB	*Oxford Dictionary of National Bibliography*, ed. H. C. G. Matthew and B. Harrison, 60 vols. (Oxford, 2004)
OEN	*Old English Newsletter*
O'Keeffe, *MS C*	*The Anglo-Saxon Chronicle. A Collaborative Edition. Volume 5, MS C*, ed. K. O'Brien O'Keeffe (Cambridge, 2001)
OMT	Oxford Medieval Texts
ON	Old Norse
Pet	*Charters of Peterborough Abbey*, ed. S. E. Kelly, AS Charters 14 (Oxford, 2008)
Raine, *York*	*The Historians of the Church of York and its Archbishops*, ed. J. Raine, 3 vols., RS 71 (London, 1879–94)
RES	*Review of English Studies*
Robertson, *Charters*	*Anglo-Saxon Charters*, ed. and trans. A. J. Robertson (Cambridge, 1939)
Roch	*Charters of Rochester*, ed. A. Campbell, AS Charters 1 (London, 1973)
RS	Rolls Series
Rumble, *Property and Piety*	Alexander R. Rumble, *Property and Piety in Early Medieval Winchester: Documents Relating to the Topography of the Anglo-Saxon and Norman City* (Oxford, 2002) [cited by document]
S	P. H. Sawyer, *Anglo-Saxon Charters: An Annotated List and Bibliography* (London, 1968) [cited by document number]
Sel	*Charters of Selsey*, ed. S. E. Kelly, AS Charters 6 (Oxford, 1998)
Shaft	*Charters of Shaftesbury Abbey*, ed. S. E. Kelly, AS Charters 5 (Oxford, 1995)
Sherb	*Charters of Sherborne*, ed. M. A. O'Donovan, AS Charters 3 (Oxford, 1988)
StAlb	*Charters of St Albans*, ed. J. Crick, AS Charters 12 (Oxford, 2007)
Stenton, *ASE*	Frank Stenton, *Anglo-Saxon England*, 3rd ed. (Oxford, 1971)
Stubbs, *Dunstan*	*Memorials of St Dunstan*, ed. W. Stubbs (London, 1874)
Symons, *RC*	*Regularis Concordia*, ed. and trans. Thomas Symons (London, 1953)
Taylor, *MS B*	*The Anglo-Saxon Chronicle. A Collaborative Edition. Volume 4, MS B*, ed. S. Taylor (Cambridge, 1983)
THSLC	*Transactions of the Historic Society of Lancashire and Cheshire*
TRHS	*Transactions of the Royal Historical Society*

VCH	*Victoria County History* (London, 1900–75; Oxford, 1976–)
Wells	*Charters of Bath and Wells*, ed. S. E. Kelly, AS Charters 13 (Oxford, 2008)
Whitelock, *Wills*	*Anglo-Saxon Wills*, ed. Dorothy Whitelock (Cambridge, 1930)
WinchNM	*Charters of the New Minster, Winchester*, ed. S. Miller, AS Charters 9 (Oxford, 2001)
WM, *Gesta Regum*	Gesta Regum Anglorum. The History of the English Kings, ed. and trans. R. A. B. Mynors, R. M. Thomson and M. Winterbottom, 2 vols. (Oxford, 1998–9)
Yorke, *Æthelwold*	*Bishop Æthelwold: His Career and Influence*, ed. B. Yorke (Woodbridge, 1988)

THE HOUSE OF ALFRED

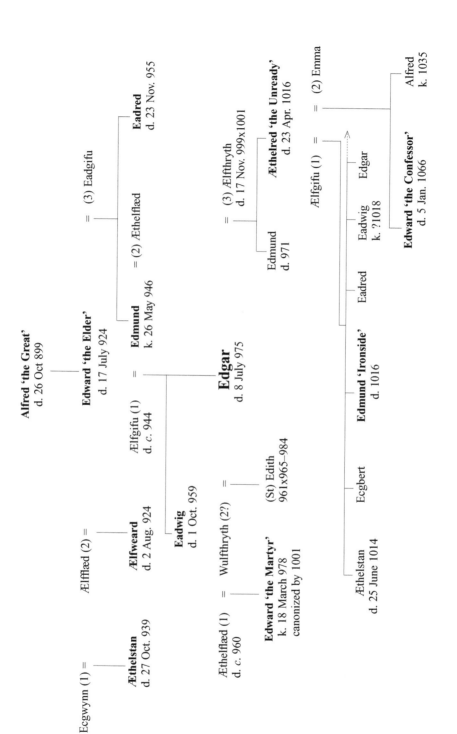

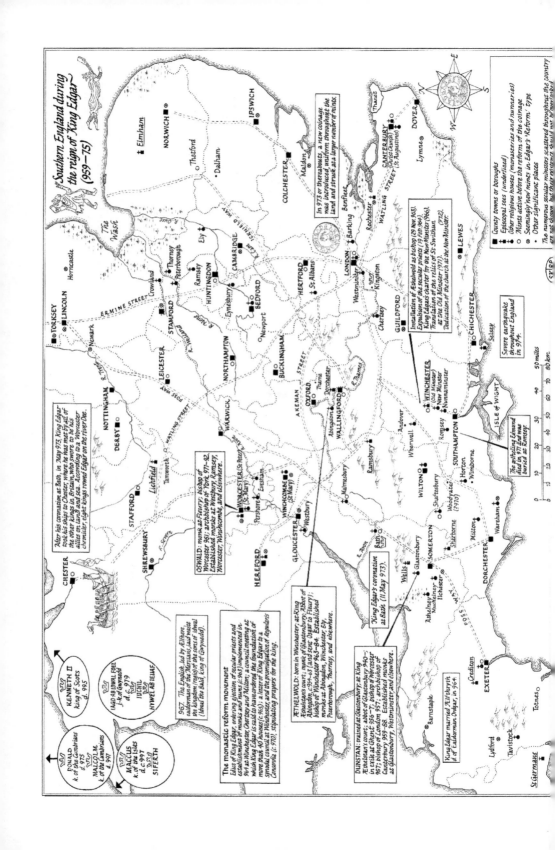

Southern England during the reign of King Edgar (959–75)

I

Documentary Evidence

1

Edgar, *rex admirabilis*

SIMON KEYNES

IN the frontispiece to his grant of privileges for the New Minster, Winchester, drawn up in 966, King Edgar is shown prostrate before Christ (see frontis. to this book);[1] and in an eleventh-century manuscript of the *Regularis Concordia*, perhaps reproducing an earlier image, he is shown flanked by two bishops, presumed to be Dunstan and Æthelwold, lending their combined authority to the text.[2] Both images depict Edgar in close association with the monastic reform movement, and symbolize the particular aspect of his reign which has come to dominate all others.

As always, it is instructive to see how the received tradition took shape. In Bishop Æthelwold's treatise on the Old English Rule of St Benedict, written probably in the 970s if not before, Edgar is praised as one who maintained his dominion (*anweald*) in such great peace and tranquility.[3] For Ealdorman Æthelweard, writing from his position of authority probably in the 980s, Edgar was *rex admirabilis*, *Anglorum insignis rex*, and *monarchus Brittannum nobilis*.[4] As the viking raids of Æthelred's reign intensified, from the 990s into the opening years of the eleventh century, Edgar came to be remembered, in the monastic houses which had been reformed or founded during his reign, as bringer of the stability, peace and good order that had been lost and was now craved;[5] and indeed, it was in this context that he first achieved a form of apotheosis.

---

[1] BL, Cotton Vespasian A. viii: *The Golden Age of Anglo-Saxon Art 966–1066*, ed. J. Backhouse, D. H. Turner and L. Webster (London, 1984), p. 47 (no. 26); see also C. E. Karkov, *The Ruler Portraits of Anglo-Saxon England* (Woodbridge, 2004), pp. 84–118, and 'The Frontispiece to the New Minster Charter and the King's Two Bodies', below, pp. 224–41.

[2] BL, Cotton Tiberius A. iii: *Golden Age*, ed. Backhouse *et al.*, p. 47 (no. 28).

[3] The treatise (appended to a manuscript of the Old English Rule) is best edited, with translation and commentary, in *Councils & Synods*, I.33. For the suggestion that it was written in the 960s, see M. Gretsch, *The Intellectual Foundations of the English Benedictine Reform* (Cambridge, 1999), esp. pp. 230–3 and 240–1.

[4] Campbell, *Æthelweard*, pp. 55–6.

[5] S. Keynes, 'England, 900–1016', *The New Cambridge Medieval History*, III: *c. 900–c. 1024*, ed. T. Reuter (Cambridge, 1999), pp. 456–84, at 479, citing Æthelwold, Lantfred, Wulfstan and Ælfric, all of Winchester, and Byrhtferth of Ramsey. For Ælfric on Edgar, see Ælfric's *Lives of the Saints* (Swithun), in M. Lapidge, *The Cult of St Swithun*, Winchester Studies 4.ii (Oxford, 2003), pp. 590–609, at 606–7.

Perhaps significantly, there is little to this effect in the earliest *Life* of St Dunstan, which has so little to say of Dunstan himself after his appointment to the see of Canterbury in 959, and little for that matter to say of Edgar as king of the English.[6] Wulfstan of Winchester, on the other hand, and Byrhtferth of Ramsey, were writing in the late 990s from two of the power-houses of the monastic reform movement, and represent the view of Edgar which by then had formed among those who owed so much to what had been achieved during his reign. In Wulfstan's *Life* of St Æthelwold, the superlatives are simply heaped upon the king: glorious, distinguished, most merciful, most powerful, unconquered, most blessed, and celebrated.[7] In Byrhtferth's *Life* of St Oswald, Edgar is represented, rather more strikingly, as one who had suppressed all of his enemies, who instilled fear in all those subject to his authority, and who could be described in the report of his death as 'glory of leaders and ruler of the whole of Albion' (*decus ducum et totius Albionis imperator*), who presided over 'a time of joy' (*tempus letitie*) since in his days all remained peaceful (*quod in eius tempore pacifice stabat*).[8] Put another way, Wulfstan, archbishop of York, looked back to Edgar's reign, from a vantage-point in 1014, as a period since when 'Christ's laws have waned and the king's laws dwindled'.[9]

It was a necessary part of the rhetoric of the Norman Conquest that the English had *deserved* to be punished and conquered in 1066, for their manifold sins. Yet there was much in their past that commanded respect, and that needed to be preserved; so attention came to be focussed on the kings of the West Saxon line who could be represented as builders of the polity taken over by the Normans. In the late eleventh and early twelfth centuries, tales of King Edgar formed around his associations with Æthelflæd, Wulfthryth, Ælfthryth, and

---

6   For B.'s *Vita S. Dunstani*, see Stubbs, *Dunstan*, pp. 3–52, which will be superseded in due course by *The Early Lives of St Dunstan*, ed. M. Lapidge and M. Winterbottom (forthcoming); excerpts in *EHD*, pp. 897–903 (no. 234). See also M. Lapidge, 'B. and the *Vita S. Dunstani*', *St Dunstan: His Life, Times and Cult*, ed. N. Ramsay *et al.* (Woodbridge, 1992), pp. 247–59. For B.'s account of the council of 'Bradford', see below, p. 8.

7   *Wulfstan of Winchester: Life of St Æthelwold*, in Lapidge and Winterbottom, *WulfstW*, chs. 13, 16 and 25.

8   For Byrhtferth's *Vita S. Oswaldi*, see Raine, *York*, I.399–475, which will be superseded by *Byrhtferth of Ramsey: The Lives of Oswald and Ecgwine*, ed. M. Lapidge (forthcoming); excerpts in *EHD*, pp. 911–17 (no. 236). I am greatly indebted to Professor Lapidge for access to his edition in advance of its publication. See also M. Lapidge, 'Byrhtferth and Oswald', *St Oswald of Worcester: Life and Influence*, ed. N. Brooks and C. Cubitt (London, 1996), pp. 64–83. For Byrhtferth on Edgar, see *Vita S. Oswaldi* (BR, *VSO*), esp. iii.10, iv.3–4 and iv.17 (Raine, *York*, pp. 425–6, 434–5 and 448); in much the same vein, see also Byrhtferth's *Vita S. Ecgwini*, iv.11. The peace was soon disturbed, first by the disputed succession and then by viking raids: BR, *VSO* iv.17 and v.4 (*ibid.*, pp. 448 and 455). For the association between Edgar and peace, in the early eleventh century, see also Adalard, *Epistola ... de Vita S. Dunstani*, *lectio* iii (Stubbs, *Dunstan*, p. 56). The style *rex ... pacificus* accorded to Edgar in S 761 (*Abing* 107) is probably anachronistic.

9   *VIII Æthelred*, ch. 37: *Die Gesetze der Angelsachsen*, ed. F. Liebermann, 3 vols. (Halle, 1903–16), I.263–8, at 267; *The Laws of the Kings of England from Edmund to Henry I*, ed. A. J. Robertson (Cambridge, 1925), pp. 116–29, at 126; *EHD*, pp. 448–51 (no. 46), at 451.

others; and his reputation as a womanizer led to the development of the story of the seven-year period of penance, which preceded the 'delayed' coronation of 973.[10] Even so, Edgar's renown as a peace-maker, formed during the reign of King Æthelred, ensured that he would be accorded his due as *rex Anglorum pacificus*, and would come to stand for the kingdom of England in its finest hour;[11] and to this end the splendid image was created of King Edgar circumnavigating his realm every summer with his fleet, going from east to west, from west to north, and from north to east.[12] A rather different line is enshrined in Sir Frank Stenton's *Anglo-Saxon England*, first published in 1943. For Stenton, the Scandinavian settlements of the late ninth and tenth centuries had interrupted the march towards the political unification of England, begun during the reign of King Offa; and in his view the reign of Edgar was seen not as a final stage in a process of political development which took place in the tenth century, but as the beginning of the 'decline of the Old English monarchy', which ended when the Normans imposed order and uniformity from above.[13] It was, however, a sign of Edgar's 'competence' as a ruler that his reign was 'singularly devoid of recorded incident'.[14]

The 'Kingdom of The English'

The political developments which took place during the first half of the tenth century, and onwards into the early 950s, form an essential part of the background to Edgar's reign. The Alfredian 'kingdom of the Anglo-Saxons' was first extended by Alfred's son, Edward the Elder,[15] and then transformed by Alfred's

[10] Osbern of Canterbury, *Vita S. Dunstani*, ch. 35 (Stubbs, *Dunstan*, pp. 111–12); and Eadmer of Canterbury, *Vita S. Dunstani*, chs. 56–8 (*Eadmer of Canterbury: Lives and Miracles of Saints Oda, Dunstan, and Oswald*, ed. A. J. Turner and B. J. Muir (Oxford, 2006), pp. 44–159, at 134–45).

[11] *William of Malmesbury, 'Gesta Regum Anglorum', The History of the English Kings*, I, ed. R. A. B. Mynors, R. M. Thomson and M. Winterbottom (Oxford, 1998), esp. pp. 240 and 262; *The Chronicle of John of Worcester*, II: *the Annals from 450 to 1066*, ed. R. R. Darlington and P. McGurk (Oxford, 1995), p. 416, etc.; *Henry, Archdeacon of Huntingdon: Historia Anglorum*, ed. D. Greenway (Oxford, 1996), pp. 318–20. See also P. Wormald, *The Making of English Law: King Alfred to the Twelfth Century*, I: *Legislation and its Limits* (Oxford, 1999), pp. 135–7, and S. Jayakumar, 'Some Reflections on the "Foreign Policies" of Edgar "the Peaceable"', *Haskins Society Journal* 10 (2002), 17–37, at 17.

[12] WM, *Gesta Regum* ii.156 (ed. Mynors *et al.*, p. 256), and JW, *Chronicon*, s.a. 975 (ed. Darlington and McGurk, pp. 424–6). Agreement of this kind between WM and JW indicates their dependence on a common source, probably a Latin chronicle compiled at Worcester in the late eleventh or early twelfth century.

[13] Stenton, *ASE*, pp. 367–72; cf. S. Keynes, 'Anglo-Saxon History after *"Anglo-Saxon England"'*, *Stenton's 'Anglo-Saxon England' Fifty Years On*, ed. D. Matthews, Reading Historical Studies 1 (Reading, 1994), pp. 83–110, at 93 and 105–6.

[14] Stenton, *ASE*, p. 368; see also E. John, 'The Age of Edgar', *The Anglo-Saxons*, ed. J. Campbell (Oxford, 1982), pp. 160–89, at 188–9.

[15] S. Keynes, 'King Alfred and the Mercians', *Kings, Currency and Alliances: History and Coinage of Southern England in the Ninth Century*, ed. M. A. S. Blackburn and D.

grandson Æthelstan into the 'kingdom of the English'.[16] After Æthelstan's death, his half-brothers Edmund and Eadred were necessarily preoccupied with the re-establishment and consolidation of their power over the Scandinavian kingdom of York. In 954 the Northumbrians seem to have decided to accept the rule of the southern English king, enabling Eadred to achieve his purpose; at which point the 'kingdom of the English' might have seemed secure. Eadred himself, however, was unwell, and on his death in 955 the responsibilities of royal office passed to the next generation, represented in the first instance by Eadwig, son of Edmund, soon joined by his younger brother Edgar. Although the evidence needs to be set out in detail, and approached with all due circumspection, the royal styles employed in charters of the period convey some impression of how these changes were regarded by those who were part and even at the centre of the political order of the day.[17] At the outset of Æthelstan's reign we encounter the Alfredian kingship 'of the Anglo-Saxons'; but this gives way (after 927) to Æthelstan's kingship 'of the English', with extension (from 931) to kingship 'of the whole of Britain', or (more rarely) 'of the whole of Albion'.[18] Not inappro-priately, given the political developments in the aftermath of Æthelstan's death, the styles employed in charters of his successors Edmund and Eadred seem to reflect greater restraint, even uncertainty about the outcome. The preferred usage in 'mainline' charters was clearly king 'of the English', with extension to include unspecified peoples round about;[19] but other views were always avail-able. The draftsmen of the so-called 'alliterative' charters, in the 940s, opted for

N. Dumville (Woodbridge, 1998), pp. 1–45, at 34–9, and 'Edward, King of the Anglo-Saxons', *Edward the Elder 899–924*, ed. N. J. Higham and D. H. Hill (London, 2001), pp. 40–66, at 57–62.

[16] For contemporary perceptions of kingship, as represented in royal charters, see Keynes, 'England 900–1016', pp. 459–74, and *The Charters of King Æthelstan (924–39) and the Kingdom of the English*, Toller Memorial Lecture 2001 (forthcoming); see also John, 'The Age of Edgar', p. 176. For a rather different view of political development, attaching par-ticular significance to the word *Angelcynn* (standard usage already in the ninth century), see S. Foot, 'The Historiography of the Anglo-Saxon "Nation-State"', *Power and the Nation*, ed. L. Scales and O. Zimmer (Cambridge, 2005), pp. 125–42, at 129.

[17] T. Reuter, 'The Making of England and Germany, 850–1050: Points of Comparison and Difference' (1998), in his *Medieval Polities and Modern Mentalities*, ed. J. L. Nelson (Cambridge, 2006), pp. 284–99, at 296–8, sets the use of royal styles in a useful context, but his account of the evidence from Anglo-Saxon England is potentially misleading. See also H. Kleinschmidt, 'Die Titulaturen englischer Könige im 10. und 11. Jahrhundert', *Intitulatio III: Lateinische Herrschertitel und Herrschertitulaturen vom 7. bis zum 13. Jahrhundert*, ed. H. Wolfram and A. Scharer, Mitteilungen des Instituts für österreichische Geschichtsforschung, Ergänzungsband 29 (1988), pp. 75–129, and H. Kleinschmidt, *Un-tersuchungen über das englische Königtum im 10. Jahrhundert*, Göttinger Bausteine zur Geschichtswissenschaft 49 (1979).

[18] The use of 'Albion' was a natural extension of the use of 'Britain', perhaps suggested by the opening sentence of Bede's *Historia ecclesiastica gentis Anglorum*. For further discus-sion, see Julia Crick, 'Edgar, Albion and Insular Dominion', below, pp. 158–70.

[19] This extension, so characteristic of the charters of Edmund and Eadred, seems to have originated in Æthelstan's charters of the late 930s; see Keynes, *Charters of King Æthel-stan*.

a particularly complex form of political analysis;[20] and the draftsman of the so-called 'Dunstan B' charters, in the early 950s, decided to run with the kingship 'of Albion';[21] and only in 955, following the political reunification of the previous year, did the draftsman of the 'alliterative' charters style Eadred 'king of the whole of Britain'. In charters issued in the name of King Eadwig, up to the division of the kingdom in 957, we find him called king 'of the Anglo-Saxons', 'of the English', 'of Albion', and 'of the whole of Britain', suggesting that the draftsmen felt less restrained than before and were beginning to reach out again for a sense of the king's and through him of their own political identity, or perhaps that there were more of them at work than before.[22] However, there were still problems within the former 'West Saxon' or 'Anglo-Saxon' but now more properly 'English' polity, which needed to be confronted and if possible resolved. One such problem was the attitude of politically active 'Mercians' to their incorporation in a unified kingdom of the English; another was the notion that monarchy was necessarily something more desirable than joint-rule, or division of the kingdom, should there happen to be more than one person eligible for royal office; and a third was the natural rivalries and competing interests which were bound to arise between particular families or among particular groups.

In 957 the kingdom of the English was divided along the line of the river Thames between Eadwig (to the south) and Edgar (to the north).[23] The clearest view of this new polity emerges from examination of the surviving corpus of charters of the period 957–9, some issued in the name of King Eadwig and others in the name of King Edgar.[24] The charter by which Eadwig granted land at Ely to Archbishop Oda, dated 9 May 957, and still extant in its original

---

[20] For the 'alliterative' charters, see S. Keynes, 'Koenwald', *Blackwell Encycl.*, pp. 273–5; Keynes, *Attestations*, table XXVIII; and S. Keynes, 'The Vikings in England, *c.* 790–1016', *The Oxford Illustrated History of the Vikings*, ed. P. Sawyer (Oxford, 1997), pp. 48–82, at 70–3.

[21] For the 'Dunstan B' charters, see Keynes, *Attestations*, table XXIX, and S. Keynes, 'The "Dunstan B" Charters', *ASE* 23 (1994), 165–93.

[22] For a basic classification of the charters issued in the name of King Eadwig in 956, see Keynes, *Diplomas*, pp. 48–69. For observations on Eadwig's reign, see Keynes, 'England 900–1016', pp. 474–6, and S. Keynes, 'Eadwig', *ODNB*, xvii.539–42; cf. Keynes, *Diplomas*, p. 62, n. 109. See also B. Yorke, 'Æthelwold and the Politics of the Tenth Century', Yorke, *Æthelwold*, pp. 65–88, at 74–9, and C. Wickham, *Problems in Doing Comparative History*, Reuter Lecture 2004 (Southampton, 2005), pp. 22–8.

[23] For the division of the kingdom in 957, see Stenton, *ASE*, pp. 366–7; C. R. Hart, 'Æthelstan "Half-King" and his Family', *ASE* 2 (1973), 115–44, repr. in his *The Danelaw* (London, 1992), pp. 569–604, at 582–5; N. Banton, 'Ealdormen and Earls in England from the Reign of King Alfred to the Reign of King Æthelred II' (unpubl. D.Phil. thesis, Univ. of Oxford, 1981), pp. 132–8 and 158; A. Williams, '*Princeps Merciorum Gentis*: The Family, Career and Connections of Ælfhere, Ealdorman of Mercia', *ASE* 10 (1982), 143–72, at 157; N. Brooks, 'The Career of St Dunstan' (1992), in his *Anglo-Saxon Myths: State and Church 400–1066* (London, 2000), pp. 154–80, at 175–7; Keynes, 'England 900–1016', pp. 477–9, and 'Eadwig'. For the view that the division was planned in the last years of Eadred's reign, and not fully implemented until 957, see F. M. Biggs, 'Edgar's Path to the Throne', below, pp. 124–39.

[24] Keynes, *Attestations*, table LII.

single-sheet form, can be seen from its witness-list to have been issued *before* the kingdom was divided in that year.[25] Some other charters in Eadwig's name, dated 957, and all of his charters dated 958 and 959, are seen in the same way to have been issued *after* the kingdom was divided. Significantly, if perhaps not unexpectedly, bishops and ealdormen whose areas of responsibility lay south of the river Thames continued to attend meetings of the *witan* convened by King Eadwig, but those whose areas of responsibility lay north of the Thames, or in East Anglia, disappear from view; interestingly, Eadwig seems also to have retained the services of almost all of the thegns who had attested his charters before the division.[26] It is especially interesting to note that whereas before the division the draftsmen of Eadwig's charters had deployed royal styles with almost gay abandon, after the division they seem in general to have restricted themselves to kingship 'of the English'. It is as if they had sobered up, or as if they were taking stock; yet kingship 'of the English' might still imply authority of some kind *beyond* the river Thames. Although no charters of King Edgar have survived from the year 957, his reign as 'king of the Mercians' (with East Anglia and Northumbria) is well represented by charters issued in 958–9.[27] Sooner or later Edgar invited Dunstan to return from exile to England, apparently having benefited from his guidance in the past; and, at a 'great assembly of council-lors' (*magnus sapientium conventus*) convened at an unidentified *Bradanford* ('Bradford', perhaps Bradford-on-Avon), Dunstan was duly ordained a bishop [in 957/8], and began to instruct Edgar in royal usage.[28] Edgar is said in one vernacular charter of the period to have been given control of all the royal pre-rogatives (*anweald ... ealra cynerihta*);[29] and he can be seen from his charters to have disposed of land and privileges across the greater part of his kingdom (the west midlands, the east midlands, Essex, and Yorkshire). In so doing, he acted independently, without reference to King Eadwig; and it is clear that his assem-blies were attended by the appropriate complements of bishops and ealdormen,

---

25 S 646 (BCS 1347): *Facsimiles of Anglo-Saxon Charters*, ed. S. Keynes (Oxford, 1991), no. 5.
26 The one thegn who can be seen to have transferred from Eadwig's to Edgar's court in 957 was Ælfwine, whose brother Ælfhere had been ealdorman of Mercia since 956, and whose brother Ælfheah was appointed an ealdorman in Eadwig's kingdom in 959; see further below, p. 33.
27 Simon Keynes, 'A Conspectus of the Charters of King Edgar, 957–75', below, pp. 60–80, at 64–5; see also below, pp. 13–14.
28 B, *VSD*, ch. 25 (Stubbs, *Dunstan*, pp. 36–7; *Councils & Synods*, pp. 86–8 (no. 24); *EHD*, p. 902). The meeting in question is placed after the death of King Eadwig; but charters show clearly that Dunstan was already a bishop in 958 (Keynes, *Attestations*, table LIV). The author of the *Vita S. Dunstani* suggests that Dunstan was initially a bishop without portfolio (cf. S 675, below, n. 53), and that it was not until after the death of Coenwald, bishop of Worcester, on 28 June ?958, that Edgar appointed him bishop of Worcester in Coenwald's place, and then bishop of London as well, in succession to Byrhthelm; see Brooks, 'Career of St Dunstan', pp. 177–8, and Keynes, 'The "Dunstan B" Charters', p. 191 (reading London for Worcester, and *vice versa*).
29 S 1447 (Robertson, *Charters*, no. 44, from Westminster), extant in its original single-sheet form.

with representation from all parts of his kingdom, including East Anglia. It is an impressive record; yet it is all the more significant, therefore, that Edgar seems not to have been empowered to issue a coinage in his own name. Indeed, it would appear that coins in the name of King Eadwig continued to be minted *north* of the Thames in the period 957–9;[30] and although Edgar might have taken a share of the profits, the implication must be that Eadwig retained some form of overall authority or control.

The Reign of King Edgar (959–75)

Following the death of King Eadwig, on 1 October 959, and his burial at the New Minster, Winchester, Edgar succeeded to the now re-united Kingdom of the English. It is not possible to construct a coherent narrative of Edgar's reign from the disjointed scraps of information provided in the available versions of the *ASC*,[31] even when supplemented by the *Lives* of Dunstan, Æthelwold and Oswald; and the perception of Edgar formulated by the monks of Winchester and Ramsey in the late tenth century, subsequently absorbed in the early twelfth century into the mainstream of English historical tradition, still exerts its influence. Of course it is not the case, however, that little else apart from monastic reform took place in Edgar's reign, or indeed that absence of incident should necessarily be interpreted as evidence of competence. Some reigns were characterized by sequences of events of a kind which ensured coverage in the available 'literary' sources, but others were marked more significantly by developments which unfolded beneath the surface of recorded incident. So, while the 'literary' sources available for Edgar's reign fail to provide a basis for anything approximating to a chronological framework, there are various themes around which it is possible to organize an approach to the period as a whole.[32]

---

[30] K. Jonsson, *The New Era: The Reformation of the Late Anglo-Saxon Coinage* (Stockholm, 1987), pp. 68–70; *CTCE*, pp. 272–80; K. Jonsson, 'The Pre-Reform Coinage of Edgar – the Legacy of the Anglo-Saxon Kingdoms', *Coinage and History in the North Sea World, c. A.D. 500–1250: Essays in Honour of Marion Archibald*, ed. B. Cook and G. Williams (Leiden, 2006), pp. 325–46, at 330–1; see also Hugh Pagan, 'The Pre-Reform Coinage of Edgar', below, pp. 192–207.

[31] A contemporary chronicler at Winchester registered some events for the years 962–4 (including the annal on the ejection of priests from the Old and New Minsters, and from Chertsey and Milton); a chronicler in the north of England provided some significant information for the years 965–9; a chronicler probably at Abingdon reported on the death of Oscetel, archbishop of York, in 971, and on his burial at Bedford; and a source which tended to focus on events of 'national' importance provided records of the death of the ætheling Edmund in 971, of the coronation of King Edgar in 973, and of the king's death in 975.

[32] For a recent survey of Edgar's reign, see A. Williams, 'Edgar', *ODNB*, xvii.698–703, with further references.

Royal government

First and foremost must be an understanding of Edgar's rule as king of the English, based squarely on the evidence of law-codes, charters and coins. Edgar was associated in the minds of his contemporaries with peace and order, perhaps in contrast with what had gone before, and with what came after, yet perhaps also because the routine business of royal government was conducted during his reign in a way that generated a sense of stability and control. The basic context for the display and exercise of royal power remained that of itinerant kingship.[33] The king and his entourage (presumably including the officials of the royal household) moved from one royal estate or town to another; and from time to time, perhaps on four or five occasions during the course of each year, major assemblies were convened by prior arrangement at particular places, often coinciding with important festivals in the Christian calendar (Christmas, Easter, Pentecost [Whitsunday], Michaelmas). It is unfortunate that more is not known of the way in which proceedings were conducted on such occasions, and of the range of business brought forward. We may presume, however, that the business would have included discussion of matters pertaining to the maintenance of order in society, the welfare of the church, the control of commerce, and the organisation of the coinage, as well as the formal ratification of grants of land and privileges, and the settlement of particular disputes; but of course we should not forget that these must also have been prime occasions for gossiping, networking, politicing and plotting, and much else besides.[34]

The most important products of the routine processes of royal government were the codes of law promulgated in the king's name. Lantfred of Winchester, writing *c.* 975, describes how in Edgar's reign 'a law of great severity was promulgated throughout the kingdom of the English', whereby any thief or robber should be comprehensively mutilated;[35] which might help to account for Edgar's reputation as one who brought peace and order to his kingdom.[36] Unfortunately, the corpus of Edgar's surviving legislation is small, and it is not even known when the extant codes were promulgated. The law-code traditionally designated 'I Edgar' is now known more appropriately as the 'Hundred Ordinance', since it has no explicit or proven association with King Edgar.[37] It is the case, however,

---

[33] See, for the sake of comparison, J. W. Bernhardt, *Itinerant Kingship and Royal Monasteries in Early Medieval Germany, c.936–1075* (Cambridge, 1993), and Reuter, 'Making of England and Germany', pp. 295–7.

[34] S. Keynes, 'The Witan and the Written Word', *Kingship and Power in Anglo-Saxon England*, ed. G. R. Owen-Crocker (Woodbridge, forthcoming).

[35] Lantfred of Winchester, *Translatio et miracula S. Swithuni*, ch. 26 (*Cult of St Swithun*, ed. Lapidge, pp. 310–12). The story was retold, in the 990s, by Wulfstan of Winchester, *Narratio metrica de S. Swithuno*, ch. 9 (*Cult of St Swithun*, ed. Lapidge, p. 514), with the addition of a passage (lines 453–65) reflecting an attitude to this law a generation later.

[36] On the incidence of 'crime' in Edgar's reign, and its punishment, see P. Wormald, 'A Handlist of Anglo-Saxon Lawsuits' (1988), *Legal Culture in the Early Medieval West: Law as Text, Image and Experience* (London, 1999), pp. 253–87, at 267 and 285.

[37] *Gesetze*, ed. Liebermann, I.192–5; *Laws*, ed. Robertson, pp. 16–19; *EHD*, pp. 429–30 (no. 39); see also Wormald, *Making of English Law*, pp. 378–9. The designation 'I Edgar'

that the draftsman refers back to King Edmund, and that the code would fit well in the context of Edgar's legislation; indeed, it may represent an early stage in a process by which Edgar imposed order on less formal or less uniform arrangements which had emerged during the reigns of his predecessors.[38] The bipartite code known as 'II–III Edgar' reflects the king's concern to protect the interests of all of 'God's churches', to ensure that the rule of law was enforced among his people, and that basic commercial controls were in place (coinage, weights and measurements, and the price of wool);[39] yet all that can be said of the circumstances of its production depends on the assumption that it represents the legislation promulgated at Andover, in Hampshire, mentioned in 'IV Edgar'. *IV Edgar* was itself promulgated as a remedy for 'the sudden pestilence' (*fǣrcwealme*) which afflicted the people throughout his dominion.[40] The meeting at which the code was issued was held at *Wihtbordesstane* (unidentified); but was this in or soon after 962, when, according to one version of the *ASC*, 'there was a very great mortality' (*micel mancwealm*), or was it on the occasion of an otherwise unrecorded plague or pestilence, some time later in the reign, as might be suggested by the arrangements made for its copying and distribution?[41] It matters for general historical purposes, because *IV Edgar* is a text in which the king makes interesting references to the 'Danes', to the northern parts of his kingdom, and to the inclusion of 'Britons' among his people. If *IV Edgar* is so 'early', that would be significant in itself, and would imply that *II–III Edgar* were even earlier. If *IV Edgar* is 'late', the question would arise whether the link between them draws *II–III Edgar* forwards, or whether the only extant

---

originated with the edition of the code in *Die Gesetze der Angelsachsen*, ed. R. Schmidt (Leipzig, 1832), 2nd ed. (Leipzig, 1858), pp. 182–5.

[38] A key issue for understanding of royal government in the tenth century, and the emergence of a unified kingdom, is by what process or stages was a shire system, long established in Wessex, extended into midland England (between the Thames and the Humber). See S. Keynes, 'Shire', *Blackwell Encycl.*, pp. 420–2, with references, and A. Reynolds, *Later Anglo-Saxon England: Life & Landscape* (Stroud, 1999), pp. 65–110.

[39] *Gesetze*, ed. Liebermann, I.194–207; *Laws*, ed. Robertson, pp. 20–9; *EHD*, pp. 431–3 (no. 40). For further discussion, see Wormald, *Making of English Law*, pp. 313–17 and 441.

[40] *Gesetze*, ed. Liebermann, I.206–15; *Laws*, ed. Robertson, pp. 28–39; *EHD*, pp. 434–7 (no. 41). For further discussion, see Wormald, *Making of English Law*, pp. 317–20 and 441–2 (on its 'imperial overtones').

[41] The reference in *IV Edg.* 15 to 'Earl Oslac', evidently in control of an earldom in northern England, is not necessarily significant, since it is possible that he was regarded as an earl in the north from 963 onwards (S. Keynes, 'The Additions in Old English', *The York Gospels*, ed. N. Barker (London, 1986), pp. 81–99, at 86–7). The crucial factor is therefore the statement that copies of the code were to be made and sent 'both to Ealdorman Ælfhere and to Ealdorman Æthelwine', who were to distribute them in all directions (*IV Edg.* 15.1), as if they were the officials principally responsible. Ælfhere held first place among the king's ealdorman throughout the reign; but the reference to Æthelwine, ealdorman of East Anglia from 962, to the exclusion of others, seems to reflect the position in 970–5 when Æthelwine was consistently second in the hierarchy (Keynes, *Attestations*, table LVI). It is possible, however, that in this form the code was only intended for circulation in the parts of the country for which these two ealdormen were responsible.

acts of Edgar's legislation were in fact several years apart. Whatever the case, an instructive contrast can be drawn between *II–III Edgar*, as a stately display of royal power, and *IV Edgar*, as a response of royal government in a moment of crisis.

The evidence of King Edgar's legislation is complemented by the evidence of his charters. The charters are perhaps not as readily accessible as the law-codes, for the very good reason that it is difficult to identify an authentic core of texts amidst all the noise and distraction generated by later fabrications; and with this in mind an attempt has been made in the second chapter of this book to reduce the corpus to a semblance of order.[42] It is clear that the extant texts represent the work or output of a number of different agencies of production, using the term 'agency' (in preference to 'draftsman' or 'scribe') so as not to privilege one aspect of production over another, and so as not to deny the possibility than an agency might comprise more than one person.[43] Much, however, depends on the position one might choose to adopt in the debate about the arrangements which existed for the production of charters in the tenth century. The matter proceeds at one level from close study of the script and other physical features of those charters preserved in their original single-sheet form, and at another level from detailed analysis of the formulation of the charters, with a view to establishing the origin, development and subsequent use of each component part (pictorial and verbal invocation, proem, dispositive section, sanction, boundary-clause, dating-clause, witness-list, and endorsement). It also involves consideration of the circumstances in which necessary arrangements were made for the authorization of a particular grant, for the making of any payment to the king by the prospective beneficiary, for the drawing up and handing over of the charter to the beneficiary himself (or herself), perhaps on the occasion of a royal assembly, and for the announcement of the grant at a meeting of a local assembly. At every stage, difficult judgements have to be made about the authenticity of particular texts, and there are bound to be differences of opinion in all matters of interpretation. It may be that the production of charters was 'decentralized', and that different 'local' agencies were acting independently of each other, each perhaps representing a different religious house. It may be that a small group of office-holders in the king's household (deacons, clerks, and priests, perhaps in association with some men not in holy orders) worked together as members of a royal writing office, producing the charters required for the purposes of a particular royal assembly. It may be that arrangements were flexible enough to allow a *combination* of such agencies to act when the whim, need or opportunity

---

42 Keynes, 'Conspectus', below, pp. 60–80.
43 The act of drafting, which might involve a process of selection or adaptation of formulas found in earlier charters, or a process of developing and using a more personal repertoire, would not necessarily have gone hand-in-hand with the act of writing; but a close association between the two activities is suggested by evidence from Æthelstan's reign (Keynes, *Charters of King Æthelstan*) and from Edgar's (Keynes, *Diplomas*, pp. 18 and 71–6, and below, pp. 14–18). The likelihood is, however, that the composition of an agency would change; and that if at certain times one man was dominant, at other times there might be a need for more manpower, producing greater variety of formulation and script.

arose, perhaps determined by the particular circumstances of a transaction, or by circumstances which prevailed at a particular meeting of the king and his councillors. Only by attempting to distinguish between the work of the several different agencies concealed behind such seemingly formulaic texts can we begin to form an estimation of how Edgar's government worked in practice; and, as we shall see, the matter also has a direct bearing on our understanding of the process of monastic reform.

The charters issued by King Edgar in 958–9, in which he is generally styled *rex Merciorum* ('king of the Mercians'), provide an instructive point of departure. The eight surviving charters issued in 958 can be resolved into two pairs, one set of three, and a singleton, representing an intriguing pattern for such a small and chronologically compact body of material. The first pair comprises a charter granting land in Huntingdonshire to the thegn Ælfheah, and a charter granting land in Nottinghamshire to the bishop of Dorchester.[44] The draftsman employed a royal style derived perhaps unthinkingly from the diplomatic norm;[45] and the inclusion of several earls or thegns with Scandinavian names among the witnesses affords a tantalizing glimpse of representatives of the Anglo-Scandinavian society of the east midlands.[46] The second pair comprises a charter granting land in Cheshire to the church of St Werburg,[47] and a charter granting land in Herefordshire to the thegn Ealhstan.[48] The link between the charters is less immediately obvious than in the case of the first pair; but it depends on the more overtly 'Mercian' nature of the royal styles, on association with the west as opposed to the east midlands, and on shared details of formulation (from the superscription to the distinctive combination of dating clause and formula introducing the witness-list).[49] In the charter for St Werburg's, the king is 'raised to the height of the kingdom of the Mercians', and attests as 'king of the Mercians and of other nations'. In the charter for Ealhstan, he holds 'the monarchy of the whole kingdom of the Mercians'; the land is said to be *in pago Magescætna*, reflecting consciousness of one of the older tribal identities in Mercia; and the king attests as *rex Merciorum et Norðanhymbrorum atque Brettonum* ('king of the Mercians and Northumbrians and of the British'). The set of three comprises charters granting land in Essex to Ealdorman Æthelstan, land in Warwickshire to the thegn Eadwald, and land in Oxfordshire to the thegn Eanwulf.[50] All three belong to the distinctive 'Dunstan B' type, associated in Eadred's reign with Glastonbury abbey;[51] and one would imagine that the use

---

[44] S 674 (*Pet* 13), and S 679 (BCS 1044), from York.

[45] Keynes, *Diplomas*, p. 69.

[46] Lesley Abrams, 'King Edgar and the Men of the Danelaw', below, pp. 171–91.

[47] S 667 (BCS 1041), from St Werburg's, Chester, issued at Penkridge in Staffordshire; see C. P. Lewis, 'Edgar, Chester, and the Kingdom of the Mercians, 957–9', below, pp. 104–23.

[48] S 677 (*Wells* 31), extant in its original single-sheet form.

[49] Keynes, *Diplomas*, p. 69, n. 137.

[50] S 676 (BCS 1037), from the Old Minster, Winchester); S 676a, from ?Coventry; and S 678 (*Abing* 82).

[51] Keynes, 'The "Dunstan B" Charters', pp. 176–7 and 190–1.

of this type for charters of Edgar drawn up in 958 reflects the continued employment of the same agency of production, albeit under circumstances which
remain obscure.[52] The singleton is a grant of land in Oxfordshire to the thegn
Æthelric, which has no obvious connection with the other seven.[53] It is arguable on this basis that the eight extant charters of King Edgar issued in 958
were the work of four agencies of production, each with its distinctive identity;
and the question arises whether these agencies worked independently of each
other, or whether we might imagine that they worked as colleagues in the royal
household. The only surviving charter issued in the name of King Edgar in
959, before the re-unification of the kingdom, is a grant of land in Yorkshire to
a woman called Quen.[54] Appropriately enough, the witness-list includes some
of the earls and thegns from the Anglo-Scandinavian north; yet in terms of its
diplomatic it is again distinctive, showing features which look forward to the
charters produced by one of the best-known draftsmen of the early 960s.[55]

One would expect Edgar's household in the 960s to have included some clerics
who had served him as king of the Mercians (957–9), and some who came into
his service from Eadwig's household when he became king of the English in
959; and no doubt matters would be complicated by Edgar's ever deepening
involvement in the progress of the monastic reform movement.[56] About half of
the surviving charters issued in Edgar's name as king of the English (959–75)
were issued in the first four years or so of his reign, between 1 October 959
and the end of December 963. A significant proportion of these charters can
be shown on a combination of palaeographical and diplomatic grounds to have
been the work of a scribe who has come to be known to modern scholarship as
'Edgar A', instantly recognizable (in charters preserved in their original single-
sheet form) from his characteristically curvaceous chrismons. It would appear
that 'Edgar A' had begun his career as a draftsman of charters while Edgar was
still king of the Mercians, in which case it may be that he had a 'Mercian' background; for two charters issued in 959, one by Edgar as king of the Mercians
and the other by Edgar as king of the English, show features of what would soon

---

52 Perhaps the most likely explanation is that the agency was connected in some way with
    Dunstan himself, who attests the charters as a bishop (of Worcester and/or London), and
    who may have been able to recover some kind of position at Glastonbury. The feature
    which remains difficult to explain is the non-inclusion of Edgar in the witness-list, as if
    he had not been present at the meeting where the grant was made. Earlier charters of the
    type had been issued in the name of King Eadred, apparently in his absence; one can but
    guess what Edgar's apparent absence might signify. See also below, p. 19.
53 S 675 (BCS 1042), from the Old Minster, Winchester. This charter is attested by Coenwald,
    bishop of Worcester, and also by Dunstan.
54 S 681 (*Pet* 14).
55 Keynes, *Diplomas*, pp. 75–6, with reference to the charters of 'Edgar A' (below, p. 15).
    The omission of a figure giving the hidage of the estate is curious, and possibly signifi-
    cant: for some other instances, see *Shaft*, p. 94, and see further below, n. 97.
56 In the *capella* of tenth-century rulers of Germany, writing charters was 'menial' work
    (T. Reuter, 'The "Imperial Church System" of the Ottonian and Salian Rulers: A
    Reconsideration' (1982), in his *Medieval Polities and Modern Mentalities*, ed. Nelson,
    pp. 325–54, at 330); but perhaps not so in Anglo-Saxon England.

become his characteristic formulation.[57] Two of five extant charters from 960, three of about ten charters from 961, and four of about twelve charters from 962 were seemingly produced by 'Edgar A'.[58] There are no fewer than seventeen surviving charters of King Edgar dated 963 (more than for any other single year of his reign), spread across ten archives. At least nine and perhaps as many as thirteen of these charters were issued *before* Abbot Æthelwold's elevation to the see of Winchester, on 29 November; and, of these thirteen charters, eight were produced probably by 'Edgar A'. The remaining four of the seventeen charters dated 963 were issued probably on a single occasion in December of that year, after Æthelwold's elevation to the see of Winchester. 'Edgar A' was probably responsible for the production of three of them, recording grants of land in Yorkshire to Earl Gunner, of land possibly in Oxfordshire to the thegn Wulfnoth, and of land in Sussex to Æthelwold himself, recently consecrated bishop of Winchester.[59] Yet while one senses that 'Edgar A' was entrusted with an increasing workload in the early 960s, clearly it was not the case that he ever operated to the exclusion of other agencies. In 963, one of these 'other' agencies produced Edgar's charter granting land in Berkshire to his *camerarius* Æthelsige;[60] and one produced a charter by which the king booked land in Wiltshire to himself.[61] A third seems to have been entrusted on various occasions in the early 960s with the production of charters for estates in the west country.[62] A fourth, no less interestingly, was the 'Mercian' draftsman who had produced two of the extant charters issued by Edgar in 958, for lands in the west midlands; it

---

[57] Keynes, *Diplomas*, pp. 75–6, with reference to S 681 (*Pet* 14) and to S 680 (BCS 1051), from the Old Minster, Winchester. Kelly (*Abing*, pp. cxix–cxx and 244–5) cites S 607 (*Abing* 57) and S 626 (BCS 920), from Glastonbury, as evidence that elements of the formulation in the two charters of 959 were in use already in 956; but although there is a curious similarity between them, both charters have seriously problematic features when judged in the context of the charters of 956. As a pair, the two charters of 959 constitute far stronger evidence of an early stage in the development of the 'Edgar A' formulation.

[58] For further details, see Keynes, 'Conspectus', below, pp. 65–7.

[59] It is not the case, therefore, that Edgar A's career 'fits very neatly between Edgar's accession and Æthelwold's elevation to the bishopric of Winchester, after which other scribes took over' (*Abing*, I.cxix).

[60] S 713, showing influence from the 'Dunstan B' formulation. For Æthelsige, see further below, p. 35.

[61] S 715. In 964 Edgar again granted land in Wiltshire to himself; see S 727 (BCS 1127), dated 964, from Romsey, perhaps produced by the same agency. King Æthelwulf had booked a large area of land in Devon to himself; see S 298 (BCS 451; *EHD*, no. 88), extant in its original single-sheet form, dated '847', from the Old Minster, Winchester. Essentially, such actions represent the conversion of folkland into bookland.

[62] S 721. This agency is otherwise represented by three charters extant in their original single-sheet form, written by different scribes: S 684 (BCS 1056), dated 960, from Exeter; S 697 (BCS 1072), dated 961, from the Old Minster, Winchester; and S 736 (BCS 1165), dated 965, from Abbotsbury, on which see also below, n. 81. See Keynes, *Diplomas*, p. 76, n. 153; P. Chaplais, 'The Royal Anglo-Saxon "Chancery" of the Tenth Century Revisited', *Studies in Medieval History presented to R. H. C. Davis*, ed. H. Mayr-Harting and R. I. Moore (London, 1985), pp. 41–51, at 50; and *Abing*, p. cxv, n. 128. Cf. S 704, dated 962, from Buckfast, and S 795, dated 974, from Crediton.

seems that he had remained in the king's service, and was made responsible in 963 for the production of two more charters, also for estates in the west midlands.[63] In December 963, 'Edgar A' produced a charter in favour of Earl Gunner which includes two 'northern' earls (Oslac and Cytelbearn) in the witness-list, both styled *dux*; but for whatever reason it seems to have been an agency other than 'Edgar A' who was made responsible for producing the charter by which the king granted land at Sherburn-in-Elmet, in Yorkshire, to 'Æslac' (Old Norse Áslákr), anglicized as Oslac,[64] and it may be that they were operating together on an occasion on which Edgar was paying particular attention to the north.[65]

At this point 'Edgar A' disappears from view, presumably because he ceased to be responsible for the production of any charters. The challenge, of course, is to ascertain his identity, and to understand in what capacity he had acted when performing this service for the king. It has been suggested that 'Edgar A' was an Abingdon scribe, perhaps none other than Abbot Æthelwold himself;[66] an alternative view is that he was a priest who had served Edgar as king of the Mercians, and who continued to serve Edgar in the early years of his reign as king of the English.[67] The argument turns in part on complex aspects of Anglo-Saxon diplomatic. We would have to establish whether the so-called 'Orthodoxorum' charters of Eadwig and Edgar for Abingdon abbey were authentic

---

[63] S 723, for an estate in Shropshire, and S 712a, for an estate in Derbyshire. These two charters may or may not have been produced on the same occasion. The style of subscription used for the king incorporates the phrase *scribere iussi*, implying that he ordered (someone) to write (the charter), which of course is normally taken for granted. The non-inclusion of abbots does not necessarily signify that none was present. S 712a includes two 'northern' ealdormen (Gunner and Myrdah), and Oslac, styled *dominus*; but their 'absence' from S 723 could be explained in various ways (e.g. determined by the amount of space available on a single sheet or in a cartulary).

[64] The basic formulation of S 712 was derived from charters of the previous decade (Keynes, *Diplomas*, p. 66, n. 125). For the sanction, cf. S 736 (BCS 1165), dated 965, which belongs to a 'west country' group (above, n. 62); and for the styles of subscription, cf. S 1213 (below, n. 74).

[65] It is possible that S 712a (above, n. 63), attested by Earls Gunner and Myrdah, and also by Oslac, styled *dominus*, was produced on the same occasion. It need not occasion concern that Oslac should be described as *dominus* in one context (S 712a), as *dux* in another (S 716), and be accorded no style in a third (S 712), since there might have been different ways of expressing his status at this stage, before his formal appointment or succession in 966 (*ASC*) and before his more regular inclusion in charters thereafter (from 968, discounting his occurrences in the Abingdon cluster of 965). It was perhaps the circumstances of Edgar's appointment of Oslac (Áslákr) that lay behind whatever was his fate in 975; see further below, p. 57.

[66] R. Drögereit, 'Gab es eine angelsächsische Königskanzlei?', *Archiv für Urkundenforschung* 13 (1935), pp. 335–436, at 416; P. Chaplais, 'The Origin and Authenticity of the Royal Anglo-Saxon Diploma' (1965), *Prisca Munimenta*, ed. F. Ranger (London, 1973), pp. 28–42, at 42; C. R. Hart, *The Early Charters of Northern England and the North Midlands* (Leicester, 1975), pp. 23–6; Chaplais, 'Royal Anglo-Saxon "Chancery" of the Tenth Century', pp. 49–50; and *Abing*, pp. lxxxiv–cxxxi. For more recent discussion, see *Historia Ecclesie Abbendonensis: The History of the Church of Abingdon*, ed. J. Hudson, 2 vols. (Oxford, 2002–7) I.cxcvii–cxcviii.

[67] Keynes, *Diplomas*, pp. 70–6, and above, p. 14.

products of the year 959, and would thus have been available, at Abingdon, to be quarried by 'Edgar A' in the early 960s; or whether it was charters of the 960s which were quarried by the draftsman of King Æthelred's 'Orthodoxorum' charter for Abingdon, in 993, and this charter which served thereafter as a model for the fabrication, at Abingdon, of the 'earlier' charters of the same type cast in the names of Edgar and Eadwig.[68] And this could only be settled by detailed analysis of the 'Orthodoxorum' charters as a group, focusing on their formulation,[69] their witness-lists,[70] and their place in the unfolding story of the monastic reform movement.[71] For what it may be worth, my own view remains that Æthelred's charter of 993, itself arising from circumstances which prevailed in the early 990s, was probably the first of its kind, and that the 'earlier' 'Orthodoxorum' charters for Abingdon, and other houses, came into existence sooner or later thereafter.[72] If so, it would follow that the charters of 'Edgar A' can be studied in their own right, as a well-defined corpus of 'literary' texts. The exercise would involve an interesting combination of disciplines (Insular Latin literature, palaeography, and diplomatic);[73] and one suspects that in this process

---

[68] The three 'Orthodoxorum' charters from Abingdon are S 658 (*Abing* 83), S 673 (*Abing* 84), and S 876 (*Abing* 124). They are so-called from the opening word of the proem in S 658 ('Ortodoxorum vigoris ecclesiastici monitu'); but it should be noted that the proem as found in S 673 and S 876 begins with an invocation of a higher authority ('Altitroni moderatoris imperio'). The other 'Orthodoxorum' charters, from Pershore, Worcester and Romsey, follow S 658; see further below, n. 216.

[69] Analysis of the origin, development and 'reception' of the elaborate proem common (with variations) to the group is just the first step. If the proem originated in S 658, it would seem to have been modified for use in S 673 and picked apart thereafter: by 'Edgar A' himself in 960–3, e.g. in S 690 (*Abing* 87), supposedly establishing a connection between 'Edgar A' and Abingdon, and in S 717 (*CantCC* 126); and by his successors, e.g. in S 764 (Glastonbury), dated 968; and it would follow that the draftsman of Æthelred's charter (S 876) took over the proem from Edgar's (S 673). It is arguably more likely that various turns of phrase which originated in charters of the late 950s and 960s were brought together for the first time in the proem found in Æthelred's charter (S 876), and mixed there with some usages of the 990s; and that S 876 itself served as a model, perhaps as early as the 990s, for other charters of this type.

[70] As comparison of the thegns will show, the witness-lists in the charters of Eadwig and Edgar are related to each other in ways which cause one to wonder whether they could be anything other than skilful concoctions; cf. *Abing*, pp. xcv–xcix. On the elaborate styles of subscription in S 690, said by Kelly to have been added to that charter at Abingdon in 961, following the styles in Edgar's 'Orthodoxorum' charter (S 673), see n. 74.

[71] The question is whether there is a context for the production of such charters for Abingdon in 959, perhaps setting a precedent for the 960s, or whether they belong more naturally in a later context.

[72] For further discussion of the authenticity of these charters, see Keynes, *Diplomas*, pp. 98–102; *Abing*, pp. lxxxiv–cxv; S. Keynes, 'Re-Reading King Æthelred the Unready', *Writing Medieval Biography 750–1250*, ed. D. Bates *et al.* (Woodbridge, 2006), pp. 77–97, at 90–3; and *Abingdon*, ed. Hudson, I.cxcix–cciv.

[73] Each text, or charter, is likely to have had direct or indirect sources of its own, and each will display features shared with other texts in the group as well as features peculiar to itself. I am indebted to Dr Rosalind Love for instructive discussion of such matters, in relation to the charters of 'Edgar A' and in relation to the 'Orthodoxorum' group; though I hasten to add that much remains a matter of interpretation.

'Edgar A' would gain due recognition as a significant figure at King Edgar's court. He would appear to have operated on the occasion of the meetings of the king and his councillors, drawing up his charters immediately in advance of the ceremony during which they would have been formally delivered to the beneficiary, but in one case leaving the text (dating-clause and witness-list) to be completed by a colleague,[74] and in another obliged to insert the boundary clause in a space originally left blank.[75] We would have to ask, at the same time, whether it is likely that evidence for a 'central' agency of such a kind, operating at meetings of the king and his councillors and catering for a wide variety of beneficiaries, should be interpreted in terms of the delegation of responsibility to an abbot, or as a more natural extension of arrangements clearly discernible since the reign of King Æthelstan.[76] We need not doubt that Æthelwold himself was fully capable of producing a charter, when he put his mind to it; but there is no compelling reason to connect the charters of 'Edgar A' with Æthelwold in particular, or indeed with Abingdon,[77] and the likelihood remains that he was so often to hand, and able to discharge this service on behalf of the king, because he was one among a number of priests in the king's household.

---

[74] The elaborate styles of subscription found in S 690 (*Abing* 87) appear to represent a usage developed in the early 960s by an agency other than 'Edgar A'; they are also found in S 689 (*Abing* 89), and in whatever lay behind S 811 (BCS 1319), issued *c.* 962, from the Old Minster, Winchester. Their effect is to raise the bishops onto a platform with the king and the archbishops, and to distinguish them from the other witnesses. It has been suggested that Oswald, as a newly appointed bishop of Worcester, might have had a hand in their formulation; see M. Lapidge, 'Æthelwold as Scholar and Teacher' (1988), in his *Anglo-Latin Literature 900–1066* (London, 1993), pp. 183–211, at 186–7. Another distinctive set of styles of episcopal subscriptions, displaying the same spirit of elaboration, is found in S 712 (BCS 1112), from York, dated 963, and in whatever lay behind S 1213 (BCS 1084), dated '962' (though with indiction for 963), from Bury St Edmunds, following the text of the latter in the abbey's Palgrave register (BL, Add. 45951), from a lost single sheet, which improves in significant respects on the text in BCS. The 'notarial' style attached in these two texts to Æthulf, bishop of Elmham, represents the origin of the formula in which one of the bishops appears to claim a role in the drafting of the text, seen also in S 730 (*Shaft* 25) and S 755 (BCS 1197); see Keynes, *Diplomas*, pp. 26–8, with nn. 39 and 46, to which S 1213 should be added. For more such styles, see S 701 (*Abing* 93). The styles found in S 690 exerted influence thereafter on the draftsman of S 876, in 993, and passed from there into S 673.

[75] Keynes, 'The Witan and the Written Word', with reference to S 690 (*Abing* 87) and S 717 (*CantCC* 126). For other views of S 690, see Chaplais, 'Royal Anglo-Saxon "Chancery" of the Tenth Century', pp. 49–50, arguing that both scribes were Abingdon; D. N. Dumville, *English Caroline Script and Monastic History* (Woodbridge, 1993), pp. 52–3, raising the possibility that the script-form seen in the section added to S 690 (Style I Anglo-Caroline) 'was being developed in the royal chancery'; and Kelly (*Abing*, pp. 358–9), to the effect that the dating-clause and the witness-list were added at Abingdon, using S 673 (Edgar's 'Orthodoxorum' charter) as a model for the styles of subscription. For S 717, see S. D. Thompson, *Anglo-Saxon Royal Diplomas: A Palaeography* (Woodbridge, 2006), pp. 126–8, with plate 3.

[76] Keynes, *Charters of King Æthelstan*.

[77] For a different view, see *Charters of Abingdon*, ed. Kelly, esp. pp. cxv–cxxii, though note that the case proceeds from the supposed 'rehabilitation' of S 658 and S 673.

The seven or eight charters which survive from the years 964–5 were evidently the work of a number of different agencies, perhaps operating in collaboration with each other, much as before.[78] The agency responsible for the 'Dunstan B' charters, which had been active in the early 950s, during the last years of Eadred's reign, and which had been active again on Edgar's behalf in 958, seems to have come back into business at this time, producing several charters in 964–7 (and more in 972–5), albeit under circumstances which remain far from clear.[79] Most of the 'Dunstan B' charters would appear to have emanated from ordinary meetings of the king and his councillors (abbots, however, being conspicuous by their absence from the witness-lists); one of them, dated 964, is remarkable for its long list of bishops, with identifications of their respective sees, and another, dated 965, represents the king as asking the beneficiary (Abbot Æscwig), and 'all those who have examined the wording (*dictamina*) of this charter', for their prayers (*oramina*).[80] The 'west country' agency active in 960–3 was also still active in 965.[81] However, it is the apparent interruption of the diplomatic tradition represented in 960–3 by 'Edgar A' that prompts further speculation. It is not inconceivable that he was a secular clerk on secondment to the king's household from the Old or New Minster at Winchester, who fell victim to reform in 964; or perhaps he was someone who fell foul for whatever reason of tension in high places occasioned by Edgar's marriage in that year to Ælfthryth, daughter of Ealdorman Ordgar and widow of Ealdorman Æthelwold, and by the status accorded quite pointedly to her thereafter as a legitimate queen. It is as well to indulge in such thoughts if only to remind oneself that the agency in question was human, and subject therefore to the vicissitudes of life.

The charters of the 'Edgar A' *type* resume as if with a vengeance in 966; and from then until the end of the reign they constitute an identifiable 'mainstream' of the diplomatic tradition.[82] The scribe so instantly recognizable as 'Edgar A' is not found among the four later charters of the 'Edgar A' type preserved in single-sheet form, so the presumption (after the gap in 964–5) is that the charters of this type, produced in 966–75, were the work of a different scribe or scribes.[83] The question remains whether the later charters of the 'Edgar A' type

---

[78] For details, see Keynes, 'Conspectus', below, pp. 69–70.

[79] Keynes, 'The "Dunstan B" Charters', pp. 176–9 and 192–3. It may or may not be significant that 'Dunstan B' did not produce charters during the 'Edgar A' years (960–3).

[80] S 726 and S 735. The king's request for prayers (*oramina*) finds an echo in the *Regularis Concordia, Proemium*, ch. 8: Symons, *RC*, pp. 5–6; and *Consuetudinum saeculi X/XI/XII monumenta non-Cluniacensia*, ed. K. Hallinger, Corpus Consuetudinum Monasticarum 7.3 (1984), 61–147, at 74.

[81] Above, n. 62. S 736 is a title-deed for an estate in Dorset; and it may or may not be significant that Ælfwold, bishop of Sherborne, is accorded a notarial form of subscription (*scribere iussi*); cf. the usage of the 'Mercian' draftsman in 958 and 963 (above, n. 63). The sanction in a development of that seen in S 712, from York, dated 963.

[82] For details, see Keynes, 'Conspectus', below, pp. 70–5.

[83] It is the case, however, that of the four charters in question (S 738, 772, 794, 801), none is accepted as unequivocally 'original'; the matter requires further investigation.

should be regarded as the work of imitators working from available models in different places, or as the work of trained protégés, perhaps organized into a single agency, and managing to maintain a degree of control over their collective output. Opinions will differ;[84] but the impression is arguably of a fully-fledged writing office that functioned effectively. Three pairs of charters will suffice to illustrate its operation, bringing us as close to a production line as we should wish to come. In 966, the king granted land in Oxfordshire and land in Buckinghamshire to his kinswoman Ælfgifu. The separate charters were evidently the work of a single agency, using standard 'Edgar A' formulation.[85] In 969, the king granted land in Bedfordshire and land in Warwickshire to his thegn Ælfwold.[86] Again, the separate charters were evidently the work of a single agency, using standard 'Edgar A' formulation.[87] In 970, the king granted land in Somerset to Bath abbey, and land in Suffolk to Ely abbey.[88] The separate charters appear to have been the work of the selfsame agency, and it is striking that the agency in question, operating at what would appear to have been a well-attended meeting of the king and his councillors, should have produced charters in favour of two religious houses, in quite different parts of the country. The formulation common to the two texts is more adventurous, and, in the case of the charter for Ely, care was taken to include some recognizably 'local' witnesses among the thegns.[89]

As had been the case in 960–3, the agency or agencies responsible for pro-

---

[84] Hart, *Early Charters of Northern England*, p. 25, suggested that 'Edgar A' was an Abingdon scribe who moved to Winchester with Æthelwold in 963, and that after the reform of the community, in 964, the scriptorium of the Old Minster took over main responsibility for the production of charters for the rest of Edgar's reign. Kelly (*Abing*, esp. pp. cxxi–cxxii) sees the continued use of 'Edgar A' formulation as a reflection of Æthelwold's 'close relationship with the king and his influential position', but also (it seems) in terms of some more 'local' production of charters at Abingdon.

[85] S 738 (BCS 1176), extant in single-sheet form, from the Old Minster, Winchester, and S 737 (*Abing* 105).

[86] S 772 (BCS 1229), extant in single-sheet form, and S 773 (BCS 1234; *EHD*, no. 113), both preserved subsequently at Worcester. The latter was one of the Somers charters (S. Keynes, 'Anglo-Saxon Charters: Lost and Found', *Myth, Rulership, Church and Charters: Essays in Honour of Nicholas Brooks*, ed. J. Barrow and A. Wareham (London, 2008), pp. 45–66, at 59).

[87] The scribe responsible for S 772 has been identified in another context: see T. A. M. Bishop, *English Caroline Minuscule* (Oxford, 1971), p. 17. Hart, *Early Charters of Northern England*, pp. 81–2, questioned the presumption that the scribe was at Worcester; but Dumville, *English Caroline Script*, pp. 70–4, argues that the charter is not likely to be original, and might have been written at Worcester in the early eleventh century.

[88] S 777 (*Bath* 18), and S 781 (BCS 1269), from Ely.

[89] The last ten thegns attesting the Ely charter are not found in the Bath charter, and are clearly distinctive (Keynes, *Attestations*, table LVII). The account in the *Libellus Æthelwoldi episcopi*, ch. 57 (*LE*, p. 115), of Bishop Æthelwold's purchase of land in Cambridgeshire from 'Heanric of Wantage', at a meeting of the king and his councillors, names among those present King Edgar, Ealdorman Ælfhere, Æthelwine and Byrhtnoth, Ælfric *cild*, Ringulf, and Thurferth. All of these men, including Ringulf, Thureferth and Heanric, are named in S 781; and it seems reasonable, on this basis, to regard the two meetings as one and the same.

ducing the charters of the 'Edgar A' type in 966–75 did not enjoy a monopoly. The charters of the 'Dunstan B' type produced in 966–7 and in 972–5 are a case in point. Even more distinctive, however, is the famous charter, written in golden letters and produced in the form of an illuminated book, which marked the expulsion of canons from the New Minster, Winchester, in 964, and their replacement by a community of monks living in accordance with the Rule of St Benedict.[90] The charter was drawn up two years later, in 966, and reads like a formal statement of the need for reform, justifying the recent action against those would now seek to undo what had been done, and extending protection to the monks themselves (chs. vii–xi). At the same time, it is made clear how the monks must 'conform to the practices of a rule', and what this entailed (chs. xii–xiii), how kings and monks should help each other (chs. xiv–xv), and how monks should be protected from persecution of other men, especially with regard to the monastery's landed property (chs. xvi–xxi). Interestingly, there is no list of the estates themselves, perhaps because a list had been removed, and not replaced, or perhaps by not naming any lands to ensure that the charter would cover them all. We otherwise find a number of ordinary title-deeds, differing from the 'Edgar A' type only in so far as they display greater variety of formulation across the component parts of the charter as a whole (perhaps reflecting the use of a wider range of models). A charter by which Edgar granted land in Derbyshire to Wulfric, bishop of Hereford, in 968, extant in its original form, is perhaps instructively anomalous.[91] The charter by which Edgar granted land at Barrow-upon-Humber, in Lincolnshire, to Bishop Æthelwold, in 971, is arguably a special case.[92] Dorothy Whitelock drew attention to compelling textual evidence that it might have been drafted by Æthelwold, bishop of Winchester;[93] and it would be entirely appropriate, in that case, that the draftsman should be aware that Barrow had been associated with St Chad, 'before the ravaging of the pagans', that Æthelwold intended to give the land to his monastery at Peterborough, and that the bishop had given the king forty pounds of tested silver, as well as a golden cross 'which he valued more than the money'. The witness-list comprises a number of bishops, abbots and ealdormen, followed by four men each styled *disc[ifer]*, evidently thegns holding office in the king's household.

---

[90] S 745 (*WinchNM* 23): A. R. Rumble, *Property and Piety*, pp. 65–97, at 81–4, and *The Liber Vitae of the New Minster and Hyde Abbey, Winchester*, ed. S. Keynes, EEMF 26 (Copenhagen, 1996), pp. 26–8. It seems likely that Bishop Æthelwold was involved in the drafting of the text: see D. Whitelock, 'The Authorship of the Account of King Edgar's Establishment of Monasteries' (1970), in her *History, Law and Literature* (London, 1981), VII.125–36, at 130–2; M. Lapidge, 'The Hermeneutic Style in Anglo-Latin Literature' (1975), in his *Anglo-Latin Literature 900–1066*, pp. 105–49, at 127–8; Lapidge, 'Æthelwold as Scholar and Teacher', pp. 189–90, with further references; Lapidge and Winterbottom, *WulfstW*, pp. lxxxix–xc; and *WinchNM*, p. 109.

[91] S 768 (*Burt* 23). The witness-list appears to have been inserted in a space originally left blank, between the main text and the dating-clause, filling the upper part of the sheet, and the boundary-clause and the sanction, filling the lower part of the sheet. Note also the designation of the first three thegns as *discifer*, and of the fourth as *pedisecus*.

[92] S 782 (*Pet* 15).

[93] Whitelock, 'King Edgar's Establishment of Monasteries', pp. 130–3.

The *disciferi* are themselves followed by the names of sixteen men not accorded any style, who would appear to have been drawn from the Anglo-Danish society of eastern England.[94] The two 'Dunstan B' charters issued in 975 are also quite instructively different;[95] indeed, it is difficult to avoid the suspicion that if only we knew more about Edgar, Dunstan, and Glastonbury, where the king was buried, we might learn more about the circumstances in which the charters of this type had been produced.[96]

None of this variety need occasion any suspicion or surprise. There are instances in Edgar's reign where the production of charters for land in a particular region, or perhaps for a particular beneficiary, was entrusted to a particular agency, or where the beneficiary himself appears to have played a leading part in the process. There are rather more instances where the work was entrusted to an agency seemingly empowered to produce charters for estates in different parts of the country and for a wide range of beneficiaries. A more extended study of the surviving corpus of Edgar's charters, whether preserved in their original single-sheet form or only in later copies, would be required in order to reveal all of the details, patterns and connections which bear in one way or another on the circumstances of their production. One question to be borne in mind is whether charters were normally produced before, during the course of, or after the assembly where a grant was made, and under what circumstances were they handed over or 'delivered' to the beneficiaries.[97] Another is how the agencies responsible for the production of Edgar's charters functioned as part of a system of royal government: whether they operated as independent bodies; or to what extent they operated as individual members of a larger agency, working in collaboration with each other; and to what extent arrangements depended on continuity from one assembly to the next.[98] The matter as a whole must form

94   Hringulf and Thureferth had been included among the witnesses to Edgar's charter for Ely in 970 (S 781, above, p. 20); Frithegist and Fræna were perhaps the men from eastern England named in the *Chronicle* as two of the three leaders who 'started the flight' in 993. Cf. S 1215 (*CantCC* 128), which distinguishes between thegns and several *rustici*, at a local meeting in Kent.

95   S 802 (BCS 1315), from the Old Minster, Winchester, drawn up at the instigation of the monk Ælfwine, appears to emanate from a meeting held at Glastonbury, in the king's absence, with the bishop of Hereford, Ealdorman Ælfhere, a group of (mainly west country) abbots, and three of the king's thegns. S 803 (BCS 1314), also from the Old Minster, is a replacement charter drawn up for the king's kinsman Osweard, attested by the king and otherwise only by a remarkably full complement of bishops.

96   It is unfortunate, of course, that fifteen charters of Edgar from the archives of Glastonbury abbey have been 'lost', since they might have helped to redress in Glastonbury's favour the balance which otherwise favours Abingdon. For details, see S 1759–73.

97   For general discussion of this matter, see S. Keynes, 'Angelsächsische Urkunden (7.–9. Jahrhundert) / Anglo-Saxon Charters (7th–9th century)', *Mensch und Schrift im frühen Mittelalter*, ed. P. Erhart and L. Hollenstein (St Gallen, 2006), pp. 97–108, at 106; and for discussion of the tenth-century evidence, from originals and cartulary copies, see Keynes, 'The Witan and the Written Word'.

98   For example, there is cross-over between charters of the 'Edgar A' type, and other charters of the period, in the use of similar memoranda of names for the witness-list and in choice of styles of subscription. S 690 (*Abing* 87) is itself symbolic of this connection

an important element in our estimation of Edgar's government, just as it affects our understanding of many other aspects of his reign; yet if the evidence points firmly towards 'centralized' production of charters as the norm, in continuation and extension of practices which had developed in the second quarter of the tenth century, common sense dictates that arrangements would need to have remained flexible in order to be effective.[99]

The evidence of law-codes and charters is complemented in important respects by Edgar's coinage, which remains a challenge to historians and numismatists alike.[100] Particular interest attaches to the arrangements which obtained in the 960s, before the reform of the coinage towards the end of his reign (*c.* 973). During the 960s and into the early 970s, moneyers in the different regions of the kingdom of the English struck silver pennies conforming to one or other of three main types, in continuation of practices which had originated in the first half of the tenth century. The 'Horizontal' types carried the king's name ('+ EDGAR REX') on the obverse, in an outer circle around a small central cross, with the moneyer's name (but not the name of the mint) on the reverse, arranged in two horizontal lines most commonly separated by three crosses.[101] The 'Circumscription' types carried the king's name and style (an abbreviated form of 'REX TOTIUS BRITANNIAE', or of 'REX ANGLORUM') on the obverse, in an outer circle around a small central cross, with the moneyer's name, and sometimes the name of the mint, in an outer circle on the reverse, around a small central cross.[102] The 'Bust Crowned' types carried the king's name around a crowned bust facing right, on the obverse, with the moneyer's name, and sometimes the name of the mint, in an outer circle on the reverse,

---

(above, n. 74); similarly elaborate styles of subscription were used for charters of the 'Edgar A' type in 966, as in S 737 and S 738.

[99] There might well have been movement of personnel from clerical or monastic communities into the king's service, and *vice versa* (N. Brooks, 'Anglo-Saxon Charters: Recent Work', in his *Anglo-Saxon Myths*, pp. 181–215, at 208–9); nor could one exclude the possibility that in certain cases an ecclesiastical beneficiary, or some other interested party, was invited, required or able to contribute to the process of production of charters, during the course of an assembly. For further discussion, see Keynes, 'The Witan and the Written Word'.

[100] R. H. M. Dolley and D. M. Metcalf, 'The Reform of the English Coinage under Eadgar', *Anglo-Saxon Coins*, ed. R. H. M. Dolley (London, 1961), pp. 136–68; J. J. North, *English Hammered Coinage*, I: *Early Anglo-Saxon to Henry III c. 600–1272* (London, 1980), pp. 109–13 [cited as N]; M. Archibald and C. E. Blunt, *British Museum, Anglo-Saxon Coins*, V: *Athelstan to the Reform of Edgar 924–c.973*, SCBI 34 (London, 1986); *CTCE*; K. Jonsson, 'The Pre-Reform Coinage of Edgar – the Legacy of the Anglo-Saxon Kingdoms', *Coinage and History in the North Sea World, c. A.D. 500–1250: Essays in Honour of Marion Archibald*, ed. B. Cook and G. Williams (Leiden, 2006), pp. 325–46; and Pagan, 'The Pre-Reform Coinage of King Edgar', below, pp. 192–207.

[101] Horizontal types (N 741, etc.): Archibald and Blunt, nos. 859–986 (plates XXXVIII–XLIII), with variant types, nos. 987–1031; *CTCE*, pp. 156–70, and plates 17–19.

[102] Circumscription types (N 748 [without mint name] and N 749 [with mint name]): Archibald and Blunt, nos. 1036–1145 (plates XLV–L); *CTCE*, pp. 172–90, and plates 20–2.

around a small central cross.[103] The overall impression (at least to the historian) is one of almost bewildering variety, yet consistent with the supposition that matters of design and production were delegated by royal authority to a number of regional agencies. A number of interesting points emerge. The use of a royal style was not usual; but one finds contracted forms of *rex totius Britanniae* on certain coins of the 'Circumscription' type, minted in the west midlands, and *rex Anglorum* elsewhere in the kingdom. The quality of die-engraving for the royal portrait in the 'Bust Crowned' type varied from excellent (at London) to abysmal (in East Anglia, where it seems to have been the only type in production or use). A large hoard of silver coins and ingots, concealed at Chester *c.* 970, comprised significant numbers of coins of Æthelstan, Edmund, Eadred and Eadwig, as well as significant numbers of Edgar's 'Horizontal', 'Circumscription' and 'Bust Crowned' types.[104] One of Edgar's law-codes (*III Edgar*, ch. 8) stipulates that there should be 'one coinage' (*mynet*) current 'through out all the king's dominion' (*ofer ealne þæs cyninges anweald*), presumably with reference to coinage patently and exclusively royal.

In the early 970s, probably in 973 or 974, the coinage was transformed. Henceforth, the silver pennies produced throughout the kingdom were to conform to a single type, as defined by the designs and inscriptions on each side of the coin, and new mechanisms were introduced to control the production of the coinage. The pre-reform coinage of King Edgar, as represented in the Chester hoard, is of the utmost importance in its own right, as evidence of the continued development during the 960s and early 970s of administrative arrangements inherited by Edgar from his predecessors; but its significance lies also in the way it provides such a telling contrast with the reformed coinage of what proved to be the last two years or so of Edgar's reign. Deep-rooted diversity, albeit under overall royal control, was replaced by an impressive and now entirely visible degree of uniformity, with all that must have been entailed in achieving that purpose. In addition to standardization of design, it was decided to adopt *rex Anglorum* as official usage for the coinage as a whole, which was no more and no less than the recognition of political reality. More practically, the reform seems to have reflected a determination on the part of the king's government to exercise much tighter control of the coinage than had been attempted before. For if the seemingly optional inclusion of a mint-signature in coins of the (pre-reform) 'Circumscription' and 'Bust Crowned' types might be taken as a sign that the mints were not then conceived as the component parts of a single network, the uniformity of Edgar's 'Reform' type, in every respect, suggests that this was indeed the coinage of a newly regulated order.

One important point that emerges clearly from the *combined* evidence of Edgar's law-codes, charters and coins concerns the contemporary perception of

---

[103] Bust Crowned types (N 750, etc.): Archibald and Blunt, nos. 1146–82 (plates L–LI); *CTCE*, pp. 195–7 and 199–201, and plate 24.

[104] C. E. Blunt and R. H. M. Dolley, 'The Chester (1950) Hoard', *British Numismatic Journal* 27 (1952–4), 125–60.

the nature and extent of his royal power.[105] As we have seen, King Æthelstan (924–39) was the first king of his line to make regular and extensive use of the styles 'king of the English' and 'king of the whole of Britain'. The circumstances and perhaps the prospects were quite different during the reigns of Edmund (939–46) and Eadred (946–55); and although both were clearly secure in their identity as kings 'of the English', the draftsman of the so-called 'alliterative' charters chose a very different way of analyzing the composition of a quadripartite kingdom. The styles accorded to Eadwig, in his charters, were initially undisciplined; but it seems to have been during the period of the divided kingdom (957–9), when the kings and their respective councillors might have had cause to reflect on the matter, that usages became more restrained. In the later of his two (undated) law-codes, Edgar refers 'to all the nation, whether Englishmen, Danes or Britons, in every province of my dominion' (*eallum leodscype ægðer ge Englum ge Denum ge Bryttum, on ælcum ende mines anwealdes*),[106] probably reflecting his recognition of the basic reality that his subjects were made up of three distinct political communities, where 'Danes' would signify the Anglo-Danish inhabitants of eastern and northern England, and where 'Britons' would appear to signify the British of Strathclyde. Yet the message of the royal styles in the charters issued by Edgar as king of the English is loud and clear. The normal usage, from the early 960s onwards, was for him to be styled *rex totius Britanniae* (*vel sim*) in the superscription, and *rex Anglorum* in the witness-list; more unusual styles, though coming to much the same thing, include 'monarch of the English of Britain' (*Britanniae Anglorum monarchus*), in the witness-list of an original charter of 961, and 'king of the English and also of the whole of Britain' (*rex Anglorum necnon et totius Brittaniae*), in the witness-list of a charter of 963.[107] The styles employed in Edgar's 'Circumscription' type reflect the same pattern, and perhaps it is appropriate that there should have been greater awareness in the west midlands of his identity as 'king of Britain'. Exactly the same idea lies behind the description of Edgar, as 'illustrious king of the English and of the other peoples dwelling within the bounds of the island of Britain', which forms the sonorous opening of the *Regularis Concordia*.[108] In short, the position from the outset to the end of Edgar's reign was that, like Æthelstan before him, he had two identities, as a 'king of the English' who could presume or claim at the same time to be a king whose rule extended over all other peoples within Britain. If we may set aside the political pretentiousness of Eadwig's charters in 955–7, and respect the restraint observed during the reigns of Edmund and Eadred, the consistent usages of Edgar's reign represent nothing less than a determined reaffirmation of the polity created by Æthelstan in the 930s.

The question arises whether the disruptions of the twenty-year period from the death of Æthelstan, in 939, to the death of Eadwig, in 959, would have un-

---

[105] Above, pp. 5–9.
[106] *IV Edgar* (above, n. 40) 2.2.
[107] S 690 (*Abing* 87) and S 712a. The remarkable style found in S 766, from Wilton, reflects the influence of the so-called 'alliterative' charters of the 940s (above, n. 20).
[108] Symons, *RC*, p. 1.

dermined any sense of continuity which could have been felt in Edgar's reign from the political order of the 930s to his own. It may be more to the point, however, that like Æthelstan before him Edgar had served his apprenticeship north of the Thames. He might well have derived a political advantage from his two years as 'king of the Mercians', and from the way his identity differed in this respect from that of his elder brother; and perhaps it should be noted, in this connection, that the regnal years in Edgar's charters, when calculated at all, were calculated from points in 959, 960 and even 973, but most often from his accession in 957.[109]

The king and his councillors

A second theme in Edgar's reign, again barely hinted at in the literary sources, is the unfolding story of the king's relations with those who might be counted among his councillors. The witness-lists incorporated in the king's charters serve as (albeit imperfect) records of attendance at the meetings where, arguably, the charters themselves were drawn up and delivered to the beneficiaries at a formal ceremony conducted in the presence of witnesses; and they can be used, by natural extension of this argument, as an indication of the changing composition of the king's council throughout his reign.[110] There was rarely a *strict* order of precedence among any group of witnesses (bishops, abbots, ealdormen or thegns), but there is enough consistency for one to be able to tell that such things were meaningful, and mattered. Indeed, the closer one studies these seemingly arid lists of obscure names, the more one learns to recognise the conventions that underlie their construction and to appreciate how, when brought together, they spring to life and generate the best image we have of the cycle of meetings which lay at the heart of the government of the kingdom of the English in the second half of tenth century.

It is not uncommon, in charters produced in the thirty years before Edgar's accession, to find a small number of 'sub-kings' accorded a prominent place in the witness-list of an Anglo-Saxon charter, indicating that rulers from elsewhere in Britain had attended the meeting of the king and his councillors at which the charter was produced.[111] It should be noted, however, that the charters which contain such attestations are in themselves highly distinctive. The extraordinary series of charters produced by the scribe known to modern scholarship as 'Æthelstan A', active between 928 and 935, project an image of Æthelstan's kingship which helped to advertise the grandeur and extent of his power, and which was doubtless intended to impress; so, alongside the Welsh *subreguli*, one

---

109 For further details, see Keynes, 'Conspectus', below, p. 61, n. 5.

110 On the composition of witness-lists in Anglo-Saxon charters, see Keynes, *Diplomas*, pp. 154–62.

111 Keynes, *Attestations*, table XXXVI (Welsh and Scottish sub-kings). It should be noted that the 'sub-kings' attended meetings at Exeter (16 April 928), Worthy [Hants.] (20 June 931), Lifton [Devon] (12 September 931), Milton [?Dorset] (30 August 932), Exeter (9 September 932), Winchester (28 May 934), Nottingham (7 June 934), and Buckingham (13 September 934); but there were evidently some meetings which they did not attend.

finds unusually 'inclusive' lists of bishops, abbots, ealdormen and thegns.[112] The so-called 'alliterative' charters, produced in the 940s and 950s, and arguably associated with Coenwald, bishop of Worcester, reflect a rather different conception of the Anglo-Saxon political order of the day, yet are similarly inclusive.[113] Against this background, it is striking that Welsh and Scottish sub-kings are conspicuous only by their *absence* from Edgar's charters; but whether we should infer that they were for some reason absent from meetings of the king and his councillors is perhaps another matter.

The attestations of the king's own family expose other important issues. It would appear from the evidence of tenth-century charters that a royal woman needed to be a person of particular importance in order to rate inclusion in the formal context of a witness-list. The first to be accorded such an accolade was Eadgifu, third wife of Edward the Elder: not, unsurprisingly, during the reign of Æthelstan, her step-son, but quite clearly in the period 940–55, during the reigns of her sons Edmund and Eadred, though again, unsurprisingly, not at all during the reign of her grandson Eadwig.[114] It is significant that Edgar's third wife, Ælfthryth, daughter of Ealdorman Ordgar, was the first such woman in the tenth century to make an impression of this kind during the reign of her own husband.[115] In 964 Edgar granted land in Buckinghamshire to Ælfthryth, styled his *lateranea*;[116] the marriage was registered in the 'northern recension' of the *ASC*, for 965;[117] and from 966 onwards she appeared from time to time in the witness-lists, not regularly but frequently enough to suggest that she commanded respect in her own right. Nor is the explanation far to seek. Edgar's marriage to Ælfthryth seems to have been contrasted, in certain quarters, with Edgar's two previous liaisons (with Æthelflæd, mother of Edward (the Martyr), and with Wulfthryth, mother of (St) Edith of Wilton),[118] suggesting that its purpose had been from the outset to secure a particular political objective. Edmund, son of Edgar and Ælfthryth, was pointedly described in the witness-list of the New Minster charter of 966 as *clito legitimus*, and is *followed* by his elder half-brother Edward, to whom the adjective *legitimus* is not applied, and then by Ælfthryth, styled *legitima … coniuncx*.[119] Similarly, Ealdorman Ælfheah made bequests in his will to Ælfthryth, the king's wife, to the elder ætheling (Edmund), described as 'the king's son and hers', and to the younger (Æthelred),

---

[112] Keynes, *Charters of King Æthelstan*, and 'England 900–1016', p. 470.
[113] For the 'alliterative' charters, see above, n. 20.
[114] Keynes, *Attestations*, table XXXIc (queens).
[115] Ælfthryth's first husband, Ealdorman Æthelwold, ceased attesting charters in 962, at which point his brother Æthelwine was appointed an ealdorman in his place (below, p. 31). See also B. Yorke, 'The Women in Edgar's Life', below, pp. 143–57.
[116] S 725 (*Abing* 101).
[117] *The Northern Recension*, ed. D. N. Dumville, Anglo-Saxon Chronicle 11 (Woodbridge, forthcoming).
[118] WM, *Gesta Regum* ii.159 (ed. Mynors *et al.*, pp. 258–60) and JW, *Chronicon*, s.a. 964 (ed. Darlington and McGurk, p. 416), probably representing a late eleventh-century Worcester source.
[119] S 745 (*WinchNM* 23).

pointedly omitting any reference to their elder half-brother Edward.[120] As it happened, the ætheling Edmund died in 971, and was buried at Romsey Abbey;[121] at which point his status as a 'legitimate prince', in contrast to Edward, would have been transferred to Edmund's younger brother Æthelred, perhaps exacerbating an already difficult position. We have to bear in mind, therefore, that resentment of Edmund, and by extension of his younger brother Æthelred, might well have been brewing, among supporters of Edward, for some time before it broke surface in the disputed succession of 975; and that under these circumstances the inclusion of Ælfthryth in a witness-list is quite likely to have been politically sensitive. The probability that there are dimensions which remain hidden to modern scholarship is suggested by the apparent significance, in the early 970s, of a king's kinsman called Osweard, of whom rather little is known.[122]

The attestations of the bishops and abbots should be taken together.[123] The lists of bishops are invariably headed by Archbishop Dunstan, which is no more than we should expect; and although he is followed in most lists by Oscetel of York, it is a nice question whether Oscetel's *absence* from an otherwise full list of bishops might indicate that a charter emanated from a meeting at which he had not been present. Again, unsurprisingly, there is more consistent representation of particular 'West Saxon' and 'Mercian' sees (Winchester, Ramsbury, London, Worcester) than of some of the more outlying sees, and although the matter is often complicated by the difficulty of 'disambiguating' between two or more bishops with the same name, one can but ask what factors might have determined a bishop's attendance at a meeting, or his relative position, or indeed his inclusion, in a list.[124] It should be noted, however, that the agency responsible for the 'Dunstan B' charters made it his business to list almost the full complement of bishops (thirteen or fourteen out of a possible seventeen or eighteen, against a much lower average in, say, the 'Edgar A' or 'Edgar A'-type

---

120 S 1485 (Whitelock, *Wills*, no. 9).

121 King Edgar seems to have regarded Romsey with special affection. He is said to have 're-founded' the abbey in 967, appointing a certain Merewenna as its abbess, and entrusting Æthelflæd, daughter of his wife Ælfthryth by her first husband Æthelwold, to her care. In 968 he gave to Romsey the royal estate at Edington, in Wiltshire (S 765). A list of the nuns of Romsey was entered in the *Liber Vitae* of the New Minster, Winchester (*Liber Vitae*, ed. Keynes, p. 96).

122 For Osweard, see S 784 (BCS 1285), dated 972, from Wilton, and S 803 (BCS 1314), dated 975, from the Old Minster, Winchester; see also Keynes, *Attestations*, table LVII (thegns).

123 Keynes, *Attestations*, tables LIV (bishops) and LV (abbots).

124 The charters of the period 928–35, produced by 'Æthelstan A', reveal the existence of a secondary tier of bishops, underlying those who represented the main sees; but it was not thereafter normal practice to include them in the witness-lists. The Bishop Sigewold, said to have been Greek in origin, who tried unsuccessfully to obtain Ely from King Edgar in the 960s, was perhaps one of these 'lesser' bishops, in eastern England. For the possibility that he can be identified as Nikephoros, bishop of Herekleia, see M. Lapidge, 'Byzantium, Rome and England in the Early Middle Ages', *Settimane di studio del centro italiano di studi sull'alto medioevo* 49 (2002), 363–400, at 386–91.

charters), in one case carefully naming their respective sees;[125] so one should not infer from the non-inclusion of, say, the bishop of Selsey, or the bishop of Cornwall, in an 'Edgar A' (-type) charter, that he was necessarily absent from the meeting. As one would expect, the attestations of abbots reflect some basic truths about the monastic reform movement. In the period 959–63, most charters include Æthelwold, abbot of Abingdon, in the witness-list, and no other abbots;[126] though there remain several charters which do not include any abbots at all.[127] There can be no doubt, in other words, that Æthelwold enjoyed special standing in the early years of Edgar's reign at meetings of the king and his councillors, which at this stage made him unique among heads of religious houses. It is tempting to imagine that Æthelwold's non-inclusion in a witness-list might denote his absence from a meeting (so that charters issued in the same year could be separated from each other on this basis); but it is more likely that the inclusion of an abbot was a matter of preference. In two charters of 963, both seemingly produced by 'Edgar A', Æthelwold was joined by three other abbots.[128] From 964 onwards, there are generally at least four abbots, and in the early 970s sometimes as many as twelve. By this time there must have been between twenty and forty abbots in office, yet it is apparent that a small number of perhaps the more senior among them were consistently accorded prominence over the rest: Ælfric of Malmesbury, Osgar of Abingdon, Æscwig of Bath, Æthelgar of the New Minster, Winchester, and Cyneweard of Milton. However, not all draftsmen of charters saw the ecclesiastical hierarchy in the same way: 'Dunstan B', who liked to be so inclusive when it came to the bishops, omitted the abbots altogether.[129]

The attestations of ealdormen and thegns in the charters of Eadwig and Edgar form an important part of a story which unfolded during their reigns at

---

[125] S 726 (BCS 1134); only S 781 (BCS 1269), among 'Edgar A'-type charters, comes close. Osulf, bishop of Ramsbury (Wilts.), is styled 'Sunnungnensis episcopus', with reference to the episcopal manor at Sonning (Berks.); see M. Gelling, *The Place-Names of Berkshire*, 3 pts, EPNS 49–51 (Cambridge, 1973–6) i.132–3 and iii.843–4.

[126] Æthelwold is included in all of the 'Edgar A' charters of the period 960–3 (of which five survive in their original form), and also in several charters drafted by other agencies during the same period (none of which, however, happens to survive in its original form).

[127] S 684 (BCS 1056); S 697 (BCS 1072); S 692 (*Bath* 15); S 694 (*Bath* 14); S 705a (Athelney); S 704 (Buckfast); S 701 (*Abing* 93); S 713 (*Abing* 97); S 715 (BCS 1118); S 723 (BCS 1119); S 712a. It is the case, therefore, that Æthelwold does not appear in the three originals of the period not written by 'Edgar A' (S 684, S 697, S 704 [all 'southwest']). Kelly (*Abing*, p. cxix) comments that 'When "Edgar A" was unavailable, then so was Æthelwold'; see also Hudson, *Abingdon*, I, p. cxcviii. Would that it were all so simple.

[128] S 708 (*Abing* 96) and S 719 (BCS 1120). In addition to Æthelwold, the other three were Ælfric of Malmesbury, Æscwig of Bath, and Ælfwold (unidentified).

[129] The significant examples from Edgar's reign are S 724 (BCS 1142), dated 964; S 735 (*Bath* 17), dated 965, in favour of Abbot Æscwig; S 720 (*Abing* 106), dated 967; S 790 (BCS 1292), dated 973; S 794a, dated 974; and perhaps S 803 (BCS 1314), dated 975. The exception is S 802 (BCS 1315), dated 975, which was seemingly a distinctive occasion (above, n. 95).

the upper levels of the secular hierarchy, though the details of the plot remain largely unknown. The major family groups or kindred-based factions which coalesced during the second and third quarters of the tenth century, and which come into sharper focus during the third, constitute a vital dimension in our understanding of the period.[130] There are inherent dangers, of course, in the process of making the necessary identifications and connections. There is also danger in presuming on affection between any one man and his parents, siblings, uncles, aunts, and other relations, let alone his in-laws, and in proceeding at all when we cannot take account of friendship between people not known to have been related to each other. The significance of a particular family or group is judged, none the less, by the closeness of its members to the royal family, or indeed to other identifiable groups, by the extent of their land holdings and thus their wealth and influence in a particular area, by the offices they held at the king's pleasure, and by the associations they cultivated with one religious house or another. The wealth, power and influence of these families or groups is then presumed to have increased further as they began to accumulate more land across southern England, in a process matched by the enlargement of their social connections, the widening of their political horizons, and the deepening of their economic interests. In the later 950s, the brothers Eadwig and Edgar found themselves faced by a body of ealdormen and thegns who represented the emergent landed aristocracy of the tenth-century 'kingdom of the English'.[131] Some among their number who were particularly close to the king, or who found themselves at the centre of activity, were rewarded with office in the king's household, or with even greater status involving high authority at a regional level. Others attended meetings of the king and his councillors when held in their part of the country, and concentrated instead on minding their own business. Whether Eadwig and Edgar were able to assert their own independence of action, or remained at the mercy of established interests at court, is unclear; but, looking forward from the second into the third quarter of the tenth century, one senses that they would have been wholly subsumed by developments over which they can have had but little control. Eadwig himself had promoted the interests of families already flourishing under royal patronage. Soon after his accession (in late 955) he appointed Æthelstan Rota, and Ælfhere (?) son of Ealdorman

---

130 Hart, 'Æthelstan "Half-King" and his Family'; Williams, 'Ælfhere, Ealdorman of Mercia'; Banton, 'Ealdormen and Earls in England', pp. 150–9; C. R. Hart, 'The Ealdordom of Essex' (1987), repr. in his *The Danelaw*, pp. 115–40, at 127–31; R. Fleming, *Kings and Lords in Conquest England* (Cambridge, 1991), pp. 22–33; and A. Wareham, *Lords and Communities in Early Medieval East Anglia* (Woodbridge, 2005).

131 The key documents in our understanding of this aristocracy are the four extant wills of tenth-century ealdormen: Ælfgar (S 1483), Æthelwold (S 1504), Ælfheah (S 1485), and Æthelmær (S 1498). These are complemented by the wills of some high-ranking women: e.g. Ælfgifu (S 1484), who is generally supposed (albeit on tenuous grounds) to have been the wife of King Eadwig, and Æthelflæd (S 1494), widow of King Edmund and wife of Ealdorman Æthelstan. Yet these documents serve not least to suggest what we miss in our ignorance of arrangements made by others of their kind.

Ealhhelm, as ealdormen in Mercia.[132] Later on in 956, Eadwig appointed Æthel-wold, son of Ealdorman Æthelstan 'Half-King', as ealdorman in East Anglia, and Byrhtnoth as ealdorman in Essex. Following the division of the kingdom in 957, these 'new' men were transferred, in effect, to King Edgar's court; and in 959 Eadwig appointed Ælfheah, brother of Ealdorman Ælfhere, as ealdorman in Wessex. There is no reason to imagine that Edgar would have been inclined or indeed that he would have been in a position to do differently from his elder brother, even if at the level of his own household he had been able (in 957) to make a fresh start; and indeed, after his brother's early death, in 959, the story seems to have continued along much the same lines as before.

The witness-lists in King Edgar's charters provide a small and clouded window into the political and social structures at court.[133] A 'primacy' of some kind was accorded throughout his reign to Ealdorman Ælfhere, disturbed only by the curious fact that in several charters of the years 968–70 Ælfhere's position was taken by Æthelstan Rota (in Mercia). It is otherwise apparent that the draftsmen of charters had at least a general sense of one ealdorman's place relative to others, in a hierarchy which involved them all.[134] In making his own appointments, Edgar showed a natural preference for those close to himself. One of the several ealdormen inherited from Eadwig's regime was Æthelwold of East Anglia, eldest son of Æthelstan 'Half-King', and thus Edgar's foster-brother; and when Æthelwold died, in 962, Edgar immediately appointed Æthel-wold's youngest brother Æthelwine to hold office in his place.[135] Another was Ealdorman Edmund, who had held office in Wessex since the late 940s, and who disappears from view in 963; he was replaced or succeeded in the following year by Ordgar, father of Ælfthryth, herself the widow of Ealdorman Æthelwold and soon to become Edgar's queen.[136] No less important, however, was Oslac (Old

---

[132] In a famous passage in *The Battle of Maldon*, lines 216–19 (*The Battle of Maldon AD 991*, ed. D. Scragg (Oxford, 1991), pp. 26–7 and 241–2), the heroic Ælfwine, son of Ælfric, claims to be 'of a great family amongst the Mercians; my grandfather was called Ealhhelm, a wise and prosperous ealdorman'. It must be admitted that the argument for identifying his father Ælfric as Ælfric *cild*, ealdorman of Mercia (983–5), and as husband of a sister of Ealdorman Ælfhere, who would thus have been a son of Ealdorman Ealh-helm, seems rather tenuous (albeit now deeply embedded in the literature).

[133] Keynes, *Attestations*, table LVI.

[134] It is the case, however, that the order of precedence observed in the charters of Edgar's son Æthelred was more stable; see Keynes, *Diplomas*, pp. 157–8, and Keynes, *Attestations*, table LXII.

[135] For the sons of Ealdorman Æthelstan 'Half-King' (Æthelwold, Ælfwold, Æthelsige and Æthelwine), see *Vita S. Oswaldi*, iii.14 (Raine, *York*, pp. 428–9), and the Ramsey *Liber benefactorum*, ch. 4 (*Chronicon Abbatiæ Rameseiensis*, ed. W. D. Macray (London, 1886), pp. 11–13). The author of the *Liber benefactorum* refers also to the fostering of Edgar by Ælfwyn, wife of Æthelstan 'Half-King' (ed. Macray, pp. 11 and 53). For Edgar's alleged complicity in the murder of Æthelwold, see WM, *Gesta Regum*, ii.157, pp. 256–8.

[136] From 960 to 964 Ordgar attested Edgar's charters as a thegn (Keynes, *Attestations*, table LVII), and was still a thegn when S 725 (*Abing* 101) was issued, in favour of Ælfthryth; he occurs from 964 to 970 as an ealdorman (*Attestations*, table LVI), and gained precedence over some of those senior to him.

Norse Áslákr), who seems to have been appointed by Edgar in the early 960s to control the southern part of a once larger earldom of Northumbria, based probably at York;[137] for the pattern of his attestations suggests that his standing at meetings of the witan increased in the later 960s, and that by the early 970s he had become a person of particular importance at court.[138] A significant change in the pattern of the ealdormen's attestations seems to have taken place in or soon after 970, and was maintained from 971 until the end of Edgar's reign in 975. The change arises directly from the seemingly simultaneous 'disappearance', in 970, of one of the king's long-serving Mercian ealdormen, Æthelstan Rota, and of both of his surviving West Saxon ealdormen, Ælfheah (brother of Ealdorman Ælfhere) and Ordgar (the king's father-in-law).[139] Henceforth, the only ealdormen attesting Edgar's charters were Ælfhere (of Mercia), Æthelwine (of East Anglia), Oslac (in the north), and Byrhtnoth (of Essex). It is possible that one or more of these ealdormen assumed much wider responsibilities, or that administrative arrangements of a different kind were made for the shires of Wessex and the south-east; it is also possible that Edgar himself took over direct control of the whole of England south of the Thames.[140]

The attestations of thegns in the charters of Eadwig and Edgar have much to reveal about matters which were bound to be of importance: for example, the identification of those who were prominent in the king's household; and the extent of continuity, or otherwise, from one reign to the next.[141] Many of Edgar's thegns made only sporadic appearances at meetings of the king and his councillors, during the reign as a whole, and it is accordingly difficult to resolve their attestations into individuals, or indeed to identify individuals in other contexts, with any degree of confidence. However, several names occur in the witness-lists with more pronounced degrees of consistency and promi-

---

[137] It would appear that Osulf of Bamborough had managed in the 950s to extend his authority southwards to York. The appointment of Oslac (above, p. 16) would thus have represented a strengthening of royal authority in York itself; but it is not clear what new arrangements were made further north. For the larger context, see D. Whitelock, 'The Dealings of the Kings of England with Northumbria in the Tenth and Eleventh Centuries' (1959), in her *History, Law and Literature* (London, 1981), III.70–88, at 77.

[138] The draftsmen of charters tended not to include 'northern' ealdormen; so Oslac's growing prominence in Edgar's reign, first in 963, and then in 966 and from 968, is particularly striking.

[139] John of Worcester reports on uncertain authority the death of Ælfheah, ealdorman of the men of Southampton, and of Ordgar, ealdorman of Devon, in 971, adding that the one was buried at Glastonbury and the other at Exeter (ed. Darlington and McGurk, p. 420). Ealdorman Ælfheah makes what on this basis would be a posthumous appearance in S 784 (BCS 1285), dated 972; so there may be complications. The day of his death (18 April) was recorded at Glastonbury; see M. Blows, 'A Glastonbury Obit-List', *The Archaeology and History of Glastonbury Abbey*, ed. L. Abrams and J. P. Carley (Woodbridge, 1991), pp. 257–69, at 265.

[140] Hart, 'Æthelstan "Half-King" and his Family', pp. 591–2, suggests that Ælfhere was responsible for England south of the Thames); see also Williams, 'Ælfhere, Ealdorman of Mercia', pp. 158–60. For Æthelweard in the early 970s, see below, p. 34.

[141] Keynes, *Attestations*, tables LI (Eadwig's thegns), LVII (Edgar's thegns) and LVIIa (selected thegns).

nence, offering plenty of scope for more detailed analysis; and in some cases they occur in associations which aid identification. It must suffice for present purposes to focus attention on the succession of 'leading' thegns, who appear to have been accorded primacy over or among the thegns for extended periods, who may have held a particular office (perhaps honorific) in the king's household, and who in certain cases can be identified as the king's kinsmen. The leading thegn at Edgar's court in 957–9 was a certain Ælfwine. He is plausibly identified as Ælfwine, brother of Ælfhere, ealdorman of Mercia (956–83), and of Ælfheah, ealdorman of Hampshire (959–70/1), and, as such, the king's kinsman;[142] he remained prominent among Edgar's thegns after the reunification of the kingdom.[143] After the death of Eadwig in 959, and Edgar's accession to the kingdom of the English, the brothers Ælfgar and Byrhtferth, who also belonged in some way to the royal family, and who had been prominent in Eadwig's household, reappeared at Edgar's court.[144] Ælfgar was immediately accorded primacy among Edgar's thegns, but vanishes from sight in 962. An entry in *ASC* A, which at this stage was at the Old Minster, Winchester, records that Ælfgar, described as 'the king's kinsman in Devon', died in 962, and was buried at Wilton.[145] The pattern thereafter is that primacy among Edgar's thegns was accorded in most charters to Byrhtferth, but in certain cases to Ælfwine, until both disappear from the witness-lists in 970.[146] It is not known what became of Byrhtferth. There was an Ælfwine, kinsman of King Edgar, who in 975, as a monk at Glastonbury, urged the king to make a grant of land in Shropshire to a certain Ealhhelm.[147] It is arguable that the association between this Ælfwine and someone called Ealhhelm might reflect an association between him and the family of an older Ealhhelm, ealdorman of Mercia in the 940s and (supposed) father of Ealdorman Ælfhere, Ealdorman Ælfheah, and Ælfwine.[148] There was also an Ælfwine who was the 'successor' of a certain Wulfric, and

---

[142] For Ealdorman Ælfheah and his brother Ealdorman Ælfhere, see S 1485 (Whitelock, *Wills*, no. 9); and for Ealdorman Ælfhere and his brother Ælfwine, see S 1276 (*CantCC* 98 (*b*)). For the presumption that they were sons of Ealhhelm, ealdorman of Mercia (940–51), see above, n. 132.

[143] For further details, see Hart, *Early Charters of Northern England*, pp. 277–8 and 328–9, and Williams, 'Ælfhere, Ealdorman of Mercia', pp. 154–5.

[144] Hart, *Early Charters of Northern England*, pp. 254–5 (Ælfgar) and 301 (Byrhtferth).

[145] *ASC* A: Bately, *MS A*, p. 75.

[146] One can but guess what the apparently simultaneous disappearance of Byrhtferth and Ælfwine, in 970, might signify, and whether, for example, it is related to the changes among the ealdormen, also in 970, or analogous to the simultaneous disappearance of Ordulf and Æthelmær in 1005.

[147] S 802 (BCS 1315), dated 975.

[148] Williams, 'Ælfhere, Ealdorman of Mercia', pp. 154–5. The case takes strength from recognition of the close association between the brothers Ælfheah and Ælfhere and Glastonbury abbey (*ibid.*, p. 167), indicated most clearly by Ealdorman Ælfheah's will (S 1485 above, n. 131) and by the fact that the brothers were buried there; cf. above, n. 139. See also Blows, 'A Glastonbury Obit-List', pp. 265 (Ælfheah) and 267 (Ælfhere); the obit for an otherwise unidentified 'Eilwinus dux et monachus Glast.' was perhaps a garbled entry for their brother Ælfwine.

who gave estates in Wiltshire, and perhaps elsewhere, to Glastonbury abbey, on his becoming a monk there.[149] This Wulfric is reasonably identified as Wulfric, brother of Dunstan, and Dunstan himself is said to have been related to a niece of King Æthelstan;[150] so, if Ælfwine is presumed to have been related in some way to Wulfric, we would have another person of that name who might be described as a royal kinsman and who became a monk of Glastonbury. In the interests of economy, the persons called Ælfwine in each of these Glastonbury contexts might reasonably be regarded as one and the same man; and on this basis one might suppose that the Ælfwine who had been so prominent in Edgar's household from 958 until 970 decided then to retire to the monastery most closely connected with his own family.[151] From 971 until 975 the primacy was generally accorded to a certain Æthelweard, who had been prominent among Edgar's thegns since 964, and who may latterly have shared this position with a certain Ælfweard, apparently his brother;[152] it seems that both continued to attest charters, as thegns, into the reigns of Edgar's sons Edward and Æthelred, when Ælfweard emerged as the more prominent of the two.[153] The possibility also exists, however, that Æthelweard was the king's kinsman (and chronicler) who was appointed an ealdorman early in the reign of Edward the Martyr and who was described in a charter of 997 as ealdorman 'of the western shires' (*occidentalium prouinciarum*).[154] It is striking that in certain cases Ælfwine, Ælfgar, Byrhtferth and Æthelweard are not accorded their ordinary status as

---

[149] S 472 (BCS 750), S 504 (BCS 800) and S 1743 (lost). All three charters appear to have been endorsed with notes to this effect; all three were entered in the *Liber Terrarum* of Glastonbury abbey (LT 43, LT 44, LT 46), but only the first two were entered thereafter in the Great Cartulary.

[150] Brooks, 'The Career of St Dunstan', pp. 160–6.

[151] Should one choose to overlook the apparent family associations of the Ælfwine known to have been a monk of Glastonbury in 975, one might conclude that this Ælfwine was Wulfric's son, and thus Dunstan's nephew; see Keynes, 'The "Dunstan B" Charters', pp. 192–3.

[152] For Æthelweard and Ælfweard as brothers, see S 796 (*Malm* 30).

[153] Keynes, *Attestations*, tables LVII, LVIII and LXIII; Keynes, *Diplomas*, pp. 182–3. The matter is complicated by the fact that S 796 (*Malm* 30) is anomalous, by the observation that the prominent Æthelweard of Edgar's reign was as often as not separate from Ælfweard, until shared status brought them together in the early 970s, and by the possibility that Æthelweard, brother of Ælfweard, was in fact the *second* Æthelweard who can be seen at Edgar's court from the mid-960s, as in S 806 (BCS 1219) and S 668 (BCS 1145).

[154] S 751 (BCS 751) and S 800 (BCS 1316) are probably unreliable as evidence that Æthelweard was appointed an ealdorman by Edgar, in the early 970s (though see above, n. 140, on Edgar and Wessex in the early 970s); in which case his first appearance as ealdorman is in charters of 976–7 (Keynes, *Attestations*, table LVIII); cf. Hart, 'Æthelstan "Half-King" and his Family', p. 592. In other words, Æthelweard would have continued on an upward trajectory after Edgar's death, and Ælfweard would have secured his own primacy among the thegns.

'thegn' (*minister*), but are treated in ways which seem to reflect special importance among the king's councillors.[155]

It would be hazardous to make very much more of the attestations of thegns in Edgar's charters. A run of attestations in the name of Æthelwine extends from 958 to 962, and then stops; so there is good reason for assigning these attestations to Edgar's foster-brother Æthelwine, son of Æthelstan 'Half-King', who succeeded his eldest brother Æthelwold in 962 as ealdorman of East Anglia.[156] On this basis, we might expect to find their brothers Ælfwold and Æthelsige among the thegns at King Edgar's court. As it happens, Æthelwine occurs on some occasions in association with an Ælfwold, and on other occasions in association with an Æthelsige; in a charter of 961, all three names occur together as if in a group, and after Æthelwine's elevation in 962 the names of Ælfwold and Æthelsige are sometimes found together. A thegn Ælfwold who received grants of land in Bedfordshire and Warwickshire, in 969, is described with unusual warmth, in the endorsement of one of his charters, as the king's 'dear and true thegn' (*leofan getreowan þegne*), and should perhaps be identified in the witness-lists as the Ælfwold who had been in Edgar's service since 958;[157] and a *camerarius* called Æthelsige, who received a grant of land in Berkshire, in 963, was doubtless one or other of the thegns of that name who attested in the 960s.[158] It is tempting indeed to presume on the further connections, and so to conclude that Edgar's foster-brothers Ælfwold and Æthelsige were also prominent at meetings of the king and his councillors, and held office in the royal household; of course Byrhtferth of Ramsey is eloquent on the particular importance of both men, not least because both were benefactors of the abbey where they lay buried.[159] A thegn called Wulfstan, evidently a person of some considerable importance at court, or in the king's household, from 962 onwards, was accorded primacy on certain occasions between 967 and 972; it is tempting to identify him as Wulfstan of Dalham, who had acted as the king's agent in 964.[160]

---

[155] S 684 (BCS 1056), dated 960, and extant in its original single-sheet form (Ælfgar, Byrhtferth and Ælfwine, no style): S 692 (*Bath* 15), dated 961 (Ælfgar and Byrhtferth, styled *consul*); S 704, dated 962 (Byrhtferth, no style); S 716 (BCS 1113), dated 963 (Byrhtferth, no style); S 668 (BCS 1145), dated '922' for ?972 (Æthelweard, no style). Cf. *Wells*, p. 120.

[156] For Æthelwine's attestations as thegn, see Keynes, *Attestations*, table LVII, and Hart, 'Æthelstan "Half-King" and his Family', pp. 591–2.

[157] For the charters, see above, p. 20; see also Keynes, *Attestations*, table LVII. Hart, 'Æthelstan "Half-King" and his Family', pp. 589–90 and 594, regards the identification as certain.

[158] S 713 (*Abing* 97), dated 963; Æthelsige *pedisecus*, in S 768 (*Burt* 23); and Hart 'Æthelstan "Half-King" and his Family', pp. 590–1.

[159] BR, *VSO* iii.14 (Raine, *York*, pp. 428–9), to the effect that Ælfwold 'was exalted with such authority that he even disdained to become an ealdorman', and that Æthelsige 'was a very powerful man, such that he acquired the authority of an ealdorman and had the distinction of exceeding importance whenever he came into the king's presence'. See further below, p. 55.

[160] WW, *VSÆ*, ch. 18 (Lapidge and Winterbottom, *WulfstW*, p. 32). For a bold attempt to provide Wulfstan of Dalham with a more complex genealogy than is perhaps warranted

Titstan, the king's *cubicularius* or *burþegn*, and Winstan, the king's *camerarius* or *cubicularius*, are also found among the beneficiaries of Edgar's charters, but neither appears among the witnesses.[161] It should otherwise be noted that charters dealing with land in eastern or northern England sometimes include some 'Scandinavian' names in the witness-list, though whether these seemingly 'local' witnesses were chosen especially for the grant, or reflected a local element at a meeting held in the region, is not immediately apparent.[162]

Social and economic consequences

A third theme around which to organize an approach to Edgar's reign might be characterized as the social and economic consequences of the political unification of the kingdom of the English in the tenth century. As political horizons widened, from the late ninth century onwards, the key players would have started to make new contacts and to extend their interests further afield. One can but imagine the consequences, for the kings themselves, for all members of the royal kin group (those identified in charters and other contexts as the 'king's kinsmen'), for the ealdormen, for those who held office in the king's household, for others of sufficient standing to be described as 'thegns', and for those who aspired to attain that status. As families expanded and dispersed, large estates would need to have been broken down into smaller parts, perhaps involving the conversion of folkland into bookland so that a man could enjoy his land on better terms, including the power of alienation outside the family. New opportunities might also have meant that accumulated reserves of gold and silver were brought out of family treasure chests and put into wider circulation. No doubt men in power locally, or who enjoyed the patronage of an ealdorman or indeed of the king, enjoyed the best prospects for advancement. Perhaps under circumstances of this kind, a veritable 'land market' (for want of a better term) seems to have developed in southern England during the second quarter of the tenth century, reflected at a superficial level by the quantity of charters surviving from the 940s, 950s and 960s.[163] Each charter appears at first sight to represent a gift of land by the king to the beneficiary, and the impression thus created is of a sustained display of royal munificence towards laymen and religious houses, presumably in the hope (on the king's part) of reward in this world or the next. It has to be understood, however, that charters are cast in terms which can conceal

---

by the evidence, see Wareham, *Lords and Communities*, pp. 33–43; see also Hart, *Early Charters of Northern England*, p. 379, and *Anglo-Saxon Ely: the 'Libellus Æthelwoldi Episcopi' and other records of Ely Abbey 970–1066*, ed. S. Keynes and A. Kennedy (forthcoming).

161 Titstan: S 706 (BCS 1083), dated 962. Winstan: S 719 (BCS 1120), dated 963, and S 789 (BCS 1286), dated 972. S 706 and S 719 relate to land at Avon Farm, in Durnford, Wilts. For the terminology of officials of the royal household, see Keynes, *Diplomas*, pp. 158–60.

162 S 674 (*Pet* 13); S 679 (BCS 1044), from York; S 681 (*Pet* 14); S 781 (BCS 1269), from Ely; S 782 (*Pet* 15).

163 For a table showing the number of surviving charters each year in the period 924–1066, see Keynes, *Diplomas*, p. 47, and *Attestations*, table XXVI.

all too easily a whole range of more complex transactions, and that it is generally impossible to tell whether a change of ownership was being effected by force, due process of law, sale, gift, bequest, or exchange; and for all we know, some charters may have represented the conversion of a particular estate from folkland into bookland, without change of ownership.[164] Unfortunately, it is very difficult to get much sense of the dynamics of English society during this period; but surviving vernacular documents, which (far more so than the royal charters in Latin) show people interacting with each other, provide glimpses of a society with significant opportunities for advancement and change.

Awareness of the general historical context in Edgar's reign creates the impression that much of this activity was connected with the monastic reform movement, as the re-founded, reformed or newly founded religious houses increased their landed endowments and thereby extended their influence in the social, economic and political networks around them. Yet of course there was more to it than that. Although the victims of the disruption in Eadwig's reign are known to have included prominent figures from the previous regime, such as Queen Eadgifu and Abbot Dunstan, it seems likely that many of those adversely affected were drawn not from the ranks of the king's ealdormen, or from among the thegns holding office in the king's household, but from the multitude of 'lesser' thegns. The key may yet emerge from the systematic analysis of the rich seams of documentation available for the tenth century, encouraged by the variety of electronic tools which are fast coming into their own.[165] It will always be impossible to reconstruct a fully articulated and animated society from the persons named in the charters themselves, whether as beneficiaries, interested parties, or witnesses; and it is scarcely any easier to track every change which took place in the ownership of land during the second and third quarters of the tenth century.[166] Clearly, however, there was more to the unification of the English people than notions of *Angelcynn*, or the *gens Anglorum*; and it is in prosopography, and estate history, that one might hope to reach the realities and complexities of political developments in the tenth century.

The first flush of enthusiasm for the newly unified kingdom of the English, in the 930s, was suspended, to some extent, after Æthelstan's death; whereupon the upheavals of the 940s and 950s created their own legacy, stretching forwards into the reign of King Edgar. The thegn Æthelgeard, for example, began his career in the early 930s, during the reign of King Æthelstan, and continued to prosper until 958, when he fades from view; curiously, there seem to have been problems in connection with several of his estates, and the question is

---

[164] See above, n. 61, for two instances of King Edgar doing this for his own benefit, which of course is why it shows up in the form of a charter by which he granted land to himself.

[165] Among the most useful electronic resources are PASE (Prosopography of Anglo-Saxon England) <www.pase.ac.uk>, 'Kemble' <www.trin.cam.ac.uk/kemble>, 'Langscape' <www.langscape.org.uk>, the databases of Anglo-Saxon coins <www.fitzmuseum.cam. ac.uk/dept/coins>, and *Fontes Anglo-Saxonici* <http://fontes.english.ox.ac.uk/>.

[166] L. Abrams, *Anglo-Saxon Glastonbury: Church and Endowment* (Woodbridge, 1996), pp. 42–265, shows the way forward.

what this might signify.[167] The tale of Wulfric *Cufing* may or may not have been analogous.[168] Of the two thegns called Wulfric who are conspicuous among the beneficiaries and witnesses to charters of Edmund, Eadred and Eadwig, in the 940s and 950s, one (Wulfric I) is probably to be identified as Wulfric *Cufing*, and the other (Wulfric II) as Wulfric, brother of Dunstan, abbot of Glastonbury.[169] Although both were prominent at the court of King Eadred, in the later 940s, Wulfric II seems to have disappeared after 951, whereas Wulfric I was still conspicuous at the beginning of Eadwig's reign, and was accorded a prominent position among the thegns attesting the king's charters on at least one occasion in 956. Wulfric I seems to have lost his standing at Eadwig's court later that year; but he began to rebuild his fortunes in 958, and in 960 paid a large sum of money to King Edgar in order to clear his name and receive a confirmation of his estates.[170] It is a tale which seems to reflect a certain lack of order, or control, in Eadwig's reign, as an important thegn fell from grace and then managed to recover his standing in certain respects. So, far from being a matter determined by Wulfric's supposed preference for Edgar in 957, the interest of the tale is how, for a price, Edgar restored order where there might previously have been confusion. It is unfortunate, of course, that we do not know more about Æthelgeard and Wulfric *Cufing* themselves, and it may be that there were others like them whose careers came unstuck in the 950s. There are several instances in the mid-tenth century where two or more charters relating to the same estate were drawn up within a few years of each other, and several others where traces can be discerned of tampering with the grantor's or the beneficiary's name.[171] Something was happening, and we don't know what it was; but one senses that Æthelgeard and Wulfric stand for more widespread dangers faced by young upwardly-mobile thegns in the politically volatile world of the new kingdom of the English.

Political developments in the second quarter of the tenth century are likely to have been matched by an increase in economic activity, as accumulated or surplus resources were put to good use and as a tenth-century equivalent of

---

167   Keynes, *Attestations*, table LI; *Liber Vitae*, ed. Keynes, pp. 86–7.
168   Keynes, *Attestations*, tables XLIII, XLVI and LI.
169   Wulfric *Cufing* is so-named in S 1491 (*WinchNM* 18), and can be identified on this basis as the Wulfric of S 687 (*Abing* 86), and thus as the beneficiary of several charters issued in the 940s and 950s. Wulfric, brother of Dunstan, is named in B's *Vita S. Dunstani*, ch. 18 (Stubbs, *Dunstan*, p. 28). For discussion, see Hart, *Early Charters of Northern England*, pp. 370–2; Brooks, 'The Career of St Dunstan', pp. 163–6; and *Abing*, pp. clxxiii–lxxxv and 351–5.
170   S 687 (*Abing* 86), extant in its original single-sheet form, written by 'Edgar A'. Kelly (*Abing*, p. clxxxiii; cf. pp. 354–5) takes the view that Wulfric Cufing may not have received any new royal grants after 951, and suggests that his forfeiture was connected with the division of the kingdom in 957, whereupon he fell out of favour until restored by Edgar in 960. Wulfric's recovery in 958 is represented by S 575 (BCS 902), for part of Woolstone, Berks., S 577 (*Abing* 77), for Boxford, Berks., and S 657 (*Abing* 81), for Denchworth, Berks.
171   Keynes, *Attestations*, table LIII; S. Keynes, 'Boundary-clauses in Anglo-Saxon Charters' (forthcoming).

the multiplier effect helped to stimulate activity further on down the line. The shire-towns, market-towns and other royal and ecclesiastical centres would have continued to prosper in their various ways, not least from access to new markets; and a vital factor must have been a growing perception among those in northern England, the west midlands, the east midlands, and East Anglia, that their longer-term interests lay in connections with southern England, perhaps especially in and around London. An annal in the 'Northern Recension' of the *ASC* recording that in 969 King Edgar 'ordered all Thanet to be ravaged' proves to be indicative of this symbolic truth; for northern annals embedded in a thirteenth-century chronicle reveal that the king took this action in order to punish the men of Thanet for their ill-treatment of some merchants from York.[172]

More is needed, however, than such generalities. Although the draftsmen of the king's charters chose only rarely to indicate that any money had changed hands, there is enough evidence to show that, in continuation of past practices, payments were sometimes (perhaps often) made in gold, silver, and precious objects. In 960, the thegn Wulfric *Cufing* gave the king 120 mancuses of pure gold (*auri probatissimi*) for the restoration of his confiscated lands; in 962, the thegn (*satraps*) Godwine gave the king five pounds of gold and silver for a hide of land in Somerset; in 970, the abbot of Bath acquired ten hides of land close to the abbey in return for a payment of 100 mancuses of gold, and ten hides elsewhere; in 971, Bishop Æthelwold gave the king forty pounds of pure silver (*meri argenti*), and a golden cross which he valued more than the money, in return for land at Barrow-upon-Humber, for Peterborough abbey; and in 972, Archbishop Dunstan bought six hides in Middlesex for seventy *solidi* of refined gold (*auri obrixi*).[173] Although it is difficult (for various good reasons) to detect a close relationship between the operative details of these transactions, it is interesting to see how sums of money were computed and expressed in Edgar's days. Payments could be made up of silver and gold, presumably reckoning 240 silver pence, or (at 30 pence to a mancus) eight gold mancuses, to a pound of money; though precious objects of special value might also be included. Clearly, there was no shortage of gold, even though so little has survived from the period. Yet there would still have been much counting of pennies, as suggested by the remarkable record of a 'private' transaction, drawn up in 968, probably at Canterbury, which brings us down to the requisite level: a swine-pasture, at Heronden, in Tenterden, Kent, was purchased by a certain Ælfwold for 1,450 pence (*denarii*), or just over 6 pounds; Ælfwold later added a further 100 pence (*panega*).[174] Such transactions must have been commonplace; and we learn from

---

[172] Stenton, *ASE*, p. 563; Roger of Wendover, *Flores Historiarum*, s.a. 974, in *EHD*, p. 284.

[173] S 687 (*Abing* 86); S 705a (unpublished); S 777 (*Bath* 18); S 782 (*Pet* 15); S 1451 (BCS 1290), from Westminster see also S 1216 (*Abing* 115).

[174] S 1215 (*CantCC* 128). The charter is preserved in its original single-sheet form, reflecting successive stages of production in a most instructive way; it is attested by several *rustici*. For further discussion, see Keynes, 'The Witan and the Written Word'.

the twelfth-century *Libellus Æthelwoldi episcopi*, giving details of transactions which took place for the most part in Cambridgeshire in the early 970s, that Bishop Æthelwold's expenditure on the endowment of Ely Abbey amounted to about 375 pounds (in gold and silver), roughly the equivalent of 90,000 silver pence.[175]

The monastic reform movement

The first, second and third themes discussed above serve to keep the fourth in its appropriate perspective. The principal motivation or driving force behind the re-establishment of religious houses in the kingdom of the English, living in strict accordance with the Rule of St Benedict, was a desire to restore to their former glory some of the ancient houses known from the pages of Bede's *Ecclesiastical History of the English People*, from other literary works, from historical traditions of the later eighth and ninth centuries, or indeed from the visible remains of buildings.[176] In his treatise on the Old English Rule of St Benedict, Æthelwold himself gives an account of what were for him the origins of the reform movement; and although the relevant part of the text is missing, the story seems to have been told therein of the young Edgar, perhaps *c.* 950, seeing the ruins of an old monastery (Abingdon), and vowing there and then that if ever he became king he would restore the place, and others like it, to their original state.[177] Our knowledge of the progress of the reform movement during the 960s and early 970s is based otherwise on the *Lives* of Dunstan, Æthelwold and Oswald, written (*c.* 1000) within ten years or so of the deaths of their respective subjects, yet looking back to a more distant past. There is an obvious danger that sources of this nature are likely to focus attention on key individuals to the exclusion of many others who contributed to the process (before, during and after the heyday of Edgar's reign), and on reformed communities, living in strict accordance with the Rule, at the expense of less regular or 'secular' counterparts. Moreover, even the slight advantage of hindsight enjoyed by someone writing at the end of the tenth century might have been enough for him to regard the events of Edgar's reign from a particular point of view: to subsume the aims, methods and aspirations of the separate protagonists into an organized movement, with a particular cause, and to mistake an outcome or effect for an item on an original agenda. Modern historians will recognize how much was owed to the monastic reform movements on the continent, and will find extra dimensions, such as a wish to extend royal influence into areas where a king of the West Saxon line might not expect his writ to run, or a more general wish to revive a sense of 'Englishness', through raising awareness of the traditions of the past. It is easy, indeed, to get

---

[175] Keynes, 'Ely Abbey 672–1109', pp. 23–7; for analysis of the separate transactions, see Keynes and Kennedy, *Anglo-Saxon Ely*.

[176] For recent accounts of the subject, see C. Cubitt, 'The Tenth-Century Benedictine Reform in England', *EME* 6 (1997), 77–94, and, with a refreshing perspective, Blair, *Church*, pp. 346–54.

[177] *Councils & Synods*, p. 145, with WM, *VSD*, ii.2.1–2 (ed. Winterbottom and Thomson, p. 238), citing what would appear to have been a complete copy of the treatise.

carried away by the interest and obvious importance of whatever was going on; but how would it have seemed at the time?

To judge from his *Life*, Dunstan was installed at Glastonbury in the early 940s, and soon set about gathering together a community.[178] In the early 950s Æthelwold, by then dean of Glastonbury, established himself with King Eadred's help at Abingdon.[179] There can be no doubt that Æthelwold continued to function as abbot of Abingdon throughout the reign of Eadwig; yet to judge from the *Life* of Æthelwold, little or no progress seems to have been made there during this period, and indeed by Æthelwold's own account it was Edgar who took matters forward.[180] It remains an interesting question, therefore, whether the several charters in which Eadwig is represented as a benefactor of Abingdon are anything more than the products of a later attempt to create a better history.[181] Matters were transformed following Edgar's accession in 959 to the kingdom of the English. One of his first actions was to advance Dunstan, by now the bishop of London and Worcester, to the archbishopric of Canterbury, in place of Byrhthelm (formerly bishop of Wells);[182] and although one hears little more of Dunstan's role at Edgar's court, one must assume that he continued to exercise an important influence on the king. Dunstan would have had every reason to organize a formal inauguration ceremony, or coronation, perhaps held some time after his return from Rome in 960. Moreover, in 961 he persuaded Edgar to appoint Oswald, recently returned from Fleury, to the now vacant see of Worcester;[183] whereupon Oswald established a monastic community in an old minster at Westbury-on-Trym, in Gloucestershire.[184] For a while, during these early years of Edgar's reign, Æthelwold himself was perhaps pointedly the only abbot accorded whatever special standing at court is implied by regular inclusion among the witnesses to the king's charters; though three other abbots, including those of Malmesbury and Bath, make appearances in 963, perhaps reflecting the further activities of Archbishop Dunstan.[185] The king's own position may have been complicated at this stage by the fact that the key bishopric

---

[178] B, *VSD*, chs. 14–15 (Stubbs, *Dunstan*, pp. 24–6); see also WW, *VSÆ*, ch. 9 (Lapidge and Winterbottom, *WulfstW*, pp. 14–16), which implies that Dunstan and Æthelwold were at Glastonbury before the end of Æthelstan's reign. For the evidence of charters, see Brooks, 'Career of St Dunstan', pp. 4–5 and 11–14.

[179] WW, *VSÆ*, ch. 11 (Lapidge and Winterbottom, *WulfstW*, pp. 18–22).

[180] WW, *VSÆ*, chs. 11 and 13 (Lapidge and Winterbottom, *WulfstW*, pp. 18–22 and 24); *Councils & Synods*, pp. 148–9. There is arguably no obvious context here for the granting of privileges to Abingdon by Eadwig and Edgar in 959; cf. below, n. 219 (Osgar).

[181] For Eadwig's charters, see *Abing*, pp. xxxvii–xxxviii and ccxiv, with S 605 (*Abing* 52), S 607 (*Abing* 57), S 663 (*Abing* 59), S 583 (*Abing* 58), S 584 (*Abing* 68) and S 658 (*Abing* 83); see also *Abingdon*, ed. Hudson, I, pp. 60–75. It emerges from Keynes, *Attestations*, table XLVIII, that three abbots (Ælfric, Ælfwold and Æthelwold) were recognised in 959: S 658 (*Abing* 83), S 586 (Wilton) and S 660 (*WinchNM* 22).

[182] B, *VSD*, chs. 26–8 (Stubbs, *Dunstan*, pp. 37–40); N. P. Brooks, *The Early History of the Church of Canterbury: Christ Church from 597 to 1066* (Leicester, 1984), pp. 243–4.

[183] BR, *VSO* iii.4–5 (Raine, *York*, pp. 419–21).

[184] BR, *VSO* iii.8 (Raine, *York*, pp. 423–4).

[185] Above, p. 29. For Ælfric, see *Malm*, pp. 110–11; and for Æscwig, see *Wells*, p. 39.

of Winchester was still in the hands of his kinsman, another Byrhthelm, with whom he was apparently on good terms;[186] and it was thus Byrhthelm's death, or removal, apparently in the autumn of 963, which created the opportunity for which some may have been waiting. Æthelwold, abbot of Abingdon, was installed as the new bishop of Winchester on 29 November, and within three months had ejected the secular clergy from the Old Minster and replaced them with monks.[187] It seems to have been at about this time that Edgar issued an order (*preceptum*) of some kind, in which he enjoined upon Dunstan, Æthelwold and Oswald 'that all monastic sites should be established with monks and likewise with nuns'.[188] If we accept the statement at face value, it was perhaps this order which lay behind the action taken in 964 to drive the secular clergy from Winchester, Chertsey and Milton;[189] and this would accord with the involvement of Wulfstan of Dalham, representing royal authority.[190] The triumvirate of monastic bishops, at Canterbury, Worcester and Winchester, took different attitudes towards the clergy in their respective sees; but there were already several other monks established in other episcopal sees,[191] and, with the active support of the king, the stage was now set for the making of further progress in the re-establishment of the monastic order in England.

From his vantage point in the late 990s, Byrhtferth of Ramsey estimated that Edgar had ordered 'more than forty' monasteries to be established.[192] If the

---

186   For Edgar and Byrhthelm, see S 693 (BCS 1054), drafted by 'Edgar A' in 960; S 695 (BCS 1076), dated 961; and S 693 (BCS 1077), a lease of episcopal property, also dated 961. See also *Liber Vitae*, ed. Keynes, p. 24.

187   WW, *VSÆ*, chs. 16–18 (Lapidge and Winterbottom, *WulfstW*, pp. 28–32); *ASC* A, s.a. 963–4.

188   BR, *VSO* iv.3, 'ut omnia monasterii loca essent cum monachis constituta pariterque cum monialibus' (Raine, *York*, p. 434). Cf. Wormald, *Making of English Law*, p. 317.

189   It is arguable that Edgar's *preceptum* should (from its context in Byrhtferth's narrative) be dated c. 966; that it should be identified with the letter in which Edgar commanded Dunstan to draw up the *Regularis Concordia*; and that on this basis the *RC* itself can be dated 966 (and thus brought into close proximity to the New Minster charter). See Julia Barrow, 'The Chronology of the Benedictine "Reform"', below, pp. 219–20, and *Byrhtferth*, ed. Lapidge, *ad loc*.

190   *ASC* A, s.a. 964; WW, *VSÆ*, chs. 16–18 (Lapidge and Winterbottom, *WulfstW*, pp. 28–32); see also A. R. Rumble, 'The Laity and the Monastic Reform in the Reign of Edgar', below, pp. 242–51, at 243, drawing attention to the possibility that Queen Ælfthryth may have assisted in the process at the New Minster, through her own representative (*mea legatione*). The order was extended to Mercia in 969: John of Worcester, *Chronicon*, s.a. 969 (ed. Darlington and McGurk, p. 418).

191   The most authoritative evidence to this effect is provided by the list of bishops who were 'brothers' of the Old Minster, Winchester: *Liber Vitae*, ed. Keynes, pp. 87–8; see also Knowles, *Monastic Order*, pp. 697–701.

192   BR, *VSO* iii.11 (Raine, *York*, p. 426): 'plusquam quadraginta iussit monasteria constitui cum monachis'. A similar kind of remark was made by Wulfstan of Winchester, in his *Vita S. Æthelwoldi*, ch. 27 (Lapidge and Winterbottom, *WulfstW*, pp. 42–4), but without venturing a number. Eadmer of Canterbury, in his *Vita S. Dunstani*, ch. 57 (ed. Turner and Muir, p. 142), and in his *Vita S. Oswaldi*, ch. 19 (*ibid.*, p. 254), gives 48; cf. the claim in the (spurious) *Altitonantis* charter (S 731) to the effect that Edgar founded forty-seven monasteries.

chronology of monastic foundation, refoundation and reform could be worked out in any detail, it would probably reveal how, after a slow beginning in the 940s and 950s, the pace quickened from the mid-960s and sustained its new momentum until Edgar's death in 975.[193] Nor would it be difficult to substantiate Byrhtferth's estimate of forty houses, assuming that it would include nunneries as well as monasteries, some houses which remain unidentified by modern scholarship (known only from attestations of their abbots), and some houses which existed in Byrhtferth's time and which he simply assumed had been founded during the reign of King Edgar. The presumption is that the religious houses were founded or refounded under the influence of one or other of the triumvirate; and that while Dunstan (Glastonbury, Westminster) concentrated his efforts in the west country, Oswald (Westbury, Worcester, Winchcombe) was active in the west midlands and at Ramsey,[194] and Æthelwold (Winchester) moved into the fenlands, refounding houses at Ely, *Medeshamstede* (Peterborough), Thorney and elsewhere.[195] It is a useful model, though it should be admitted that the evidence is very uneven and that the hypothesis implies a degree of co-ordination which might well misrepresent the actual nature of the process. In reality, the circumstances in which a house was re-founded or founded, and the particular way in which it flourished thereafter, or perhaps failed to flourish, varied greatly from one place to another. Houses also suffered different fates at the time of the Norman Conquest, and maintained of variety of record-keeping practices thereafter. Yet our knowledge of the Anglo-Saxon past depends heavily on the records of these religious houses, and on their perceptions of what that past should be; and it is not least for this reason that so much importance attaches to an understanding of the separate histories of religious houses in the tenth and eleventh centuries.

The fullest and most instructively circumstantial account of the foundation of a monastery in the 960s is Byrhtferth's narrative of the early history of Ramsey. The story originated in Oswald's wish to find a more suitable home for the small community of monks which, soon after he became bishop of Worcester in 961, he had assembled at Westbury.[196] Oswald attended a meeting of the king and his councillors, held over the Easter festival at an unspecified place, in an unspeci-

---

[193] The story is summarized by D. Knowles, *The Monastic Order in England*, 2nd ed. (Cambridge, 1963), pp. 48–52 and 721 (table); see also Hart, 'Æthelstan "Half-King" and his Family', p. 596, n. 103, D. Hill, *An Atlas of Anglo-Saxon England* (Oxford, 1981), p. 151 (map), and C. Holdsworth, 'Benedictine Monks and Nuns of the 10th Century', *Studies in the Early History of Shaftesbury Abbey*, ed. L. Keen (Dorchester, 1999), pp. 73–98, at 96–7.

[194] BR, *VSO* iv.4 (Raine, *York*, p. 435), for Worcester and Winchcombe; and *VSO* iv.8 (*ibid.* pp. 438–41), for Pershore (under Abbot Foldbriht), among 'seven' in the province of the Hwicce. One should bear in mind that Winchcombe was an ancient religious house, and probably by this time the centre of a shire.

[195] WW, *VSÆ*, chs. 23–4 (Lapidge and Winterbottom, *WulfstW*, pp. 38–42); see also HH, *Historia Anglorum*, v.25 (ed. Greenway, p. 321). Æthelwold is said to have been ordered by King Edgar to institute monasteries, apparently with reference to those 'destroyed' by Ealdorman Ælfhere after the king's death (*ASC* DE, s.a. 975).

[196] BR, *VSO* iii.8 (Raine, *York*, pp. 423–4).

fied year, possibly in 965 or perhaps thereafter.[197] According to Byrhtferth, the king was moved on this occasion by the assembled company of bishops, abbots and abbesses, with their respective followings, singing divine service; and it is in this context that Byrhtferth says of the king that he ordered more than forty monasteries to be established with monks. After the others had dispersed, Oswald stayed back and asked the king if he had a place where he might be able to assemble his monks. Edgar offered him a choice of three monasteries, at St Albans (Hertfordshire), Ely (Cambridgeshire), and Benfleet (Essex); so Oswald went at once to inspect them, and then returned home. Yet he also had a fourth option. It had so happened, during the course of the Easter meeting, that a distinguished king's thegn (*inclytus miles regis*) had died. At the funeral, the king ordered that the body should be taken away to its place of burial; Oswald accompanied the procession, and, after the burial, another distinguished thegn (*miles egregius*), called Æthelwine, identified as one of the sons of Ealdorman Æthelstan Half-King, approached Oswald for his blessing. In the course of their conversation Æthelwine remarked that he had a suitable place for the establishment of a monastery, at Ramsey, where there were already three men eager to follow the monastic life. Within a few days Oswald had inspected Ramsey as well, and was so impressed by its suitability, expressed in terms of its natural resources, that he instructed the priest Eadnoth to move there from Westbury and to make the place habitable. Work continued apace during the spring and summer; and in August, when all was ready, Oswald himself led his monks across the country to Ramsey.[198] Necessary preparations were made for the first winter, and in the following spring foundations were laid for stone buildings, including the church.[199] Oswald pressed on thereafter, with help from Ealdorman Æthelwine.[200] As soon as the monastery was completed, apparently at about the time of King Edgar's death in 975, it was consecrated by Archbishop Oswald, assisted by Ælfnoth, bishop of Dorchester.[201] Byrhtferth chooses to indicate in this connection that Oswald provided his community at Ramsey with many gifts,

---

[197] There is no reason to believe that this meeting was anything other than an ordinary meeting of the king and his councillors. For some further discussion, see J. Barrow, 'The Community of Worcester, 961–c.1100', *St Oswald of Worcester*, ed. Brooks and Cubitt, pp. 84–99, at 94–5.

[198] BR, *VSO* iii.9–17 (Raine, *York*, pp. 424–31). The remark about forty monasteries may have been part of Byrhtferth's general encomium of the king, rather than a reference to a specific order made on a particular occasion. The identity of the thegn who died during the course of the meeting is not known; but according to Ramsey's twelfth-century *Liber benefactorum*, the funeral took place at Glastonbury. Byrhtferth was evidently under the impression that Æthelwine himself was a young man at the time, and so still a thegn (iii.15); and perhaps he would not have known that Æthelwine had succeeded his brother in 962 and would thus already have been an ealdorman at the time of his meeting with Oswald. For the suggestion that the funeral was in fact that of Ealdorman Æthelmund (here loosely styled *miles*), who does indeed disappear from the witness-lists in 965, see *Byrhtferth*, ed. Lapidge.

[199] *VSO* iv.1–2 (Raine, *York*, pp. 433–4).

[200] *VSO* iv.8 (Raine, *York*, pp. 438–9).

[201] *VSO* iv.15 (Raine, *York*, pp. 446–7).

including books, vestments, and other items necessary for the religious life;[202] and he indicates in another context that Ealdorman Æthelwine also gave many gifts, and promised to give 200 hides of land.[203]

One learns from all this, unsurprisingly, that the foundation of a monastery was a long and complex process. In the case of Ramsey, the building work seems to have extended over a period of almost ten years; and it seems that the acquisition of a landed endowment took even longer. Much would depend on the resources of the founders themselves, or on their willingness to expend their resources for such a purpose; yet much might also depend on a monastery's 'identity' or profile within its own locality, and on its success, or otherwise, in becoming a focal point of attention. Perhaps there is a contrast to be drawn here between a place like Ramsey, which depended to a great extent on the patronage of a particular family, and a place like Ely, which had been refounded by the bishop of Winchester, which enjoyed royal patronage, and which had the undoubtedly special attraction of its association with St Æthelthryth to generate extra support. That is not to say, however, that Ely's extraordinary success in the early 970s was necessarily to its advantage; for the greater the success, the greater the impact on local society, and so the greater the resentment after Edgar's death – as we read in the *Libellus Æthelwoldi episcopi.*

It is scarcely surprising that after several years of separate initiatives the need should have been felt for some overall control. It is not known for certain when Edgar convened the 'synodal council' at Winchester described in the prologue to the *Regularis Concordia*, and suggestions range from a date in the mid-960s, perhaps 966,[204] to a date in the early 970s, perhaps 973.[205] King Edgar addressed a letter, to the synodal council of Winchester, 'set forth magnificently on parchment', in which he urged 'all to be of *one mind* as regards monastic usage ... lest differing ways of observing the customs of *one Rule* and *one country* (*unius regulae ac unius patriae*) should bring their holy conversation into disrepute'.[206] There is an analogy to be pressed here with the reform of the coinage, and with the background to the events at Bath and Chester in 973; but perhaps the more compelling argument in favour of the later date is that such action might not have been required before the early 970s.

This is not the place to pursue the monastic reform movement into its second generation, in the late tenth and early eleventh centuries, except to say again how dependent we are on views of the 'movement', in the central decades of the

---

[202] *VSO* iv.15 and v.10 (Raine, *York*, pp. 446–7 and 462–3).

[203] *VSO* v.14 (Raine, *York*, pp. 467–8); see also Hart, 'Æthelstan "Half-King" and his Family', pp. 596–7.

[204] Barrow, 'Chronology', below, pp. 211–23. The suggestion arises from the identification of Edgar's *preceptum* about the establishment of monasteries (*VSO* iv.3: above, p. 42), in force in the mid-960s, as the letter addressed to the council of Winchester which led to *Regularis Concordia.*

[205] T. Symons, '*Regularis Concordia*: History and Derivation', *Tenth-Century Studies*, ed. D. Parsons (Chichester, 1975), pp. 37–59 and 214–17, at 39–42.

[206] *Regularis Concordia, Proemium*, ch. 4 (Symons, *RC*, pp. 2–3; *Consuetudinum saeculi X/XI/XII monumenta non-Cluniacensia*, ed. Hallinger, pp. 70–1).

tenth century, which were formed in the context of conditions which had come to prevail in the 990s. The earliest *Lives* of Dunstan, Æthelwold and Oswald have for this reason to be treated with all due circumspection. Yet perhaps there is more to it than that. It would be interesting to know how widely Bishop Æthelwold's treatise on the Old English Rule of St Benedict might have been read, and what influence it might have exerted on the communities of religious houses in times of trouble, when they would have been brought under ever in-creasing pressure from the secular powers. Reflecting concerns expressed else-where in the New Minster charter, Æthelwold exhorts his successors to observe the Rule, and, more strikingly, impresses upon them the need to protect God's property against the kind of losses from which churches had suffered in the past, whether through acts of robbery perpetrated by evil men or through the actions of those who were in charge of the churches themselves.[207] One can almost see the genesis, here, of a natural inclination for heads of houses to ensure that their landed endowments and their privileges were protected by the necessary or most effective forms of documentation, with threats and curses of every kind; and there were reasons, in the 990s, why for their part the secular powers might have been minded to promote the same cause.[208] We are led back, unavoidably, to the controversy surrounding the authenticity of the so-called 'Orthodoxorum' charters in the names of Eadwig and Edgar.[209] If genuine, they would bear di-rectly on the course of monastic reform from 959 onwards, and the tenor of the summary given above would have to be adjusted. If spurious, King Æthelred's charter for Abingdon abbey, dated 993, would take its place at the head of the series, and much else would follow. The basic formula employed in Edgar's charters of the 960s and early 970s for the operative element in grants of land to religious houses was *ad usus monachorum* (or a variation on that theme), found in charters of 'Edgar A' and of the 'Edgar A' type for Abingdon, Shaftes-bury, Glastonbury, Romsey, Wilton, Bath, and Ely;[210] different forms of words

207 *Councils & Synods*, pp. 152–4. If in the preface to the *Regularis Concordia* King Edgar was represented as protector of monks, Æthelwold's remarks in this context seem to reflect an awareness of more complex realities; and for the way in which Ælfric moved in the same direction, see C. A. Jones, *Ælfric's Letter to the Monks of Eynsham* (Cambridge, 1998), pp. 43–6.

208 Keynes, *Diplomas*, pp. 189–93, and 'An Abbot, an Archbishop, and the Viking Raids of 1006–7 and 1009–12', *ASE* 36 (2007), pp. 151–220. For Æthelweard and his son Æthelmær, see also M. Gretsch, 'Ælfric, Language and Winchester', *A Companion to Ælfric*, ed. M. Swan and H. Magennis (Leiden, forthcoming).

209 Above, pp. 16–17.

210 Among charters for Abingdon, the formula *ad monachorum usus inibi regulariter de-gentium dominoque nostro deuote seruientium* occurs in S 690 (*Abing* 87), dated 961, and occurs also in S 688–9; the formula *ad usus ibidem fratrum Deo seruientium* occurs in S 682, dated 960, S 708, dated 963, and S 732–4, dated 965; and the formula *ad usus monachorum Dei inibi degentium* occurs in S 757–60, dated 968; cf. S 700, dated 962, S 701, dated 962, and S 724, dated 964. For similar usages in 'Edgar A' charters for other houses, see S 744, dated 966 (Shaftesbury), S 764, dated 968 (Glastonbury), S 765, dated 968 (Romsey), S 766–7, dated 968 (Wilton), S 777, dated 970 (Bath), and S 780–1, dated 970 (Ely).

are found in charters of the 'Dunstan B' type, for Bath and Glastonbury, and in other charters for the Old Minster, Winchester, and for Peterborough.[211] Yet Edgar's charter for the New Minster, Winchester, dated 966, demonstrates quite clearly that general privileges of such a kind were not out of place in his reign; and, since Wulfstan of Winchester refers to royal charters for Abingdon, apparently produced during the abbacy of Æthelwold's successor Osgar (963–84),[212] and also to a charter for Ely,[213] one might suppose that the New Minster charter was not unique. The question arises, nonetheless, whether *any* of Edgar's charters of foundation or refoundation, or general grants of privileges, apart from the New Minster charter, can be accepted as authentic.[214] Some among them may have come into existence in the closing decades of the tenth century, in recognition of a need to provide a monastery with useful documentation, perhaps extending to a respectably ancient identity, at a time when its lands and privileges were coming under threat. At Westminster, for example, the monks produced a charter intended to secure the endowment received in Edgar's reign (invoking ancient charters of King Offa);[215] the fact that Edgar's 'Orthodoxorum' charter for Pershore abbey survives in single-sheet form, written probably not later than the end of the tenth century,[216] suggests that some if not all of the other 'Orthodoxorum' charters, including those of Eadwig and Edgar for Abingdon, came into existence at about the same time; and Edgar's charter for Ely abbey, also extant in single-sheet form (probably of the later eleventh century), is given not only in Latin but in an Old English version which has been attributed to Ælfric of Eynsham.[217] A composite text, representing Edgar's role as benefactor of the Old Minster, Winchester, was conceivably put together in Æthelred's reign;[218] some of the charters of King Edgar said by Wulfstan of Winchester to have

---

[211] For usages in 'Dunstan B' charters for Bath and Glastonbury, see S 694, S 735, S 743, S 785 and S 791; the usage in S 735 (*Bath* 17) is especially interesting (above, p. 19). See also S 699, dated 961 (Old Minster, Winchester), and S 782, dated 971 (Peterborough).

[212] WW, *VSÆ*, ch. 21 (Lapidge and Winterbottom, *WulfstW*, p. 36); but see further below, n. 000.

[213] WW, *VSÆ*, ch. 23 (Lapidge and Winterbottom, *WulfstW*, pp. 38–40).

[214] For the charters in question, see Keynes, 'Conspectus', pp. 63–4. They range from problematic to patently spurious; but there is much to learn from the circumstances in which each was produced, and from the relationship between them.

[215] S. Keynes, 'Wulfsige, Monk of Glastonbury, Abbot of Westminster (c.990–3), and Bishop of Sherborne (c.993–1002)', *St Wulfsige and Sherborne*, ed. K. Barker *et al.* (Oxford, 2005), pp. 53–94, at 56–7, with reference to S 670 (BCS 1048), S 1450, MS. 1 (BCS 1351), and S 1451 (BCS 1290).

[216] S 786 (BCS 1282), with the letter from Godfrey, archdeacon of Worcester, to the pope, in BL, Cotton Augustus ii. 7; see also Thompson, *Anglo-Saxon Royal Diplomas*, pp. 142–5, and P. Stokes, 'King Edgar's "Orthodoxorum" Charter for Pershore Abbey', *ASE* (forthcoming).

[217] S 779 (BCS 1266–7); see J. Pope, 'Ælfric and the Old English Version of the Ely Privilege', *England before the Conquest*, ed. P. Clemoes and K. Hughes (Cambridge, 1971), pp. 85–113.

[218] S 814–19 + 821–7, for which see Rumble, *Property and Piety*, pp. 98–135, at 103, and a forthcoming study by Sophie Rixon.

preserved at Abingdon in his own day might have been produced more recently than he might have supposed;[219] and Professor Lapidge suggests that Edgar's charter for Ramsey, dated 974, contains traces of Byrhtferthian Latinity, raising the possibility that the need for such a charter might have been felt, at Ramsey, in the late tenth or early eleventh century.[220] It is arguable that few of the monasteries which came into being during Edgar's reign did so in circumstances for which a straightforward charter of foundation or endowment, or a grant of privileges, would have been expected, or indeed appropriate; but different conditions prevailed in Æthelred's reign, and of course at later dates. The question, therefore, is whether some religious houses might have turned sooner rather than later, under these circumstances, to the fabrication of charters, not just in the name of King Edgar, or his immediate predecessors, but also in the names of kings from the more distant and venerable past.

The events of 973

A fifth and final theme, which also needs to be approached in its wider context, arises in the early 970s. In 1943 Sir Frank Stenton expressed his view that 'the first event of [Edgar's] time which made a strong impression on his contemporaries was his long-deferred coronation, which took place at Bath, on Whit Sunday 973'.[221] The medieval notion was that Edgar's coronation was deferred as penance for his sins;[222] and a modern notion has arisen that Edgar's solemn anointing was deferred until he reached the canonical age (thirty) for ordination into the priesthood (in fact he was in his twenty-ninth year). It is now perhaps generally assumed that Edgar would have been crowned and consecrated king by Archbishop Dunstan in 960, not long after Dunstan's return to England on receiving his pallium from Pope John XII at Rome in September of that year;[223]

---

219   The view in the late tenth century was that Abingdon was enriched (*ditatus*), following the appointment of Osgar as abbot (in 963), with at least 600 hides, and strengthened (*suffultus*) with charters of eternal liberty, written with divine and royal authority, which, 'sealed with gold leaves' (*laminis aureis sigillata*), were preserved there 'to the present day' (WW, *VSÆ*, ch. 21, Lapidge and Winterbottom, *WulfstW*, p. 36). The allusion seems to be to a number of separate charters, which between them are rather unlikely to have amounted to an endowment of this order of magnitude (cf. *Abing*, pp. clxv–clxvi, and *Historia Ecclesie Abbendonensis*, ed. Hudson, I, cxxxvii–cxliii); but it remains unclear what might have been meant by the reference to their being 'sealed with gold leaves', unless no more than a flight of fancy, perhaps suggested by *II Chron*. iii.8, with reference to Solomon's temple, overlaid with gold – *laminis aureis* – amounting to 600 talents.

220   S 798 (BCS 1311); see *Byrhtferth*, ed. Lapidge. The 'original' charter was displayed at Ramsey in the 1530s; see Keynes, 'Anglo-Saxon Charters: Lost and Found', pp. 50–1.

221   Stenton, *ASE*, p. 368; see also John, 'The Age of Edgar', pp. 188–9, and A. Jones, 'The Significance of the Regal Consecration of Edgar in 973', *Journal of Ecclesiastical History* 33 (1982), 375–90.

222   WM, *Gesta Regum* ii.158 and 160.1 (ed. Mynors *et al.*, pp. 258 and 260); EC, *VSD*, chs. 56 and 58 (ed. Turner and Muir, pp. 136 and 142–4).

223   For this line of argument, see J. L. Nelson, 'Inauguration Rituals' [1977], reprinted in her *Politics and Ritual in Early Medieval Europe* (London, 1986), pp. 283–307, at 296–303. A copy of the privilege of Pope John XII accompanying the grant of a pallium to Arch-

and of course it is an assumption which has a significant impact on the interpretation of the events at Bath in 973. The evidence of law-codes, charters and coins indicates that there was nothing deficient about Edgar's kingship during the 960s; yet there is no mistaking the contemporary perception of his 'second' coronation in 973 as a symbolic event of the utmost significance in its day, which in some sense marked a new beginning.[224] So what did it signify? For reasons which are not entirely clear, Byrhtferth of Ramsey remarks in his *Vita S. Oswaldi* that Edgar sent Æscwig, abbot of Bath, to Germany, accompanied by the thegn Wulfmær, bearing wonderful presents (*mira munera*) for the emperor (presumably Otto I), and returning with even more wonderful gifts (*mirabiliora munera*) and a treaty of peace (*pactum ... pacis*).[225] The date of the mission is not specified; but it seems likely that it took place in the closing months of 972, after the emperor's return from Italy.[226] It would be interesting, therefore, to know whether Æscwig and Wulfmær were still present in Germany for either or both of the major assemblies convened by Otto in March 973, first at Magdeburg (Palm Sunday [16 March]) and then at Quedlinburg (Easter Sunday [23 March]); but alas the evidence fails us.[227] It is difficult to resist the thought that Æscwig was reminded by whatever he saw in Germany of the value of grand ceremonial, and that he was instrumental in applying this lesson for the meeting convened at Bath over Pentecost (11 May) in 973.[228] There is no reason to believe that a special version of the coronation service was devised for use specifically on this occasion, representing a significant change from earlier liturgical usage or indeed in the conception of Edgar's kingship;[229] so it is essentially

bishop Dunstan, dated 21 September 960, is entered in the 'Pontifical of St Dunstan'; see *Councils & Synods*, no. 25, and Keynes, 'Wulfsige', pp. 62–6.

[224] The principal sources are the entries in *ASC*; see also BR, *VSO* iv.6–7 (Raine, *York*, pp. 436–8). For the poem in *ASC ABC*, see Mercedes Salvador-Bello, 'The Edgar Panegyrics in the *Anglo-Saxon Chronicle*', below, pp. 252–72. The entry in the 'northern recension' (*ASC* DE) contains the same basic information, but continues with a connected reference to the event at Chester.

[225] BR, *VSO* iv.4 (Raine, *York*, p. 435, but following Lapidge in reading 'Æscuuium' for Raine's 'Ætherium'). Æscwig attests Edgar's charters as abbot (of Bath) from 963 onwards (Keynes, *Attestations*, table LV); see also *The Heads of Religious Houses: England and Wales*, I: *940–1216*, ed. D. Knowles *et al.*, 2nd ed. (Cambridge, 2001), p. 28. A thegn called Wulfmær was the beneficiary of a charter in 962 (S 707) and again in 973 (S 793); attestations of a Wulfmær occur in 968 and 972 (Keynes, *Attestations*, table LVII).

[226] K. Leyser, 'The Ottonians and Wessex', in his *Communications and Power in Medieval Europe: The Carolingian and Ottonian Centuries*, ed. T. Reuter (London, 1994), pp. 73–104, at 95–7.

[227] For the assemblies at Magdeburg and Quedlinburg, see D. A. Warner, *Ottonian Germany: The Chronicon of Thietmar of Merseburg* (Manchester, 2001), pp. 114–15; see also T. Reuter, *Germany in the Early Middle Ages 800–1056* (London, 1991), pp. 174–5.

[228] *ASC*, s.a. 973; see also BR, *VSO* iv.6–7 and 11 (Raine, *York*, pp. 436–8). The connection was made by Leyser, 'Ottonians and Wessex', p. 97, unaware that the abbot in question was in fact the abbot of Bath; see also *Byrhtferth*, ed. Lapidge.

[229] This argument was propounded by P. Schramm, *A History of the English Coronation* (Oxford, 1936), pp. 19–22, and adopted by Stenton, *ASE*, p. 368. It is now recognized

the repetition of the ritual, and its location at Bath, that must be indicative of its intended meaning, together with the fact that it was associated with a ceremony which took place at Chester immediately afterwards. A contributor to the northern recension of the *ASC*, writing perhaps twenty-five years after the event, remarked in this connection that six kings came to meet Edgar, 'and gave him pledges that they would be his allies on sea and on land'; or, as Ælfric put it (without identifying the occasion), 'all the kings who were in this island, of the Welsh and of the Scots, came to Edgar – on one such day eight kings – and they all submitted to Edgar's rule'.[230] For his part, Byrhtferth of Ramsey had a clear view of the extent of King Edgar's power: he subjected all peoples 'whom the ocean surrounds' to his authority, conquered 'the ferocious and foolish kings of the Scots and Welsh' (*feroces ac stolidos reges Scottorum atque Cumbriensium*), and glittered thereafter.[231] In these various sources the rulers in question are left unnamed; but the kings who came to Edgar at Chester were identified in the later eleventh- or early twelfth-century source which lies behind the chronicles of John of Worcester and William of Malmesbury,[232] and are seen on this basis to lend substance to the notion of Edgar's much vaunted supremacy throughout Britain. Modern post-colonial interpretation has reinvented the ceremony at Chester as a 'peace summit', or a conference of the 'Great Powers', casting Edgar as little more than a genial host or chairman.[233] It might be different if the draftsmen of Edgar's charters had chosen, like some of their predecessors, to include sub-kings in the witness-lists, and thus have given a better sense of the background in the 960s; for it is difficult to see in the events of 973 very

that the significant developments in the history of the Anglo-Saxon coronation service took place in the late ninth or early tenth century; see esp. J. L. Nelson, 'The Second English Ordo', in her *Politics and Ritual*, pp. 361–74, and 'The First Use of the Second Anglo-Saxon Ordo', *Myth, Rulership, Church and Charters*, ed. Barrow and Wareham (forthcoming).

230 *ASC* DE, s.a. 973; Ælfric's *Lives of the Saints*, in *Swithun*, ed. Lapidge, pp. 606–7.

231 BR, *VSE* iv.11 (ed. Lapidge, forthcoming). It is not clear what Byrhtferth may have meant by the *Cumbrienses*; but perhaps more than the men of Cumbria (or Strathclyde). For the background, see A. Woolf, *From Pictland to Alba 789–1070*, New Edinburgh History of Scotland 2 (Edinburgh, 2007), pp. 152–7.

232 JW, *Chronicon*, s.a. 973 (ed. Darlington and McGurk, pp. 422–4), and WM, *Gesta Regum* ii.148.2 (ed. Mynors *et al.*, pp. 238–40); see also S 808 (*CantCC* 129). The Malcolm *dux* seen in S 779 (BCS 1266), from Ely, was presumably Malcolm of Strathclyde.

233 Jayakumar, 'Reflections on the "Foreign Policies" of King Edgar', pp. 31–5; D. Thornton, 'Edgar and the Eight Kings, AD 973: *Textus et Dramatis Personae*', *EME* 10.1 (2001), 49–79; J. Barrow, 'Chester's Earliest Regatta? Edgar's Dee-Rowing Revisited', *EME* 10.1 (2001), 81–93; and A. Williams, 'An Outing on the Dee: King Edgar at Chester, AD 973', *MScand* 14 (2004), 229–43. For more recent discussion, see S. Matthews, 'King Edgar, Wales and Chester: the Welsh Dimension in the Ceremony of 973', *Northern History* 44 (2007), 9–26, re-emphasizing larger political dimensions; A. Breeze, 'Edgar at Chester in 973: A Breton Link?', *Northern History* 44 (2007), 153–7; Woolf, *From Pictland to Alba*, pp. 207–9, on the 'Welsh' context; and C. Downham, *Viking Kings of Britain and Ireland: The Dynasty of Ívarr to A.D. 1014* (Edinburgh, 2007), pp. 124–7.

much less than the ceremonial reaffirmation and public celebration of Edgar's rule throughout Britain.[234]

A curious tract on the Anglo-Saxon kingdoms, compiled apparently at Durham in the 1120s, ends with a brief account of the earls of Northumbria which reveals what may be another dimension of the same story.[235] According to this source, Earl Oslac [of York] and Earl Eadwulf 'Yvelcild' [of Bamborough], with Bishop Ælfsige [of Chester le Street], escorted Cinaed, king of Scots [Kenneth II (*c.* 971–95)], to a meeting with King Edgar; whereupon, in return for his homage, Edgar gave Kenneth the land called Lothian (between the Tweed and the Forth).[236] Oslac was evidently a major player in the north at this time; Eadwulf, his more northerly colleague, is found among the witnesses to Edgar's charters only in 968–70,[237] yet enough to lend some credence to the possibility that Edgar tried in the later 960s and early 970s to bring the far north under some semblance of control. There is good reason to believe that Bishop Ælfsige, for his part, was in the heart of Wessex in 970, but it would be hazardous to press this evidence too far.[238]

The aftermath of King Edgar's death
Edgar died on 8 July 975, and was buried, like his father Edmund before him, at Glastonbury.[239] The place of a king's burial was always a matter of importance, whether to a king before his death, or to those who had reason to control his

---

[234] Stenton, *ASE*, pp. 369–70; Nelson, 'Inauguration Rituals'; Keynes, 'England 900–1016', pp. 481–2; Wormald, *Making of English Law*, pp. 441–2. It should be emphasized, of course, that Edgar had been styled 'king of the whole of Britain' from the outset of his reign (above, pp. 24–5).

[235] The tract (*De primo Saxonum adventu*) is edited from BL, Cotton Domitian A.viii, in *Symeonis Monachi Opera Omnia*, ed. T. Arnold, 2 vols. (London, 1882–5), I.365–84, at 382, and *EHD*, p. 284, n. 6. For further discussion, see Whitelock, 'Dealings of the Kings of England', pp. 76–9.

[236] For discussion, see Stenton, *ASE*, p. 370; M. O. Anderson, 'Lothian and the Early Scottish Kings', *Scottish Historical Review* 39 (1960), 98–112; B. Meehan, 'The Siege of Durham, the Battle of Carham and the Cession of Lothian', *Scottish Historical Review* 55 (1976), 1–19; D. Broun, 'Kenneth II', *ODNB* xxxi.279–80; and Woolf, *From Pictland to Alba*, pp. 208–11.

[237] Keynes, *Attestations*, table LVI.

[238] In a note in the tenth-century 'Durham Ritual' (Durham Cathedral A.IV.19, p. 167; facsimile in M. P. Brown, *Manuscripts from the Anglo-Saxon Age* (London, 2007), p. 111), Bishop Ælfsige is reported to have been present, in a tent, at a place south of 'Woodyates at Oakley in Wessex', on St Lawrence's Day (10 Aug.), a Wednesday, when the moon was five nights old. The indications would be compatible with 970; and it is the case that Bishop Ælfsige makes his sole appearance in Edgar's reign in a charter dated 970 (S 781, from Ely: Keynes, *Attestations*, table LIV). For further discussion, see *Rituale Ecclesiae Dunelmensis / The Durham Collectar*, ed. A. H. Thompson and U. Lindelöf, Surtees Society 140 (Durham, 1927), pp. xiv–xix and 185, and Ker, *Catalogue*, pp. 144–6 (no. 106). Whether this was the only occasion on which Ælfsige came south is of course another matter.

[239] JW, *Chronicon*, s.a. 975 (ed. Darlington and McGurk, p. 424); WM, *Gesta Regum* ii.160 (ed. Mynors *et al.*, p. 260).

remembrance;[240] and in Edgar's case, the choice of Glastonbury is perhaps to be read in terms of the closeness of the relationship between the king and his archbishop, stretching back to Edgar's reign as king of the Mercians. The death of King Edgar also had immediate and dramatic consequences of various kinds, and from the nature of these consequences we learn much about the reign which had just ended. The aftermath was described by one contemporary observer as a period of dissension (*dissensio*), trouble (*tribulatio*), and sedition (*seditio*);[241] another referred to 'most unhappy times' (*infelicissima ... tempora*).[242] On the face of it, the explanation is not far to seek. The succession to Edgar's throne was immediately disputed between supporters of Edward and supporters of Æthelred; and there were at the same time widespread attacks on the recently reformed monasteries, labelled by modern scholarship as 'the anti-monastic reaction'. The question is whether or to what extent these matters might have been connected, and whether there were other issues at stake.[243]

The fact that the succession was disputed on Edgar's death, and that it was not the kingdom that was divided, is perhaps a sign of what Edgar had achieved in the 960s and early 970s. Certainly, the kingdom represented by the reformed and impressively uniform coinage of the closing years of Edgar's reign would seem to have been less readily divisible than the kingdom represented by the coinage of the 950s and 960s. The fullest account of the disputed succession is provided by Byrhtferth of Ramsey, writing about twenty years after the event, during the reign of King Æthelred, and presenting a view which cannot have been far removed from the official line of the day: some of the chief men (*primates*) wanted the elder son Edward, but several of the nobles (*principes*) disliked Edward and preferred Æthelred; Edward and Æthelred were on good terms with each other; the murder of Edward was a heinous crime perpetrated by treacherous and deranged men, who later received their just deserts; and the victim was the Lord's anointed, who became a martyr.[244] Although Dunstan is said by later writers to have acted decisively in support of Edward,[245] there seems little reason to believe that Edward's party was identified as one of monastic reform, still less that the supporters of Æthelred sought to harm Edward's position by or-

---

[240] For the burial-places of the kings of the West Saxons, and their successors in the tenth and eleventh centuries, see *Blackwell Encycl*, pp. 511–16.

[241] BR, *VSO* iv.17 (Raine, *York*, p. 448).

[242] S 1451 (BCS 1290), from BL, Stowe Ch. 32 (written in the late tenth century).

[243] Keynes, *Diplomas*, pp. 163–74.

[244] BR, *VSO* iv.18–21 (Raine, *York*, pp. 449–52). It is conceivable that Byrhtferth intended a distinction here between *primates*, denoting high-ranking ecclesiastics, and *principes*, denoting high-ranking laymen; distinctions of apparently the same kind are made in his *Vita S. Ecgwini*, i.10, iii.4, and iii.6. For the early development of the cult of St Edward, and the role of Ælfric (bishop of Ramsbury and archbishop of Canterbury), Wulfstan (bishop of London and archbishop of York), and Germanus (abbot at Ramsey and of Cholsey), see S. Keynes, 'King Alfred the Great and Shaftesbury Abbey', *Studies in the Early History of Shaftesbury*, ed. Keen, pp. 17–72, at 50–3, and 'The Cult of Edward the Martyr during the Reign of King Æthelred the Unready' (forthcoming).

[245] OC, *VSD*, ch. 37 (Stubbs, *Dunstan*, p. 114); EC, *VSD*, ch. 59 (ed. Turner and Muir, p. 144); WM, *VSD*, ii.18.2 (ed. Winterbottom and Thomson, p. 268).

chestrating an attack on monasteries.[246] The dispute arose from Edgar's successive marriages, and seems to have been essentially personal. There was support
in some quarters for the natural priority of Edward, son of Edgar and Æthelflæd,
over Æthelred, son of Edgar and Ælfthryth. Others, probably including Bishop
Æthelwold, took the view that Ælfthryth was a 'legitimate' queen, and so that
Æthelred was the surviving legitimate heir. Edward's coronation should have
settled the issue, at least for the time being; but some among Æthelred's thegns
preferred their own lord, leading about two and a half years later to the murder
of King Edward, on 18 March 978.[247]

More significant, perhaps, than the disputed succession were the changes in
the secular hierarchy precipitated by Edgar's death. We saw above that from
about 970 until the end of Edgar's reign there were ealdormen holding office
in Mercia (Ælfhere), East Anglia (Æthelwine), Essex (Byrhtnoth), and Northumbria (Oslac). The ealdormen of Mercia, East Anglia and Essex retained
their positions. According to the *ASC* for 975, Earl Oslac was driven from the
country; the implication seems to be that he was closely identified with Edgar's
regime, and effectively went with it.[248] Yet what should we make of the apparent
lack of representation for the whole of England south of the river Thames, in
the early 970s? It may be that Edgar's perceived strength as a ruler was to some
extent a function of the degree of power or personal influence that he was able
to exercise, latterly, in this area; in which case his death would have left a gaping
void which had to be filled. At least three new appointments were soon made
to cover the area in question: Æthelweard of west Wessex, Æthelmær of Hampshire, and Eadwine of Sussex (and Kent).[249] If the peace and stability in Edgar's
reign had depended to such an extent on his own ability to hold structures in
place, one begins to understand why it might have proved so difficult, during the
short reign of Edward the Martyr, for the authorities to keep control, and why
so many might have taken advantage of the situation in order to protect, assert
and advance their own interests. A chapter-heading in the unique manuscript
of Ealdorman Æthelweard's *Chronicle* suggests that he intended to provide a
chapter on the reign of Edward, and on his murder.[250] It would be most inter-

---

[246] D. J. V. Fisher, 'The Anti-Monastic Reaction in the Reign of Edward the Martyr', *Cambridge Historical Journal* 10 (1950–2), 254–70; Keynes, *Diplomas*, pp. 163–74.

[247] Cf. D. N. Dumville, 'The Death of King Edward the Martyr – 18 March, 979?', *Anglo-
Saxon* 1 (2007), pp. 269–83; and for further discussion, see Keynes, 'The Cult of Edward
the Martyr'.

[248] Eadulf of Bamborough is not heard of after the early 970s, and may have been eclipsed
or indeed replaced by Oslac of York. Oslac was soon replaced by Thored, who attests
from 979; and Waltheof makes a solitary appearance in 994 (Keynes, *Attestations*, table
LXII). For Oslac, see also below, p. 57.

[249] Keynes, *Attestations*, table LVIII, and (e.g.) S 828 (*Abing* 117). Æthelmær 'of Hampshire' and Eadwine 'of Sussex' both died in 982 (*ASC*); for Eadwine's role in Kent, see
S 1457 (*Roch* 36). The ealdorman Leofwine seen in S 830 and 832 was perhaps also from
the west country; he is otherwise unknown. The 'ealdorman' Ælfric who occurs in S 828
(*Abing* 117) was perhaps in fact Ælfric, abbot of Malmesbury.

[250] Æthelweard, *Chronicle*, iv, Chapter-headings, p. 34.

esting to know where he stood on this matter, but if the chapter was ever written alas it has not survived.

Closer examination of the troubles unleashed in the immediate aftermath of Edgar's death brings us closer to what may have been the truth. Although the troubles sprang from various roots, they manifested themselves most obviously as an attack on the interests of the newly reformed monasteries. An entry in verse, written during Edward's reign and serving as the annal for 975 in *ASC* ABC, refers to the attacks as widespread in Mercia, indicating that God's servants were dispersed and his rights violated.[251] Another chronicler chose to associate the troubles with Ealdorman Ælfhere (of Mercia), referring to the destruction of monasteries which Edgar had ordered Bishop Æthelwold to institute.[252] Ælfhere was no enemy of monks in general, or indeed on principle; but it is not unlikely that he had friends among the disaffected secular clergy, or that some of his interests as ealdorman of the Mercians had been affected by the refoundation of religious houses within his province. For their part, some of the dispossessed secular clergy were doubtless prompted by Edgar's death to try to recover whatever they had lost whenever their respective monasteries had been 'reformed'. It is clear also that there were many laymen in different parts of the country who for whatever reason were resentful of the way in which certain monasteries, or perhaps particular churches of any kind, had been able to increase their wealth and power, and for whom Edgar's death was an opportunity to undo what they now thought ought not to have been done. In Byrhtferth's view, by the king's death 'the condition (*status*) of the whole kingdom was shaken: the bishops were thrown into confusion (*commoti*), the ealdormen (*principes*) made angry (*irati*), the monks struck with fear (*timore concussi*), and the people terrified (*pauefacti*); the clerics were made happy (*leti effecti*), because their time had come'.[253] He refers in particular to the expulsion of Abbot Germanus and his monks from Oswald's foundation at Winchcombe; and, like the chronicler, he identifies Ælfhere, ealdorman of the Mercians, as a leader in anti-monastic hostility. When the action began to spread from the west towards 'the eastern peoples of the Mercians' (*ad orientales Merciorum populos*), in other words towards the eastern midlands,[254] all of the more noble thegns (*milites nobiliores*), and the distinguished sons of ealdormen (*incliti filii*

---

[251] *ASC* ABC, s.a. 975. The entry for 975 (covering the death of Edgar, the departure or death of Bishop Cyneweard, the trouble in Mercia, the exile of Oslac, a comet, and famine) is in alliterative verse, 'of a quality to make one glad that the chroniclers mainly used prose' (Whitelock). The presence of the annal in MS. B indicates that it was written during Edward's reign. For further discussion, see T. A. Bredehoft, *Textual Histories: Readings in the 'Anglo-Saxon Chronicle'* (Toronto, 2001), pp. 106–8, and Salvador-Bello, 'The Edgar poems in the *Anglo-Saxon Chronicle*'. Bishop Cyneweard is said to have 'left Britain', ten days before Edgar died. This might signify that he died (cf. JW, *Chronicon*, s.a. 975), or that he chose to leave Britain, e.g. for Rome, without any intention to return, or that he was driven from the country for personal or political reasons.

[252] *ASC* D (in style of Archbishop Wulfstan) and EF.

[253] BR, *VSO* iv.11 (Raine, *York*, p. 443).

[254] *VSO* iv.11–12 (Raine, *York*, p. 444).

principum), came to Ealdorman Æthelwine, in order to discuss the matter.[255] Æthelwine was supported by his brother Ælfwold, and by Ealdorman Byrhtnoth. The story was told of an unnamed person who had laid claim to certain estates which belonged to Bishop Æthelwold's foundation at Peterborough, and who, at the meeting, spoke up strongly against Ælfwold in particular; and although Byrhtferth's account can be read in different ways, it was apparently Ealdorman Æthelwine who at some later stage gave orders that the man should be killed, for which the ealdorman was required to do penance before the bishop at Winchester.[256]

Byrhtferth's account of the 'anti-monastic reaction' represents the view from Ramsey abbey, and probably needs to be taken in a wider context. It is not difficult to imagine that there were many who had cause to regret or to resent what had been done during the reign of King Edgar; whose regret or resentment had been effectively contained during the king's lifetime; and for whom Edgar's death in July 975 created an opportunity to take advantage of a temporary weakening of royal power in order (as they saw it) to set matters right. Those who had been expelled from religious houses in the mid-960s, when replaced by monks, might well have persisted in their resentment of the way in which they had been treated, only ten years before. Moreover, the true faith displayed by some in promoting the cause of a particular religious house would have left others with disappointed expectations. Again, a powerful layman closely identified with the fortunes of one house might take action against other houses with which he had no connection, if their interests encroached upon his own. The early twelfth-century work known as the *Libellus Æthelwoldi episcopi*, based on vernacular records which had accumulated at Ely abbey in the late tenth century, affords a remarkable view of the process by which the abbey had accumulated its endowment in the early 970s, and at the same time it exposes the disruption occasioned by Edgar's death, illustrated by the way in which some men sought to renege on earlier transactions and others sought to recover what they considered to be rightfully theirs.[257] Much the same construction can be put on the tale of Brihtric, who, seeing the opportunity presented by Edgar's death, persuaded his kinswoman that they should try to undo a deal which she had recently concluded with the bishop of Rochester; so they applied to Ealdorman Eadwine, 'and the section of the public which was the adversary of God', and managed to compel

---

[255] *VSO* iv.13 (Raine, *York*, pp. 444–6).

[256] *VSO* iv.14 (Raine, *York*, p. 446). The enemy of Peterborough is generally identified as Leofsige, who is mentioned in the *Libellus Æthelwoldi episcopi*, chs. 10–11 (*LE*, pp. 84–6), as one who had seized land at Peterborough, Oundle and Kettering from Peterborough abbey. However, this identification should not be taken for granted, not least because Peterborough, like other houses, would have had many such enemies at this time. It is further supposed that it was Ælfwold who ordered the killing and who did the penance; yet the person doing penance is described as a *dux*, and then seemingly as *princeps Orientalium Anglorum*, presumably with reference to Æthelwine. Elsewhere Edgar is *decus ducum* (iv.17), perhaps a poeticism meaning 'best of all leaders'.

[257] Keynes, 'Ely Abbey 672–1109', pp. 26–7; see also Keynes and Kennedy, *Anglo-Saxon Ely*.

the bishop to give up various estates.[258] There is a clear analogy here with the challenges faced by Ely, yet the victim was the bishop or the bishopric of Rochester, and the indications are that the matter was perceived quite simply as a challenge to the previously established and properly constituted order.

No doubt there were also personal rivalries and animosities, all but contained during Edgar's lifetime and waiting to be unleashed upon his death. On a presumption of family ambition and group solidarity, the leading players are fondly imagined to have vied with one another in their relentless pursuit of power; and it has become almost axiomatic that the family of Ælfhere, ealdorman of Mercia (956–83), was pitched against the family of Æthelwine, ealdorman of East Anglia (962–92), in just such a struggle. So while Ealdorman Æthelwine, his brother Ælfwold and Ealdorman Byrhtnoth are seen to have stood firm against Ealdorman Ælfhere on what was represented by Byrhtferth of Ramsey as a 'monastic' issue, the question is whether they were protecting their own interests against the threatened extension of Ælfhere's activities eastwards into regions which had once been controlled by Æthelstan Half-King, father of Æthelwine, and which fell outside Ælfhere's own territory. It is an approach which can be taken too far; yet since members of less successful families might have harboured resentment towards the king himself, or towards the representatives of his regime, it is also an approach which in our ignorance may not always be taken far enough.

Conclusion

For all the praise that was heaped upon Edgar from the late tenth century onwards, there is much about him that remains a mystery. Perhaps the most difficult problem is to understand what Wulfstan, archbishop of York (1002–23), had in mind when he expressed a significant reservation in the short account of Edgar inserted in the 'northern recension' of the *ASC*:[259]

> Ane misdæde he dyde þeah to swyðe, þæt he eldeodige unsida lufode,]
> heþene þeawas innan þysan lande gebrohte to fæste,] utlændisce hider in
> tihte,] deriende leoda bespeon to þysan earde.

> Yet he did one ill-deed too greatly: he loved evil foreign customs and brought too firmly heathen manners within this land, and attracted hither foreigners and enticed harmful people to this country.

William of Malmesbury interpreted this remark to mean that crowds of 'foreigners' (named as Saxons, Flemings and Danes) who had come to England during Edgar's reign had exerted a bad influence on the English themselves,[260] thereby contributing to the decline which set in after his death. Wulfstan was

---

258 S 1457 (*Roch* 36).
259 *ASC* D, s.a. 959 (Cubbin, *MS D*, p. 45); see also *Northern Recension*, ed. Dumville.
260 WM, *Gesta Regum* ii.148.3 (ed. Mynors *et al.*, p. 240); see also HH, *Historia Anglorum*

writing at a time when the English were suffering from sustained viking attack, and it is likely that he would have been looking to the past for any explanation of their present troubles; and he does not mince his words. The references to 'evil foreign customs', 'heathen manners', 'foreigners' and 'harmful people' appear in combination to indicate that he had the Danes firmly in mind, and that he regarded the renewal of viking raids during Æthelred's reign as in some way a consequence of whatever Edgar had done to encourage them hither. The implication seems to be that there was a significant movement of people from Scandinavia (and perhaps from Denmark in particular) to England in the 960s and 970s, of a nature and under circumstances wholly unknown. This need not have had anything in particular to do the Scandinavian settlements in the Danelaw, although of course it can be taken that way.[261] It might well relate, on the other hand, to the employment of Scandinavian mercenaries in strategic places throughout the kingdom, as part of a protective force, and also to the presence of Scandinavian merchants in many of the same places. There is no direct evidence pointing to the presence of Scandinavian mercenaries or merchants in England, during Edgar's reign;[262] yet Wulfstan's remark, if correctly interpreted, carries considerable weight. What was it, one has to ask, about Earl Áslákr, or Oslac, who seems to have controlled Northumbria from his centre of power in York, that led one chronicler to describe him (albeit in verse) as 'a courageous man ... wise and skilled in speech' (*deormod hæleð ... wis J wordsnotor*), and another to describe him as 'the famous earl' (*se mæra eorl*), and yet led those who ruled the land after Edgar's death to drive him out of the country; and where, for that matter, did he go?[263] It is not difficult to imagine a situation in which people who had enjoyed the king's protection during his lifetime found themselves resented, and without such protection, after his death; and, if we may speculate further, on this basis, that they were forced in the aftermath of Edgar's death to return whence they came, it may be that they were soon able to put their skills, and their knowledge of the country, to a satisfactorily productive use.

In 1052 Æthelweard, abbot of Glastonbury, opened King Edgar's grave and found his body to be incorrupt; it was then placed in a silver-gilt casket, over the altar, with relics of St Apollinaris and St Vincent, and miracles followed.[264] Edgar had done well from his association with the monastic reform movement,

---

v.24 (ed. Greenway, pp. 318–20), and compare the unqualified panegyric in JW, *Chronicon*, s.a. 959 (ed. Darlington and McGurk, p. 412).

[261] Stenton, *ASE*, p. 371, n. 2; Bredehoft, *Textual Histories*, pp. 107–8; Downham, *Viking Kings*, p. 124.

[262] For discussion of some indirect evidence, see Jayakumar, 'Reflections on the "Foreign Policies" of Edgar', pp. 24–31.

[263] For Danish merchants in York, in the late tenth century (but probably before), see BR, *VSO* v.3 (Raine, *York*, p. 454). For the rise of Oslac in the 960s, see above, pp. 16 and 31–2.

[264] WM, *De Antiquitate Glastonie*, chs. 62 and 66 (*The Early History of Glastonbury: An Edition, Translation and Study of William of Malmesbury's 'De Antiquitate Glastonie Ecclesie'*, ed. J. Scott (Woodbridge, 1981), pp. 130 and 134); see also WM, *Gesta Regum* ii.160.2 (ed. Mynors *et al.*, pp. 260–2).

first when Wulfstan of Winchester and Byrhtferth of Ramsey began to look back on his reign from the 990s, and later when the Anglo-Norman historians fastened on Edgar as a fine example of firm rulership. Under the influence of their writings, Edgar's reign came to be regarded as a period when the king promoted the interests of monastic reform, consolidated his rule throughout a newly unified kingdom, and brought peace to his people. Edgar was indeed a powerful, determined and effective ruler; but in achieving his purposes he made enemies as well as friends, and generated resentment as well as admiration and affection. His reign was, as Stenton put it, 'singularly devoid of recorded incident'. Not so the reigns of his sons; and perhaps, in a way, that is precisely the point.

Table 1.1: Charters of King Edgar (by year and by archive), based on the conspectus

	Abbotsbury	Abingdon	Athelney	Bath	Buckfast	Burton	Bury St Edmunds	Canterbury (CC)	Canterbury (StA)	Chertsey	Chester	Coventry (?)	Crediton	Crowland	Ely	Evesham	Exeter	Ghent, St Peter's	Glastonbury	London, St Paul's	Malmesbury	Muchelney	Paris, Saint-Denis	Pershore	Peterborough	Ramsey	Rochester	Romsey	St Kew	Sherborne	Thorney	Uncertain	Wells	Westminster	Wilton	Winchester (NM)	Winchester (OM)	Worcester	York	TOTAL
BA series	•	•		•		•		•	•											•	•				•		•			•			•			•			•	—
957											1	1													1								1				2		1	8
958		1																																						1
959			1	2													1																		1		1			1
960		2				1																															1			5
961		<5		1		1																															5			<12
962		3		1		2											1															1	1	1	1					10
963		4		1			1	1											1									1									3		2	17
964		2																																		1		1		5
965	1	<3																																						<5
966		1				1													2															1			1			8
967		1													2				1																2		2			6
968		<6				1													1			1						1									1	2		<14
969								1									1		1	1																	1			5
970		1																							1															5
971																																			2		1			1
972				1		1													2															1			1			6
973													1																					2						3
974																																				1	4			3
975																																								4
Suspect		3					1	1	1					3	2	1		1	1	1	2	1	1	1	1	1	1	1	1	1	1			3	1	1	6	3		
Lost	•				•		•	•	•						•				15	2						•										•	3	1		

2

A Conspectus of the Charters of King Edgar, 957–75

SIMON KEYNES

THE standard catalogue of Anglo-Saxon charters, compiled by Peter Sawyer and first published in 1968,[1] now available in a revised, updated and expanded form,[2] registers the existence of about 160 charters in the name of King Edgar, including four 'new' charters (dated 958, 962, 963 and 974) which have come to light in more recent years.[3] The corpus comprises about ten charters which purport to have been issued during Edgar's reign as king of the Mercians (957–9), and about 150 charters from Edgar's reign as king of the English (959–75). To these should be added a number of 'lost' or incomplete texts, most of which are of uncertain date.[4] The surviving charters were preserved in the archives of about forty religious houses, which establishes an effective cross-archival basis for analysis, comparison and judgement; among them, the archives of Abingdon and Winchester (Old Minster) are especially well represented, in part reflecting the quality of the cartularies from these houses but perhaps also reflecting a predisposition to fabricate charters of Edgar at two places where he was held in especially high esteem. The archives of Glastonbury would also be well represented, were it not for the fact that its eleventh-century *Liber Terrarum* has not survived.

The list below is intended to convey an impression of the nature and distribution of the surviving corpus of Edgar's charters. Most of Edgar's charters are

---

[1] P. Sawyer, *Anglo-Saxon Charters: An Annotated List and Bibliography*, Royal Historical Society Guides and Handbooks 8 (London, 1968), conventionally cited as Sawyer, or S, with number of document.

[2] Work on the 'Revised Sawyer', funded by the Arts and Humanities Research Council (AHRC), and conducted under the auspices of the British Academy–Royal Historical Society Joint Committee on Anglo-Saxon Charters, was undertaken initially by Susan Kelly, and has been taken further, as the 'Electronic Sawyer', by Rebecca Rushforth and others. The 'Revised Sawyer' is available in electronic form from the 'Kemble' website <www.trin.cam.ac.uk/kemble/>, and in due course will be published in book form.

[3] The charters of King Edgar are registered as S 667–827. The more recently-discovered texts are registered in the 'Revised Sawyer' as S 676a, S 705a, S 712a and S 794a; for further details, see S. Keynes, 'Anglo-Saxon Charters: Lost and Found', pp. 52–5.

[4] For the 'lost' and incomplete charters, see below, pp. 79–80.

dated only by year and indiction, though some are also dated by regnal year;[5] in the case of charters issued in 962, 963 and 964, it happens to be possible to introduce a useful element of relative dating within the year by analysis of witness-lists. Each entry indicates in which archive a charter was preserved, its date (and, if given, its place of issue), and its main content; the royal style accorded to Edgar represents the usage in the superscription, but a different style is often used in the subscription. The brief notes, in italic, serve simply to characterize a charter in terms of its formulation, and to draw attention to those preserved in single-sheet form. S 672 is omitted, since it is clearly a charter of King Eadwig (956), with alterations.

The charters are cited by their number in 'Sawyer', followed in brackets by citation of a printed text. The new edition of the corpus of Anglo-Saxon charters, prepared under the auspices of the British Academy–Royal Historical Society Joint Committee on Anglo-Saxon Charters, and published by the British Academy, is now well under way, and when complete will comprise about thirty volumes, each containing the charters formerly preserved in the archives of a particular religious house, or group of houses. Editions of charters are cited by their number in a particular volume of the series, or, if the volume has not yet been published, by their number in Birch's edition (for the period to 975) or in Kemble's edition (for the period 975–1066). For these purposes, the following abbreviations are used:

Abing   *Charters of Abingdon Abbey*, ed. S. E. Kelly, 2 pts, AS Charters 7–8 (Oxford, 2000–1)

Bath   *Charters of Bath and Wells*, ed. S. E. Kelly, AS Charters 13 (Oxford, 2007)

BCS   W. de G. Birch, *Cartularium Saxonicum*, 3 vols. (London, 1885–93)

Burt   *Charters of Burton Abbey*, ed. P. H. Sawyer, AS Charters 2 (Oxford, 1979)

CantCC   *Charters of Christ Church, Canterbury*, ed. N. Brooks and S. E. Kelly, 3 pts, AS Charters (Oxford, forthcoming)

CantStA   *Charters of St Augustine's Abbey, Canterbury*, ed. S. E. Kelly, AS Charters 4 (Oxford, 1995)

KCD   J. M. Kemble, *Codex Diplomaticus Ævi Saxonici*, 6 vols. (London, 1839–48)

LondStP   *Charters of St Paul's, London*, ed. S. E. Kelly, AS Charters 10 (Oxford, 2004)

---

[5] Four of the charters issued by Edgar while king of the Mercians incorporate regnal years: S 674 (Peterborough), S 679 (York), S 667 (Chester), and S 677 (Wells), all dated 958, in the king's 2nd year. A calculation from 957 was clearly preferred thereafter for charters dealing with land north of the Thames: S 723 and S 712a, both dated 963, in the king's 7th year [963–4]; S 712 (York), dated 963, in the 6th year [*recte* 7th] of the king's *imperium*; S 776 (Ely), dated 970, in the 13th year of his reign; and S 782 (Peterborough), dated 971, in the 15th year of his earthly *imperium*. Interestingly, a calculation from 957 was also used for a Kentish charter: S 1215 (*CantCC* 128), dated 968, in 11th year of his reign. For calculations from Edgar's accession in October 959 or from a coronation in 960, see S 725 (*Abing* 101), dated 964, in the king's 5th year; and S 755 (BCS 1197), dated 967, in the 7th year of the king's *imperium*. Regnal years are relatively common among those charters here deemed 'problematic' (below, pp. 75–9), including instances where Edgar's reign was calculated from his coronation in 973.

Malm   *Charters of Malmesbury Abbey*, ed. S. E. Kelly, AS Charters 11 (Oxford, 2005)
Pet   *Charters of Peterborough Abbey*, ed. S. E. Kelly, AS Charters 14 (Oxford, 2008)
Roch   *Charters of Rochester*, ed. A. Campbell, AS Charters 1 (London, 1973)
Sel   *Charters of Selsey*, ed. S. E. Kelly, AS Charters 6 (Oxford, 1998)
Shaft   *Charters of Shaftesbury Abbey*, ed. S. E. Kelly, AS Charters 5 (Oxford, 1995)
Sherb   *Charters of Sherborne*, ed. M. A. O'Donovan, AS Charters 3 (Oxford, 1988)
StAlb   *Charters of St Albans*, ed. J. Crick, AS Charters 12 (Oxford, 2007)
Wells   *Charters of Bath and Wells*, ed. S. E. Kelly, AS Charters 13 (Oxford, 2007)
WinchNM   *Charters of the New Minster, Winchester*, ed. S. Miller, AS Charters 9 (Oxford, 2001)

Texts (without critical apparatus and commentary) are also available on the 'Electronic Sawyer', which can be approached through the 'Kemble' website <www.trin.cam.ac.uk/kemble/>.

The abiding difficulty with any set of Anglo-Saxon charters is to separate a core of authentic texts from those charters in the same set which are not likely to be authentic in their received or transmitted form, and in this way to distinguish the signal from the noise. The complications arise from the multiplicity of circumstances in which charters were drafted in the first place, the different purposes for which they came to be used, and the variety of conditions in which they were copied and subsequently preserved; but even the most disreputable charter might have some seemingly authentic documentation behind it, or prove to be of some interest for some purpose. Accordingly, the judgements which have to be made range across a wide spectrum, and need in most cases to be expressed in narrative form rather than handed down as verdicts or pronouncements.[6]

While it is necessary to respect the differences between the individual texts, one has to bear in mind at the same time that they constitute the component parts of a larger whole. Of the surviving corpus of about 160 charters issued in King Edgar's name, most of those issued by him as king of the Mercians, and about 100 of those issued by him as king of the English, are substantially authentic, distributed unevenly across a period of about eighteen years, with apparent peaks in 961–3 and 968. These charters are grouped together below, in sections A (pp. 64–5) and B (pp. 65–75). The majority of them are seemingly straightforward records of grants of land to religious houses, or to individuals

---

[6]   T. Reuter, 'The Making of England and Germany, 850–1050: Points of Comparison and Difference' (1998), in his *Medieval Polities and Modern Mentalities*, ed. J. L. Nelson (Cambridge, 2006), pp. 284–99, at 297, bemoaned the fact that 'Anglo-Saxon diplomatists persist in the belief that it is possible to be slightly dead or partly pregnant'; but it does not always help to judge the Anglo-Saxon evidence from a Carolingian, Ottonian or Salian perspective. Relatively few charters survive in their original single-sheet form, as against a much higher proportion in cartulary copies; and perhaps there was a greater tendency, in England, to fabricate charters in the service of a variety of different purposes.

(whether ecclesiastics or laymen), more or less 'standard' in form and preserved because they served as title-deeds for the estates in question. Among them are three clusters of charters in favour of Abingdon (961, 965, 968), which might be interpreted as evidence of contemporary production at the abbey, but which might alternatively raise questions of later in-house fabrication.[7] One should add that eight charters of Edgar, dated between 958 and 967, belong to a series of predominantly tenth-century charters, preserved at Abingdon, which have no apparent connection with the abbey's endowment; and in their case the question arises whether some of them might have been deposited at the abbey for safe-keeping.[8] A few of the charters are less than straightforward. One is King Edgar's charter granting privileges to the New Minster, Winchester (S 745, dated 966), which conveys a very particular image of Edgar's kingship, fulfilling the intentions of its creator every time its frontispiece (frontis. in this book)) is reproduced, but which, although iconic, is wholly atypical. Two documents preserved in original single-sheet form afford rare glimpses of how business might be conducted at 'local' meetings attended by the king (as opposed to major assemblies of the king and his councillors): a 'private' charter recording a transaction at Canterbury; and a note added to a late ninth-century charter, also Kentish, recording how the king handed over the charter to a certain Leofric, in the presence of a group of witnesses.[9] Other non-standard charters represent transactions of a more complex nature.[10]

About 40 charters which purport to have been issued during Edgar's reign, including several 'private' (non-royal) texts, might be described as problematic in their received or transmitted form. These charters are grouped together below, in section C (pp. 75–9). Many of the charters in question purport to affirm the privileges of a particular religious house, or to confirm a house in its posses-sion of a substantial number of estates, or to mark its foundation: charters for

---

7   If the king wished to grant estates in different places to a single beneficiary, on a single occasion, it would have been only sensible to make a single agency responsible for the production of separate charters for each estate, and only natural that the charters should be cast in identical (or near identical) terms (e.g. S 737 and S 738, dated 966; S 772 and S 773, dated 969); but the apparent instances of this practice found among the Abingdon charters are rather less than convincing, especially when judged in relation to each other and in their larger archival context. For extended discussion (more inclined to give them the benefit of the doubt), see *Abing*, pp. lxxi–lxxxiv, cxv–cxxxi (esp. cxxiii–cxxiv), 363 and 366–7 (961), 412–14 (965) and 435–6 (968), and *Historia Ecclesie Abbendonensis: The History of the Church of Abingdon*, ed. J. Hudson, 2 vols. (Oxford, 2002–7) I, esp. pp. xxviii–xxx, cxxxix, and cxcv–ccviii; cf. Keynes, *Diplomas*, pp. 10–13, at 11, nn. 16–17.

8   For extended discussion, see *Abing*, pp. cxxxviii–cxli, and *Historia Ecclesie Abbendon-ensis*, ed. Hudson, I, esp. pp. xxviii–xxix, xlvii–xlix, cxxvi–cxxxi and cxcvi–cxcvii; cf. Keynes, *Diplomas*, pp. 10–13, at 12, n. 19.

9   S 1215 (*CantCC* 128), dated 968, and S 1276 (*CantCC* 98), which is undated (963 x 971), and which is registered below under the year 971. The endorsement on S 1276 represents a practice also represented among charters of King Edgar by the endorsements to S 717 (*CantCC* 126) and S 795 (BCS 1303).

10 S 687 (*Abing* 86), restoring land to Wulfric; S 693 (BCS 1077), leasing a Winchester estate; S 701 (*Abing* 93), granting produce and dues from various places to Abingdon Abbey; S 715 (BCS 1118) and S 727 (BCS 1127), granting land to himself.

Muchelney (S 729, dated 964), Crowland (S 741, dated 966), Chertsey (S 752, dated 967), Westminster (S 774, dated 969), Ely (S 779, dated 970), Glastonbury (S 783, dated 971), Peterborough (S 787), Thorney (S 792, dated 973), Ramsey (S 798, dated 974), and Wilton (S 799, dated 974); the notorious 'Altitonantis' charter from Worcester (S 731, dated 964); the so-called 'Orthodoxorum' charters for Abingdon (S 673, dated '958'), Pershore (S 786, dated 972), Worcester (S 788, dated 972), and Romsey (S 812); and a series of seemingly 'incomplete' charters from the Old Minster, Winchester, lacking dating-clause and witness-lists, treated here as a single composite text (S 814–19 + 821–7). Such charters are by no means without interest in their own right, for they belong to the development of Edgar's reputation, from the late tenth century onwards, as a founder and benefactor of monasteries.

Charters known once to have existed, but no longer extant, are deemed to be 'lost', and charters of which only parts have been preserved are deemed to be 'incomplete'. All such charters are important because their former existence has to be borne in mind when making any judgement based on texts which happen to have survived. For further details, see section D (pp. 79–80).[11]

A. CHARTERS OF EDGAR AS KING OF THE MERCIANS 957–9

Charters of 958

S 674 (*Pet* 13), from Peterborough. AD 958 (2nd yr). Edgar, king of the English, grants 5 hides at Orton, Hunts., to Ælfheah, his thegn. *Related to S 679.*

S 679 (BCS 1044), from York. AD 958 (2nd yr). Edgar, king of the English, grants 10 hides at Sutton, Notts., to Oscytel, bishop of Dorchester. *Related to S 674.*

S 667 (BCS 1041), from Chester. AD 958 (2nd yr), at Penkridge, Staffs. Edgar, king of the Mercians, grants 17 hides at various places in Flint and Cheshire to the community of St Werburg's Abbey, Chester. *Probably 'improved'; but based on a charter by Edgar's 'Mercian' draftsman.*

S 677 (*Wells* 31), from Wells. AD 958 (2nd yr). Edgar, king of the Mercians (and of the Northumbrians and British), grants land *in pago Magescætna*, namely 6 hides at Staunton, Heref., to Ealhstan, his thegn (for 40 mancuses of gold). *Single sheet (probably original), written by a scribe not otherwise identified, with formulation by Edgar's 'Mercian' draftsman.*

S 675 (BCS 1042), from Winchester (Old Minster). AD 958. Edgar, king of the Mercians, grants 20 hides at Wootton, Oxon, to Æthelric, his thegn.

S 678 (*Abing* 82), from Abingdon. AD 958. Edgar, king of the Mercians, grants 14 hides at Ducklington, Oxon, to Eanulf, his thegn. *'Dunstan B' formulation; not attested by the king.*

---

[11] For further details, see Keynes, 'Anglo-Saxon Charters: Lost and Found'.

S 676 (BCS 1037), from Winchester (Old Minster). AD 958. Edgar, king of the Mercians, grants 5 hides at Ham, Essex, to Æthelstan, his ealdorman (*comes*). *'Dunstan B' formulation; not attested by the king.*

S 676a ('Kemble'), from ?Coventry. AD 958. Edgar, king of the Mercians, grants 3 hides at Coundon, Warwicks., to Eadwald, his thegn. *'Dunstan B' formulation; not attested by the king.*

Charters of 959

S 681 (*Pet* 14), from Peterborough. AD 959. Edgar, ruler of the whole *provincia* of Mercia, grants [...] hides at Howden and (Old) Drax, Yorks., to Quen, his *matrona. Proto-'Edgar A' formulation.*

B. CHARTERS OF EDGAR AS KING OF THE ENGLISH 959–75

Charters of 959

Eadwig died on 1 October, and was buried at the New Minster, Winchester. He was succeeded by Edgar, who was then 16 years old [calculated from 943].

S 680 (BCS 1051), from Winchester (Old Minster). AD 959. Edgar, ruler of the whole of Albion, grants 10 hides at West Clere, Hants., to Ælfwine, his thegn. *Proto-'Edgar A' formulation.*

See also S 670 (Westminster), S 673 (Abingdon) and S 1293 (Westminster), in section C.

Charters of 960

S 685 (BCS 1053), from Wilton. AD 960. Edgar, ruler of the English, grants 20 hides at Stanton (St Bernard), Wilts., to Osulf, bishop [of Ramsbury].

S 683 (BCS 1054), from Winchester (Old Minster). AD 960. Edgar, king of the whole kingdom of Britain, grants 10 hides at Itchen Stoke, Hants., to his kinsman Brihthelm, bishop [of Winchester]. *'Edgar A' formulation.*

S 687 (*Abing* 86), from Abingdon. AD 960. Edgar, ruler of the whole of Britain, restores land at various places in Berks., Sussex and Hants. to Wulfric, his thegn (for 120 mancuses of gold). *Single sheet (original), written by 'Edgar A'.*

S 682 (*Abing* 85), from Abingdon. AD 960. Edgar, king of the whole of Albion, grants 20 hides at Drayton, Berks., to Abingdon Abbey (previously given by King Eadred to his thegn Eadwold).

S 684 (BCS 1056), from Exeter. AD 960. King Edgar grants 9 hides at Tywarnhayle and 2 hides at Bosowsa, Cornwall, to Eanulf, his thegn. *Single sheet (probably original), written by a scribe not otherwise identified, with 'southwestern' formulation.*

See also S 686 (Paris, Saint-Denis), in section C.

Charters of 961

Two of the charters listed below (S 688–9), in favour of Abingdon Abbey, have to be treated with caution; see above, p. 63.

S 690 (*Abing* 87), from Abingdon. AD 961. Edgar, ruler of the whole of Britain, grants 22 hides at Ringwood, Hants., to Abingdon Abbey. *Single sheet (original), with main text written by 'Edgar A'; dating-clause and witness-list added, after folding, by another hand.*

S 688 (*Abing* 88), from Abingdon. AD 961. Edgar, ruler of the whole of Britain, grants 20 hides at Burbage, Wilts., to Abingdon Abbey. *'Edgar A' formulation. (Abingdon cluster.)*

S 689 (*Abing* 89), from Abingdon. AD 961. Edgar, king of the whole of Albion, grants 50 hides at Hurstbourne (Tarrant), Hants., to Abingdon Abbey. *(Abingdon cluster.)*

S 691 (*Abing* 90), from Abingdon. AD 961. Edgar, king of the English, grants 9 hides at Ardington, Berks., to Ælfric, his thegn. *Attestation of Bishop Æthelwold not possible.*

S 698 (*Abing* 91), from Abingdon. AD 961. Edgar, ruler of the whole of Britain, grants 3 hides at *Hamstede*, to Eadric, his thegn. *'Edgar A' formulation. Attestation of Bishop Æthelwold not possible*

S 699 (BCS 1068), from Winchester (Old Minster). AD 961. Edgar, king of the English, grants 5 hides at Avington, Hants., to the Old Minster, Winchester.

S 696 (BCS 1071), from Winchester (Old Minster). AD 961. Edgar, king of the English, grants 5 hides at Ebbesborne, Wilts., to Byrnsige, his thegn. *'Edgar A' formulation.*

S 695 (BCS 1076), from Winchester (Old Minster). AD 961. Edgar, king of the whole English region, grants 7½ hides at Easton, Hants., to his kinsman Byrhthelm, bishop [of Winchester].

S 693 (BCS 1077), from Winchester (Old Minster). AD 961. Edgar, ruler of the whole of Britain, grants a lease of 10 hides at Kilmeston, Hants., to Athulf, his thegn, and two successors, with Bishop Brihthelm's permission and in return for a specified annual payment.

S 697 (BCS 1072), from Winchester (Old Minster). AD 961. Edgar, king of the whole island of Albion, grants 4 hides at Withiel (Florey), Somerset., to Cenulf, his man. *Single sheet (probably original), written by a scribe not otherwise identified, with 'south-western' formulation.*

S 692 (*Bath* 15), from Bath. AD 961. Edgar, king of the whole of Albion, grants 1 hide at Evesty, Somerset, to Æthelwold, his thegn. *Distinctive formulation.*

S 694 (*Bath* 14), from Bath. AD 961. Edgar, king of the whole of Albion, restores 5 hides at (South) Stoke, Somerset, to St Peter's Abbey, Bath. *'Dunstan B' formulation; attested by the king. Probably spurious in this form.*

Charters of 962

In 962 Ælfgar, the king's kinsman in Devon, died, and was buried at Wilton. Charters dated 962 can be organized into sub-groups by analysis of their witness-lists. S 705a, S 700, S 703 and S 669 were attested by Ælfgar, and were thus issued before his death;

S 702 and S 704 were issued probably after Ælfgar's death, but before the death of Ealdorman Æthelwold; S 701, S 706 and S 705 were issued after the death of Ealdorman Æthelwold, and after the appointment of his successor Æthelwine.

S 705a ('Kemble'), from Athelney. AD 962. Edgar, king of the English people, grants 1 hide at Ilton, Somerset, to Godwine, his *satraps* (for 5 pounds of silver and gold).

S 707 (*Burt* 19), from Burton. AD 962. Edgar, king of the English, grants 10 hides at Hilmarton and at Littlecott, Wilts., to Wulfmær, his thegn. *For formulation, cf. S 1214 (in section C).*

S 700 (*Abing* 92), from Abingdon. AD 962. Edgar, king of the whole of Britain, grants 3 hides at Hendred, Berks., to Abingdon Abbey. *'Edgar A' formulation; but possibly spurious.*

S 703 (BCS 1082), from Bury St Edmunds. AD 962. Edgar, ruler of the whole of Britain, grants 7 hides at Chelsworth, Suffolk, to Æthelflæd, his *matrona*. *Single sheet (original), written by 'Edgar A'.*

S 669 (BCS 1103), from Exeter. AD '951' for ?962. Edgar, king of the whole of Britain, grants 1 hide at Clyst (St Mary or St George), Devon, to Æthelnoth, his man. *Single sheet; spurious in this form, but with witness-list drawn from a charter of 962.*

S 702 (BCS 1085), from Westminster. AD 962. Edgar, king of the whole of Britain, grants 10 hides at Sunbury, Middlesex, to his kinsman Ælfheah, his *fidelis*. *Single sheet (s. x ex), modeled on a charter written by 'Edgar A'.*

S 704 ('Kemble'), from Buckfast. AD 962. Edgar, king of the English, grants 3 *perticae* at Seeley (in Churchstow), Devon, to Æthel[...], his thegn. *Single sheet (probably original), written by a scribe not otherwise identified.*

S 701 (*Abing* 93), from Abingdon. AD 962. Edgar, king of the whole of Britain, grants a vineyard at Watchet, Somerset, and some royal dues, etc., to Abingdon Abbey. *'Edgar A' formulation, in part.*

S 706 (BCS 1083), of uncertain provenance (?Wilton). AD 962. Edgar, king of the whole of Britain, grants 8 hides at Avon (in Durnford), Wilts., to Titstan, his chamberlain (*cubicularius*). *Single sheet (original), written by 'Edgar A'.*

S 705 (*Abing* 94), from Abingdon. AD 962. Edgar, king of the English, grants 20 hides at Moredon (in Rodbourne Cheney), Wilts., to Eadwine, his thegn.
See also S 811 (Winchester), S 833 (Abingdon) and S 1214 (Evesham), in section C.

Charters of 963

In 963 Æthelwold, abbot of Abingdon, was consecrated bishop of Winchester on 29 November. Charters dated 963 can be organized into sub-groups by analysis of their witness-lists. S 708, S 717, S 720, S 711, S 718, S 709, S 719, S 713 and S 715 were attested by Æthelwold as abbot, or by two bishops called Byrhthelm (one of whom would have been Æthelwold's predecessor as bishop of Winchester), and must therefore have been produced at a meeting or meetings held before Æthelwold's consecration as bishop. S 712, S 716, S 722 and S 714 were all issued after Æthelwold's elevation to the see of Winchester, perhaps on a later occasion in December. S 710 and S 721 have truncated witness-lists; S 723 and S 712a have only one bishop Byrhthelm, and do not contain attestations of any abbots.

S 708 (*Abing* 96), from Abingdon. AD 963. Edgar, king of the whole kingdom of Albion, grants 4 hides at Easthall, Sussex, to Abingdon Abbey. *'Edgar A' formulation.*

S 717 (*CantCC* 126), from Christ Church, Canterbury. AD 963. Edgar, king of the whole of Britain, grants 7 hides at Vange, Essex, to Ingeram, his thegn. *Single sheet (original), written by 'Edgar A', with inserted bounds; endorsed with note to the effect that Ingeram gave the charter, with the land, to Archbishop Dunstan.*

S 720 (*Burt* 20), from Burton. AD 963. Edgar, king of the English, grants 3 hides at Duddeston, Warwicks., and 3 at *Ernlege*, to Wulfgeat, his thegn. *'Edgar A' formulation.*

S 711 (*Bath* 16), from Bath. AD 963. Edgar, king of the whole of Britain, grants 2½ hides at Stanton (Prior), Somerset, to Ælfsige, his 'decurion'. *'Edgar A' formulation.*

S 718 (BCS 1114), from Winchester (Old Minster). AD 963. Edgar, king of the whole of Britain, grants 8 hides at Ambersham, Sussex, to the church of St Andrew at Meon. *'Edgar A' formulation.*

S 709 (*Wells* 32), from Wells. AD 963. Edgar, king of the whole of Britain, grants 1 hide, less ½ a *pertica*, at Manworthy (in Milverton), Somerset, to Ælfric, his thegn. *'Edgar A' formulation.*

S 719 (BCS 1120), from Wilton. AD 963. Edgar, king of the whole of Britain, grants 3 hides at Avon (in Durnford), Wilts., to Winstan, his chamberlain (*camerarius*). *'Edgar A' formulation.*

S 713 (*Abing* 97), from Abingdon. AD 963. King Edgar grants 10 hides at Sparsholt, 1 hide at Balking, and a mill at *Hirdegrafe*, Berks., to Æthelsige, his chamberlain (*camerarius*). *Formulation influenced by 'Dunstan B'.*

S 715 (BCS 1118), from Winchester (Old Minster). AD 963. Edgar, king of the English, grants 5 hides at Patney, Wilts., to himself. *Draftsman has provided additional computistical data in dating clause.*

S 710 (*Shaft* 24), from Shaftesbury. AD 963. Edgar, king of the whole of Britain, grants 5 hides at Orchard, Dorset, to Ælfsige, his thegn. *'Edgar A' formulation.*

S 721 (BCS 1104), from Glastonbury. AD 963. Edgar, king of the whole of Albion, grants 2 hides at Ottery (St Mary), Devon, to Wulfhelm, his thegn. *'South-western' formulation.*

S 723 (BCS 1119), from Winchester (Old Minster). AD 963 (7th yr). Edgar, king of the whole of Britain, grants 6 hides *in provincia Wrocensetna*, at Plaish (in Cardington) and at (Church and Chetwynd) Aston, Salop, to Wulfric, his thegn. *Edgar's 'Mercian' draftsman.*

S 712a ('Kemble'), of uncertain provenance (?Burton). AD 963 (7th yr). King Edgar grants 5 hides *in pago Pecset*, at Ballidon, Derbys., to Æthelferth (for 20 mancuses of pure gold). *Edgar's 'Mercian' draftsman.*

S 712 (BCS 1112), from York. AD 963 ('6th' yr). Edgar, king of the English people, grants 20 hides at Sherburn (-in-Elmet), Yorks., to Oslac (*Æslac*).

S 716 (BCS 1113), from York. AD 963. Edgar, king of the whole of Britain, grants 30 hides at Newbald, Yorks., to Gunner, his ealdorman. *'Edgar A' formulation.*

S 722 (*Abing* 99), from Abingdon. AD 963. King Edgar grants 5 hides at *Hocan edisce* to Wulfnoth, his thegn. *'Edgar A' formulation.*

S 714 (*Abing* 98), from Abingdon. AD 963. Edgar, king of the whole of Britain, grants 23 hides at Washington, Sussex, to Æthelwold, bishop [of Winchester]. *'Edgar A' formulation.*

See also S 1213 (Bury St Edmunds), in section C.

Charters of 964

In 964 King Edgar drove out the priests from the Old and New Minsters at Winchester, from Chertsey and from Milton, and replaced them with monks; and he appointed Æthelgar abbot of the New Minster, Ordberht abbot of Chertsey, and Cyneweard abbot of Milton. S 725 was issued while Ordgar was still a thegn; S 724 was issued after his appointment as an ealdorman.

S 727 (BCS 1127), from Romsey. AD 964. Edgar, king of the whole of Britain, grants [...] hides at (Steeple) Ashton, Wilts., to himself. *Dated 964, but lacks witness-list.*

S 730 (*Shaft* 25), from Shaftesbury. AD 964. Edgar, king of the English, grants 5 hides at Teffont, Wilts., to Sigestan, his thegn.

S 725 (*Abing* 101), from Abingdon. AD 964 (5th yr). Edgar, king of the English, and of the barbarians and gentiles, grants 10 hides at Aston (Upthorpe), Berks., to Ælfthryth, his consort (*lateranea*).

S 724 (*Abing* 100), from Abingdon. AD 964. Edgar, king of the English, grants 10 hides at Hendred, Berks., to Abingdon Abbey.

S 726 (BCS 1134), from Worcester. AD 964. Edgar, king of Albion, grants 2 hides at Cookley (in Wolverley), Worcs., to Byrhtnoth, his ealdorman (*comes*). *'Dunstan B' formulation; attested by the king. Note identification of the bishops' sees.*

See also S 728 (Ghent), S 729 (Muchelney), S 731 (Worcester), in section C.

Charters of 965

In 965 King Edgar took Ælfthryth, daughter of Ealdorman Ordgar, as his queen (cf. S 724–5, dated 964). Three of the charters listed below (S 732–4) form a cluster of identical charters in favour of Abingdon Abbey, with a witness-list apparently derived from a charter of 970, and should be treated with caution; see above, p. 63.

S 734 (*Abing* 102), from Abingdon. AD 965. Edgar, king of the whole of Albion, grants 50 hides at Marcham, Berks., to Abingdon Abbey. *Probably spurious.*

S 732 (*Abing* 103), from Abingdon. AD 965. Edgar, king of the whole of Albion, grants 5 hides at Beedon, Berks., to Abingdon Abbey. *Probably spurious.*

S 733 (*Abing* 104), from Abingdon. AD 965. Edgar, king of the whole of Albion, grants 2 hides at Denchworth, Berks., to Abingdon Abbey. *Probably spurious.*

S 736 (BCS 1165), from Abbotsbury. AD 965. Edgar, monarch of the whole island of Britain, grants 3 *virgae* at Cheselbourne, Dorset, to Wulfheard, his

man. *Single sheet (probably original), written by a scribe not otherwise identi-fied, with 'south-western' formulation.*
S 735 (*Bath* 17), from Bath. AD 965. Edgar, king of the whole of Albion, grants 7½ hides at Stanton (Prior), Somerset, to Abbot Æscwig for St Peter's, Bath. *'Dunstan B' formulation, incorporating a request for prayers; attested by the king.*

Charters of 966

In 966 Oslac succeeded to the aldormanry of Northumbria (cf. S 712, S 712a and S 716, dated 963, and S 732–4, dated 965).

S 744 (*Shaft* 26), from Shaftesbury. AD 966. Edgar, king of the whole of Britain, grants 10 hides at Up Piddle, Dorset, to Shaftesbury Abbey (the land given by his grandmother Wynflæd, though the earlier charter had been lost). *'Edgar A' formulation.*
S 738 (BCS 1176), from Winchester (Old Minster). AD 966. Edgar, king of the English, grants 10 hides at Newnham (Murren), Oxon, to his kinswoman Ælfgifu, *matrona*. *Single sheet (probably original), written by a scribe not oth-erwise identified, with 'Edgar A' formulation; witness-list based on same memo-randum as used for S 737.*
S 737 (*Abing* 105), from Abingdon. AD 966. Edgar, king of the English, grants 10 hides at Linslade, Bucks., to his kinswoman Ælfgifu, *matrona*. *'Edgar A' formulation; witness-list based on same memorandum as used for S 738, appar-ently also used as a model for the witness-list in the Abingdon cluster of 968.*
S 740 ('Kemble'), from Muchelney. AD 966. Edgar, king of the whole of Albion, grants 10 hides at Isle (Abbots), Somerset, to Ælfwold, bishop [of Sherborne or Crediton].
S 739 (*Burt* 21), from Burton. AD 966. Edgar, king of the whole of Albion, grants 10 hides at Parwich, Derbys., to Ælfhelm, his thegn. *Attested by Edward (the Martyr) and Ælfthryth.*
S 742 (BCS 1177), from Glastonbury. AD 966. Edgar, king of the whole kingdom on this side of the sea (*citra mare*), grants 15 hides at Buckland (Newton), Dorset, to 'Ethelred' (Ælfthryth), his wife. *Not in the 'Liber Terrarum' (below, p. 79); entered in the 'Great Cartulary'.*
S 743 (BCS 1188), from Glastonbury. AD 966. Edgar, king of the whole of Albion, grants 2 hides at (Podimore) Milton, Somerset, to Glastonbury Abbey. *'Dunstan B' formulation; attested by the king.*
S 745 (*WinNM* 23), from Winchester (New Minster). AD 966. Edgar, king of the English, affirms that the community of the New Minster will follow the Rule of St Benedict. *Original (written in gold letters, in book form), with a frontispiece showing King Edgar presenting the charter to Christ.*
See also S 746 (New Minster, Winchester), S 741 (Crowland) and S 1294 (Crowland), in section C.

Charters of 967

S 747 (BCS 1196), from Glastonbury. AD 967. Edgar, king of the whole of Britain, grants 20 hides at Merton and 5 hides at Dulwich, Surrey, to Ælfheah, ealdorman (*comes*), and his wife Ælfswith. *'Edgar A' formulation.*

S 748 (BCS 1199), from Winchester (Old Minster). AD 967. Edgar, king of all the English people, grants 5 hides at *Eastune*, to Ælfsige, his thegn. *'Edgar A' formulation.*

S 754 (BCS 1200), from Winchester (Old Minster). AD 967. Edgar, king of the whole of Albion, grants 8 hides at Meon and at Farnfield (in Privett), Hants., to Wynflæd, *matrona*. *'Edgar A' formulation.*

S 755 (BCS 1197), from Exeter. AD 967 (7th yr). Edgar, king of the English, grants 3 hides at Lesneage and 1 acre at Pennare, Cornwall, to Wulfnoth Rumuncant, his *vasallus*. *Later copy on single sheet (s. xi.2).*

S 750 (*Abing* 106), from Abingdon. AD 967. Edgar, king of the English, grants [...] hides at (Cold) Brayfield, Bucks., to Byrhtnoth, his ealdorman (*comes*). *'Dunstan B' formulation; attested by the king.*

S 753 (BCS 1198), from Westminster. AD 967. Edgar, king of the whole of Albion, grants 1½ hides at *Cealvadune* (?Chaldon, Surrey) to Dunstan, archbishop [of Canterbury], being the half part of the estate forfeited by Eadwold (with bounds of the whole). *Single sheet (possibly original), written by a scribe not otherwise identified, with 'Dunstan B' formulation; attested by the king (but Oswald is styled 'archbishop' too early).*

See also S 752 (Chertsey), in section C.

Charters of 968

Four of the charters listed below (S 757–60) form a cluster of identical charters in favour of Abingdon Abbey, with a witness-list apparently derived from a charter of 966, and have to be treated with caution; see above, p. 63.

S 764 (BCS 1214), from Glastonbury. AD 968. Edgar, king of the whole of Britain, grants 30 hides at Sturminster (Newton), Dorset, to Glastonbury Abbey. *'Edgar A' formulation.*

S 765 (BCS 1215), from Romsey. AD 968. Edgar, king of the whole of Britain, grants land at Edington, Wilts., to Romsey Abbey. *'Edgar A' formulation; but lacks witness-list.*

S 767 (BCS 1216), from Wilton. AD 968. Edgar, king of the whole of Britain, grants 2 hides near Wilton, Wilts., to Wilton Abbey (formerly held by Regenweard *mercator*). *'Edgar A' formulation.*

S 762 (*Shaft* 27), from Shaftesbury. AD 968. Edgar, king of the whole of Britain, grants 3 *iugera* of farmland and 20 *iugera* of woodland at *Ealderes cumbe* to Brihtgifu, *femina*. *'Edgar A' formulation.*

S 766 ('Kemble'), from Wilton. AD 968. Edgar, king of the English, with Northumbrians, pagans and British, grants land at five places in Wiltshire, with appurtenant land in the Isle of Wight, to Wilton Abbey, previously leased to Wulfthryth [abbess of Wilton]. *'Edgar A' formulation.*

S 757 (*Abing* 111), from Abingdon. AD 968. Edgar, king of the whole of Britain, grants 30 hides at Cumnor, Berks., to Abingdon Abbey. *'Edgar A' formulation. Probably spurious.*

S 758 (*Abing* 110), from Abingdon. AD 968. Edgar, king of the whole of Britain, grants 25 hides at Fifield, Berks., to Abingdon Abbey. *'Edgar A' formulation. Probably spurious.*

S 759 (*Abing* 112), from Abingdon. AD 968. Edgar, king of the whole of Britain, grants 20 hides at Hanney, Berks., to Abingdon Abbey. *'Edgar A' formulation. Probably spurious.*

S 760 (*Abing* 113), from Abingdon. AD 968. Edgar, king of the whole of Britain, grants 10 hides at Oare, Berks., to Abingdon Abbey. *'Edgar A' formulation. Probably spurious.*

S 763 (BCS 1217), from Winchester (Old Minster). AD 968. Edgar, king of the whole of Britain, grants 20 hides at Moredon (in Rodbourne Cheney), Wilts., to Eadwine, his thegn. *The draftsman used the formulation in a charter of the 950s: cf. S 638, issued by King Eadwig in 956, for the same estate.*

S 769 (*Abing* 109), from Abingdon. AD 968. Edgar, king of the English, grants 10 hides at Whistley, Berks., to Wulfstan, his thegn. *The draftsman used the formulation from a charter of the 950s: cf. S 603 (Abing 61) and S 611 (Abing 73), in the name of King Eadwig. The witness-list appears to be from a charter of 966.*

S 761 (*Abing* 107), from Abingdon. AD 968. Edgar, king of the English, grants 10 hides at Boxford, Berks., to Ælfwine, his thegn. *Problematic, given Edgar's style ('rex pacificus') and occurrence of (Archbishop) Oswald.*

S 768 (*Burt* 23), from Burton. AD 968. Edgar, king of the English, grants 1 hide at Stanton (in the Peak), Derbys., to Wulfric, bishop [of Hereford]. *Single sheet (probably original), written by a scribe not otherwise identified; witness-list inserted after main text and sanction.*

S 1215 (*CantCC* 128), from Christ Church, Canterbury. AD 968 (11th yr). Record of a sale of land in Kent by Æthelflæd (and Eadwold) to Ælfwold (for 1,450 pennies), produced at a meeting attended by the king, Archbishop Dunstan, and others. *Single sheet (probably original), written by a scribe not otherwise identified, in different stages.*

See also S 756 (Abingdon) and S 806 (Winchester), in section C.

Charters of 969

S 770 (BCS 1231), from Exeter. AD 969. Edgar, king of the English, grants 2 hides and 1 *pertica* at Lamorran and Trenowth (in Probus), Cornwall, to Ælfheah Gerent, *homo*, and his wife Moruurei. *Single sheet (s. xi.2), with formulation related to S 704 (962), from Buckfast.*

S 771 (BCS 1230), from Winchester (Old Minster). AD 969. Edgar, king of the whole of Britain, grants 30 hides at Witney, Oxon, to Ælfhelm, his thegn. *'Edgar A' formulation.*

S 772 (BCS 1229), from Worcester. AD 969. Edgar, king of the whole of Albion, grants 15 hides at Aspley (Guise), Beds., to Ælfwold, his thegn. *Single sheet (possibly original), with 'Edgar A' formulation; cf. S 773.*

S 773 (BCS 1234), from Worcester. AD 969. Edgar, king of the whole of Albion, grants 10 hides at Kineton, Warwicks., to Ælfwold, his thegn. *Somers charter (lost), with 'Edgar A' formulation; cf. S 772.*

S 1795 (*LondStP* 17), from London (St Paul's). AD 969. Edgar, king of the English, grants 40 hides at Hadham, Herts., to (his stepmother) Æthelflæd, widow and nun. *'Edgar A' formulation.*

See also S 774 (Westminster), in section C.

Charters of 970

S 777 (*Bath* 18), from Bath. AD 970. Edgar, king of the whole kingdom of Britain, grants 10 hides at Clifton, Somerset, to Bath Abbey (under Abbot Æscwig), in exchange for 100 mancuses of gold and 10 hides at Compton (Chilcompton or Compton Dando), Somerset. *'Edgar A' formulation; cf. S 781.*

S 781 (BCS 1269), from Ely. AD 970. Edgar, king of the whole kingdom of Britain, grants 10 hides at Stoke (by Nayland), Suffolk, to Ely Abbey (under Bishop Æthelwold). *'Edgar A' formulation; cf. S 777. According to the 'Libellus Æthelwoldi', ch. 51, Bishop Æthelwold bought the land from the king for 100 mancuses.*

S 775 (BCS 1259), from Glastonbury. AD 970. Edgar, 'emperor' of the whole of Albion, grants 10 hides at Idmiston, Wilts., to Ælfswith, widow and nun, for services rendered *a primeva usque in presentem ... etatem.*

S 778 (*Abing* 114), from Abingdon. AD 970. Edgar, king of the English, grants 7 hides at Kingston (Bagpuize), Berks., to Brihtheah, deacon. *Formulation from a charter of the 950s; cf. S 650.*

S 780 (BCS 1268), from Ely. AD 970. Edgar, king of the whole of Britain, grants 10 hides at Linden (End), Cambs., to Ely Abbey. *'Edgar A' formulation.*

See also S 776 (Ely) and S 779 (Ely), in section C.

Charters of 971

S 782 (*Pet* 15), from Peterborough. AD 971 (15th yr). Edgar, king of the whole British island, grants land at Barrow (-upon-Humber), Lincs., to Æthelwold, bishop [of Winchester], for Peterborough Abbey, in return for 40 pounds of silver and a gold cross. *Elements of 'Edgar A' formulation.*

S 1276 (*CantCC* 98*b*), from Christ Church, Canterbury. Undated (963 x 971). King Edgar transfers a charter to Leofric, with witness-list. *A note added s. x.2 to a charter preserved in single-sheet form.*

See also S 783 (Glastonbury) and S 787 (Peterborough), in section C.

Charters of 972

S 789 (BCS 1286), from Wilton. AD 972. Edgar, king of the whole of Britain, grants 4 hides on the river Avon, Wilts., to Winstan, his chamberlain (*cubicularius*). *'Edgar A' formulation.*

S 784 (BCS 1285), from Wilton. AD 972. King Edgar grants 10 hides at Kennet,

Wilts., with the permission of Osweard, to Ælfflæd, *femina. For Osweard, cf. S 803 (king's kinsman).*

S 749 (*Burt* 22), from Burton. AD '967' for ?972. Edgar, king of the whole of Britain, grants 3 hides at Breedon (-on-the-Hill), and 10 hides at three other places, Leics., to Æthelwold, bishop [of Winchester], not to be taken from the church of Breedon. *Elements of 'Edgar A' formulation.*

S 785 (*Bath* 19), from Bath. AD 972. Edgar, king of the whole of Albion, grants 10 hides at Corston, Somerset, to Bath Abbey. *'Dunstan B' formulation; attested by the king.*

S 668 (BCS 1145), from Winchester (Old Minster). AD '922', for ?972. Edgar, king of the English, grants 10 hides at *Winterburnan*, to Eadric, his thegn.

S 805 (BCS 1309), from Westminster. AD '878' for ?972. Edgar, king of the whole of Britain, grants 5 hides at Hampstead, Middlesex, to Mangoda, his thegn. *'Edgar A' formulation.*

See also S 786 (Pershore) and S 788 (Worcester), in section C.

Charters of 973

In 973, on the day of Pentecost (11 May), at Bath, Edgar was consecrated king, in the thirteenth year after he succeeded to the kingdom [calculated from 960], and in the thirtieth year of his life [calculated from 943].

S 793 (BCS 1291), from Glastonbury. AD 973. Edgar, king of the English, grants 5 hides at Berrow, Somerset, to Wulfmær, his thegn. *Elements of formulation recur in S 834, dated 979, from Peterborough.*

S 790 (BCS 1292), from Winchester (Old Minster). AD 973. Edgar, king of the whole of Albion, grants 7 hides at Harwell, Berks., to Ælfric, his thegn. *'Dunstan B' formulation; attested by the king.*

S 791 (BCS 1294), from Glastonbury. AD 973. Edgar, king of the whole of Albion, grants 7 hides at (High) Ham, Somerset, to Glastonbury Abbey, in exchange for land at Braunton, Devon. *'Dunstan B' formulation; attested by the king.*

See also S 792 (Thorney), in section C.

Charters of 974

S 794 (BCS 1305), from Westminster. AD 974. Edgar, king of the whole of Britain, grants 2½ hides at (West) Wratting, Cambs., to Ælfhelm, his thegn. *Single sheet (probably a non-contemporary copy), written by a scribe not otherwise identified, with 'Edgar A' formulation.*

S 794a ('Kemble'), from Westminster. AD 974. Edgar, king of the whole of Albion, grants 9 hides at Brickendon, Herts., to Ælfhelm, his thegn. *'Dunstan B' formulation; attested by the king.*

S 795 (BCS 1303), from Crediton. AD 974. Edgar, king of the whole of Britain, grants 3 hides at *Nymed* (Woolfin, in Down St Mary), Devon, to Ælfhere, his thegn. *Single sheet (probably original), written by a scribe not otherwise identified; with an intriguing gap in the witness-list.*

See also S 796 (Malmesbury), S 798 (Ramsey) and S 799 (Wilton), in section C.

Charters of 975

S 800 (BCS 1316), from Winchester (Old Minster). AD 975. Edgar, king of the whole of Britain, grants 5 hides at Fyfield, Hants., to Ælfweard, his thegn. *'Edgar A' formulation.*
S 801 (BCS 1312), from Winchester (Old Minster). AD 975. Edgar, king of the whole of Britain, grants 3 hides at Madeley, Staffs., to Æthelwold, bishop [of Winchester]. *Single sheet (possibly original), written by a scribe not otherwise identified, with 'Edgar A' formulation.*
S 802 (BCS 1315), from Winchester (Old Minster). AD 975, at Glastonbury. Edgar, king of Albion, grants 3 hides at Aston (in Wellington), Salop, at the request of his kinsman, the monk Ælfwine, to Ealhhelm, his thegn. *'Dunstan B' formulation; not attested by the king.*
S 803 (BCS 1314), from Winchester (Old Minster). AD 975. Edgar, king of the whole of Albion, grants 4 hides at (South) Stoke, Sussex., to his kinsman Osweard (replacing a charter lost by fire). *'Dunstan B' formulation; attested by the king. For Osweard, cf. S 784, dated 972, from Wilton.*

C. 'PROBLEMATIC' CHARTERS

The charters grouped together in this section are separated from the charters listed above because they are for one reason or another 'problematic', in the sense that they do not appear to be acceptable in their received form. In several cases the charters are demonstrably spurious; in other cases, the inclusion of a charter in this section is a matter of judgement. Many are texts of the kind which Edgar's reputation as a supporter of the cause of monastic reform was bound to attract to his name, in a process which probably began in the late tenth century (above, p. 47). Also included in this group are a number of charters from outside the main series: S 833 (Abingdon); S 1213 (Bury St Edmunds); S 1214 (Evesham); S 1293 (Westminster); S 1294 (Crowland); in some of these cases, significant elements of formulation appear to have been derived from authentic texts.

S 670 (BCS 1048), from Westminster. AD '951' for ?959, enacted at Glastonbury Abbey. Edgar, king of the whole of Albion, grants 5 hides (on the river Thames), to the church of St Peter at Westminster (for 120 gold *solidi*); with reference to an ancient charter of King Offa. *Single sheet (s. x ex), with elements of 'Dunstan B' formulation; lacks a witness-list.*
S 673 (*Abing* 84), from Abingdon. AD '958'. Edgar, king of the English, restores four estates in Berkshire to Abingdon Abbey, with affirmation of the community's right, after the death of Abbot Æthelwold, to choose a successor from among their own number, and with affirmation of privileges and lands as granted to the abbey in the past. *An 'Orthodoxorum' charter in the name of King Edgar; cf. S 658 (Abing 83), dated 17 May 959, in the name of King Eadwig.*
S 1293 (BCS 1050), from Westminster. AD 959 (4th yr). Dunstan, bishop of

London, announces King Edgar's instigation of grants of privileges and lands to Westminster Abbey. *A twelfth-century forgery.*

S 686 (BCS 1057), from Paris, Saint-Denis. AD 960, 26 December (2nd yr), at York. Edgar, king of the English, restores land in Sussex to St Denis.

S 1214 (BCS 1092), from Evesham. AD 962. 'Private' charter, by which 'Ufa the Hwede', sheriff of Warwick, granted 6½ hides at Wixford and (Temple) Grafton, Warwicks., to Evesham Abbey. *Spurious, but with formulation and witness-list drawn from a charter of 962; cf. S 707.*

S 833 (*Abing* 95), from Abingdon. AD 962. 'Æthelred', king of the English, grants woodland near the Claybrook, Leics., to Leofric, his thegn. *Spurious in this form, but based on a charter of 962, with 'Edgar A' formulation.*

S 810 ('Kemble'), from St Kew. Undated (?961 x 962). Edgar, king of the Anglo-Saxons, grants 2 hides at Lanow (in St Kew), Cornwall, to the minster [at Plympton, Devon], with reversion to the minster of SS Dawe and Kew.

S 811 (BCS 1319), from Winchester (Old Minster). AD '8[...]'. Edgar, ruler of the English, renews grant of 65 hides at Meon, Hants., to his grandmother Eadgifu (replacing a charter which she had entrusted to him when an ætheling, and which he had lost). *Spurious in this form, but with witness-list drawn from a charter of 962.*

S 1213 (BCS 1084), from Bury St Edmunds. AD 963. 'Private' charter, by which Wulfstan grants 4 hides at Palgrave, Suffolk, to St Edmund's Abbey. *Spurious, but with elements of formulation and witness-list drawn from a charter of 963.*

S 728 ('Kemble'), from Ghent (St Peter's). AD 964 (6th yr). Edgar, king of the English, restores land in Kent to St Peter's, Ghent.

S 729 ('Kemble'), from Muchelney. AD 964. Edgar, king of the whole of Britain, grants privileges to Muchelney Abbey: that Bishop Ælfwold [of Sherborne or Crediton] should govern the community during his lifetime, and that after his death the community should choose a successor from among their own number; with confirmation of all the abbey's estates (not specified). *Probably spurious, but with elements drawn from authentic charters of Edgar.*

S 731 (BCS 1135), from Worcester (St Mary's). AD 964, 28 December (6th yr), at Gloucester. Edgar, king of the English, gives an account of recent history, including the foundation of 47 monasteries, and affirms the creation of *Oswaldeslaw. A famous forgery, known as the 'Altitonantis' charter.*

S 732–4, from Abingdon, in section B (965), with witness-list from a charter of 970.

S 741 (BCS 1178), from Crowland. AD 966. Edgar, king of the whole of Britain, grants privileges and lands to Crowland Abbey. *Patently spurious.*

S 1294 (BCS 1179), from Crowland. AD 966, at St Paul's, London. Archbishop Dunstan, Archbishop Osketel, with the bishops of Winchester, Worcester and Dorchester, make known the grant of privileges and lands to Crowland Abbey. *Patently spurious.*

S 746 (*WinNM* 24), from Winchester (New Minster). AD 966. Edgar, king of the English, grants 5 hides at Donnington, 28 hides at Southease, and 10 hides at Telscombe, Sussex, and 2 hides at Winterburna (in Maddington), Wilts., to the New Minster. *'Edgar A' formulation.*

S 752 (BCS 1195), from Chertsey. AD 967. King Edgar confirms privileges and lands to Chertsey Abbey. *Patently spurious, although it incorporates some interesting information.*

S 756 (*Abing* 108), from Abingdon. AD '958' or '968'. Edgar, king of the English, grants 72 hides at Bedwyn, Wilts., to Abingdon Abbey. *Patently spurious, using a witness-list from 968.*

S 757–60, from Abingdon, in section B (968), with witness-list from a charter of 966.

S 806 (BCS 1219), from Winchester, Old Minster. AD '978' (Easter), ? for 968 (10th yr), at Cheddar. Edgar, king of the English, renews the liberty of Taunton, Somerset, as previously granted to the Old Minster by his grandfather, Edward (the Elder); with a record of Bishop Æthelwold's payment to King Edgar and to (Queen) Ælfthryth. *Anomalous in form and content; using witness-list drawn from a charter of c. 968.*

S 774 (BCS 1264), from Westminster. AD 969 (13th yr). Edgar, king of the English, confirms Westminster Abbey in its possession of lands and privileges. *Patently a twelfth-century forgery.*

S 776 (BCS 1265), from Ely. AD 970, Easter (13th yr), at Woolmer, Kent. Edgar, king of the whole of Albion, grants Ely Abbey to Æthelwold, bishop of Winchester, with land at Melbourn and Armingford, Cambs., in exchange for land at Harting, Sussex.

S 779 (BCS 1266), from Ely. AD 970 (13th yr), at Woolmer, Kent. Edgar, king of the whole of Albion (etc.), confirms the establishment of Ely Abbey by Æthelwold, bishop of Winchester, with grant of land at Melbourn and Armingford, Cambs., and Northwold, Norfolk, in exchange for land at Harting, Sussex. *Bilingual charter (Latin/Old English).*

S 783 (BCS 1277), from Glastonbury. AD 971, at London. Edgar, king of the English, grants privileges to Glastonbury Abbey. *Patently spurious; not in the 'Liber Terrarum' (below, p. 79).*

S 809 (*CantStA* 29), from Canterbury (St Augustine's). Undated (963 x 971). Edgar, king of the English, grants 4 sulungs at Plumstead, Kent, to St Augustine's Abbey, Canterbury. *The formulation is archaic (cf. S 332).*

S 787 (*Pet* 16), from Peterborough. AD 970/972 (10th/16th yr). King Edgar grants privileges and lands to Peterborough Abbey. *Patently spurious, although it incorporates some interesting information.*

S 786 (BCS 1282), from Pershore/Worcester. AD 972. Edgar, king of the English, for the church of Pershore: that after the death of Abbot Foldbriht the members of the community shall choose a successor from among their community, in accordance with the Rule of St Benedict; with a grant of privileges on the same terms as established by King Coenwulf for Ealdorman Beornoth, in the old charter, and with a list of estates in Worcestershire and Gloucestershire. *An 'Orthodoxorum' charter in the name of King Edgar; single sheet, written s. x/xi.*

S 788 (BCS 1284), from Worcester. AD 972. Edgar, king of the English, for the church of Worcester, in similar terms (but without a list of estates). *An 'Orthodoxorum' charter in the name of King Edgar; probably modeled on S 786 (Pershore).*

S 671 (*Roch* 29), from Rochester. AD '955', ?for 973. Edgar, king of the English, grants 10 hides at Bromley, Kent, to the church of Rochester, in return for payments from Bishop Ælfstan and the reeve Wulfstan. *Single sheet (s. x/xi), presumably fabricated at Rochester.*

S 812 (BCS 1187), from Romsey. Undated. Edgar, king of the English, for the church of Romsey: that after the death of Abbess Merewenne the members of the community shall choose a successor from among their community, in accordance with the Rule of St Benedict; a wood given in exchange for 900 gold mancuses in a beautifully made bowl. *An 'Orthodoxorum' charter in the name of King Edgar.*

S 792 (BCS 1297), from Thorney. AD 973 (1st yr of royal dedication). Edgar, king of the English, grants privileges and lands to Thorney Abbey. *A spurious foundation charter, although it incorporates some interesting information.*

S 751 (BCS 1201), from Worcester. AD '967', ?for 973 (13th yr). Edgar, king of the English, grants 2 hides at *Suthtune* (?Ullington in Pebworth, Gloucs.) and at Bickmarsh, Warwicks., to Byrhtnoth, his thegn, with assignment (with Byrhtnoth's son) to the church of Worcester.

S 808 (*CantCC* 129), from Canterbury (Christ Church). Undated (?973), Pentecost, at Bath. Edgar, king of the whole of England, grants land at Sandwich, Kent, to the church of Canterbury. *A fabrication reflecting awareness of literary accounts of the submission to Edgar at Chester in 973.*

S 798 (BCS 1310), from Ramsey. AD 974. Edgar, king of the English, grants privileges and lands to Ramsey Abbey. *A spurious foundation charter, although it incorporates some interesting information.*

S 799 (BCS 1304), from Wilton. AD 974 (15th yr, and 34th yr of his age). Edgar, king of the whole of Britain, to Wulfthryth, abbess, and Wilton abbey: affirmation of privileges, confirmation of Chalke, Wilts., and of other lands (not specified).

S 796 (*Malm* 30), from Malmesbury. AD 974 (14th yr of reign, and 1st of coronation). Edgar, king of the whole of Albion, restores 10 hides at Eastcourt (in Crudwell), Wilts., to Ælfric, abbot of Malmesbury. *Interestingly anomalous in various respects, and not certainly spurious; see also S 797.*

S 797 (BCS 1300), from Crowland. AD 974 (1st yr of coronation). Edgar, king of the whole of Albion, restores land at *Nene* to Ælfric, abbot of Malmesbury. *A bowdlerized version of S 796 (974), from Malmesbury.*

S 820 (BCS 1307), from Winchester (Old Minster). Undated ('17' years after his accession, in the first of his coronation, ? for 973–4). Edgar, king of the whole of Albion, grants 45 hides at Crondall, Hants., to the Old Minster. *Based in part on 'Edgar A' formulation.*

S 807 (BCS 1302), from Winchester (Old Minster). AD '984', for ? 974. Edgar, king of the whole of Britain, grants land in Winchester to the Old Minster, New Minster, and Nunnaminster, Winchester.

S 804 (BCS 1313), from Winchester (Old Minster). AD 975. Edgar, king of the English, grants 5 hides at Bleadon, Somerset, to the Old Minster. *Seriously spurious.*

S 813 (*Sherb* 10), from Sherborne. Undated. King Edgar grants 5 hides at

Oborne, Dorset, to Sherborne. *Ostensibly derived from an entry in a gospel-book.*

S 814–19 + 821–7 (BCS 1150, etc.), from Winchester (Old Minster). Edgar, king of the English, grants, confirms, or restores land in various counties (Hants, Wilts, Somerset, Surrey) to the Old Minster.[12]

D. 'LOST' CHARTERS OF KING EDGAR

Examples of 'lost' or 'incomplete' charters in the name of King Edgar have been noted among records relating to the archives of Abbotsbury, Buckfast, Canterbury (Christ Church), Canterbury (St Augustine's), Ely, Glastonbury, London (St Paul's), Ramsey, Winchester (Old Minster), Winchester (New Minster), and Worcester; many of them are registered in Sawyer's catalogue (1968), and full details will be found in the 'Revised Sawyer' (above, p. 60).

The most significant group of lost charters comprises those formerly preserved at Glastonbury Abbey.[13] The *Liber Terrarum* of Glastonbury, a cartulary compiled probably in the late eleventh century and known only from a list of its contents drawn up in 1247 (Cambridge, Trinity College R.5.33, fol. 77rv), contained the texts of 16 charters of King Edgar. Four of these charters (*LT*, nos. 82–3, 103, 113) are known by virtue of their inclusion in the thirteenth-century 'Great Cartulary' of Glastonbury (Longleat House, Wiltshire, 39), and are thus included in section B above (S 743, 747, 775, 791); 12 others (*LT*, nos. 70, 71, 72, 74, 80, 81, 86, 90, 111, 114, 117, 119) are now lost (S 1759–70). Many of the charters preserved at Glastonbury were still extant in single-sheet form in 1247, when they were listed (Cambridge, Trinity College R.5.33, fols. 77v–78v). Of those in the name of King Edgar, two had been entered in the *Liber Terrarum* (S 747, S1762); five appear in the 'Great Cartulary' (S 721, S 747, S 764, S 783, S 793); and two others, not included in *LT* or *GC*, are otherwise unknown (S 1771–2). One other charter of King Edgar, not included in the *Liber Terrarum* and not listed in 1247, appears in the 'Great Cartulary' (S 742). Of the fifteen lost charters of Edgar from the Glastonbury archive, 11 were in favour of laymen, and four (including three in the *Liber Terrarum*) were in favour of Glastonbury.

In certain cases it is not clear whether a lost charter seemingly of King Edgar would have been one issued in his name, or an older title-deed which changed hands in the context of a transaction known to have taken place during

---

[12] For text and translation, see Rumble, *Property and Piety*, pp. 98–135; and for further discussion, see Sophie Rixon, 'Monastic Foundation Charters' (PhD dissertation, Univ. of Cambridge), in preparation.

[13] For a more detailed presentation and discussion of this material, see L. Abrams, *Anglo-Saxon Glastonbury: Church and Endowment* (Woodbridge, 1996), pp. 14–27, with pp. 31–4 (list of the contents of the *Liber Terrarum*), 35–7 (lists of the single-sheet charters still extant in 1247), and 38–9 (charters included in a fifteenth-century inventory).

his reign.[14] In other cases we are on different ground. Three charters of Edgar were registered by John Chase among single sheets seen by him at Winchester in 1643 (S 1814–16); another was registered by William Dugdale among single sheets seen at Worcester in the same year, and, most interestingly, is said to have been a charter, dated 970, by which Edgar granted 7 hides at Bishampton, Worcs., to Ely Abbey (S 1844); at least two more were among those excerpted by seventeenth-century antiquaries investigating the archives of St Paul's (*LonStP* 17–18).

[14] E.g. *Libellus Æthelwoldi episcopi*, chs. 5 (charter for 40 hides at Hatfield, Herts., given by Edgar to Ely Abbey) and 49 (charter for land at Sudbourne, Suffolk, given by Edgar and Ælfthryth to Bishop Æthelwold, on condition that he translate the Rule of Benedict into English, and then given by Æthelwold to Ely); see *LE*, pp. 79 and 111, and *Anglo-Saxon Ely: the 'Libellus Æthelwoldi Episcopi' and other records of Ely Abbey 970–1066*, ed. S. Keynes and A. Kennedy (forthcoming).

II

Edgar before 959

3

Eadwig and Edgar: Politics, Propaganda, Faction

SHASHI JAYAKUMAR

THE difficulty with Edgar's regime is not just that so little is known about it, but that the monastic memory of him sought to plug a gaping hole by imposing its own image. In some ways Edgar was similar to Edward the Confessor – an iconic figure representing a golden age and 'the good law'.[1] The aim of this chapter is to shed light on comparatively neglected aspects of Edgar's rule – on the principals at court and the relations between the nobility and the king.

A great deal of the politics of Edgar's reign has its roots in the years immediately preceding, and the issue must first be touched on. Eadwig's rule very quickly came under a type of *damnatio memoriae*: it clearly became politic under Edgar to mount a campaign against his predecessor. In his *Preface* to the English translation of the Benedictine Rule (written *c*. 970–3), Bishop Æthelwold wrote

> It was not before long his brother [Eadwig] ended the time of this transitory life, who through the ignorance of childhood dispersed his kingdom and divided its unity, and also distributed the lands of the holy churches to rapacious strangers.[2]

This, of course, represents the earliest of many character attacks on Eadwig and the basis for the much-repeated assertion by medieval writers that Eadwig was no friend of the church. This accusation was developed by later writers, some of whom tended to portray Eadwig as being hostile to monasticism as a whole. William of Malmesbury followed this line and made Eadwig responsible for the introduction of secular canons at Malmesbury as well as at other houses.[3]

The most technical piece of evidence can be dealt with first. An investigation

---

[1] In the twelfth century for example Eadmer was to open his *Historia Novorum* with a glowing panegyric on Edgar along just such lines. Eadmer, *Historia Novorum in Anglia*, ed. M. Rule (London, 1884), p. 3.

[2] *Councils & Synods*, pp. 142–54, at 146. Æthelwold's authorship of this tract was established by D. Whitelock, 'The Authorship of the Account of King Edgar's Establishment of Monasteries', *Philological Essays in Honour of Herbert Dean Meritt*, ed. J. L. Rosier (The Hague, 1970), pp.125–36.

[3] William of Malmesbury, *Gesta Regum Anglorum*, ed. R. Mynors, R. Thompson and M. Winterbottom, 2 vols. (Oxford, 1998–9), I.238–9.

into the lands mentioned in Eadwig's charters shows the extreme difficulty in identifying any estate granted out to a layman when the land in question had been given to the church at any time earlier in the century. There are instances where the estates booked to laymen were claimed by religious houses in charters of dubious value,[4] but it is revealing that monastic forgers do not seem to have been averse to selecting Eadwig as the grantor in their own concoctions. The Abingdon monks later forged a diploma which had Eadwig grant the community an estate at Ginge (Berks.); they also seem to have had their eye on Tadmarton (Oxon.) and they set about forging a charter where Eadwig let them have that estate as well.[5] Eadwig had in fact granted land to Abingdon, with King Æthelred's *orthodoxorum* charter in favour of Abingdon also naming Eadwig as one of the abbey's chief benefactors.[6] Significantly, while early sources such as Dunstan's biographer, known as 'B', and Byrhtferth of Ramsey charge Eadwig with misgovernment, cronyism and adultery, spoliation of the church does not figure among his crimes.[7] Close to his own time, then, Eadwig was probably not especially renowned for his 'hostility to monasteries'.[8]

This makes the later accusations all the more intriguing – why was so much vitriol later directed against Eadwig and (as we shall see) some of his coterie? In order to answer this question it is worth making an attempt to identify this group of supporters, and then to see how Edgar dealt with them.

Eadwig's Court

Ælfhere of Mercia became an ealdorman in 956 after just two authentic attestations, an unprecedented feat in the tenth-century.[9] He appears as a thegn in an Eadwig charter which, given its date of 955, represents the earliest of Eadwig's surviving charters. The temptation is to think that the unusually lengthy witness list represents a large gathering: it is conceivable that it was produced at the witan marking his accession late in that year. Eadwig's closest associates

---

4 S 584 and S 630.
5 S 583 and S 584. See S 630 for similar goings-on at Shaftesbury (a charter, unacceptable in its present form, which has Eadwig granting to Shaftesbury land at Donhead in Wiltshire).
6 See S 605, S 607 and S 663 for Eadwig's grants to Abingdon. King Æthelred's Orthodoxorum charter is S 876.
7 'B', *Vita Dunstani*, in Stubbs, *Dunstan*, pp. 35–6; Byrhtferth's *Vita Oswaldi*, in Raine, *York*, I.402–3.
8 For an interesting (and neglected) reference to Eadwig's generosity to the 'holy men' at Bampton, see J. Blair, 'St Beornwald at Bampton', *Oxoniensa* 49 (1984), 47–55, at 47.
9 S 555 (grant by Eadred in 951 of land at Buckland in Somerset to his kinsman Ælfhere), and S 582 from 955, Eadwig's earliest surviving charter. Some of the text of S 582 may be interpolated but the exceptionally long witness-list should probably be accepted as it stands See *Shaft*, p. 88. The methodology for much of what follows – the analysis of court politics through the royal charters and their witness lists – was pioneered in Keynes, *Diplomas*; see esp. pp. 48–83 for discussion of royal charters in the reigns of Eadwig and Edgar.

are singled out in this charter: Ælfhere is remarkably described as 'ex parentela regis' while Ælfheah is 'frater ejus'. Ælfhere and his brothers are elsewhere described in charters as royal kinsmen.[10] By the time of S 597, an early
charter from 956, Ælfhere's elevation has taken place and he attests as *comes*
(ealdorman).[11] Ælfhere's father, Ealhhelm, is an obscure figure who had been
ealdorman in Mercia under Edmund. Besides Ælfhere and Ælfheah, Ealhhelm
had two other sons, Ælfwine and Eadric. The only one of these four brothers
who was an important figure in his own right prior to 955 was Ælfheah, who
is the beneficiary of several charters.[12] Given that Ealhhelm's family does not
seem to have been long-established at court, it may be that the origins of its link
with the royal house were quite recent. It is possible that there was a kinship-
link with the female side of the royal family. Ealhhelm could for example have
married Wynflæd, the maternal grandmother of Eadwig and Edgar.[13] This might
explain Ælfhere's appearance as *ex parentela regis* in S 582, and it might also
shed light, indirectly, on why Ælfric *Cild*, possibly Ælfhere's brother-in-law,
appears in another charter from 956 as *adoptivus parens*.[14] Ælfric might have
had a hand in raising the young Eadwig.

Bishop Ælfsige of Winchester appears to have been a particular friend to
Ælfhere's brother, Ælfheah. The latter is described as *minnan leofan freond* and
made the executor of Ælfsige's will (955 x 958). Bishop Ælfsige also bequeathed
to Ælfheah an estate at Crondall in Hampshire.[15] The bishop also seems to
have been close enough another Eadwig man, Wulfric *Cufing* (whom we shall
presently deal with), to bequeath him land at Tichborne (Hunts.). Ælfsige was

---

[10] See for example S 555, S 570. A. Williams, '*Princeps Merciorum Gentis*: The Family,
Career and Connections of Ælfhere, Ealdorman of Mercia, 956–83', *ASE* 10 (1982),
143–172, is the definitive dissection of Ælfhere and his family.

[11] For dates of these charters (meaning how they should be 'grouped' relative to each other),
see Keynes, *Diplomas*, pp. 48–69; this should be supplemented with reference to the relevant tables in Keynes, *Attestations*.

[12] Ælfheah was probably appointed seneschal by Eadwig. He is called *cyninges discðen* in
S 1292 (an Old English memorandum from Abingdon to be dated 956 x 957 which, as
I will argue below, is important as it records the names of some of Eadwig's adherents).
The charters which have Ælfheah as beneficiary concern lands at Knoyle, Wilts. (S 531
from 948), *Norðune* (S 554 from 951) and Compton Beauchamp, Somerset (S 570 from
95 3x 955). For S 462 from 940, which was probably a grant by Edmund to Ælfheah and
his wife, see Williams, 'Ælfhere', pp. 147–8.

[13] Following the suggestion of L. N. Banton, 'Ealdormen and Earls in England from Alfred
to Ethelred the Unready', unpublished D.Phil. thesis, Univ. of Oxford, 1981, pp. 142–4.
See Yorke, 'Æthelwold', p. 75, for an alternative explanation.

[14] The charter in question, S 597, sees Eadwig granting to the same Ælfric the estate at
Hanney. On the Ælfric–Ælfhere connection we have suggestions but no certainty. Ælfric
Cild's son is named as Ælfwine in the *Battle of Maldon* where the latter mentions his
ancestor Ealhhelm; it was this Ælfwine who received an estate from Ælfheah in his will
(Williams, 'Ælfhere', p. 161, n. 90). For Ælfric *Cild* see also *Abing*, I.cxc–cxci. John of
Worcester says that Ælfric *Cild* was a son of Ælfhere, which is probably a mistaken infer-
ence drawn from the fact the Ælfric succeeded Ælfhere to the Mercian ealdordom. JW,
Chronicon, II.435.

[15] Whitelock, *Wills*, no. 4.

appointed by Eadwig to succeed Archbishop Oda of Canterbury when the latter died in 958, only to freeze to death in the Alps en route to collect his pallium. Ælfsige was a target of reformers of Edgar's time – Byrhtferth of Ramsey recounts in his *Vita Oswaldi* how Ælfsige insulted the grave of Archbishop Oda, a story which is repeated by William of Malmesbury in his *Gesta Pontificum*, and in his *Life* of Dunstan.[16]

Another kin group which should be considered is that of Byrhtnoth, the hero of Maldon.[17] Byrhtnoth's origins and advancement yield crucial insights into the make-up of Eadwig's regime. Previous studies of this man have tended to neglect the fact that he was an Eadwig appointee. In an early charter from 956 Eadwig granted an estate to the church at Worcester. In the text Eadwig (highly unusually) makes it clear that the grant has been facilitated by 'precibus et suasionibus Brihtnothi regalis presidis'.[18] Byrhtnoth goes on to become an ealdorman towards the end of 956 without once attesting a charter as a thegn, in a close parallel with Ælfhere's meteoric rise. Despite the speed of his elevation, Byrhtnoth may not have been a complete *parvenu*. The name stem 'Byrht-' was by no means uncommon among (predominantly Mercian) members of the nobility and royal family in the ninth century.[19] It has been suggested in the past that Byrhtnoth may have been descended from the Mercian royal family. The ætheling Beorhtnoth, whose son Byrhtsige died fighting Edward the Elder at the battle of the Holme, may have been Byrhtnoth's ancestor – possibly his great-grandfather.[20]

The likelihood is that the royal kinsman named Byrhthelm, appointed by Eadwig to succeed bishop Ælfsige to Winchester, was closely related to Byrhtnoth's family. There are several bishops Byrhthelm who attest during this period. But to summarize scholarly opinion: after Ælfsige's death en route to Rome, two separate Byrhthelms succeeded to the sees of Canterbury and Wells respec-

---

16 William of Malmesbury, *Gesta Pontificum*, p. 25; Stubbs, *Dunstan*, p. 294; *Vita Oswaldi*, p. 408. In his *Gesta Pontificum* William states that Ælfsige purchased the archbishopric of Canterbury, Hamilton, *Gesta*, p. 165.

17 For general treatments for Byrhtnoth and his family, C. Hart, 'The Ealdordom of Essex', *An Essex Tribute presented to Frederick G. Emmison*, ed. K. Neale (London, 1987), pp. 57–84; M. A. L. Locherbie-Cameron, 'Byrhtnoth and his Family', *The Battle of Maldon, A.D. 991*, ed. Donald Scragg (Oxford, 1991), pp. 253–62, and P. Stafford, 'Kinship and Women in the World of *Maldon*: Byrhtnoth and his Family', *The Battle of Maldon: Fiction and Fact*, ed. J. Cooper (London, 1993), pp. 225–36.

18 S 633.

19 See *The Crawford Collection of Early Charters and Documents*, ed. A. S. Napier and W. H. Stevenson (Oxford, 1895), pp. 85–6 and n. 4.

20 *ASC* A, s.a. 904 (= 902/3); Locherbie-Cameron, 'Byrhtnoth and his Family', p. 253. In addition, Byrhtnoth did already have connections at court. He replaced the mysterious ealdorman Byrhtferth – who attests only in 955 and 956. It has usually been accepted that Byrhtferth was some sort of relation to Byrhtnoth; he might have been an uncle or some other male relative. See H. M. Chadwick, *Studies on Anglo-Saxon Institutions* (Cambridge, 1905), pp. 179–80; Hart, 'Ealdordom of Essex', p. 131. Byrhtferth had himself been preceded by Ælfgar, Byrhtnoth's father-in-law. Ælfgar's will, which can be dated to 946 x 951, makes no mention of Byrhtferth, although it does include references to his son-in-law Byrhtnoth. Whitelock, *Wills*, no. 2.

tively.[21] The Byrhthelm who succeeded to Winchester was a royal kinsman.[22] Byrhthelm also makes an appearance in a charter from 957 where he attempts to secure the see of Selsey.[23] This charter marks one of Byrhtnoth's very earliest attestations as ealdorman. In addition, a document in the vernacular from Eadwig's reign which records an exchange of lands between Byrhthelm, *presbyter*, and Abbot Æthelwold should be considered.[24] There are only a handful of witnesses (including unique appearances for Ælfgifu, the king's wife, and Æthelgifu, her mother), with one of those attesting being the ealdorman Byrhtnoth. This would seem to reinforce the idea of a link between Byrhtnoth and the *presbyter* Byrhthelm who was later to be elevated to Winchester.[25] There is a Byrhthelm who turns up in charters in 956–7 among the bishops but without being identified as one; which cements the impression that Eadwig's priest and kinsman was in some sense a bishop-in-waiting at this time.[26]

The foundation charter of Eynsham Abbey – S 911 dated 1005 – suggests a kinship link between Byrhtnoth, a Bishop Byrhthelm and the family of the ealdorman Æthelweard (the 'Chronicler' and future ealdorman).[27] S 911 states that 'a certain Bishop Byrhthelm' had granted estates at Esher and Thames Ditton, Surrey, to his *propinquus* Æthelweard. The logical candidate would be Byrhthelm of Winchester, who is known to have been a *propinquus* of Edgar. It needs to be emphasised that Æthelweard himself first found advancement under Eadwig.[28] This was almost certainly because he was the brother of Eadwig's wife, Ælfgifu. In her will dating from the later half of Edgar's reign (*c.*966x975), Ælfgifu grants several estates to the king; she also refers to a man named Æthel-

---

21 On the various Bishops Byrhthelm of the period, see P. Wormald, 'The Strange Affair of the Selsey Bishopric 953–63', *Belief and Culture in the Middle Ages: Studies presented to Henry Mayr-Harting*, ed. R. Gameson and H. Leyser (Oxford, 2001), pp. 128–41, and D. Whitelock, 'The Appointment of Dunstan as Archbishop of Canterbury', *Otium and Negotium. Studies in Onomatology and Library Science Presented to Olaf Von Feilitzen*, ed. F. Sandgren (Stockholm, 1973), pp. 232–47.

22 See S 683 and S 695 for the identification of the Winchester Byrhthelm as a royal kinsman.

23 S 1291. Byrhthelm is likely to have been intended by Eadwig for (or even provisionally appointed to) Selsey, but Ælfsige at Winchester had swallowed up Selsey and its endowments. Wormald, 'The Strange Affair', pp. 128ff; *Sel*, no. 20.

24 S 1292. This document is a memorandum in the vernacular from Abingdon. *Anglo-Saxon Charters*, ed. and trans. A. J. Robertson, 2nd ed. (Cambridge, 1956), p. xxxi.

25 Robertson, *Charters*, 2nd ed., p. xxxi.

26 S 630 and S 639. Patrick Wormald also shows that the royal kinsman at Winchester is likely to have been the same man as the bishop-elect, Eadwig's kinsman, granted land at Stowe in Northamptonshire in 956 (S 615).

27 For S 911 see *The Eynsham Cartulary*, ed. H. E. Salter (Oxford, 1907–8), i, p. 20. See also Robertson, *Charters*, 2nd ed. pp. 386–7. The text makes it clear that certain estates granted by Edgar to Byrhtnoth eventually descended to Æthelweard's family. The fact that Byrhtnoth's widow Ælfflæd refers in her will to Æthelmær (the son of Æthelweard) as her husband's kinsman further illustrates the point. See Whitelock, *Wills*, pp. 40–1.

28 Æthelweard first begins to attest charters in Eadwig's reign. He appears in S 594, S 672, S 630 and S 616 from 956, and S 658, S 660, and S 586 from 959. Note that his brother Ælfweard attests next to him in S 616.

weard who appears to have been her brother.[29] It has usually been accepted that this is Æthelweard the Chronicler, and this connection would explain a great deal as Æthelweard refers in his *Chronicon* to his descent from King Æthelred I.[30] Æthelweard makes Æthelred I his *atavus* or great-great-grandfather, so if Ælfgifu was his full sister, she would have been Eadwig's third cousin once removed.[31]

Dynastic History

The rise of a kin-group linked to Eadwig through his new wife was no accident. Eadwig's marriage was *the* issue at court at this time – Archbishop Oda was later to separate Eadwig and Ælfgifu, on the grounds of consanguinity according to the 'D' text of the *Chronicle*.[32] Although we shall never know what the precise objections were in 955/6, the key lies not in canonical principle, but in dynastic history which goes back to the time of Alfred and his son Edward the Elder. Æthelred I's son, the ætheling Æthelwold, had chafed at being denied part of the kingdom in 899, the year Edward the Elder succeeded Alfred. He revolted and was only killed in 902 (or possibly early in 903) at the battle of Holme.[33] Æthelwold came perilously close to fracturing the West-Saxon state, for it was the Danes who 'remained in possession of the battle-field' at Holme, as the chronicler admits.[34] Perhaps only Æthelwold's death on the battlefield prevented a dynastic disaster. Some of the 'establishment' view of these events can be seen in the make-up of the *Chronicle*. In all its rescensions the ealdorman of Kent, Sigehelm, is a conspicuous casualty of the battle of Holme, killed fighting on the West-Saxon side. Edward the Elder married Sigehelm's daughter Eadgifu *c*. 916, probably after the death of his second wife Ælfflæd, though we cannot be certain of this. In any case, after King Æthelstan's death in 924 Eadgifu was probably *the* powerbroker at court, supported latterly by Dunstan.[35] It was the issue of Eadgifu and Edward – Edmund, Eadred and their heirs – who ruled after the death of Æthelstan (who appears himself to have been the son of Edward by yet another woman).[36] The emergence of Ælfgifu, descendent of the ætheling

---

29 Whitelock, *Wills*, no. 8; Yorke, *Æthelwold*, p. 76.

30 Campbell, *Æthelweard*, pp. 38–9.

31 Yorke, *Æthelwold*, p. 77.

32 Cubbin, *MS D*, s.a. 958.

33 *ASC* A, s.a. 904 (=902/3).

34 *ASC* A, s.a. 904.

35 On Eadgifu in general see Stafford, 'The King's Wife', in her *Unification and Conquest* (London, 1989), pp. 42–4. Eadgifu had been on good terms with Dunstan at least since Eadred's time. Dunstan had on one occasion refused the offer of the bishopric of Crediton, despite the efforts of Eadgifu to persuade him to accept it: Stubbs, *Memorials*, pp. 29–30. Note that Eadgifu does not witness Æthelstan's diplomas, and it is possible that relations between the two were not good. Eadgifu appears to have been despoiled of some of her estates with the cognizance of Æthelstan and his councillors. *Select English Historical Documents of the Ninth and Tenth Centuries*, ed. F. E. Harmer (Cambridge, 1914), xxiii, 67.

36 See below, n. 89.

Æthelwold, did not just threaten Edgar's position – it represented a *revanche* to a line and a lineage with royal claims of its own. How were the Eadgifu/Dunstan axis and their supporters to deal with the emergence of the families of Ælfhere, Byrhtnoth and Æthelweard which were themselves linked by ties of kinship and *amicitia*? The ancestors of Byrhtnoth and Æthelweard had in all likelihood fought together with Æthelwold on the *Danish* side at the battle of Holme, the opposite side to that which Eadgifu's father Sigehelm had fought for.

Faced with powerful vested interests at court, Eadwig himself would have needed his own support base. While several of Eadwig's supporters were related to him, those 'new men' such as Ælfhere, Byrhtnoth and perhaps Byrhthelm who rose most quickly (and highest) seem to have been bound to each other and to him by especially close ties to each other. The 'consimiles' said by 'B' to have been favoured by Eadwig might not be simply 'those like himself', but his kinsmen.[37] Prior to Eadwig's reign, the attestations of Ælfhere are limited to just one or two appearances in authentic charters. Ælfhere's sudden elevation to an ealdormanry under Eadwig parallels what Eadwig did for Byrhtnoth. These men repaid Eadwig with support on key issues. Æthelweard for example would not have found advancement if he had not supported the Eadwig–Ælfgifu match. Although Æthelweard does not mention Ælfgifu's marriage to Eadwig in his *Chronicon*, he does break with other writers and offers the earliest positive view of that king.[38] Others such as Æthelwold, then abbot of Abingdon, also supported the marriage. It is in S 1292, an Abingdon document which we have already dealt with, that Ælfgifu is described as *ðæs cininges wif*.[39] Others who appear in this document include Byrhtnoth, the brothers Ælfheah and Eadric, Bishop Ælfsige and Bishop Osulf of Ramsbury. It cannot be doubted that these people too supported the marriage between Eadwig and Ælfgifu, a union which proved so much of a threat to the prospects of the aetheling Edgar. It is also

---

[37] Cyril Hart's translation of 'B's criticisms should perhaps be preferred to the version in *EHD* – Eadwig was 'losing the shrewd and wise who disapproved of his folly, *and eagerly annexing men of his own kin*'. C. Hart, *The Early Charters of Northern England and the North Midlands* (Leicester, 1975), p. 322. We should note that other royal kinsmen also came to the fore at this time. An example is Leofwine *propinquus regis* attesting at the head of the thegns in S 582 (the charter which mentions Ælfhere *ex parentela regis*). Leofwine has not appeared before and does not seem to have been able to cement his position afterwards in Eadwig's reign. However, he may be the same Leofwine who attests next to Æthelweard or Ælfweard in Edgar's reign. This individual would probably then be the same Leofwine who appears in King Æthelred's charter for Eynsham Abbey (S 911, 1005): the charter makes clear that Leofwine was part of the kin-group of Æthelweard 'the Chronicler' and was also linked to the ealdorman Byrhtnoth.

[38] '... he for his great beauty got the name "All-fair" from the common people. He held the kingdom continuously for four years, and deserved to be loved'. Æthelweard, *Chronicle*, p. 55.

[39] S 1292. Æthelwold was also a beneficiary of Ælfgifu's will. Æthelwold's support for the marriage is dealt with by Yorke and I do not intend to dwell on it here. My debt to her masterly unpicking of court politics will be obvious, see Yorke, *Æthelwold*, esp. at pp. 76–7 and 80.

no coincidence that Eadgifu's discomfiture and Dunstan's flight and exile from court coincide with Ælfgifu's rise and that of her supporters.[40] It was this axis that won out in 955–6.

I do not intend to dwell on the division of the kingdom itself except to point out that the schism in the heart of the West-Saxon polity probably owed much to the political faction sketched above.[41] The division appears to have been a negotiated settlement whereby Edgar was to rule England north of the Thames.[42] What this actually means is that the thegns and ealdorman who habitually attended the West-Saxon court may not have had a great deal of choice in where their fortunes now lay. Byrhtnoth, Æthelwold and Ælfhere were all Eadwig appointees; they left Eadwig's court because this was presumably what had been agreed between the two factions. It is worth noting however that a variant orthodoxy began developing at an early stage as to exactly what had happened in 957. There is an intriguing reference in an Old English document from Edgar's reign to the election of Edgar by the Mercian council.[43] The case concerns a land dispute involving the estates of Sunbury and Send in Middlesex. The document, an 'original' in the Westminster archive, should be associated with Dunstan and his circle, as it records at the end his (ultimately successful) efforts to purchase Sunbury and Send from the ealdorman Ælfheah sometime in the 960s. Reference is made in the document to how an individual named Æthelstan, unhappy with the judgement he received at the hands of Eadwig and his councillors, took his case to Edgar, who had just been chosen by the Mercians as their king and had been handed control of 'all the royal prerogatives'. It is however difficult to see how the Mercian nobility could themselves have engineered the breakaway on their own. Charter attestations seem to indicate that Edgar was continually at the West-Saxon court from 955 to 957. The young ætheling could have had precious little interaction with the nobility outside Wessex.[44] It perhaps reflects the developing orthodoxy in the 960s as to just what had happened in 957 (ultimately established in 'B's account), with the focus laid squarely on Eadwig and the northern peoples.

---

[40] See Stubbs, *Dunstan*, p. 36 for reference to the confiscation of Eadgifu's estates. We shall never know how much of the incident at Eadwig's coronation feast has a basis in fact. But Dunstan's flight is real enough: it was described also by Adelard who adds some important information when he tells us that the 'certain prince' was Arnulf I of Flanders, who installed Dunstan at St Peter's in Ghent, Stubbs, *Dunstan*, pp. 59–60.

[41] I intend to examine the issue of the divided kingdom and politics from 957 to 959 in a subsequent paper.

[42] Stubbs, *Dunstan*, pp. 35–6; JW, *Chronicon*, II.406–7.

[43] Robertson, *Charters*, 2nd ed., p. xliv. The events described in the text stretch from 955–6 (when Earl Byrhtferth, who is referred to, held office) to *c.* 968.

[44] As Stafford notes, 'Had Mercian separatism played the major role, it was folly to have chosen a West Saxon prince whose claims and desire to rule the entire kingdom remained strong …'. P. Stafford, *Unification and Conquest* (London, 1989), p. 49.

The Reign of Edgar

After this lengthy (but necessary) excursus, we can turn to what happened once the kingdom was unified after Eadwig's death. The post-reunification grants of 959–960 themselves do not fit into any specific pattern; the likelihood is that there are several that have been lost, without which we do not have the whole picture that might make clear just who profited most from Edgar's accession (and who did not). But what is certain that Eadwig's death on 1 October 959 and Edgar's subsequent accession in 959 saw a settling of scores. There are a few men who completely cease to attest charters from the precise moment of Edgar's accession. The ealdorman Ælfric, probably of Kent and Sussex, who was appointed by Eadwig only in 957, ceases to attest immediately and does not reappear.[45] Eadwig's highest-ranking ealdorman in 957–9 had been Eadmund (probably of the Western Shires). He continues to attest, in a much inferior position, until 963. Edgar appears to have been capable of more direct forms of action. In 960, he restored forfeited lands at Berkshire and Sussex to Wulfric *minister*, in return for 120 mancuses of gold.[46] This individual is to be identified with the Wulfric *Cufing* who appears in the will of Bishop Ælfsige as the recipient of land at Tichborne (Hants).[47] Going by his charter attestations, Wulfric was another of the top-ranking thegns under Eadwig, and a prominent landowner in the Berkshire region. The sum he paid to redeem his lands is extremely high, and makes it likely that it was Edgar himself who effected this dispossession, agreeing to restore the estates only at an exorbitant cost. Wulfric's attestations during the 960s are extremely sporadic and after a few years he fades away altogether.[48]

Others appear to have suffered a similar fate. The thegn Æthelgeard is a case in point. Æthelgeard first makes an appearance in Æthelstan's reign and was, going by his charter attestations, one of the most prominent thegns at court for a quarter of a century, receiving over a hundred hides of land from four different kings. He remained at Eadwig's court after the division in 957 and continued to witness until sometime in 958. He is one of the few members of the nobility who disappears at the precise moment of Edgar's accession, sug-

---

[45] Ælfric's all too brief career is conveniently tracked in Keynes, *Attestations*, tables L, LII.

[46] S 687.

[47] *Abing*, I.clxxiv–clxxxv; see S 1491 for the will of Bishop Ælfsige, and also Whitelock, *Wills*, no. 4.

[48] Wulfric owned several other estates which are *not* in the restitution charter S 687. One of them, Welford, was granted by Eadwig to Eadric in 956 (S 622). Kelly notes that the Welford estate is not in S 687 as it had already been alienated to another by Eadwig; this might seem to imply that it was Eadwig who deprived Wulfric of his estates, *Abing*, I.clxxxiii–clxxxiv). But Wulfric cannot have been deprived as early as 956, as he continued attesting in a high position until late in 958, as well as receiving estates.

gesting that his ties with Eadwig were very close indeed.[49] There is reason to believe that Æthelgeard's estates were up for grabs, so to speak, in the years immediately following his death. Three charters from the Winchester archive, which purport to be grants to Æthelgeard have been heavily modified (or forged outright) by the Winchester monks.[50] These are all controversial documents, but as Keynes notes, 'their existence suggests that there were complications surrounding the descent of some of Æthelgeard's estates which involved recourse to forgery, perhaps in the wake of the division and re-unification of the kingdom in 957–9'.[51] There is also interesting interplay between those who gained by the accession of Edgar and those who fell by the wayside. In 959, Edgar granted ten hides at Highclere in Hampshire to his thegn Ælfwine (S 680), who, as noted above, was the brother of Ælfhere of Mercia. In his will (to be dated 955 x 8) the unfortunate Bishop Ælfsige had bequeathed this estate to his kinsmen.[52] Ælfwine had, according to his attestations, been one of the most important of the *ministri* at Edgar's Mercian court from 957–9 and Edgar seems to have used the moment of his accession to the undivided kingship as an opportunity to reward such loyalty, through the gift of an estate which had been in the possession of one of Eadwig's chief confidants. Ælfwine was also to profit from Wulfric *Cufing*'s misfortunes. In 968 (S 761) Ælfwine received Boxford which had previously been in Wulfric's hands.[53] Ælfwine attests as one of the two or three highest-ranking thegns throughout the 960s, and attests S 768 from 968 as *discifer*.[54]

---

[49] Although his attestations had already become intermittent by 958 – it could be argued that he died or retired in this year.

[50] S 511, 517 and 536. S 511 – a charter of Edmund concerning land at Tisted, but dated '960'; S 517 – a charter of Eadred concerning land at Brightwell, Sotwell, Mackney and the 'castellum' at Wallingford in Berkshire, but dated '945', and S 536, a charter of Eadred (948) concerning land at Mackney, Sotwell and the 'castellum' at Wallingford. For discussion, see *The Liber Vitae of the New Minster and Hyde Abbey, Winchester*, ed. S. D. Keynes, EEMF 26 (Copenhagen, 1996), p. 87 for discussion. Æthelgeard's landed interests were mainly in the vicinity of Winchester, and it is there that his charters came to be kept. He was probably the Æthelgeard *preng* whose name appears as one of the benefactors of the New Minster. *Liber Vitae: Register and Martyrology of New Minster and Hyde Abbey, Winchester*, ed. W. D. G. Birch (Hampshire Record Society, 1892), p. 22.

[51] Keynes, *Liber Vitae*, p. 87.

[52] S 1491. Whitelock, *Wills*, no. 4 and p. 115. Another estate in Bishop Ælfsige's will, Ringwood, was bequeathed to the Old Minster. Edgar seems to have had no intention of respecting the terms of this will. Instead he granted the estate to Abingdon (S 690).

[53] S 761. See also S 577 for Eadwig's grant of Boxford to Wulfric.

[54] By the early 970s he seems to have retired to become at monk at Glastonbury. See Williams, 'Ælfhere', p. 154. The identification of the Glastonbury Ælfwine with Ælfhere's brother is confirmed by the charter S 802 (AD 975) where Edgar granted three *mansiunculae* at Aston, Shropshire, to Ealhhelm *minister*, at the request of the king's venerable kinsman, the monk Ælfwine. Ealhhelm (a name not unknown in Ælfwine's family) was probably Ælfwine's son. Ælfwine appears to have been the same man who had connections with another Wulfric, Dunstan's brother – he facilitated the bequests of the latter to Glastonbury Abbey. His connection with Wulfric *Cufing* complicates matters; the issue is discussed in *Abing*, I.clxxxiv–clxxxv.

Reconstructing the fortunes of Ælfhere's family at this time poses particular problems. Ælfhere prospered under Eadwig. He attests most of Edgar's charters as the leading ealdorman and one surmises that he must have used the period of the division of the kingdom to build ties with the young king. In addition, Ælfheah's appointment to an ealdormanry, one of Eadwig's last acts, was confirmed by Edgar.[55] But the generosity to members of Ælfhere's family was not unequivocal. Edgar's 'Orthodoxorum' charter to Abingdon in 959 restores numerous estates to Abingdon.[56] The Longworth estate mentioned in the charter had been granted to Eadric by Eadwig in 958.[57] It is interesting that the 'Orthodoxorum' charter refers to estates seized by the ungodly: Edgar also deplores the fact that new charters had been created to legitimize claims over lands taken from the abbey.[58] Eadric (who received well over 200 hides of land from previous kings, including Eadwig) attests charters during the 960s, and was the recipient of Edgar's largesse on one occasion, in 961, when he was granted three hides at *Hamstede*.[59] However, his attestations become infrequent after 961 and it cannot be certain that the thegn with this name who attests very infrequently later in the 960s and 970s is the same man. With Eadric one should bear in mind Eadwig's prior generosity to him. Among the many estates granted to Eadric by Eadwig was an estate at Meon, which seems to have infringed upon the boundaries of the land bequeathed by Eadred to Eadgifu in his will.[60] This might help to explain Edgar's treatment of him. Eadric's steady decline reflected in the witness lists during the 960s is in many ways similar to the fate that befell Wulfric *Cufing*.

Some light on Edgar's relations with leading families at court can be shed by an examination of the one family besides Ælfhere's which could claim an equal footing in terms of status – that of Æthelstan 'Half-King' who was ealdorman of East Anglia from 932 until 957. This family was by this time closely associated with Dunstan and Eadgifu.[61] In Eadwig's reign, Æthelstan retired to Glastonbury

---

[55] What of Ælfric *Cild*, who was Ælfhere's brother-in-law and future successor to the Mercian ealdordom? As noted above, Eadwig addresses him as *adoptivus parens* in S 597, the diploma which conveys to Ælfric the estate an Hanney. Edgar chose to nullify this grant and hand the estate over to Abingdon (S 759). There have been doubts raised over the authenticity of S 759, but the existence of the charter demonstrates that Abingdon did have a claim to the estate. The abbey held ten hides at Hanney in 1086, which corresponds to Edgar's grant of ten hides in 968. (But in the later manuscript of S 759 this has been altered to twenty hides, the purpose of which may have been to cover the whole estate granted to Ælfric in 956. See *Abing.* no. 112.)

[56] S 673. For discussion of the charter's date and authenticity, see *Abing*, no. 84.

[57] S 654.

[58] The title to these estates had probably been a contentious issue before this. In 955 (S 567) Eadred had also restored three of these estates (Ginge, Goosey and Longworth) to Abingdon.

[59] S 698.

[60] See Williams, 'Ælfhere', pp. 151 and 153.

[61] On the whole I am in agreement with Hart's reconstruction. See Hart, 'Half-King', pp. 127–8, 130–4. For the links with Dunstan and Eadgifu see Yorke, *Æthelwold*, at pp. 74–81.

to become a monk, at the precise point when the kingdom was divided in 957. His son Æthelwold succeeded to the ealdormanry of East Anglia. By 960 Æthelwold and his three brothers, Æthelwine, Æthelsige and Ælfwold were fixtures at court. One brother, Æthelwine was to succeed his brother Æthelwold to the ealdormanry of East Anglia in 962. The Half-King's links with the royal house were close – the charters make it clear that he was a royal kinsman, though like Ælfhere the exact nature of his links to the House of Wessex are unknown. Some attention needs to be paid here to the Half-King's wife, Ælfwynn. She seems to have been of royal blood – Byrhtferth of Ramsey specifically cites her royal lineage even before the 'Half-King' is mentioned.[62] The possibility needs to be seriously considered that she was the same woman who was the daughter of ealdorman Æthelred and Æthelflæd, Lady of the Mercians who, according to the *Mercian Register*, was carried off into Wessex by Edward the Elder in 919.[63] This would explain why she was considered suitable to be a foster-mother to the ætheling Edgar.[64] It may even explain why Edgar was considered in 957 suitable to rule Mercia. In any case, we would expect the sons of the 'Half-King' to have been particularly favoured by their foster-brother Edgar when he became king.[65]

The fact is, however, that even in Edgar's reign, the position of the Half-King's family was never as strong as it had been in the days of the 'Half-King' himself. Byrhtferth of Ramsey, Oswald's biographer, strongly hints that two of the brothers – Ælfwold and Æthelsige – were deserving of honours, or even ealdormanries, which eluded them.[66] This should be supplemented by a more concrete example of the shabby treatment of the Half-King's family. The incident in question is described by the *Libellus Æthelwoldi*, the portion of the *Liber*

---

[62] '... progenitus ex regali prosopia inclytem genealogiam habuit in parte matris quam laudans Dunstanus archepiscopus, benedictam esse dixit mulierem genusque ipsius', Raine, *York*, p. 428.

[63] *ASC* s.a. 919.

[64] *Chronicon Abbatiae Ramesiensis*, ed. W. D. Macray (London, 1886), pp. 11–12. It is not of great significance that Æthelwine's maternal uncle Æthelsige attests documents without any hint that he was of royal descent (*Chron. Rams.*, p. 75, and Robertson, *Charters*, p. xxxix). In all likelihood the less that was said of the Mercian royal house, the better. This may also account for Byrhtferth's ambiguity when dealing with Ælfwynn.

[65] Ælfwold and Æthelwine had been brought to court right at the end of Eadred's reign. They appear in the undated S 579, which has traditionally been placed right at the close of the reign in 955. The fact that the 'Half-King' managed to remain on reasonable terms with Eadwig at least initially can be seen from the fact that Æthelwold (the eldest), was to be appointed ealdorman in mid-956, where he may have understudied his father before finally taking over the East Anglian ealdordom when his father retired to Glastonbury. See Hart, 'Half-King', pp. 127–8.

[66] 'tantae potestatis auctoritate erat sublimatus ut dux fieri dedignaretur' (of Ælfwold), and 'ducis possideret auctoritatem et honorem haberet potestatis eximae cum ad regis praesentiam veniret' (of Æthelsige)', Raine, *York*, pp. 428–9. (See Banton, 'Ealdormen and Earls', p. 152.) The reference to Æthelsige in the royal presence is to my mind a reference to his position as *camerarius* (see S 713 for a diploma of Edgar in favour of Æthelsige his *camerarius*). Byrhtferth could on occasion be suprisingly accurate, in an indirect way, on the goings-on at court.

Eliensis that is based on vernacular documents dating from the time of Bishop Æthelwold:

> [Edgar] granted to God and St Æthelthryth, together with the charter, forty hides of land in that district known as Hatfield, which a certain powerful man (*vir potens*) called Ordmær and his wife Ealde bequeathed to him when they died … the brothers then held this land without challenge while the king lived. But when the king died, and the affairs of the kingdom thrown into disorder, and the peace of the land was violated, powerful men came forward, namely Æthelwine, styled ealdorman, by which is meant *princeps* or *comes*, and his brothers, and they laid claim to the land. They said that their father, Ealdorman Æthelstan, had acquired the land in exchange for his inheritance, which was in the region called Devon, but King Edgar had forcibly deprived him of both. …[67]

This is by no means a clear-cut case. Edgar could *not* have been the one who initially dispossessed the 'Half-King' of his patrimony as by the time he came to power the ealdorman was already a monk at Glastonbury. In my view, the one point in time that would fit the available evidence is in late 957, when the 'Half-King' retired and withdrew to Glastonbury, and Edgar was only king of the Mercians. The ealdorman's patrimony in Devon would certainly have been at risk at this point, as the area fell within Eadwig's kingdom. This could explain why he would have been willing to exchange this presumably large holding for forty hides at Hatfield in Hertfordshire. I think what almost certainly happened is that the Devon patrimony fell into Eadwig's hands and then perhaps to Ordmaer, and perhaps Edgar gave the ealdorman and his sons the estate at Hatfield as compensation. Later when Edgar became sole king in 959 it looks like he held on to the patrimony and took Hatfield away for some reason that remains unknown.[68] The Hatfield affair was an involved case but one thing stands out – Edgar's cavalier treatment of a family that had been part of the court elite since the time of King Æthelstan.[69]

---

[67] *Libellus*, ch. 5 (*LE*, pp. 79–80). My translation is taken from a typescript kindly lent to me by Professor Keynes. Aspects of the Hatfield episode are discussed in A. Wareham, 'The Aristocracy of East Anglia, c.970–c.1154' (unpubl. Ph.D. thesis, University of Birmingham, 1992) at pp. 11–14; see also A. Kennedy, 'Law and Litigation in the *Libellus Æthelwoldi episcopi*', *ASE* 26 (1995), pp. 131–83, at 135–6 (and nn. 21 and 22).

[68] For a different interpretation see Hart, 'Half-King', p. 130. The presence of Ælfhere of Mercia at the shire-court (in one of only two appearances in the *Libellus*) indicates the seriousness of the dispute brought on by Æthelwine's claim. The fact that the shire-court met at Slaughter in Gloucestershire, within Ælfhere's ealdordom, might perhaps be taken as an indication of some factional infighting at court after Edgar's death where Ælfhere outmanoeuvred his rival. It is difficult to see Æthelwine being amenable to the venue.

[69] It is true that Æthelwold continued to hold high office under Edgar, and after his death Æthelwine was raised to the East Anglian ealdormanry. This suggests that Edgar felt the continuing need to have a member from this family as the ealdorman of East Anglia (and as a high-ranking counsellor). But the power of Æthelwine never came close to equalling that of his father under Edmund and Eadred. During Edgar's reign he consistently witnesses diplomas below Ælfhere of Mercia, and in the early 960s Ælfhere, his brother Ælfheah as well as Æthelstan 'Rota' all exceed him in terms of status.

Matters may have turned over an incident which concerns one of Edgar's marriages. There is a tradition which implicates Edgar in the death of the ealdorman Æthelwold, the eldest son of the 'Half-King', and who ceases to attest royal charters in 962. Two years later Edgar married his widow, Ælfthryth.[70] The two main sources for this are the twelfth century historians William of Malmesbury and Gaimar. Both of these men appear to have had access to a common stock of legend and scurrilous ballads dealing with Edgar's private life. The gist of both stories is the same: Æthelwold was entrusted by Edgar with the task of ascertaining the truth of the widespread reports of the noblewoman Ælfthryth's beauty. Æthelwold duped the king and married her himself, but Edgar consumed with passion then killed Æthelwold or had him killed. Dunstan then forced Edgar to undertake a penance of seven years.[71]

One aspect of the Edgar–Ælfthryth legend is the parallel to the biblical David–Uriah–Bathsheba triangle. But is all this purely legendary? To me, what appears to clinch the whole matter is Ælfric's homily *De Oratione Moysi* (*c.* 995). In it there is a cryptic reference to the 'sin of David' – David's people having been almost destroyed as a result of the king's sin.

> ... Again, David the king, though he were pleasing to God
> sinned very greviously, and then God sent to him
> the prophet Gad, saying these words to him,
> 'Choose thee now a punishment, since thou are deserving
> either a three years' famine, or three months' war ...'
>
> God would not slay the guilty David
> Though he had sinned, because very often he had done,
> Both before and afterward, very excellent things
> to the satisfaction of God ...[72]

Modern scholars have usually linked this in some way to a general criticism of Æthelred's policies.[73] But Ælfric's work was usually apolitical. It is possible that he was making coded reference to the Edgar–Ælfthryth affair.[74] The homily

[70] Ælfthryth has received a great deal of attention in modern times. See Stafford, 'The King's Wife', in her *Queen Emma and Queen Edith* (Oxford, 1997), pp. 23–4, and also her 'Queens, Nunneries and Reforming Churchmen', *Past and Present* 163 (1999), 1–35, at 24–32.

[71] WM, *Gesta Regum*, i.257–9; Gaimar, *L'Estoire Des Engleis*, ed. A. Bell (Oxford, 1960), lines 3587–9. For examinations of the legend, see Freeman, 'The Mythical and Romantic Elements', *Historical Essays*, 1st ser. (London, 1896), pp. 16–24; C. E. Wright, *The Cultivation of Saga in Anglo-Saxon England* (Edinburgh 1939), pp. 147–58; and A. Bell, 'Gaimar and the Edgar–Ælfthryth Story', *Modern Language Review*, 21 (1926), 278–87.

[72] *LS*, I.301–3.

[73] For the standard treatment of *De Oratione*, see M. Godden, 'Apocalypse and Invasion in Late Anglo-Saxon England', *From Anglo-Saxon to Middle English. Studies presented to E. G. Stanley*, ed. M.Godden *et al.* (Oxford, 1994), pp. 130–62, at 136.

[74] Certainly this homily was not the only instance where Edgar would have been likened to David in a similar sense: in describing Edgar's lustful pursuit of the nun Wulfhild, Goscelin says that Edgar eventually becomes aware he is attempting to injure a spouse holier than Uriah – a nun already betrothed to the lord, *La Vie De Sainte Vulfhilde par*

might thus show that those who came soon after Edgar (and perhaps some of his contemporaries) were convinced of his guilt. (Like another famous royal murder, that of Edgar's son Edward, the point is not so much ascertaining guilt – which is patently unrecoverable – but to get an insight into the mindsets and suspicions of those people on the ground close to the event itself.) Perhaps Æthelwold did indeed die violently, and this was one reason why accusations implicating Edgar/Ælfthryth would eventually attach to the incident. And if contemporary opinion in the 960s placed much of the blame on Ælfthryth, she could all the more easily by implicated in the death of her stepson a decade later.

In my view it is likely that the murky circumstances surrounding Æthelwold's death and Edgar's marriage to his widow (or even a perceived complicity of Edgar/Ælfthryth in the death of the ealdorman) was a key issue at court during the later 960s, on which political allegiances turned. It is this that is the most likely reason for the ealdorman Æthelwine's enmity to Ælfthryth, the new queen (we should note here that as brother to the deceased ealdorman Æthelwold, Æthelwine would have been Ælfthryth's former brother-in-law). And, as Barbara Yorke has shown, factions at court coalesced around the issue of the succession to Edgar: Æthelwine supported Edward, who was the son of Edgar by an earlier union with a noblewoman called Æthelflæd 'The White', whom we know almost nothing about.[75] Æthelwine's decision to back Edward in 975 put him in opposition to Ælfthryth.[76] Others such as Bishop Æthelwold and Ælfhere probably supported Ælfthryth and the claims of her son Æthelred.[77] It is apparent that accusations and smear campaigns must have been going on even at this time, an example being the conflicting sets of stories touching on Edgar's wives and the throneworthiness of Edgar's children. The catalyst for this type of gossip was court propaganda.[78] These stories were repeated by later writers such as William of Malmesbury, just as they were for another serial monogamist, Edward the Elder: at Edward's court, there were similar issues at stake – the throneworthiness of the æthelings and the legitimacy of the royal wives.[79]

Goscelin de Cantorbery, ed. M. Esposito, *Analecta Bollandiana* 32 (1913), 10–26, at 16.

[75] Yorke, *Æthelwold*, pp. 81–5.

[76] One suspects that there may have been more than meets the eye to Æthelwine's support for Æthelflæd 'the White' – certainly a kinship connection should not be ruled out between the family of the 'Half-King' and that of Ordmær, father of Æthelflæd. It is also entirely possible that the Ordmær mentioned in the Hatfield episode is the same individual (i.e. Æthelflæd's father). See Hart, 'Half-King', pp. 129–30.

[77] Detailed by Yorke, *Æthelwold*, pp. 81–2.

[78] See also the Prior Nicholas–Eadmer exchange: Stubbs, *Dunstan*, pp. 422–4. Prior Nicholas reports that Æthelflæd was never crowned as queen, while Ælfthryth was. Nicholas was probably reciting objections advanced against Edward by Æthelred's supporters in 975.

[79] Æthelstan's mother seems to have been a victim of a smear campaign which made her out to be inferior in status to Ælfflæd. William of Malmesbury called Ecgwynn the daughter of a shepherd, although he then described her as an 'illustrious woman'. Hamilton, *Gesta*, I.199 and 225–6. Hrosvitha of Gandersheim contrasted Edward the Elder's union with Ecgwynn unfavourably with the Ælfflæd match. Hrosvitha, *Gesta Ottonis* II, verses 66–124, in *Hrosvithae Opera*, ed. P. Winterfield, *MGH Scriptores Rerum Germanicarum*

A point to note is that the two most important ealdormen by 962–3 (going by their charter attestations) were the royal kinsmen Ælfhere and Ælfheah. The allegiances of some ealdormen in the early 960s (Æthelmund, Æthelstan 'Rota' and Edmund) are not known, but at court Æthelwine must have had few close supporters after the death of his brother. Byrhtnoth, who according to the *Vita Oswaldi* opposed Ælfhere in the 'anti-Monastic reaction' that followed Edgar's death, appears by his attesting position to have been the most junior ealdorman and was frequently absent from court. In all likelihood, Ælfhere's kin-group had the king's ear; leaving aside the ealdorman Æthelwold story one might speculate that the Ælfhere kin-group may even have canvassed the Ælfthryth match. Relations between Ælfthryth and this kin-group were good; Ælfheah was to refer in his will to Ælfthryth as his *gefæðeran* – indicating possibly that Ælfthryth was godparent to one of Ælfheah's children.[80]

But what of Edgar? The evidence suggests that he trusted neither of the key families at court. The key development in the structure of court in his reign (and, arguably, in the administration of the kingdom) is that some ealdormen do not seem to have been replaced after they finally ceased to attest. Going by tenth-century standards, by 970 the situation with regard to numbers of ealdormen is quite unusual. By 970 there are only four ealdormen, and their attesting order, usually a sign of prominence or influence, is Ælfhere, followed by Oslac or Æthelwine, and then Byrhtnoth. On the face of it, this might seem to have strengthened the hand of someone like Ælfhere, who now appears to have governed all of Mercia. But Ælfhere's younger brother Eadric had suffered a severe setback, and his brother Ælfheah's ealdormanry in Wessex appears to have been allowed to lapse. Edgar does not seem to have wanted any more ealdormen, with those who remained being kept on a tight leash.

If Edgar did not trust any of the key noble kin-groups, he may have attempted to bring in others. One of them is of course the west-country thegn Ordgar, who becomes ealdorman of the south-west at the exact point of the marriage of his daughter Ælfthryth to Edgar in 964.[81] Edgar showed especial favour to the nobility of this region. The number of men with west-country connections at court in Edgar's final years tells us something about the politics going on in Edgar's reign and after his death. Is it possible that Edgar was attempting to mitigate the power of over-mighty families by bringing in or favouring his own men, men who had no significant ties to the key ealdormen established at court?[82]

(Berlin, 1902), pp. 206–8. For a modern discussion, see K. Leyser, 'The Ottonians and Wessex', *Communications and Power in Medieval Europe*, ed. T. Reuter, 2 vols. (London, 1994), I.76–7.

80 Yorke, *Æthelwold*, p. 84.

81 Ordgar's final attestation as a *minister* occurs in S 725, the diploma of 964 where Ælfthryth first appears as Edgar's consort (*lateranea*). In S 724, another diploma of 964 (presumably later that year) he attests for the first time as *dux*.

82 The brothers Byrhtferth and Ælfgar, for example, are amongst the highest-ranking thegns at court in Edgar's reign. Ælfgar clearly becomes more important in Eadred's reign, while Byrhtferth's attestations only become consistent in Eadwig's reign. The relationship between the brothers Byrhtferth and Ælfgar is made

One of these men should be considered here. When the ealdorman Ordgar died *c.* 970, the ealdordom of the Western Shires appears to have lapsed. The decision not to fill the ealdordom immediately leaves one again with the impression that Edgar may have been trying to balance the claims of noble families. Eventually, Æthelweard ('The Chronicler') was appointed to the ealdordom but only in the reign of Edward the Martyr. Æthelweard first appears in the early stages of Eadwig's reign and his rise was in all likelihood a result of royal favour, given the likelihood that his sister married Eadwig. Still, some sort of settlement with Edgar must have been possible. Æthelweard only becomes genuinely important (going by his charter attestations) in 963–4. Æthelweard and his brother Ælfweard become more prominent as thegns in Edgar's reign until they are among the highest-ranking *ministri*, going by their charter attestations.[83] One receives the impression that Æthelweard played his cards right in Edgar's reign, perhaps by treading warily and using the same maddening discretion that one finds in his *Chronicon*. Æthelweard can be shown to have had a version of the *Anglo-Saxon Chronicle* which for the last years of Alfred's reign (as well as for some of Edward the Elder's campaigns) was more accurate than any rescension which has come down to us.[84] What he does *not* do is mention Æthelwold, although he describes the battle of Holme as a fight against the 'eastern enemy'. But the point is that Æthelweard could hardly have been unaware of the battle of Holme and its significance. The likelihood is that he deliberately chose to omit any mention of Æthelwold, who would certainly have been seen by other members of the House of Wessex as a black sheep in the royal family. Indeed Æthelweard's *Chronicon* is, unfortunately for us, a model of discretion – he omits almost all mention of dynastic disputes or court politics.[85] It is unlikely however that Æthelweard was above the fray altogether. One can imagine that

clear in a charter of Eadwig, S 651 (from 958). Ælfgar also attests that charter as *regis propinquus*, which makes it likely that he was the 'king's kinsman in Devon' who according to the *Chronicle* died in 962 and was buried at Wilton, *ASC* A, s.a. 962. Ælfgar was clearly someone important. Highly unusually, the two brothers are singled out in S 692 from 961 (a west-country charter from the Bath archive) as 'consul', sandwiched between the *duces* and the *ministri*.

[83] In my view Æthelweard was probably a west-country man, although this cannot be proved beyond doubt. A clue may lie in the fact that the prominent thegn Ælfsige usually attests next to Æthelweard or his brother Ælfweard in Edgar's reign (S 715, S 714, S 725, S 732, S 733, S 734, S 737, S 738, S 767, S 757, S 758, S 759, S 769, S 769, S 716, S 778, S 789, S 786, S 805, S 794, S 799, S 800, S 801, S 804). He is the beneficiary of S 711 from 963, where he is granted an estate at Stanton Prior in Somerset – he is also called 'decurio' in the text. He is also the recipient of two other estates: Orchard in Dorset in the same year (S 710), and another at *Eastune* (unidentified, S 748) in 967. Ælfsige also witnesses S 782 from 971 as 'discipulus', as do Æthelweard and Ælfweard. Ælfsige was probably a west-country thegn and possibly one of Edgar's retainers. In all probability he was also related to Æthelweard, the future ealdorman. He does not show up in Ælfgifu's will, which makes it likely that he was not Æthelweard's brother but a more distant relative – perhaps a cousin.

[84] See F. M. Stenton, 'Æthelweard's Account of the Last Years of King Alfred's Reign', *Preparatory to Anglo-Saxon England*, ed. D. M. Stenton (Oxford, 1970), pp. 8–13.

[85] In his one other allusion to the history of his own family connections, Æthelweard does

two men left competing for the ealdormanry of the Western Shires on Ordgar's death would have been Ordgar's son, whose name was Ordulf, and Æthelweard himself.[86] Given that one of Edward's first acts on his accession was to fill the vacant ealdormanry with Æthelweard, it seems that Æthelweard almost certainly supported Edward in the succession issue. Æthelweard may have been busy cultivating the young ætheling Edward in the early 970s, even as he had ingratiated himself with Edgar.[87]

Conclusions

The period immediately following the accession of a new king could be a tricky affair. Men rushed to secure their own estates, or to claim what they coveted. Others sought justice for long-held grievances. The backlash which followed Eadwig's death could perhaps be seen in this light. But the main reason for Edgar's actions was political and punitive. Too many of the victims can be shown to have been Eadwig's favourites for it to have been otherwise. It is clear that some of these men (Eadric, the deceased Bishop Ælfsige, Wulfric *Cufing*) had to a degree at least thrown in their lot with Eadwig, and paid the price for it. It should be stressed however that individual thegns and ealdormen probably made what terms they could with the king in 959 on the basis of details which have been lost to us. This is why some of Eadwig's men, like Ælfhere and Byrhtnoth, did extremely well for themselves in the 960s when others did not find the king's favour. Despite the lack – or loss – of evidence, it is reasonably clear that those of Eadwig's favourites who did prosper, or survive temporarily, under Edgar usually had that something extra which weighed in their favour – like kinship to the king. Royal kinship was undoubtedly what saved the one ecclesiastical appointee of Eadwig known to have found favour under Edgar. Byrhthelm of Winchester attests until 963, and received lands from the king on two occasions. In both charters he is named as the king's kinsman.[88] However, he was replaced by Æthelwold in 963 and there is some evidence that the episcopal lists attempted to suppress the record of his incumbency. Only one text records Byrhthelm's tenure there.[89]

One other reason for the survivals of Eadwig's men into Edgar's time (and

---

also venture the statement that Alfred only received the kingdom after all his brothers had died (p. 39).

[86] For Ordgar's family see H. P. R. Finberg, 'The House of Ordgar and the Foundation of Tavistock Abbey', *EHR* 58 (1943), 190–201.

[87] S 832, a diploma from 976, sees Edward the Martyr granting estates in Cornwall to the ealdorman Æthelweard – reinforcing the impression that there were ties between the two.

[88] S 683 (from 960) – grant to Byrhthelm, the king's venerable kinsman, of land at Bishopstoke, Southampton; S 695 (961) – grant to Byrhthelm (*presuli michi carnalis prosapiae nexu copulato*) of land at Easton in Southampton.

[89] Corpus Christi College, Cambridge 140. See R. I. Page, 'Anglo-Saxon Episcopal Lists', *Nottingham Medieval Studies* 9 (1965), 71–95, at 77–9.

beyond) is the likelihood that some men were simply too powerful to remove. There are hints that Edgar may have had to tolerate the presence of Ælfhere's kin-group during the 960s and early 970s, when there are indications that his choice of personal favourites lay elsewhere. Others may have been too *useful* to remove. Æthelwold may have survived through his personal links with his former student Edgar, or he may simply have been too versatile to be got rid of in the 960s.[90] His role in overseeing the production of royal diplomas during this time is a case in point.[91] Æthelwold was of course adept at *realpolitik*. Although he sided with Eadwig on many key issues in the late 950s, he is later to be found besmirching the dead king's name in the *Preface* to the Benedictine Rule. In contrast, Bishop Ælfsige of Winchester, raised to Canterbury by Eadwig himself, never got a chance to protest his loyalty to the post-959 regime – or to prove it.

This brings us to the question of what light these fragments can shed on the issue of 'faction' in late Anglo-Saxon England. What fuelled the various disputes were the allegiances of various kin-groups. Very little is known of the structure of these groups.[92] Politically these close kinsmen bore similar loyalties. Ælfhere's kin-group supported Eadwig–Ælfgifu, as they did Ælfthryth and her issue. Æthelwine's kin-group on the other hand did not. However, it would be a mistake to assume that the *extended* kin acted as a political unit in its own right. In this context it is important to bear in mind that most, if not all, of the major kin-groups may have been ultimately inter-bound by ties of kinship, if distant. For example, in the *Maldon* poem, an Ælfwine claims Ealhhelm (Ælfhere's father) as his grandfather, while at the same time naming Byrhtnoth as his *mæg*.[93] However, if Byrhtferth of Ramsey is to be believed, Byrhtnoth and Ælfhere were at odds in the aftermath of Edgar's death. What can be taken away from the fragmentary evidence is this: core kin-groups did exercise considerable influence on the make-up of individual loyalties, but faction was not a monolithic concept and still less a static one. While there may have been reasons to associate Ælfgifu with the Ælfhere kin-group in Eadwig's reign, her brother Æthelweard ('the Chronicler') was probably a key supporter of Edward in 975, whereas Ælfhere was not.

Those who fell by the wayside because they incurred the very personal enmity of the king, or of those closely connected with them, had little chance in the long run of keeping their reputations. For memory could itself be used as a weapon. While Edgar 'dispossessed' some of the men prominent under his brother, others such as Eadwig and Ælfgifu, and Bishop Ælfsige could be

---

[90] For Æthelwold's tutelage of Edgar, See Symons, *RC*, p. 1.

[91] See *Abing*, I.cxv–cxxxi for a persuasive argument.

[92] See H. R. Loyn, 'The King and the Structure of Society in Late Anglo-Saxon England', *History* 42 (1957), 87–100; *idem*, 'Kinship in Anglo-Saxon England', *ASE* 3 (1974), 197–209; T. Charles-Edwards, 'Anglo-Saxon Kinship Revisited', *The Anglo-Saxons from the Migration Period to the Eighth Century: An Ethnographic Perspective*, ed. J. Hines (Woodbridge, 1997), pp. 171–204.

[93] *The Battle of Maldon*, ed. D. G. Scragg (Manchester, 1981), lines 218 and 224.

reached through the *damnatio memoriae* visited upon them.[94] Ælfgifu appears to have made some sort of peace with Edgar.[95] But after her death, monastic tradition actively began the process of blackening her name, as well as that of her mother, in earnest.[96] The vitriol and scurrilous gossip poured on Eadwig, Ælfgifu and Bishop Ælfsige should be placed at the door of their enemies (such as Dunstan) and their propaganda machines in the form of traditions of houses that these ecclesiastics were associated with.[97] They could just as easily be turned on other individuals such as Ælfthryth when political circumstances shifted, when for example various parties sought to influence the succession to Edgar.

The sense one gets is that Edgar was capable of ruling by personal diktat if he had to. Edgar could intervene in the affairs of his subjects with more ferocity than one might otherwise glean from a reading of the extant law-codes, which

---

[94] The fact that Eadwig did not receive a bad press at the New Minster must be connected in some way with his links to Bishop Ælfsige. The *Liber Vitae* of Hyde Abbey says of Eadwig 'flebilis occidit multis suorum lacrimis'. See *Liber Vitae* (ed. Birch), pp. 7 and 57, for Eadwig and Ælfgifu. The highly laudatory notice of Eadwig in Henry of Huntingdon's work may derive from a similar tradition which escaped the *damnatio memoriae* later applied to Eadwig's reign, Henry of Huntingdon, *Historia Anglorum*, ed. and trans. D. Greenway (Oxford, 1996), p. 319. See also Yorke, *Æthelwold*, p. 87 for the counter-establishment view of Ælfgifu at the New Minster, and in general on Winchester's involvement in tenth-century politics.

[95] She was granted by him in the 960s: S 737, an estate at Linslade (Bucks.); S 738, an estate at Newnham Murren (Oxon.). Both grants date from 966 and are made by Edgar to his 'devoted kinswoman'. Ælfgifu addresses Edgar in obsequious terms in her will, and these two estates are bequeathed to the royal family (Whitelock, *Wills*, no. 8).

[96] The kernel is in the earliest *Vita Dunstani* (Eadwig's absence from his feast that followed his anointing in order to enjoy the caresses of Æthelgifu and her daughter; Stubbs, *Dunstan*, pp. 32–4). But later elaborations show that the tale took on a life of its own. Osbern's *Vita Dunstani* has a fantastic episode relating how Æthelgifu was captured and killed near Gloucester, after the northerners had revolted. Stubbs, *Dunstan*, p. 102. In his *Vita Odonis*, Eadmer takes up Osbern's story and relates how Oda had one of the two women branded and exiled to Ireland; when she dared to return she was put to death at Gloucester. *Anglia Sacra*, ed. H. Wharton (London, 1691), p. 84. Similar elaborations occur in Eadmer's *Vita Dunstani* and his *Vita Oswaldi* (Stubbs, *Dunstan*, pp. 192–3; Raine, *York*, II.4). Despite the legendary accretions in all these accounts, the 'Canterbury tradition' still shows that there was a long memory concerning such matters: the record of Eadwig's accession in *ASC* A for 955 was interpolated some time in the eleventh century by a Canterbury scribe who added 'and exiled St. Dunstan from the land'.

[97] Bishop Ælfsige in his will refers to his 'young kinsman', presumably an illegitimate son by his 'kinswoman' This was probably the Godwine of Worthy, described as the son of Bishop Ælfsige, killed in battle against the Danes in 1001. See *ASC* A, s.a. 1001. As Whitelock, *Wills*, no. 4, and pp. 114–15, notes, 'It is conceivable that the Bishop would shrink from directly mentioning a son [in his will].' It was all the more easy for later reformers to create the image of Eadwig not being a friend to monasticism, given his associations with churchmen who committed such indiscretions and who were not monks. Another example is Bishop Osulf of Ramsbury, who appears with Eadwig, Eadwig's wife Ælfgifu and Ælfgifu's mother, Æthelgifu, as well as Bishop Ælfsige, in S 1292. He was later accused by the *Evesham Chronicle* of despoiling the church there of its lands, when it is unlikely he did anything of the sort, Williams, 'Ælfhere', p. 146.

tell only part of the story.[98] This helps to put into context Stenton's oft-cited comment that Edgar's competence meant that his reign was 'singularly devoid of recorded incident'. The comment is fascinatingly similar in tone to the verdict pronounced on Henry I by Southern: 'Nothing happened of sufficient size to concentrate the attention of historians and to draw together the scattered impressions left by a multitude of unimportant details.'[99] One receives the distinct impression that these two quite separate periods where 'nothing happened' encompass similar strands – most importantly, a type of rulership that might be called vindictive or even (occasionally) despotic. It would not be stretching the comparison to note that Henry I, like Edgar, employed mutilation as a punishment for those who crossed him. This helps to put into perspective the so-called anti-Monastic reaction which followed Edgar's death. The tremendous release of pressure which followed his death should be seen as a pivotal factor in the lawlessness that ensued. Similar disintegrations can be glimpsed at other critical junctures in English history (the death of Henry I for example). The relaxation of strong rulership was enough for the populace to give vent to the seething frustrations that had lain dormant for the best part of the reign. Edgar 'the Peaceable' was a king who was not averse to violence or punitive dispossessions as a tool to punish his enemies. Such methods were sufficient to keep opposition and resentments in check – but only for as long as he lived.[100]

---

[98] Cf. the ravaging of Thanet on Edgar's orders, *ASC* D, s.a. 969.

[99] Stenton, *ASE*, p. 368; W. Southern, 'The Place of Henry I in English History', *Proceedings of the British Academy* 48 (1962), 127–56, at 128 and 156.

[100] This paper has profited immensely from discussions with participants at the Manchester conference on King Edgar. My thanks to Don Scragg for tracking me down, inviting me to give a paper, and for accepting the paper for publication late when most would have given me up. I also thank the British Academy for a generous subsidy to attend the conference. This paper is written in memory of my supervisor Patrick Wormald, who inspired my research on Edgar and who indeed made me feel that it was the only thing worth doing. I miss him often.

4

Edgar, Chester, and the Kingdom of the Mercians, 957–9

C. P. LEWIS

EDGAR's diploma of 958 for the minster church of St Werburgh in Chester is one of few charters of the mid-tenth century for an unreformed house of secular clerks. It opens a small window on the obscure affairs of Mercia during the period 957–9 when the English kingdom was divided, Edgar ruling north of the Thames and his brother Eadwig in Wessex. More obviously it provides evidence for the early history of the community at Chester.

Yet the charter has been relatively little studied, despite the existence of a good edition by Tait and consensus on its authenticity.[1] And although the division of the kingdom in 957 has been a recurrent focus of interest, far less has been written on Edgar's government of Mercia or on how this period fits within the longer history of the reign. The latter is a notable gap, because the Chester charter shows Edgar, the proponent of Benedictine Reform and supporter of monks, making a major gift to a minster staffed by canons. Moreover his involvement with Chester in 958 foreshadows his later and more celebrated interaction with the city, the supposed outing on the Dee in 973.

Edgar

Edgar's position in 958 goes a long way towards explaining the particularities of the charter. What follows takes current thinking about the events of the 950s and pushes the implications for the government of Mercia as far as seems reasonable.[2] The evidence, thin anyway, is made more difficult by the need to set aside

---

1 *The Chartulary or Register of the Abbey of St. Werburgh, Chester*, ed. James Tait, 2 vols., Chetham Society ns 79, 82 (1920, 1923), I, no. 1; S 667. Charter research for this paper was made possible by the 'Electronic Sawyer' (see above, p. 60, n.2), and Sean Miller, *The New Regesta Regum Anglorum: A Searchable Edition of the Corpus of Anglo-Saxon Royal Diplomas, 670–1066* (2001) <http://www.trin.cam.ac.uk/chartwww.NewRegReg.html>.
2 I have used esp. Stenton, *ASE*, pp. 364–72; Cyril Hart, 'Athelstan "Half-King" and his Family', *ASE* 2 (1973), 115–44, as reprinted with many changes in his *The Danelaw* (London, 1992), pp. 569–604; Pauline Stafford, *Unification and Conquest: A Political and Social History of England in the Tenth and Eleventh Centuries* (London, 1989),

the picture of the 950s drawn two decades later in the years of Edgar's maturity and after his death in 975. By the 970s the Benedictine Reform programme had struck deep roots at court and among many bishops and ealdormen, and its protagonists did not resist the temptation to rewrite the 950s in the light of later developments and current concerns. In particular they presented Edgar's accession as a triumph for the morality of the Benedictine party against the unfit rule of his brother. The St Werburgh's charter, by contrast, seems to show how unimportant Reform was as an issue for Edgar and his Mercian advisers in 958.

Edgar's early life was shaped by family complications of which he can hardly have been unaware as he grew up, his expectations in boyhood and youth changing almost by the year.[3] He was born in 943, very probably in the summer or later since he is likely not to have reached his thirtieth birthday when he was crowned at Bath on 11 May 973 (the point of delaying coronation so long being to imitate the age at which Christ began his ministry).[4] Edgar was the second son of a young king, Edmund, preoccupied with incessant military campaigns to recover control of the Southern Danelaw and Northumbria. His brother, Eadwig, cannot have been much older. Of his many paternal uncles (one had been the illustrious King Æthelstan), only Eadred was still living. Those of his aunts who were alive were either nuns in English monasteries or had been sent overseas into dynastic marriage alliances. Edgar's grandfather had been Edward (899–924), conqueror of the Danelaw; his great-grandfather Alfred, saviour of the English and first creator of a kingdom which united the West Saxons and the Mercians.

Both boys had much family history to live up to, and few family members to guide them. Their mother died when they were infants; their father remarried but had no more children before he was murdered in 946, when Edgar was three. The only adult male in the family, the boys' uncle Eadred, was crowned. He was perhaps sickly (though not incapacitated from leading the army), since he never took a wife and had no children. Edgar would have known from almost his earliest memories that the future of Alfred's dynasty and the kingdom lay with him and his brother. Their stepmother remarried but played no part in their upbringing; presumably the marriage deliberately shuffled her out of court circles. Edgar was instead removed from his uncle's court and fostered with the family of the most powerful ealdorman, Æthelstan Half-King of East Anglia.

---

pp. 45–56; Eric John, *Reassessing Anglo-Saxon England* (Manchester, 1996), pp. 99–123; Simon Keynes, 'Kingdom of the Anglo-Saxons', *Blackwell Encycl.*, pp. 37–8; Simon Keynes, 'England, 900–1016', *The New Cambridge Medieval History, III: c. 900–1024*, ed. Timothy Reuter (Cambridge, 1999), pp. 456–84, at 473–81; Shashi Jayakumar, 'The Politics of the English Kingdom, *c.* 955–*c.* 978, unpubl. Oxford Univ. D.Phil. thesis, 2001, pp. 14–79. I am greatly indebted to Dr Jayakumar for sending me a copy of his thesis.

[3] Basic data about family relationships and dates from *Handbook of British Chronology*, ed. E. B. Fryde, D. E. Greenway, S. Porter, and I. Roy, 3rd ed. (London, 1986), pp. 26–7; Ann Williams, 'Edmund I', 'Eadred', 'Edgar', *ODNB*; Simon Keynes, 'Eadwig', *ODNB*; Cyril Hart, 'Æthelstan [Half-King]', *ODNB*; Pauline Stafford, 'Eadgifu', *ODNB*.

[4] John, *Reassessing Anglo-Saxon England*, p. 135 (but unconvincingly sceptical about Edgar's real age in 973).

His grandmother, King Edward's widow Eadgifu, also had a role, sending him to be educated by the renowned scholar Æthelwold, at Glastonbury under Abbot Dunstan. Dunstan was important to Edgar throughout his life.[5]

When Edgar was twelve his uncle died, and the court tore into factions given shape by the fact that the only king-worthy members of the family were the two young brothers. The older, Eadwig, was crowned and married, raising the possibility that Edgar would be cut out of the succession altogether, an alarming prospect for the circle forming round him. Eadwig's first full year as king, 956, was marked by an unparalleled number of royal charters, a splurge of royal munificence which looks driven by an urgent wish to buy friends.[6] To many at court, even the beneficiaries, it may have seemed ill-conceived and reckless. There are other signs that affairs were falling badly apart. The king's grandmother, Eadgifu, lost all her lands. Old and long-serving ealdormen retired, notably Æthelstan Half-King, and new ones were promoted. Abbot Dunstan and his kinsman Bishop Cynesige of Lichfield were exiled. If we peer through the drifting smoke of later moralizing about Eadwig's unfitness to rule, we can surely make out a dangerously unstable government and a court in deep crisis, and we may well suspect that many important men were frightened by how quickly things were slipping beyond their ability to control them.[7]

The senior members of the court proved capable of conjuring up a surprisingly workable solution, though it was drastic in its potential implications for the kingdom fashioned by Alfred and his descendants. In 957, when Edgar turned fourteen, there was an agreed division – no doubt brokered by the ealdormen and bishops – in which Eadwig retained the style of king of the English (and a monopoly over keeping his name on the coinage) but ruled only the shires south of the Thames. Edgar was allowed to call himself king, and ruled over the Mercians and Northumbrians. Charter attestations also bifurcated, the Mercian and Northumbrian bishops and ealdormen named only on Edgar's diplomas, those in the south only on Eadwig's. Either the northerners had actually left Eadwig's court or it was thought necessary to create the fiction of separate political communities either side of the Thames. They amount to much the same thing in terms of how dual rule by two kings was supposed to be perceived. Further, the arrangements seem intended (if not from the first then very soon) to lead eventually to Edgar's rule over all the English, since in 958 Eadwig was separated from his wife, childless, at the insistence of the archbishop of Canterbury, and was not allowed to remarry, or at any rate did not do so. In the event Edgar had to wait only until the autumn of 959 for his brother to die. He was still only sixteen.

In 957 Edgar at fourteen had thus become king of the Mercians and Northumbrians, with a separate sphere of power and seemingly regarded as heir to the

---

5   Nicholas Brooks, 'The Career of St Dunstan', *St Dunstan: His Life, Times and Cult*, ed. Nigel Ramsay, Margaret Sparks, and Tim Tatton-Brown (Woodbridge, 1992), pp. 1–23.
6   Keynes, *Diplomas*, pp. 46–69.
7   This interpretation reverses that of Stafford, *Unification and Conquest*, pp. 47–8, which places the crisis in 957.

whole kingdom. An adolescent king needed the steady hand of advisers, but the willingness of the ealdormen and bishops to contemplate so drastic a step as the one they had taken suggests they had confidence in Edgar's upbringing, character, and prospective abilities, especially since Edgar's was the harder share of the kingdom to govern. His, not Eadwig's, was the task of retaining the loyalty of the Scandinavian earls and thegns of the Danelaw and Northumbria; he, not Eadwig, guarded the borders between the English and their neighbours in Scotland, Cumbria, and Wales.

Edgar had grown up under the tutelage of a circle of aristocratic monastic reformers led by Æthelwold and Dunstan, but in 957 neither was yet a bishop, and although the Benedictine project was far enough advanced for the Rule (probably) already to have been translated into English,[8] the only houses for men yet placed under it were Glastonbury and Abingdon, both of which lay in Eadwig's share of the kingdom. It is difficult to say what personal input the youthful Edgar might have had into the affairs of his short-lived Mercian and Northumbrian kingdom over barely thirty months between summer 957 and October 959. Probably we should reckon that government was directed by a conclave of older men, gradually drawing Edgar into real leadership. Although the ealdormen surely had their own regional concerns, they also had much to gain from the orderly management of the dual kingdom and (eventually) an orderly transition back to a united England. That was even more true of the Mercian bishops, whose archbishop was based in Eadwig's half.

The key figures in Mercia can be seen heading the subscriptions of laymen and clergy to the small number of royal diplomas which survive from the period.[9] The longest serving ealdorman in Edgar's kingdom was Æthelmund, who had been appointed to north-west Mercia in 940,[10] and was thus responsible for Chester, but he had never been prominent at court and was outranked in the subscription lists by Ælfhere of Mercia, one of three new appointments under Eadwig who rematerialized at Edgar's court. On the clerical side the senior figures were Archbishop Oscytel of York, Bishop Cynesige of Lichfield (the diocesan for Chester), and Dunstan, brought back from exile in Ghent. Dunstan can hardly have returned against the ealdormen's wishes, and very likely they were mindful of his influence over Edgar. Dunstan's standing is evident from his immediate appointment to the bishopric of Worcester and rapid translation to London, arguably the most important Mercian see, and even more from his subsequent promotion to the archbishopric of Canterbury as soon as Edgar succeeded his brother in 959, not least because Dunstan's elevation required the delicate manoeuvre of deposing Archbishop Byrhthelm and sending him back to Wells, whence he had arrived in the metropolitan cathedral only a few months earlier. No sources reveal exactly when Dunstan returned to England, but there

8 Mechthild Gretsch, 'Benedictine Rule, OE', *Blackwell Encycl.*, pp. 60–1, and bibliography listed there.
9 S 674–679, S 676a, S 681.
10 A. T. Thacker, 'Early Medieval Chester, 400–1230', *VCH Cheshire* V (1) (2003), 16–33, at 22; Keynes, *Attestations*, tables XLII, XLV, L.

is a telling gap of several months between Edgar's assumption of power in 957 and the first charters issued in his name in 958, presumably while his court and government settled into new routines.

The government of Mercia by this group of ealdormen and bishops (as indeed of Wessex by their counterparts) gives every appearance of normality. Even more remarkably it looks as if faction had been abolished. Edgar's charters were witnessed only by men with office in Mercia and Northumbria; Eadwig's only by those based in the south. More striking still is the fact that the flood of charters dried up at both courts. Still, it was an odd sort of normality to have two kingdoms of the English. We should further infer that Edgar's kingdom was under the direction of men with highly developed political skills who were prepared to co-operate with one another in the wider common interest.

Such ideological aspirations as can be read into Edgar's Mercian charters (variously from the identity of the recipients, the choice of wording, and the naming of witnesses) thus seem likely to have been formulated with deliberation to express a political consensus. They included a careful approach to Danelaw sensibilities; a stress on Mercian identity; a willingness to make quite large claims – but with at times a studied ambiguity – about the geographical extent of Edgar's kingdom; and a notable acknowledgement of regional sensibilities within Mercia. The charter for St Werburgh's allows us to unpick some of the Mercian strands in this mixture.

The Charter

Edgar's charter for St Werburgh's was preserved in the archive of the Benedictine abbey which succeeded the minster at Chester in the 1090s under the patronage of the Norman earl of Chester, Hugh d'Avranches. Its survival is significant in itself. The fabric of the minster church was swept away so thoroughly, probably in Earl Hugh's initial building campaign, that no certain archaeological trace of it has yet been found.[11] The minster itself had in effect disappeared from the abbey's memory by the mid-twelfth century, when an elaborate monastic foundation charter was concocted, largely from authentic materials, to tell the story of a new foundation in 1093, richly endowed by Earl Hugh and his men, but also mystifyingly confirmed in possession of estates whose earlier ownership was left vague; in reality they had belonged to the canons of the forgotten minster church.[12]

---

[11] Alan Thacker, 'The Early Medieval City and its Buildings', *Medieval Archaeology, Art and Architecture at Chester*, ed. Alan Thacker, British Archaeological Association Conference Transactions 22 (2000), 16–30, at 19, 24–5; Richard Gem, 'Romanesque Architecture in Chester c. 1075 to 1117', *ibid.*, 31–44, at 32–8; Simon Ward, 'Recent Work at St John's and St Werburgh's', *ibid.*, 45–56, esp. 52–3.

[12] *Chartulary*, ed. Tait, I, no. 3, discussed more recently in *The Charters of the Anglo-Norman Earls of Chester, c. 1071–1237*, ed. Geoffrey Barraclough, Record Society of Lancashire and Cheshire 126 (1988), no. 3 (pp. 2–11).

The archival context in which the text of the charter was preserved has a bearing on its status as a document which has not been fully explored. The only medieval copy is in a fourteenth-century register of Chester abbey charters.[13] There are also several early-modern antiquarian copies, one of which (that printed by Dugdale in *Monasticon Anglicanum*) Tait suggested may have been taken from a different medieval copy.[14] In fact, all the early-modern copies must be derived at one or more removes from the register, since every one reproduces its defective opening, where the corner of the folio has been cut away to leave the charter starting with an incomplete word ... *ens pater Spes vnica Mundi . fabricator celi . Conditor orbis* ('... ty Father, only Hope of the World, Maker of Heaven, Creator of Earth'). Tait thought that the missing word was *Omnipotens*, on the grounds that the first part of the charter's proem was closely modelled on two lines of the fifth-century poet Sedulius's *Carmen Paschale*, 'Omnipotens aeterne Deus, spes unica mundi, / Qui caeli fabricator ades, qui conditor orbis'.[15] Since the charter did not quote the first phrase as closely as those following, its opening word could as well have been *Cunctipotens*, as in the diplomatically related charter of the same year conveying land in Herefordshire to the thegn Ealhstan, which survives as a single-sheet original.[16]

The manuscript into which the charter of 958 was copied is not a full cartulary but a register of the abbey's title-deeds written soon after 1310. The register is rough and informal in comparison with the only fragment which survives of a proper abbey cartulary.[17] Only two leaves of the cartulary are intact, but they are larger, more carefully prepared, more finely written, and better planned than the register, preserving a consistent topographical arrangement of the documents. The register is crude in comparison: a booklet of low-quality parchment, irregularly made up from quires of eight, six, and six bifolia and four loose leaves, unevenly ruled, a working document rather than a fine book for the abbey library. The order of its contents has no overall plan, and it must have been compiled from loose original charters, not by copying an existing volume. It would have been infuriating to use without the index which was added at the front almost immediately.

The register was written to start (on what is now fol. 4) with the Benedictine abbey's supposed foundation charter of 1093, known to historians from its opening words as *Sanctorum prisca*. After the register was finished, Edgar's charter was copied on the leaf facing *Sanctorum prisca* (now fol. 3v). It must have been entered quite soon, as the handwriting is very similar to that of the register itself, but not immediately, since it was added after the index had been

13 BL, Harley 1965.
14 *Chartulary*, ed. Tait, I.10.
15 Sedulius, *Carmen Paschale*, book 1, lines 60–1 <http://www.thelatinlibrary.com/sedulius.html> [accessed 29 Oct. 2006].
16 S 677: + *Cunctipotens pater arce superna sedens pronam.*
17 BL, Harley 2071, fols. 38–9.

written and after a neater and finer copy had been made of the whole register,[18] Edgar's charter being absent from both. Whether Edgar was added to the register as an antiquarian curiosity or by way of correcting *Sanctorum prisca*'s impression of the community's origins is for a historian of St Werburgh's in the later Middle Ages to decide. But the charter's casual preservation in the register does seem to point to the existence of a single-sheet version at the abbey in the early fourteenth century.

Whether that single sheet was 'authentic' is a difficult question, and the materials for answering it not yet to hand. Tait, advised by W. H. Stevenson, thought there were several places where words had been copied carelessly or even altered deliberately.[19] There are certainly uncorrected slips of the pen, but only a few: *flagrantibus* received a couple of extra letters (*flagragantibus*), *comit* was wrongly extended (*comitur*), *scripturarum* inadvertently shortened (*scriptarum*), and *ceterarumque* lost its suffix (*ceterarum*). The diplomatic could do with expert attention, but for the moment at least, it is arguable that the register gives us an essentially accurate transcript of an authentic charter. Given the history of St Werburgh's between 958 and the twelfth century, it is difficult to find an occasion when the minster might have wanted to improve Edgar's diploma. The Benedictine abbey had its own title deeds (the earliest ones heavily manipulated in the mid-twelfth century) and the charter of 958 had no part in its claims or traditions. Equally, the text of Edgar's diploma itself shows that the canons never touched it up to reflect their losses and gains between 958 and 1086, since several of the estates given by Edgar were neither held nor claimed in Domesday Book, and the charter fails to mention many more properties which were theirs in 1066 and might have benefited from written title.

The scribe of the register omitted most of two whole sections of the charter. The clause which would have described the estate boundaries in Old English is curtailed after its Latin introduction: *Est autem hec terra circumcinta terminis etc.* ('And this land is encompassed with [these] boundaries, etc.'). The list of witnesses stops short after the subscription of the king himself, given in full: *Ego Eadgarus Rex Merciorum ceterarum[que] nacionum concensi et scribere iussi, et cum signo sancte crucis confirmaui et corroboraui* ('I Edgar, King of the Mercians and other peoples have agreed and ordered [this charter] to be written, and have confirmed and corroborated [it] with the sign of the holy cross'). The charter was not shortened for any lack of space in the register: it occupied less than a column on a two-column page, leaving most of the folio blank (afterwards filled with part of an inspeximus of a charter of Henry II). The use of 'etc.' at the end of the boundary introduction, and the fact that the wording of Edgar's subscription was given in full, both suggest that the scribe was abbreviating a full text, omitting details which he thought irrelevant to the needs of a working register. Indeed he abbreviated most charters in the register, some of them much more drastically and nearly always omitting all the

---

18 BL, Harley 2062, now much mutilated. The relationship of the two registers was established by Tait, *Chartulary*, I.xxxi–xxxiii.

19 *Chartulary*, ed. Tait, I.10–13.

witnesses. All this suggests the scribe's lack of interest in the diplomatic detail of Edgar's charter, consistent with any further carelessness in copying which might be detected through fuller analysis in the future.

The Estates

The detail of what Edgar gave to St Werburgh's in 958 explains why the donation was so significant in the history of the minster, and what that might tell us about the policies of Edgar's Mercian government.

Edgar's donation comprised six estates totalling 17 hides spread across western Cheshire. Closest to Chester were Upton, immediately north of the city, and Huntington and its southern neighbour Cheaveley, a couple of miles outside the east gate towards the south round the bend of the river Dee. Barrow was not much further away, less than five miles along the Roman road going east from Chester and just over the crossing of the river Gowy. Aston was quite a bit further east, on the far bank of the river Weaver fourteen miles from Chester. Hoseley lay in the other direction, some eight miles south and a little west of the city on the western side of the Dee. This was a scattered grant, not a consolidated territory.

The charter gives only a total hidage, not individual figures for the six estates. All six places were named in Domesday Book, where their combined assessments amounted to 15 hides, 2 hides short of the charter's total.[20] The two 'missing' hides can probably be accounted for by two holdings of 1 hide apiece which had become separate estates between 958 and 1066, at Aston and Newton. St Werburgh's holding at Aston was called *Midestune* ('Middle Aston') in Domesday Book and was rated at 1 hide, but there was another hide adjoining it, called *Estone* ('Aston') and in lay hands. Probably Edgar gave the whole two hides in 958. During the twelfth century St Werburgh's holding was normally called 'Aston' rather than 'Middle Aston', and there are other pointers to the original unity of the two Astons: William fitz Nigel held both in 1086 (Middle Aston from the church and Aston from Earl Hugh); Middle Aston's boundaries were those of a piece cut out of Aston; and it was not taxed separately in the Middle Ages.[21] The other 'missing' hide was probably that at Newton by Chester, a separate holding in Domesday Book but surrounded by the manor of Upton by Chester; very likely it was literally a 'new *tūn*' separated from Upton some

---

[20] To facilitate use of any of the editions of Domesday Book, references are in the form GDB [for Great Domesday Book] with the folio, a or b [for recto or verso], 1 or 2 [the column], and the place-name, followed (in parentheses) by the shire and entry number in the Phillimore edition: *Domesday Book*, ed. John Morris, 34 vols. in 39 (Chichester, 1975–86). GDB 263a2 Cavelea, Hunditone, Midestune, Odeslei, 264a1 Optone, 266a1 Bero (Ches. A/3–4, 17, 19; 1/34; 9/5).

[21] GDB 263a2 Midestune, 266a2 Estone (Ches. A/17; 9/19); John McN. Dodgson, *The Place-Names of Cheshire*, 5 vols. in 7, EPNS 44–8, 54, 74 (1970–97), II.161; John Rylands University Library of Manchester, Tatton 345 [Cheshire mise book, 1405], fol. [5].

time after 958.[22] In 1066 St Werburgh's owned only part of Edgar's grant. It retained Huntington, Cheaveley, half of Aston, and Hoseley (7½ hides) but had lost the other half of Aston and the whole of Barrow and Upton with Newton (9½ hides). The minster's total endowment in Cheshire nonetheless amounted to almost 28 hides.[23]

Edgar's selection of the six estates given in 958 is informative both about the purpose of the grant and about the distribution of royal estates in tenth-century Cheshire. In the first place, the estates were dispersed across five different hundreds: Hoseley in Exestan, Cheaveley and Huntington in Dudestan, Upton in Wilaveston, Aston in Tunendune, and Barrow in Riseton. The scattering looks deliberate: together with the urban hundred of Chester, the charter ensured that the minster had a stake in fully half of the shire's twelve hundreds. Secondly, some tentative conclusions can be drawn about the sources of the lands granted, by working backwards from the evidence of Domesday Book, later township and parish boundaries, and place-names, and in light of the likely history of estate structures in Cheshire in the tenth and eleventh centuries.[24] The most notable features of that history were the existence in the early tenth century of large royal estates which formed the cores of the twelve Cheshire hundreds, their eventual transfer to the local ealdormen and earls, and their gradual break-up as individual townships were acquired by thegns. Almost the only pointer to the chronology of those changes is that the whole of Wirral, forming the Domesday hundred of Wilaveston, appears to have been a single estate when the magnate Wulfric Spot left it to his brother and nephew soon after 1000.[25]

The two most distant and smallest properties given to St Werburgh's in 958 were probably fragments newly cut from large royal estates. Hoseley had surely been part of Gresford (it was barely a mile from Gresford church and afterwards in Gresford parish), the estate at the core of Exestan hundred. Gresford still accounted for 12 hides of the 20 at which the hundred was assessed in 1066 and was very large by Cheshire standards though then in private hands (those of an important thegn, Thorth).[26] Aston was the 'east *tūn*' of the royal estate centred on the early tenth-century fortification at Runcorn. As at Gresford, the core of the estate remained intact in 1066, in the shape of the 10-hide manor of Halton, and again it was in the hands of an important thegn, Orm.[27]

Barrow, which St Werburgh's had lost by 1066, looks from the parish boundaries to have been cut out of Tarvin, and a case could be made that it once formed a block of 20 hides with Tarvin parish (i.e. the separate Domesday

---

22 GDB 266a1 (Ches. 9/1); *PN Cheshire* IV.145–6; for the boundaries: *A New Historical Atlas of Cheshire*, ed. A. D. M. Phillips and C. B. Phillips (Chester, 2002), map in end pocket.

23 GDB 263a2–b1 (Ches. A/1–22).

24 A. T. Thacker, 'Anglo-Saxon Cheshire', *VCH Cheshire* I (1987), 237–92, at 263–8; N. J. Higham, *The Origins of Cheshire* (Manchester, 1993), pp. 126–81.

25 *Burt*, no. 29 and pp. xviii, xxiv.

26 Melville Richards, *Welsh Administrative and Territorial Units, Medieval and Modern* (Cardiff, 1969), pp. 80, 153; GDB 268a1 Gretford (Ches. 27/3).

27 GDB 266a2 Heletune (Ches. 9/17).

estates of Tarvin, Ashton, Clotton, and Stapleford), Iddinshall, and Willington.[28] The largest Domesday estate in the block was the bishop's manor of Tarvin, and perhaps Bishop Cynesige surrendered Barrow in 958 as part of the grant to St Werburgh's. Huntington and Cheaveley, later a single township, were afterwards always part of the inner core of monastic property, passing to the Benedictine monks at the refoundation, later part of the abbey manor of Saighton, and always within the abbey parish of St Oswald.[29]

The largest estate given in 958 was Upton, probably covering what in 1066 were the separate manors of Upton (4½ hides) and Newton (1 hide), neither of which St Werburgh's still owned. The later tenurial history of the area shows that the estate included the whole of the later townships of Upton by Chester, Moston, Caughall, Hoole, Newton by Chester, and Bache, besides land within the city liberties stretching south from Flookers brook to the city walls.[30] St Werburgh's held none of it in 1066, not even the land immediately beyond the city walls, adjoining the monastic precinct inside the walls. Upton belonged to Earl Edwin and Newton to a thegn. St Werburgh's made no claim to any of this land during the Domesday inquest (compare the claims which it did record to lands recently lost at Stanney and Burwardsley)[31] but the Benedictine abbey acquired much of it in later years: Newton and Hoole from their Domesday holders William fitz Nigel and Herbert the jerkin-maker; the tithes of Upton and a mill at Bache perhaps from Earl Hugh (d. 1101); the 'land of Wulfric the reeve outside the Northgate' from Earl Richard (1101–20); and the manor of Upton, including Bache and Moston but not Caughall, from Earl Ranulph I (1120–9).

Edgar's charter was not explicitly a confirmation but seemingly a new grant, and the evidence tends against the idea that St Werburgh's had much of a landed endowment before 958. To substantiate that suggestion, we have to look at the pattern of estates held in 1066 and guess how it might have evolved. The minster then had twenty-three separate properties in Cheshire (including the urban core), amounting to just under 28 hides and worth a little short of £10, besides the small manor of Fauld (Staffs.), which included the church at Hanbury where the remains of St Werburgh had lain before translation to Chester.[32] By comparison with other urban minsters of broadly similar wealth in Mercia, St Werburgh's estates were extremely dispersed, occupying probably as many as seventeen distinct blocks of land radiating from Chester. For comparison, St Alkmund's in Shrewsbury had a larger endowment of 31 hides in only eleven manors and eight

---

[28] GDB 263a1 Terve, 263a2 Etingehalle, 265a1 Estone, 265a2 Winfletone, 267a2 Stapleford, 267b1 Clotone (Ches. B/4; A/6; 5/1; 7/1; 21/1; 23/3); Higham, *Origins of Cheshire*, pp. 149–50; for parish and township boundaries: *New Historical Atlas*, map in end pocket.

[29] George Ormerod, *The History of the County Palatine and City of Chester*, revised and enlarged ed. by Thomas Helsby, 3 vols. (London, 1882), II.770.

[30] Ormerod, *History of Cheshire*, II.772, 773, 776, 816, 818, 819–20; C. P. Lewis, 'Herbert the Jerkin-maker: A Domesday Tenant Identified', *THSLC* 131 (1982, for 1981), 159–60.

[31] GDB 264a1 Stanei, 264b1 Burwardeslei (Ches. 1/35; 2/21).

[32] GDB 263a2–b1 (Ches. A/1–22); 248b1 Felede (Staffs. 10/6–7); *VCH Staffs.* X (2007), 122–4, 128, 137–8.

blocks of territory; St Oswald's in Gloucester 46 hides in only seven manors and probably five blocks.[33] The contrasting estate geographies of dispersal at Chester and compactness at Shrewsbury and Gloucester surely point to radically different patterns of endowment over the course of the tenth and eleventh centuries.

The core of St Werburgh's lands in 1066 was the block on the east bank of the Dee upstream from Chester, about half of which was formed by Huntington and Cheaveley (granted in 958) and half by Boughton and Saighton. There is no evidence to indicate whether Boughton and Saighton were already in the church's hands in 958 or a later acquisition. The only other sizable holding was Ince on the Mersey estuary, assessed at 3 hides, to which the same observation applies.

Of the more distant estates held in 1066, only Clifton, another hide carved off Runcorn-Halton, looks much like the fragments of large royal estates given in 958 at Hoseley and Aston. As many as ten of the other sixteen properties were small holdings (in all but one case of 1 hide or less) at places where there was a second manor in lay hands in 1066. In some cases the township was divided equally by hidage; at Wervin and Neston the church had a third share. None of the vills concerned had its economic resources arranged in the same proportions as its hidage, which would have been a sign of recent division. St Werburgh's had quite a lot of property at the southern end of Wirral which was probably still in a single great estate as recently as 1000. On the whole it seems likely that St Werburgh's interests in all these townships came about through pious gifts by thegnly owners in the first half of the eleventh century rather than at an earlier period before the break-up of the royal and comital estates. A more recent gift seems to be implied only at Stanney, where in 1066 Ragenald held 1 hide but the church had what was called the 'fifth acre' (*quinta acra*).

Edgar's grant did not in any sense found the monastery in Chester; it was, explicitly, a grant to an existing monastic household (*familia*). The word was almost entirely restricted in charter usage to the communities of old and well known houses, though St Werburgh's was not of any great antiquity. In the early fourteenth century the Chester monk Ranulph Higden believed that the relics of St Werburgh had been moved to Chester when the Danes wintered at Repton (873–4) but that a college of canons existed only from the time of King Æthelstan (924–39); in the early sixteenth century his successor Henry Bradshaw dated the translation 875 (his years apparently two out) and attributed the foundation of a minster to Æthelflæd, Lady of the Mercians (911–18) and her brother Edward the Elder (899–924). Recent scholarship has discounted the tradition of a ninth-century translation as unreliable and associated the removal of Werburgh's cult to Chester with Æthelflæd, arguing that she relocated it along with the cult of St Oswald at or soon after her refortification of Chester in 907 and in parallel

---

[33] GDB 253a1, 258a2 Caurtune, 260b2 Wistanestou (Salop. 3G/1–11; 4.20/19; 9/1); GDB 164b1–2 (Glos. 2/1–3, 5–7, 9, 11–13).

with her known foundation of a minster dedicated to Oswald at Gloucester.[34] The earlier date nonetheless retains its attractions, not least because it is difficult to see why any developing tradition would attach the foundation to a period in Mercian history which was both obscure and inglorious rather than to the time of Æthelflæd's rule.

An alternative view of the foundation of St Werburgh's follows the element common to the two later but conflicting traditions, namely that the monastic community at Hanbury fled to Chester with her body when the Vikings wintered at Repton in 873–4 and toppled the Mercian king Burgred. Hanbury was on the new Mercian-Viking frontier in the 870s, the church occupying a spectacular site overlooking the Dove valley where the boundary of the two territories was drawn and barely ten miles from Repton, an ancient centre of Mercian authority. Æthelflæd's role may have been to add relics of St Oswald to an existing monastery in Chester. If she had been the sole founder of the minster, we might have expected its dedication to Oswald, as at Gloucester. Instead, at Chester, the cult of Oswald was installed within an existing church, or perhaps in a new church within the monastic precinct. Oswald's cult at Chester remained subsidiary to Werburgh's: his name never ousted hers as the primary focus of the monastic church, though it eventually became the dedication of the extensive parish served in the twelfth century and afterwards by a parochial altar in an aisle of the Benedictine abbey and by a parochial graveyard on abbey lands outside the city's Northgate.[35] Perhaps that came about because Æthelflæd's importation of the cult of Oswald was the moment at which parochial territories outside the walls were assigned to the city's churches.

Because the charter of 958 gave both the estate outside the Northgate and over half of what in 1066 was the core property upstream from the city it is difficult to see what St Werburgh's might already have held before Edgar's time, unless it were Boughton and less obviously Saighton and Ince. That is speculative, and a contrary speculation would make the 8 hides at Boughton, Saighton, and Ince a later acquisition in exchange for 9½ hides lost at Upton and Barrow. St Werburgh's was almost certainly poorly endowed before Edgar's time, not at all like Æthelflæd's splendid foundation at St Oswald's, Gloucester, and more in keeping with a work of the turbulent 870s.[36]

Edgar's gift in 958 was in any case a turning point in the history of the minster: it reaffirmed royal patronage, secured any existing estates, and extended them with (for Cheshire) lavish new grants. It may have been accom-

---

[34] *Polychronicon Ranulphi Higden Monachi Cestrensis*, ed. C. Babington and J. R. Lumby, Rolls Series 41, 9 vols. (1865–86), VI.126–8, 366; *The Life of Saint Werburge of Chester, by Henry Bradshaw*, ed. Carl Horstmann, EETS os 88 (London, 1887), pp. 149–52; A. T. Thacker, 'Chester and Gloucester: Early Ecclesiastical Organization in Two Mercian Burhs', *Northern History* 18 (1982), 199–211, at 203–4; *VCH Cheshire* V (1), 19.

[35] A. T. Thacker, 'Medieval Parish Churches: St. Oswald', *VCH Cheshire* V (2) (2005), 149–53.

[36] Carolyn Heighway and Richard Bryant, *The Golden Minster: The Anglo-Saxon Minster and Later Medieval Priory of St. Oswald at Gloucester*, Council for British Archaeology Research Report 117 (York, 1999).

panied by a privilege hardly paralleled elsewhere, namely the exemption of the church's estates from the three 'common burdens' of providing men for army service, constructing bridges, and garrisoning fortresses.[37] The text in the register does grant such exemption *ab omni aggravatione secularis servicii ꝺ ab omni censu ꝺ expedicionis profectione pontisque constructione ꝺ arcis munitione* ('from all burden of secular service and from all customary payments and going on military service and constructing bridges and garrisoning fortresses'), though Tait may well have been right to suggest that an abbreviation for *preter* ('except') was changed (inadvertently?) to the cipher (ꝺ) standing for *et* ('and') with the effect of exempting the church from the three common burdens instead of reserving them for the king's use.[38] The only parallel adduced by Tait was a similar exemption in Æthelstan's charter of 930 granting Sandford (Devon) to the *familia* of Bishop Eadulf of Crediton, but that charter has since been recognized as having been written in the early eleventh century and likely to include an improvement in the terms of the grant.[39] Even without exemption, Edgar's grant to St Werburgh's elevated it well above the norm for royal minsters in Mercian shire towns such as St Juliana's and St Mary's in Shrewsbury, St Mary's in Stafford, and St Frideswide's in Oxford.

Edgar and Mercia

The Chester charter, like some of the others issued in the same year, took account of Mercian sensibilities. Three aspects require further exploration: Edgar's royal titles, the invocation of his forebears, and the place where the charter was issued.

The eight charters dated 958 and one from 959 were drafted by scribes with different diplomatic habits and expressed Edgar's kingship in various ways.[40] One scribe who had written charters for Eadred in 946 and for Eadwig in 956–7 carried on using exactly the same elaborate phrase for Edgar in two charters of 958, *industrius Anglorum rex ceterarumque gentium in circuitu persistentium gubernator et rector*, seemingly without any consciousness that it might be inappropriate for a king who did not rule the whole of England.[41] The expected translation would be 'assiduous king *of the English* and governor and ruler of

---

[37] Nicholas Brooks, 'The Development of Military Obligations in Eighth- and Ninth-Century England', *England before the Conquest: Studies in Primary Sources Presented to Dorothy Whitelock*, ed. Peter Clemoes and Kathleen Hughes (Cambridge, 1971), pp. 69–84; Richard P. Abels, *Lordship and Military Obligation in Anglo-Saxon England* (London, 1988), pp. 52–7.

[38] *Chartulary*, ed. Tait, I.11.

[39] S 405; *Facsimiles of Anglo-Saxon Charters*, ed. Simon Keynes, Anglo-Saxon Charters, Supplementary Series 1 (Oxford, 1991), no. 27a (discussed pp. 8–9).

[40] This section draws heavily on Cyril Hart, 'Danelaw and Mercian Charters of the Mid Tenth Century', *The Danelaw*, pp. 431–53; Keynes, *Diplomas*, pp. 69–70.

[41] S 674, S 676a, S 679; Simon Keynes, 'The "Dunstan B" Charters', *ASE* 23 (1994), 165–93.

other peoples living around them', but *Anglorum rex* might have been taken instead to signify 'king of the Angles' and thus fitting, if archaic, for a king of the Mercians and Northumbrians. Another scribe ('Dunstan B') who had also drafted texts for Eadwig modified his earlier wording of *rex et primicerius Anglorum* ('king and chief of the English') to *rex et primicerius Merciorum* ('king and chief of the Mercians').[42] A third, writing the Chester charter, expressed Edgar's subscription as 'king of the Mercians and of other peoples' (*Rex Merciorum ceterarumque nacionum*), a more generalized variation of his style in the charter relating to Staunton on Arrow (Herefs.), 'king of the Mercians and the Northumbrians and the Britons' (*rex Merciorum et Norðanhymbrorum atque Brettonum*).[43] The other scribes had yet more variants. Taken together, the titles signal a willingness to make large claims for Edgar's position in 957–9, but perhaps also some uncertainty about quite what that position might be at the present or imply for the future. They may well have been produced by scribes working to the instructions of different individuals at Edgar's court, and very likely on different occasions, but because there was a stable group of bishops, ealdormen, and a few thegns who witnessed all the charters of 958–9, they are likely collectively to reflect an agreed position.

Edgar's charter to St Werburgh's paid respects to his Mercian forebears in an odd phrase, explaining his motivation as being 'for the salvation of my soul and [the souls] of my predecessors Edmund, famous king of the English and my father, and also Æthelstan of blessed memory, most noble king of the same people' (*pro expiacione anime mee meorumque predecessorum Eadmundi videlicet incliti Anglorum Regis et genitoris mei ; necnon et beate memorie Ethelstani eiusdem gentis Regis nobilissimi*). The word *expiatio* rightly meant 'atonement' and was correctly used in charters of the eighth and ninth centuries (and one of King Eadred in 955) with words referring to the remedying of royal (and in one case archiepiscopal) 'sins', 'transgressions', 'misdeeds', and 'crimes' (*criminum, delictorum, facinorum, peccaminum, piaculorum,* and *scelerum*).[44] Apart from the Chester charter of 958 and same scribe's Shropshire charter of 963, the phrase *pro expiatione animæ meæ* occurs only in a group of six supposed charters of King Æthelstan from the Exeter archive, diplomas of uncertain reliability because they were actually written in the eleventh century to replace ones lost when the Danes burnt Exeter in 1003.[45]

If the choice of words was unusual, so, in a sense, was the sentiment they expressed. Pious gifts to churches were commonly made for the sake of the donor's soul but rarely (until later) for the souls of other family members.

---

[42] S 676, S 678.

[43] S 677; for a later charter by the same scribe (S 712a): Nicholas Brooks, Margaret Gelling, and Douglas Johnson, 'A New Charter of King Edgar', *ASE* 13 (1984), 137–55, at 142–8.

[44] S 92, S 96, S 140, S 144, S 168, S 202, S 262, S 263, S 264, S 270, S 287, S 300, S 316, S 323, S 330, S 567, S 1264.

[45] S 386–390, S 433; P. Chaplais, 'The Authenticity of the Royal Anglo-Saxon Diplomas of Exeter', *BIHR* 39 (1966), 1–34.

Furthermore, Edgar here selected only his father Edmund and uncle Æthelstan, naming both as kings 'of the English'. Edgar's advisers were surely here
positioning their young charge as Edmund's and Æthelstan's heir in the whole
of the kingdom; they excluded the equally illustrious Alfred and Edward the
Elder (both of whom had ruled as kings of 'the Anglo-Saxons'),[46] Ealdorman
Æthelstan and the Lady Æthelflæd (who had ruled *only* Mercia), Edgar's uncle
Eadred (whose rule over Northumbria was unsteadily maintained), and – most
pointedly of all – Edgar's brother, King Eadwig. The choice of just two among
Edgar's predecessors, and the terms in which Edmund ('famous king of the
English') and Æthelstan ('of blessed memory, most noble king of the same
people') were remembered, had the effect of placing Edgar squarely in the line
of kings of *all* the English (West Saxons, Mercians, and Northumbrians), even
though for the moment he ruled only some of them.

Another of the distinctive habits of the scribe of the Chester charter was to
specify the historic district of Mercia in which a grant was situated. Thus, in
the Herefordshire charter of 958, Staunton-on-Arrow was said to lie *in pago
Magesætna*, while in two charters postdating the reunification of 959 Plaish
and Church Aston (Salop.) were *in provincia Wrocensetna* and Ballidon (Derb.)
in pago Pecset.[47] The allusions to the provinces of the Magonsætan, Wreocen-
sætan, and Pecsætan are highly unusual in charter diplomatic. It may well be
that the ancient subdivisions of Mercia still had some functions even after shires
centred on Hereford, Shrewsbury, Derby, and other towns had been created as
territories; but it was not usual for charter-writers to locate an estate in its territory at all, yet this scribe went out of his way to do so. The Old English of
the boundary clause in the Ballidon charter shows the scribe's native dialect to
have been Mercian. The choice of a Mercian scribe to write the diploma for St
Werburgh's is unlikely to have been accidental.

Although he did not designate the territory for the six estates given to St
Werburgh's, that scribe did name the location where the charter was issued,
Penkridge (Staffs.), and moreover as a 'famous place' (*in loco famoso qui dicitur
Pencric*). Most tenth-century royal charters did not say where they were issued.
The proportion which did fell sharply from 35 per cent under Edward the Elder
and Æthelstan (899–939) to only 5 per cent under the next five kings (939–78).
Almost four times as many charters survive from the second period as from
the first, so that the absolute numbers involved are more equal.[48] The change in
diplomatic practice came abruptly with the accession of Edmund in 939. Quite
why some charters stated the place of issue is not clear and has never been
investigated. By the time of Edgar's charter for St Werburgh's it was a very

---

[46] Simon Keynes, 'Anglo-Saxons, Kingdom of the', *Blackwell Encycl.*, pp. 37–8; Keynes,
   'England, 900–1016', *New Cambridge Medieval History, III*, 459–66.
[47] S 677, S 723, S 712a.
[48] Figures calculated from the Electronic Sawyer: Edward the Elder 12 of 29; Æthelstan
   24 of 74; Edmund 4 of 57; Eadred 4 of 68; Eadwig 3 of 87; Edgar 8 of 164; Edward the
   Martyr 1 of 5.

unusual feature, and we should be open to the possibility that it has some special explanation.

More sparing still is the phrasing that a diploma was issued in a *famous* place (*in loco famosa/famoso*). The locution was more common in the ninth century (nine examples) than the tenth (four). Ninth-century Mercian charters alluded to the fame of Canterbury, Tamworth, and Bath;[49] ninth-century West Saxon charters to Kingston (Surr.), Mereworth, and Wye (both Kent);[50] and in the first half of the tenth century we have a charter of Æthelstan issued at famous Exeter and one of Eadred at famous Somerton.[51] The Penkridge charter is the last in the series apart from the great privilege in favour of the newly refounded Benedictine abbey at Ely, which Edgar ordered written 'in the royal estate which the inhabitants call by the famous name of Woolmer' (*in villa regali que famoso vocabulo a solicolis Wlfamere nominatur*).[52] The idea of famous places remained current in the vocabulary of charter-writers into the eleventh century but it was restricted to identifying the fame of the monastic communities which received royal largesse (Malmesbury, Chertsey, the New Minster at Winchester, Sherborne, Athelney),[53] or of the locations of lands granted (Worcester, Winchester, Whitchurch (Oxon.), the Weald, Oxford).[54]

Was Penkridge really famous in the 950s, and if so, why? It lay two miles off what was arguably the principal road of the Mercian kingdom, Watling Street, which linked London and Chester. Edgar's grandfather, Edward the Elder, had died at Farndon, at the Chester end of the same road. The Mercian episcopal see at Lichfield and the great Mercian royal centre of Tamworth were equally close to the road, an easy day's journey towards London. Penkridge itself was on a side road which led to the fortified borough of Stafford, which had a mint and important pottery workshops. Penkridge was well sited but not, at first sight, in the same league.

The evidence for Penkridge's status in the tenth century is fragmentary and tantalizing. The place-name suggests continuities between Roman and British territorial arrangements in the area, and then between British and English. A Roman station on Watling Street was called *Pennocrucium*, latinizing the British description of a nearby burial mound;[55] the name remained in use as *Pennocruc* in the British language after the Romans had gone; and it was adopted straight into English when the Anglo-Saxons took over the area.[56] The name was trans-

---

[49] S 164, S 193, S 199, S 208, S 210.
[50] S 281, S 293, S 296, S 297.
[51] S 418a, S 549.
[52] S 779.
[53] S 796, S 797, S 940, S 956, S 975, S 979.
[54] S 786, S 788, S 845, S 927, S 950, S 964.
[55] A. L. F. Rivet and Colin Smith, *The Place-Names of Roman Britain* (London, 1979), pp. 436–7; Margaret Gelling and Ann Cole, *The Landscape of Place-Names* (Stamford, 2000), p. 159.
[56] J. P. Oakden, *The Place-Names of Staffordshire, Part 1*, EPNS 55 (1984), pp. 87–8; David Horovitz, *The Place-Names of Staffordshire* (Brewood, 2005), p. 432; Richard Coates

ferred to the river on which Penkridge stands,[57] and from there to a district covering the river basin, with the name Pencersætan surfacing as the name of the people of the district in the boundary clause of a ninth-century charter.[58] When western Mercia was divided into hundreds in the early tenth century the meeting-place of one of them, Cuttlestone, was fixed just outside Penkridge.[59] In 1066 Penkridge was divided between a fairly extensive (but beneficially hidated) royal manor and a smaller manor belonging to the nine clerks of Penkridge.[60] The clerks were clearly the community of an important minster church which survived into the Middle Ages as a royal free chapel controlling a large mother-parish.[61] Parochial and manorial arrangements in the area around Penkridge suggest that the minster's territory was once even more extensive.[62] The settlement plan of Penkridge itself hints at a minster precinct lying at its heart.[63]

Penkridge was clearly a royal centre of some importance in the tenth century, irrespective of whether the minster was ancient, a new establishment of the tenth century, or re-established on ancient foundations. It was significant enough to be the place for the royal assembly at which the charter for St Werburgh's was issued, and for those involved in drafting the charter to wish to draw attention to the fact. In the Anglo-Saxon period the ordinary Latin word for 'a place' (*locus*) was sometimes used with the specific meaning of 'monastery/minster', and in the tenth century the English equivalent (*stow*) was the normal word for a religious establishment,[64] so perhaps the scribe of the Chester charter meant to refer specifically to the famous minster of St Michael at Penkridge. It seems again to pay his respects to the historic structures of ancient Mercia.

The nine charters which happen to survive from 958 and 959 can give only an incomplete and perhaps misleading impression of how Mercia was governed between 957 and 959. They show that Edgar and his advisers gave lands to a bishop, an ealdorman, and thegns, besides St Werburgh's; that royal grants were spread right across Mercia from east to west and north to south; that all the Mercian bishops and ealdormen were associated with Edgar's court; and that

---

and Andrew Breeze, *Celtic Voices, English Places: Studies of the Celtic Impact on Place-Names in England* (Stamford, 2000), pp. 269, 334.

[57] Eilert Ekwall, *English River-Names* (Oxford, 1928), pp. xlvi, 322.

[58] S 199, S 1272; Della Hooke, *The Landscape of Anglo-Saxon Staffordshire: The Charter Evidence* (Keele, 1983), pp. 10–12, 14–19; Della Hooke, *The Anglo-Saxon Landscape: The Kingdom of the Hwicce* (Manchester, 1985), pp. 85–6.

[59] S. A. H. Burne, 'Cuttlestone Hundred', *VCH Staffs.* IV (1958), 61–3, at 61; Oakden, *PN Staffs.*, I.24–6; Horovitz, *PN Staffs.*, pp. 46–7, 221.

[60] GDB 246a2 Pancriz; 247b2 Pancriz (Staffs. 1/7; 7/17).

[61] Dorothy Styles, 'The Early History of Penkridge College', *Collections for a History of Staffordshire* (1954, for 1950–1), pp. 1–52; Dorothy Styles, 'The College of St. Michael, Penkridge', *VCH Staffs.* III (1970), 298–303.

[62] Culling information from histories of Cannock, Cheslyn Hay, Lapley, Penkridge, Shareshill, Stretton, and Teddesley Hay in *VCH Staffs.* IV and V; and derivations of place-names from Oakden, *PN Staffs.*, I, and Horovitz, *PN Staffs.*

[63] Plan of 1754 (Staffordshire Record Office, D.260/M/E353) reproduced in *VCH Staffs.* V, facing p. 104.

[64] Blair, *Church*, pp. 110, 217 n. 145.

large groups of thegns with regional interests attended when business concerned their area. The limited number of charters suggests careful husbanding of royal largesse by the king's advisers, quite different from the reckless generosity of 956. In other words, despite their small numbers they amply illustrate the fact that the normal business of tenth-century rule operated in Edgar's truncated kingdom. What they demonstrate in particular about the place of St Werburgh's is due to the charter's chance survival, copied as an afterthought by a four-teenth-century scribe. There are no known pre-Conquest charters for a long list of other important Mercian minsters. At many of them, far-reaching post-Conquest changes dislocated communities and interrupted traditions even more severely than at Chester, perhaps leading to the loss of their charters. So, it is perfectly possible in theory that Edgar's grant to St Werburgh's was part of a wider programme of minster endowment in Mercia, though on the evidence of landholdings in 1066 it can only have been on a limited scale other than at St Alkmund's, Shrewsbury.

Insofar as St Werburgh's was singled out by the king's advisers it directs attention to what was special about Chester in the mid-tenth century. Edgar's vicarious association with the city in 958 prefigures his appearance there in 973, though the scantiness of the evidence for his reign makes it unsafe to assume that there were not many other involvements during the intervening period. The events of 973 have attracted a huge literature which has rarely, if ever, drawn on Edgar's earlier relations with Chester.[65] In 973 the king proceeded directly from a royal coronation at Bath to some kind of 'imperial' assembly at Chester, in a progress which must have been conceived and stage-managed as a whole by the king and his advisers. Precisely what happened at Chester has been irretrievably obscured by the embellishments of twelfth-century historians, who elaborated the story that Edgar was rowed by a party of submissive Celtic and Scandinavian kings from a royal palace to the episcopal minster of St John's and back. St John's does not appear in the story before John of Worcester's version, and then *only* in that version and not in the almost contemporary account by William of Malmesbury. There seems no warrant for it; we simply do not know how Edgar moved through the city in 973, though it is fair to point out that the diploma of 958 had made him patron of a church far better endowed than St John's.

The pairing of Bath and Chester in 973 was rich in symbolism. Both were 'imperial' cities with substantial and visible Roman remains, charged with high emotional meaning for the English elite. Bath had its Aachen-like Roman complex enclosing hot springs, but at Chester, too, a very large Roman baths building still stood as a prominent urban feature, together with long stretches of Roman walls and the remains of other large stone structures including the am-

---

[65] David E. Thornton, 'Edgar and the Eight Kings, AD 973: *textus et dramatis personae*', *EME* 10 (2001), 49–79; Julia Barrow, 'Chester's Earliest Regatta? Edgar's Dee-Rowing Revisited', *EME* 10 (2001), 81–93; Shashi Jayakumar, 'Some Reflections on the "Foreign Policies" of Edgar "the Peaceable"', *HSJ* 10 (2002, for 2001), 17–37, at 19–21, 31–5; Ann Williams, 'An Outing on the Dee: King Edgar at Chester, A.D. 973', *MScand* 14 (2004), 229–43.

phitheatre and an enigmatic elliptical building. Both towns had been refortified during the formative years of the English kingdom, Bath probably by Alfred, Chester certainly by his daughter Æthelflæd of the Mercians. Each housed an important royal monastery, Bath's trumping St Werburgh's in the historical depth of its royal associations, which included patronage by the Mercian kings Offa and Ecgfrith in the 770s and 790s and revival under Edgar's father Edmund in the 940s.[66] The ceremonies of 973 also played on the symbolism of complementarity, moving in 973 from Wessex to Mercia and from a Benedictine to a non-Benedictine environment. Both towns were free of the other allegiances which might have complicated assemblies held at Winchester, York, or Canterbury. At Chester, 973 was a renewal of the direct royal lordship asserted for Edgar through the charter for St Werburgh's in 958.

Chester's location, at what has been called 'the crossroads of the British Isles',[67] made it the obvious place to gather the kings of the north and west in 973, but no less attractive as a focus of royal interest in 958. It lay nearer Anglesey and Man than Lincoln or Oxford, nearer Dublin than Winchester or London. By sea it was quicker to reach Chester from Dumbarton than from Bath. The charters of 958–9 as a whole laid claim to Edgar's dominion over the peoples of the outer Irish Sea zone; whatever happened at Chester in 973 created a real relationship between him and many of their rulers.

In favouring St Werburgh's, one among many similar quite poorly endowed minsters in Mercian shire towns, Edgar's advisers were consciously building on Æthelflæd's involvement in the region fifty years earlier. Perhaps, too, they had in mind Æthelstan's local fame if indeed the battle of Brunanburh was fought at Bromborough on Wirral only twenty years previously.[68] Nor should we neglect the extent to which they might also have been thinking forward to how Mercia would fit in a reunited kingdom of the English once Eadwig was gone, by creating at St Werburgh's a significant royal resource in an important provincial centre at a pivotal location in the islands of Britain. What they were not anticipating was the Benedictine Reform. St Werburgh's was re-endowed under royal patronage without turning its clerks into monks, in a way which became impossible later in the reign. That tells us much about the limited objectives of the Benedictine reformers in the 950s, and perhaps about Dunstan's inclinations when operating independently of Abbot Æthelwold. Reform became a far-reaching programme at the heart of government only when the adult Edgar took it up. The adolescent Edgar of 958, guided by Dunstan and the ealdormen of Mercia, was not yet the Benedictine Edgar of *Regularis Concordia* or the refoundation of the New Minster.

Limits to the Benedictine Reform were geographical as well as chronological.

66 John Blair, 'Bath', *Blackwell Encycl.*, p. 54; A. T. Thacker, 'Topography 900–1914: Early Medieval, 900–1230', *VCH Cheshire*, V (1), 206–9.

67 C. P. Lewis, 'The City of Chester', *VCH Cheshire*, V (1), 1–8, at 3.

68 Donald Scragg, '*Battle of Brunanburh*', *Blackwell Encycl.*, pp. 54–5; *PN Cheshire*, IV 237–40; Paul Cavill, Stephen Harding and Judith Jesch, 'Revisiting *Dingesmere*', *EPNSJ* 36 (2004), 25–38.

Great landowners in north-west Mercia were not participants in the Reform movement until the eleventh century, and never enthusiasts in the manner of many of their peers in southern Mercia and Wessex. Mercia remained different from Wessex, and north-west Mercia different again from other parts. The Mercianness of the St Werburgh's diploma and others of 958 should nevertheless be qualified. Their meaning certainly goes deeper than the existence of one Mercian charter-writer with an informed interest in his province's history and geography. Edgar's government as a whole was attuned to its Mercian setting and prepared to countenance the rehearsal of Mercian sensibilities. At first sight the flattering references to Mercia, its regions, and its ancient minsters might be taken for an older identity supposedly left behind in Alfred's and his successors' reshaping of English identities. It might even be thought that the special circumstances of the dual kingdom in 957–9 allowed a submerged Mercian identity to resurface, perhaps with separatist resonances. In reality it was a Mercian identity articulated in the full knowledge that Edgar's half-kingdom was a temporary expedient in the affairs of the English, though one with an uncertain life expectancy. The Mercianness of Edgar's kingdom of the Mercians was a clever and courtly shaping of political rhetoric to the immediate situation. Nonetheless, if a separate kingdom of the Mercians and Northumbrians was expected to pass, the grant to St Werburgh's would endure into the reunited kingdom and make Chester a centre of royal authority in times to come.

5

Edgar's Path to the Throne

FREDERICK M. BIGGS

ONE of the more puzzling questions associated with Edgar's reign concerns his path to the throne between 23 November 955 when his uncle, King Eadred, died and 1 October 959 when his elder brother, King Eadwig, passed away, leaving Edgar in control of all of England then held by the West Saxons. The problem arises because there is strong evidence that Edgar first assumed power, as *ASC* BC report,[1] in Mercia in 957: how are we to interpret this stepped ascent to rule especially in light of the laconic and often contradictory contemporary written sources as well as the even more bewildering evidence of charters and coins? The aim of this paper is to explore the possibility that the discrepancies in the historical record and, indeed, much of the assumed drama surrounding Edgar's succession may be explained by considering an older practice, opposed, I shall argue, by the Church but apparently still politically viable even in the mid-tenth century, joint kingship.

Modern scholarly opinion, anticipating my argument, has gradually been turning away from positing a sharp political break in 957 to assuming a more gradual shift in power between Eadwig and Edgar. Sir Frank Stenton expresses the older view when he begins his discussion of these events with the remark that 'it was probably through mere irresponsibility that within two years of his accession Eadwig lost the greater part of his kingdom'.[2] He admits that 'there is no trace of any particularist feeling behind this revolution' and that 'it was not followed by any important change in the distribution of the great provincial governments', and then dismisses the claim of Dunstan's earliest biographer that his rejection was caused by 'his folly in choosing young advisers as thoughtless as himself'.[3] Stenton, however, concludes: 'The probability is that in the society of his West Saxon friends he fell completely out of touch with the local aristocracy

---

[1] See Taylor, *MS B*, p. 54; O'Keeffe, *MS C*, p. 80; and *EHD*, p. 225.
[2] Stenton, *ASE*, p. 366. See also E. John, *Orbis Britanniae and Other Studies* (Bristol, 1966), p. 158; and P. Stafford, *Unification and Conquest: Political and Social History of England in the Tenth and Eleventh Centuries* (London, 1989), pp. 47–50.
[3] Stenton, *ASE*, pp. 366–7.

of remoter parts.'[4] David Dumville adopts much the same line,[5] while, in contrast, Barbara Yorke downplays the drama when she explains that 'Edgar seems to have been able to use the bad feeling in some quarters against Eadwig, and probably the incipient nationalism of the Mercians, to draw important concessions from Eadwig', and raises a very different possibility by suggesting that in doing so Edgar 'strengthened his position as heir presumptive'.[6] Simon Keynes has gone further, as his chapter at the beginning of this book makes clear (see above, pp. 3–59).[7] Ann Williams joins with these more recent interpretations, commenting, 'it may be that the division of 957 was simply a recognition of Edgar's position as his brother's heir'.[8] It is, I would like to add, the tradition of joint kingship that may allow us to see this explanation as probable rather than possible: what happened in 957 was less important than what was established in 955, when at their uncle's death the two brothers became joint kings in different parts of the realm as a way of clarifying the next step in the succession. In doing so, they followed a tradition more common in early Anglo-Saxon England, and indeed much of the confusion in the sources can be attributed both to the Church's disapproval of this practice and to its increasingly infrequent use in the later period.

Joint Kingship

Although recent studies have shown that joint kingship was common particularly in early Anglo-Saxon England, they have not noted that the Church, while not specifically condemning the practice, expressed its disapproval by ignoring it when possible. It would, of course, be wrong to assume that there was a single model of joint kingship, any more than there was a single model of kingship,[9] that existed throughout the Anglo-Saxon period and among all its ruling groups. Yet some common elements may be perceived. In a review of the early rulers of the south-east Midlands, Dumville has explained two situations under which joint kingship might have arisen: when two or more sons succeeded a single ruler, in which case 'they may have ruled as a committee, but that is not to say that they were all equal'; and when one king deliberately associated himself with another, 'who was both subordinate and responsible for a separate

---

[4] Stenton, *ASE*, p. 367.

[5] 'The Ætheling: A Study of Anglo-Saxon Constitutional History', *ASE* 8 (1979), 1–33, at 30.

[6] 'Æthelwold and the Politics of the Tenth Century', Yorke, *Æthelwold*, pp. 65–88, at 78.

[7] See also his 'England, c. 900–1016', *The New Cambridge Medieval History*, Vol. 3, *c. 900–1024*, ed. T. Reuter (Cambridge, 1999), pp. 456–84, at 478.

[8] 'Edgar', *ODNB*. See also her *Kingship and Government in Pre-Conquest England c. 500–1066* (Basingstoke, 1999), p. 87; and 'Some Notes and Considerations on Problems Connected with the English Royal Succession, 860–1066', *Proceedings of the Battle Conference on Anglo-Norman Studies* 1(1978), 144–67 and 225–33.

[9] See S. Keynes, 'England, 700–900', in *The New Cambridge Medieval History*, Vol. 2, *c.700–c. 900*, ed. R. McKitterick (Cambridge, 1995), pp. 18–42, at 20.

unit (often a conquered one) within the kingdom'.[10] Scattered references in Bede's *Ecclesiastical History* provide evidence particularly of the first case: for example, Sæberht, who ruled Essex at the time of Augustine's mission, 'left three sons as heirs to his temporal kingdom'; Bede tells the story of them acting together to expel bishop Mellitus for refusing to give them 'holy bread' until they were baptized.[11]

Yet what others, particularly Yorke, have added is that joint kingship also figured in designating a successor. Focusing on early Kent, she finds evidence for joint kingship under a variety of circumstances: close-kinsmen holding the throne, less close kinsmen sharing power, even outside conquerors such as Offa allowing the practice to continue, and she relates it to the issue of succession:

> When one compares Kent with other early Anglo-Saxon kingdoms one is struck by the persistence of joint reigns and the long survival of one branch of the royal house. Scarcely any of the other Anglo-Saxon kingdoms were ruled in 750 by a direct descendant in the male line of the king who had ruled in 600. The success of the descendants of Aethelbert I in keeping the kingship in their branch of the royal house may well be connected with the continued existence of joint reigns as, in effect, they enabled the chief king to nominate his successor during his lifetime and for the nominee to build up a following and a reputation while in the junior position.[12]

In a later study, Yorke discusses the evidence for joint kingship in early Wessex,[13] and the tradition may play a part in the bewildering events that eventually brought Alfred to the throne in 871. This case is too complex to do more than mention here,[14] but let me note that Æthelwulf, Alfred's father, ruled in Kent (from perhaps 826 but certainly by 828),[15] while his father, Egbert, was on the throne of Wessex, before ascending the throne of Wessex himself (in 839). Moreover, his eldest son, Æthelstan also ruled this eastern kingdom between c. 838 and c. 850. Æthelstan died before Æthelwulf, and so we cannot know if he would have followed his father in Wessex, but Asser relates that Æthelwulf established that at his death the kingdom would be divided between his eldest sons, Æthelbald (in Wessex) and Æthelberht (in Kent).[16] Moreover, when Æthelbald died in 860 (two years after his father), Æthelberht became king of Wessex.

---

10 'Essex, Middle Anglia, and the Expansion of Mercia in the South-East Midlands', *The Origins of Anglo-Saxon Kingdoms*, ed. S. Bassett (London, 1989), pp. 123–40, at 138.
11 *Bede's Ecclesiastical History of the English People*, ed. B. Colgrave and R. A. B. Mynors (Oxford, 1969), pp. 152–3.
12 B. A. E. Yorke, 'Joint Kingship in Kent c. 560–785', *Archæologia Cantiana* 99 (1983), 1–19, at 17. See also her *Kings and Kingdoms of Early Anglo-Saxon England* (London, 1990), esp. pp. 169–70.
13 *Wessex in the Early Middle Ages* (London, 1995), pp. 24 and 98.
14 See Stenton, *ASE*, pp. 233–6, and 245; Keynes, 'England, 700–900', 38–41.
15 See S. Keynes, 'The Control of Kent in the Ninth Century', *EME* 2 (1993), 111–31, at 121.
16 *Asser's Life of King Alfred together with the Annals of Saint Neots*, ed. W. H. Stevenson, new impression with article on recent work on Asser's Life of Alfred by D. Whitelock (Oxford, 1959), pp. 14–15; and *Alfred the Great: Asser's Life of King Alfred and Other*

That Mercia at the beginning of the tenth century came to play the same role as Kent had in the ninth may initially have been due to chance.[17] As Keynes writes, at the death of Edward the Elder on 17 July 924 'the kingdom "of the Anglo-Saxons" appears to have fractured into two of its component parts: Æthelstan "was chosen by the Mercians as king",[18] and his half-brother Ælfweard appears to have gained recognition as king in Wessex'.[19] Yet Keynes also notes the possibility 'that the Mercians were simply acknowledging a second successor to Edward'.[20] In any case, Ælfweard died, according to *ASC* D,[21] after sixteen days (2 August 924) and Æthelstan became king in Wessex as well as Mercia. Yet, if in effect before, the tradition of joint kingship does not appear to have survived Edgar's reign. According to Byrhtferth's *Life of St Oswald*, following Edgar's death on 8 July 975, a dispute over the succession was resolved first by his son's, Edward's, election to the throne but then three years later by Edward's murder at the hands of thegns in support of his brother, Æthelred.[22] While Mercia played a significant role in Byrhtferth's account, the events both as he recounts them and as they can be reconstructed from other sources indicate a contested succession rather than one ordered by a tradition of joint kingship.[23]

If, however, joint kingship was so prominent particularly in early Anglo-Saxon England, and survived, as argued here, even as late as the mid-tenth century, why is it not more fully recognized in the written record? The answer, I propose, is to be found in the Church's attitude toward the practice, which can be teased out of Bede's *Ecclesiastical History*.[24] While not a matter of explicit doctrine, raised, for example, by a son marrying his father's widow, joint rule appears to have disconcerted Bede because it seemed contrary to a Christian ideal of kingship where succession, under God's control, should simply be a legitimate son following his father to the throne. His relative silence cannot, I would argue, be explained by his writing ecclesiastical rather than political history since the close relationship between Church and State begun with Augustine's conversion of Æthelberht would seem to make the tradition hard to ignore. Indeed, one of Yorke's compelling arguments for joint kingship in Kent was the creation of a bishopric in Rochester as well as in Canterbury, which implies 'a major admin-

---

Contemporary Sources, trans. S. Keynes and M. Lapidge (Harmondsworth, 1983), pp. 72–3 and 236–7.

[17] On the relationship between Wessex and Mercia in the ninth century with a discussion of its implications for the politics of the tenth, see S. Keynes, 'King Alfred and the Mercians', *Kings, Currency and Alliances: History and Coinage of Southern England in the Ninth Century*, ed. M. A. S. Blackburn and D. N. Dumville (Woodbridge, 1998), pp. 1–46.

[18] Keynes's reference is to the *Mercian Register*, *EHD*, p. 218.

[19] 'England, c. 900–1016', p. 467. See also Keynes, 'King Alfred and the Mercians', p. 38 and n. 164 for further bibliography.

[20] 'England, c. 900–1016', p. 467.

[21] Cubbin, *MS D*, p. 41; *EHD*, p. 218.

[22] Raine, *York*, I.443–51; trans. *EHD*, pp. 912–16.

[23] On these events, see D. J. V. Fisher, 'The Anti-Monastic Reaction in the Reign of Edward the Martyr', *Cambridge Historical Journal* 10 (1950–2), 254–70.

[24] Bede's writing is significant for my argument not only because he is the main source for the early period but also because it influences later accounts.

istrative division within the kingdom' from 'the early years'.[25] Here as elsewhere Bede records the ecclesiastical reality but covers up its political cause, the tradition of joint kingship.

In this context, the case of Sæberht, mentioned above, deserves further scrutiny. Bede discusses his division of his kingdom among his three sons immediately after telling of Eadbald of Kent, who on ascending the throne renounced Christianity and 'took his father's wife', acts that Bede strongly condemns, and identifies as leading to Eadbald's 'divine punishment'.[26] While not attracting Bede's explicit censure, there are two hints in addition to this context that suggest he considers Sæberht's division wrong: the opening sentence contrasts the *regna perennia* ('eternal kingdom') which Sæberht sought on dying with his 'temporal kingdom' that he left to his three sons as heirs (*regni temporalis heredes*) and the entire account (and chapter) concludes with the remark that even following the death of the three, the East Saxons did not return *ad simplicitatem fidei et caritatis, quae est in Christo*.[27] While the explicit problem is that the three renounced Sæberht's faith, Bede also suggests that, like God's kingdom, earthly ones should be unified.

Other allusions to joint kingship in the *Ecclesiastical History* are brief. The mention of Hengist and Horsa, as Yorke notes, tells us more about the prevalence of the practice in the eighth century Kent, 'when the foundation legends were definitely in circulation' than it does about fifth century events.[28] In any case, Bede refers to them simply as *duces* (leaders) and immediately records that Horsa 'was killed in battle by the Britons',[29] avoiding the question of whether they reigned together. In a note, Colgrave and Mynors comment on the oblique reference to the earliest known rulers of the Hwicce, 'Eanfrith and his brother Eanhere were joint kings of the Hwicce under the overlordship of Æthelred of Mercia';[30] Patrick Sims-Williams, however, is more cautious, stating that the passage 'implies that Eanhere had been king and perhaps that Eanfrith had ruled jointly with him'.[31] Bede tells us only that Eafe, queen of the South Saxons, 'was the daughter of Eanfrith Eanhere's brother, both of whom were Christians, as were their people'.[32] While later in the *History* Bede does mention that Berhthun and Andhun 'held' (*tenuerunt*) the kingdom of the South Saxons, they came to power not through an orderly succession, but rather following the slaying of the previous king, Æthelwealh (Eafe's husband), by Cædwalla, whom they drove out of the kingdom.[33] It is telling that Bede identifies their rank only before they assumed power in the phrase *a ducibus regiis* ('by royal leaders')[34] and, as

25 'Joint Kingship in Kent', p. 5.
26 *Bede's Ecclesiastical History*, ed. Colgrave and Mynors, pp. 150–1.
27 *Ibid.*, pp. 154–5; 'to the simplicity of faith and love which is in Christ'.
28 Yorke, 'Joint Kingship in Kent', 4.
29 *Bede's Ecclesiastical History*, ed. Colgrave and Mynors, pp. 50–1.
30 *Ibid.*, p. 373.
31 'Hwicce, Kings of the', *ODNB*.
32 *Bede's Ecclesiastical History*, ed. Colgrave and Mynors, p. 373.
33 *Ibid.*, pp. 380–1.
34 *Ibid.*, pp. 380–1; they translate 'by two of the king's ealdormen'.

in the case of Horsa, immediately mentions that Berhthun was later killed by Cædwalla. Finally, Kent in Bede's day presents some problems that were difficult to overlook. The years 686–90 are particularly problematic because no one descended from Æthelbert occupied either throne; Bede glosses over this period with the phrase *regnum illud aliquot temporis spatium reges dubii uel externi disperdiderunt, donec legitimus rex Uictred, id est filius Ecgbercti, confortatus in regno, religione simul et industria gentem suam ab extranea inuasione liberaret* ('various usurpers or foreign kings plundered the kingdom for a certain space of time until the rightful king, Wihtred, son of Egbert, established himself on the throne and freed the nation from foreign invasion by his devotion and zeal').[35] Yet in the next book, he notes that Berhtwold became archbishop in 692 *regnantibus in Cantia Uictredo et Suaebhardo* ('while Wihtred and Swaefheard were ruling in Kent').[36] Apparently Bede considers Swæfheard a foreign king or usurper.[37] Bede does mention that at his death in 725 Wihtred 'left his three sons Æthelberht, Eadberht, and Alric, heirs of the kingdom' (*filios tres Aedilberctum, Eadberctum et Alricum reliquit heredes*).[38] Yet even here he does not specify how they reigned, or even that they reigned, together and he adds later in the chapter that all the kingdoms he has discussed and 'the other southern kingdoms which reach right up to the Humber, together with their various kings, are subject to Æthelbald, king of Mercia'.[39] Even if there was joint rule in Kent at this time, it was under the unified rule of Mercia. In all these cases, then, Bede avoids drawing attention to what was apparently common practice in his day.

Written Sources

Both the tradition of joint kingship and the Church's inclination against it provide a context for assessing the written records of Edgar's coming to power. Central are the three sharply diverging accounts in the *Chronicle*, which may be introduced here by referring only to the most significant witnesses: D, representing a more secular northern position, acknowledges the shared rule of Eadwig and Edgar established at Eadred's death; A, written from a southern stance, overlooks the division altogether much as Bede might have; and B (more significant for this argument than C because it is closer in date to the events), perhaps reflecting Æthelwold's and Dunstan's disapproval of the division, places the event two years into Eadwig's reign. Around these, other documents may be grouped, with the Æthelweard's *Chronicle* supporting A just as Æthelwold's account of Edgar's establishment of monasteries and the 'Life of Dunstan' agree with B. Indeed this grouping of the relevant documents may allow us to see the 'Sunbury Charter' (discussed below), which might at first appear to be an

---

[35] *Ibid.*, pp. 430–1.
[36] *Ibid.*, pp. 474–5.
[37] See Yorke, 'Joint Kinghsip in Kent', 7–8.
[38] *Bede's Ecclesiastical History*, ed. Colgrave and Mynors, pp. 556–7.
[39] *Ibid.*, p. 559.

unbiased confirmation of B's version of events, as also reflecting Æthelwold's and Dunstan's views. Once their differing agendas are understood, these written versions as a whole indicate that as Eadwig assumed control of the entire Anglo-Saxon kingdom in 955, Edgar was appointed his successor by assigning him rule in Mercia although he did not take up his position in the north until 957.

As the best witness to joint kingship having been planned in 955 and to the lack of any significant change in this scheme before 959, *ASC* D may serve as our starting point. Although the complicated question of its sources will require further attention in a moment, it is significant that scholars have long recognized D's ties to northern England; G. P. Cubbin, its most recent editor, credits Ealdred, bishop of Worcester from *c.* 1046 to 1062 and bishop of York from 1061 to 1069, 'not just for the creation of our MS but, through the exchanges of material involved, for giving a wider impulse to work on the *Anglo-Saxon Chronicle* generally in the late eleventh century'.[40] Its entry for 955 differs markedly from all the other versions:

> Her forðferde Eadred cyning,] he rest on Ealdan Mynstere.] Eadwig feng to Westseaxena rice,] Eadgar his broðor feng to Myrcena rice,] hi wæron Eadmundes suna cyninges] sancte Ælfgyfe.[41]

D also contains entries for both 957 (correctly 956) and 958 (correctly 957) but neither mentions Edgar:

> Her forðferde Wulfstan arcebiscop on .xvii. kalendas Ianuarii,] he wæs bebyrged on Undelan.] on þam ylcan geare wæs Dunstan abbod adræfed ofer sæ.
> Her on þissum geare Oda arcebiscop totwæmde Eadwi cyning] Ælgyfe, for þæm þe hi wæron to gesybbe.[42]

While none of these entries notes Edgar's subordinate role to Eadwig or his designation as Eadwig's successor, they do indicate an immediate division of the kingdom in 955, a kingdom that then remained stable until Eadwig's death in 959.

The entry for 955 in D is all the more remarkable in light of the comparable entries in *ASC* EF. In this case, E corresponds more closely to B, although this may be coincidence rather than proof of some direct relationship: 'Her Ædred cyning forðferde,] feng Eadwig to rice Eadmudes sunu.'[43] Missing here, obvi-

---

40 Cubbin, *MS D*, p. lxxi.

41 *Ibid.*, p. 45; 'In this year King Eadred died, and he rests in the Old Minster, and Eadwig succeeded to the kingdom of the West Saxons, and his brother Edgar to the kingdom of the Mercians. They were the sons of King Edmund and St Ælfgifu.' Translations from *ASC* here and elsewhere are from *EHD*.

42 Cubbin, *MS D*, p. 45; 'In this year Archbishop Wulfstan died on 16 December, and he was buried in Oundle. And in the same year Abbot Dunstan was driven across the sea. In this year Archbishop Oda separated King Eadwig and Ælfgifu, because they were too closely related.'

43 Irvine, *MS E*, p. 56; 'In this year King Eadred died and Eadwig, Edmund's son, succeeded.' See also the entry for 955 in the *Historia Regum*, attributed to Simeon of Durham: 'King

ously, is any reference to Edgar's attaining the throne in Mercia, but this may be due to accidental omission or a conscious simplification. In any case, E does not follow B's entry for 957, which asserts that Edgar became king of Mercia in that year, but does agree with D in recording Archbishop Wulfstan's death in 956 (957 in D) and, as will be discussed in a moment, in providing an expanded entry for 959. It may also be worth noting that in identifying Eadwig as Eadmund's son, E corresponds with D rather than B. Moreover the entry for 955 in F suggests that its common source with E may have included material similar to D:

> Her Eadred cing forðferde at Frome on sancte Clementes dæi, '] his lic restað [on] Ealdmyn[stre]'] he rixode teoðe healf gear;] þa feng Eadwi Eadmundes cinges sunu '] sancte Ælgiue' to ⟨Westse[xana rice]⟩ '] Eadgar 'his broðer' to M[y]rcena rice. Hi wæra[n]. ...'] he aflymde sancte Dunstan ut of lande.[44]

This entry is obviously a conflation of several traditions, and indeed the phrase in question is an insertion;[45] yet it supports D's claim that Edgar became king of the Mercians in 955. Like E, F then mentions only the death of Wulfstan (identifying him as archbishop of York) before including the expanded entry on Edgar's rule also found in D and E (dated 958 not 959).

All the versions of the *Chronicle* begin their entries on 959 (958 in A and F) noting Eadwig's death and Edgar's succeeding to the kingdom. Yet D, E and F continue with surprisingly long summary of Edgar's reign.[46] Whitelock notes that 'this passage is written in alliterative prose', and suggests that it 'is in the style of Archbishop Wulfstan of York' and that it 'is influenced by' a remark by Ælfric in his epilogue to Judges.[47] If these suggestions are correct, the passage as we have it would not have been written until the late tenth century, and so does not itself represent a contemporary response to the events of 959. Yet its placement in these versions of the *Chronicle* requires explanation, since it reads like a concluding judgment on a reign rather than the account of a single year. This perspective, I would argue, if not all the details in the entry as it now stands, would have made sense in Mercia in 959 as Edgar moved south

---

Eadred died, and Eadwig, son of the Edmund who had reigned before him succeeded', trans. *EHD*, p. 280. Keynes describes this section as the Second Set of Northern Annals (annals 888–957); see his *Anglo-Saxon England: A Bibliographical Handbook for Students of Anglo-Saxon History*, 6th ed. (Cambridge, 2005). k, p. 15 (B34).

44 Baker, *MS F*, p. 81; 'In this year King Eadred died at Frome on St. Clement's day and his body rests in the Old Minster, and he ruled nine and a half years; and then Eadwig, the son of King Eadmund and of St. Ælfgifu, succeeded to the kingdom of the West Saxons, and his brother Edgar to the Kingdom of the Mercians. They were ... And he drove St. Dunstan from the land.'

45 In the first edition of *EHD*, Dorothy Whitelock noted this reading in F and commented, 'it may have been in the archetype of "E"' (p. 205, n. 2); in the second edition, she comments only that 'this clause occurs as a marginal entry in "F"' and that 'the division of the kingdom did not take place until 957' (p. 224).

46 Cubbin, *MS D*, p. 45; translation in *EHD*.

47 *EHD*, p. 225, n. 4.

to assume command of the entire kingdom: a briefer record at this point in a common source for D, E and F may well have led to the substitution of a later and fuller summation. By representing a northern view, D and, to a lesser extent, E and F confirm that Edgar became king of Mercia in 955.

While not actually mentioning Edgar before 959, the A version provides some support for this interpretation, suggesting as it does that from a southern perspective nothing significant happened between the deaths of Eadred and Eadwig. Although still a matter of dispute, many scholars have associated this version with Winchester, and indeed Janet Bately, its most recent editor, notes that the section from 924–975 'contains a number of annals found in A only, many of them containing material with Winchester connexions'.[48] Even in the entry for 955, its south-western leanings in the tenth century and later provenance in Canterbury may be suggested by the identification of the place, Frome in Somerset, of Eadred's death and by the record, added in a late eleventh-century hand,[49] of Dunstan's expulsion from England:

> Her forþferde Eadred cining on Sancte Clementes mæssedæg on Frome, ꝺ he rixsade teoþe healf gear; ꝺ feng Eadwig to rice, Eadmundes sunu cinges [ꝺ aflæmde Sancte Dunstan ut of lande.][50]

Although lacking D's remark about the burial of Eadred in Old Minster, A preserves the local knowledge of when (St Clement's day) and where the king actually died; at the end of the next century a Canterbury scribe saw fit to add that the former archbishop, Dunstan, had been expelled by the new king. The authority of the initial entry is of course enhanced by likelihood that its writing is contemporary with the events described. In any case, the next entry in A corresponds to the first sentence from D (959), yet also specifies the day Eadwig died: 'Her forðferde Eadwig cyng on kalendas Octobris, ꝺ Eadgar his broðor feng to rice'.[51] A, then, provides no evidence for any political transition in the north in 957. Indeed, by presenting the reigns of Eadred, Eadwig, and Edgar as one following the next it engages in some political propaganda of its own, refusing to admit that any division or joint rule occurred.

A similar view of Eadwig's unbroken reign appears in Æthelweard's *Chronicle*, written perhaps by Eadwig's brother-in-law.[52] Following Eadred's death, it relates:

---

48 Bately, *MS A*, pp. xc–xci. She also cites Malcolm Parkes's suggestion that Bishop Ælfheah II of Winchester may have brought the manuscript to Canterbury when he became archbishop in 1006; see p. xiv.

49 Bately writes in a note, 'Addition in hand 7 on the same line as the annal-number "956" but in fact continuing annal 955'; *MS A*, p. 75.

50 Bately, *MS A*, pp. 74–5; 'In this year King Eadred died on St Clement's day at Frome and he had ruled nine and a half years; and then Eadwig, the son of King Edmund, succeeded to the kingdom [and exiled St Dunstan from the land].'

51 Bately, *MS A*, p. 75; 'In this year King Eadwig died and his brother Edgar succeeded to the kingdom.'

52 See the entry on him by P. Wormald, *ODNB*.

Quin successor eius Eaduuig in regnum, qui et præ nimia etenim pulchritudine Pancali sortitus est nomen a uulgo secundi. Tenuit namque quadriennio per regnum amandus.[53]

As in A, there is no mention of any revolt in the north; instead Æthelweard praises Eadwig's rule and suggests he was well-liked.

By asserting that Edgar began to rule in Mercia in 957, *ASC* B presents a serious challenge to the claim that joint kingship was planned for Eadwig and Edgar in 955. Yet there are, I believe, several related ways to respond to this evidence. The first is to acknowledge that something did happen in this year, although, I would argue, it was nothing more than Edgar's actual taking up of his position, already determined in 955, as king of Mercia. If so, even the B version, standing as it does between D and A, provides some support for joint rule. Moreover, the entries themselves do not indicate the division was contentious and indeed by identifying Edgar as an ætheling they may even suggest that it was part of a pre-arranged plan.[54] Yet it still seems likely to me that these entries have been influenced by sentiments similar to those of Æthelwold and Dunstan, both of whom (on the evidence of the Old English account of Edgar's establishment of monasteries and B's *Vita S. Dunstani*) used the Church's inherent bias against joint kingship to disregard the initial decision in 955, instead focusing on the events of 957 as a way to criticise Eadwig.

The B version, like A, is a particularly important witness because its section on this period was written at around the same time as the events it describes. Although surrounded by entries both attributed to 956, the one for 957 states clearly that Edgar came to the Mercian throne in this year:

Her forðferde Eadred cing, ⁊ Eadwig feng to rice.
Her Eadgar æþeling feng to Myrcna rice.
Her forðferde Eadwig cing; ⁊ Eadgar his broðor feng to rice ægðer on Westseaxum ge on Myrcum ge on Norðhymbrum, ⁊ he wæs þa .xvi. wintre.[55]

Here, as indeed in the *Chronicle* as a whole and elsewhere, *feng to rice* is used when a king's rule begins and so these entries cannot be used to claim that Edgar merely took up his responsibilities (already conferred two years earlier) in 957.[56]

---

[53] Campbell, *Æthelweard*, p. 55; 'His successor in the kingdom was Eadwig, and he for his great beauty got the nick-name 'All-fair' from the common people. He held the kingdom continuously for four years, and deserved to be loved.'

[54] On this term, see Dumville, 'Ætheling'.

[55] Taylor, *MS B*, p. 54; '955 In this year King Eadred died and Eadwig succeeded to the kingdom. 957 In this year the atheling Edgar succeeded to the kingdom of the Mercians. 959 In this year King Eadwig died and his brother Edgar succeeded to the kingdom both in Wessex and in Mercia and in Northumbria and he was then 16 years old.'

[56] See *DOE*, s.v., 12.a. Relevant to this discussion is the use of the phrase to describe Edward's accession in 975 even though, as the poem *The Death of Edgar* specifies, he was *cild unweaxen* (11b; 'a child ungrown') at the time; *MS A*, ed. Bately, p. 77.

Yet the term ætheling at least draws attention to Edgar's eligibility to the throne, and could reflect his position in line to succeed his brother.[57]

In any case, by placing the division of the kingdom two years into Eadwig's reign, this version of the *ASC* corresponds to the position taken by two of the leading religious reformers of the day, Æthelwold and, assuming that his biographer represents his position, Dunstan. In his account of Edgar's establishment of monasteries, Æthelwold contrasts Eadwig, who 'þurh his cildhades nyteness þis rice tostencte] his annesse todælde',[58] and Edgar, who,

> þurh Godes gyfe ealne Angelcynnes anweald begeat] þæs rices twislunge eft to annesse brohte,] swa gesundlice ealles weold þæt þa þe on æran timan lifes wæron] his hyldran gemundon] heora dæda gefyrn tocneowan, þearle swiðe wundredon] wafiende cwædon: 'Hit is la formicel godes wunder þæt þysum cildgeongum cynincge þus gesundfullice eallu þing underðeodde synt on his cynelicum anwealde.'[59]

Æthelwold had found ways to accommodate Eadwig, even apparently acknowledging his marriage to Ælfgifu, whom he was forced to give up in 958.[60] Yet this contrast between the two brothers suggests that the mechanics of joint kingship seems to him to have implied a division of the kingdom that is at odds with the idea of divine rule.

B's *Life of Dunstan*, as one might expect given the animosity between Eadwig and Dunstan,[61] makes this criticism even harsher. It begins its account of these events first by disparaging Eadwig as 'a youth indeed in age and endowed with little wisdom in government' and then states, in contradiction to *ASC* D, that when he came to power 'he filled up the numbers and names of kings among both peoples' (*in utraque plebe regum numeros nominaque suppleret*), a clause Whitelock explains as meaning he ruled over both Wessex and Mercia.[62] It then offers a detailed account of the division of the kingdom that continues to denigrate Eadwig now in contrast to Edgar:

> Factum est autem ut rex præfatus in prætereuntibus annis penitus a brumali populo relinqueretur contemptus, quoniam in commisso regimine insipienter egisset, sagaces vel sapientes odio vanitatis disperdens, et ignaros qosque sibi consimiles studio dilectionis adsciscens. Hunc ita omium conspiratione

---

57 *DOE*, s.v.; and Dumville, 'Ætheling'.
58 *Councils & Synods*, p. 146; 'had through the ignorance of childhood dispersed his kingdom and divided its unity'.
59 *Councils & Synods*; 'obtained by God's grace the whole dominion of England, and brought back to unity the divisions of the kingdom, and ruled everything so prosperously that those who had lived in former times and remembered his ancestors and knew their deeds of old, wondered very greatly and said in amazement: It is indeed a very great miracle of God that all things in his royal dominion are thus prosperously subjected to this youthful king.'
60 See Yorke, *Æthelwold*, pp. 78–80.
61 This source provides the account of Eadwig leaving his coronation feast to cavort with a mother and daughter, and Dunstan escorting him back to the assembly; see *EHD*, p. 901.
62 *EHD*, p. 900; see n. 7 for Whitelock's literal translation.

relictum, elegere sibi, Deo dictante, Eadgarum ejusdem Eadwigi germanum in regem, qui virga imperiali injustos juste percuteret, benignos autem sub eadem æquitatis virgula pacifice custodieret. Sicque universo populo testante publica res regum ex diffinitione sagacium sejuncta est, ut famosum flumen Tamesæ regnum disterminaret amborum.[63]

The suggestion here that the division itself is wrong becomes clearer in B's account of Edgar's reuniting of the realm:

> Interea germanus ejusdem Eadgari, quia justa Dei sui judicia deviando dereliquit, novissimum flatum misera morte exspiravit; et regnum illius ipse, velut æwiid jæres ab utroque populo electus, suscepit, divisaque regnorum jura in unum sibi sceptrum subdendo copulavit.[64]

The dynamics of the division are more spectacularly portrayed, but the sentiment is the same: a divided kingdom is not part of God's plan.

The complicated history of an estate at Sunbury (Middlesex), which might at first appear to offer a disinterested, and therefore reliable, confirmation of the division of the kingdom midway through Eadwig's reign, should, I would argue, be viewed in this same manner. Indeed, the document that recounts this history survives as charter VIII in the collection of Westminster Abbey (S 1447),[65] presumably because Dunstan gave the estate to the monks;[66] in any case, internal evidence establishes that it was written after Dunstan bought the estate, probably in 968,[67] and perhaps after a further challenge to his ownership of it.[68] The events at issue in this paper are mentioned because, on ascending the throne, Eadwig asserted his right to the estate since Æthelstan, the person living on it,

---

[63] Stubbs, *Dunstan*, pp. 35–6; 'It came about that the aforesaid king in the passage of years was wholly deserted by the northern people, being despised because he acted foolishly in the government committed to him, ruining with vain hatred the shrewd and wise, and admitting with loving zeal the ignorant and those like himself. When he had been thus deserted by the agreement of them all, they chose as king for themselves by God's guidance the brother of the same Eadwig, Edgar, who should strike down the wicked with the imperial rod, but peacefully guard the good under the same rod of equity. And thus in the witness of the whole people the state was divided between the kings as determined by wise men, so that the famous river Thames separated the realms of both', trans. Whitelock, *EHD*, p. 901.

[64] Stubbs, *Dunstan*, p. 36; 'Meanwhile the brother of this same Edgar, because he turned from and deserted the just judgments of his God, breathed his last by a miserable death, and Edgar received his kingdom, being elected by both peoples as true heir, and united the divided rule of the kingdoms, subjecting them to himself under one sceptre', trans. *EHD*, p. 902.

[65] See S 406. More recent information can be found in *The New Regesta Regum Anglorum: A Searchable Edition of the Corpus of Anglo-Saxon Royal Diplomas 670–1066*, devised by S. Miller (2001); available at http://www.trin.cam.ac.uk/chartwww/NewRegReg.html.

[66] *History of Middlesex*, ed. J. S. Cockburn, H. P. F. King and K. G. T. McDonnell (London, 1969) [Victoria History of the Counties of England, ed. R. B. Pugh], p. 108.

[67] I follow the analysis of A. J. Robertson, who notes that Edgar's grant of ten hides at Sunbury to Ælfheah (S 702) survives and is dated 962; our document tells us that Dunstan purchased the estate from Ælfheah six years later; see Robertson, *Charters*, p. 338.

[68] See Robertson's note on lines 15f, *Charters*, p. 399.

had failed to pay a fine to his uncle, King Eadred; Eadwig then gave it to one of his followers who ejected Æthelstan. The story continues,

gemang þam getidde þæt Myrce gecuran Eadgar to cynge .] him anweald ge-sealdan ealra cynerihta . þa gesohte Æðelstan Eadgar cyng] bæd domes.[69]

Although the language here indicates an abrupt shift in the rule of Mercia during Eadwig's reign, Æthelstan's action may have been motivated by nothing more than Edgar's assuming his responsibility at this time. Moreover, while Edgar did not return the estate to Eadwig's choice, he too insisted that Æthelstan pay the fine and, when he could not, Edgar awarded the estate to Earl Æthelstan, suggesting some continuity in policy.

In any case, since these events prove to be marginal to Dunstan's claim to the land they reinforce the fact that the charter was written from Dunstan's perspective. Earl Æthelstan then sold the estate to Ecgferth, who 'unequivocally committed both the estate and the title-deeds, with the cognisance of the king to Archbishop Dunstan, in order that he might act as guardian to his widow and child'.[70] Yet the land still did not come under Dunstan's control because at Ecgferth's death and in opposition to Dunstan's direct request Edgar again took possession of it, granting it to Earl Ælfheah, from whom Dunstan finally purchased it for 200 mancuses. Dunstan's perspective is evident and so it is not surprising that the charter reflects his slant on the events of 957 as well: this is simply the way Dunstan tells this story.

Charters

More than 120 charters survive from the final years of Eadred's reign (950–5) to Edgar's ascent to the throne of all of Wessex in 959 and so a full review of this material is beyond the scope of this essay.[71] Yet, a few points culled mainly from others, particularly Simon Keynes, should be discussed since the charters do establish that some division took place in 957. Yet they also provide some support for the claims that Eadwig and Edgar were treated similarly in Eadred's final years; that Edgar played an active and supportive role during the first two years of his brother's rule; that Edgar's status as heir apparent was recognized; and that after taking up his responsibilities in Mercia, Edgar still viewed his rule more generally as over the English. This evidence, then, is compatible with the establishment of Eadwig and Edgar as joint kings in 955.

In discussing the charters of Eadred issued between 950 and 955, Keynes notes several distinctive features, but 'the most curious', he asserts, 'is the

---

[69] *Ibid.*, pp. 90–1; 'In the meantime it happened that the Mercians chose Edgar as king, and gave him control of all the royal prerogatives. Then Æthelstan betook himself to King Edgar and asked for judgment.'

[70] *Ibid.*, p. 93.

[71] In this discussion of the charters, I have relied on the *New Regesta Regum Anglorum* for both primary and secondary materials.

absence of the king's name from the list itself, as if he had not been present when the diploma was drawn up'.[72] He suggests that 'the explanation may lie either in the king's illness or in the turbulent political history of the period: perhaps King Eadred was too ill to attend meetings of his councillors, or if he was not, he was possibly preoccupied with the subjugation of the Northumbrian kingdom, and in either case he may have authorized an agency independent of his own entourage to draw up diplomas on his behalf'.[73] During such troubled times, it may well have seemed sensible to use joint kingship to clarify the next two steps in the succession. Moreover, several of these charters indicate that Eadwig and Edgar were indeed being treated as equals. A grant (S 565) of land to Ælfsige, bishop of Winchester, in 955 is attested by Eadwig *cliton* and, immediately following (as in the other cases cited here), Eadgar *cliton*; another (S 569) to Uhtred (also in 955) by Eadwig *cliton* and Eadgar atheling; and a third (S 570) to Brihtric (956 for 953–5) by Adwi *cliton* and Adgar *cliton*.[74] While other charters from this period list only Eadwig as *cliton* or atheling and Edgar as his brother (S 566, 571, and 572), there is some evidence that the two were being treated in a way compatible with joint kingship.

Around sixty charters survive from the first year of Eadwig's reign, and Edgar witnessed most of them, usually immediately following his brother although sometimes his name is third. In most (around forty) he is identified as Eadwig's brother, and nine of these (S 583, 587, 588, 595, 602, 609, 622, 624 and 625) specify that he attested *celeriter*, 'quickly' and so, presumably, with enthusiasm. If not a forgery, one of the other charters (S 605) from this group, perhaps from 955 or early 956, is particularly interesting because it identifies Edgar not only as *clito* but also with the phrase *adolphus deuotus*, 'devoted brother'. In any case, Edgar is identified in eleven others (S 589, 591, 593, 594, 597, 614, 629, 630, 637, 661 and 666) with the phrase *indoles clito* (or sometimes either *indoles* or *clito*). The impression created by these attestations is that Edgar played an active and supportive role in Eadwig's government, which in return recognized his special status.

There are many fewer charters from 957, some eleven in total, but they too present a suggestive picture since Edgar does not appear in roughly half (S 639, 640, 642, 644 and 647). He is always identified as Eadwig's brother in the ones he attested (S 641, 643, 645, 646 and 649), and all also specify that he did so *celeriter*. Yet perhaps the most remarkable of these charters is the grant of forty hides of land to Archbishop Oda at Ely (S 646) on 9 May since it indicates, as Dorothy Whitelock and Simon Keynes have noted,[75] that Edgar's move to Mercia took place sometime after this date. As one might expect, Edgar did not attest any of the charters from the remaining years of Eadwig's reign and

---

[72] Keynes, *Diplomas*, p. 46.

[73] *Ibid.*

[74] See also S 576, which cannot be authentic as it stands, yet contains the suggestive attestation, 'ego Eadwig et Eadgar indoles hec confirmauimus'.

[75] Reported by *CTCE*, p. 278.

according to Whitelock and Keynes the witnesses on these documents were all from south of Thames.[76]

Edgar's own charters of 958–9 confirm that he ruled in Mercia but contain some suggestions that he considered himself more generally as a king of the English. Whitelock has pointed out that they do not refer to Eadwig nor does Eadwig witness them; and Whitelock and Keynes have noted that they are attested by officials from north of the Thames.[77] In most, as one would expect, Edgar is identified as King of the Mercians, but there are a few in which he claimed a more general title. In two grants of 958, one to Ælfheah (S 674) and the other to Oscytel (S 679), he appears as 'industrius Anglorum rex' in the text and attested as 'rex Anglorum'. Similar titles appear in three more doubtful charters (S 670–3). Taken as a whole, then, the charter evidence indicates not only that Edgar ruled in Mercia from 957 but that this transition was planned in the last years of Eadred's reign and was put into effect with little or no disruption to the state.

Coins

Since they establish that Eadwig remained in control of the mints both south and north of the Thames throughout the period, the many coins from 955–9 are compatible with the theory that joint rule was planned from the beginning; yet recognizing this possibility may allow numismatists to understand some anomalies. Working under the assumption that the kingdom was divided in 957,[78] Blunt, Stewart and Lyon specifically looked for evidence of coins minted by Edgar, but did not discover them.[79] Instead, what they found was a volume of coins minted by Eadwig that was simply too great to force into a two-year period as well as a mule that spans the coinage of Eadwig and Edgar, indicating Eadwig's continued minting in the north after 957.[80] It seems unlikely that Edgar would wrest control of Mercia from Eadwig only then to allow him to continue minting his own coins. On the other hand, recognizing their shared power may offer new explanations for cases such as Hunred, a moneyer active under Eadred, who apparently all but stopped minting under Eadwig, yet who then minted some coins for Edgar.[81] Under a joint rule we could imagine some coins minted for Edgar perhaps even as early as 955.

---

[76] *Ibid.*
[77] *Ibid.*
[78] Although it should be noted again that their correspondence with Whitelock and Keynes introduced the approach developed in this paper.
[79] *CTCE*, p. 280.
[80] *Ibid.*, p. 278.
[81] *Ibid.*, p. 148.

Conclusion

Recognizing joint kingship at the core of the events that led to Edgar's sole rule over the Anglo-Saxons allows us to understand the competing claims of the written record and may provide new opportunities for assessing the related charters and coins. The D version of the *Chronicle* suggests that joint rule was planned in 955; A indicates that Eadwig's reign continued uninterrupted until his death in 959; and B allows us to perceive that Edgar's responsibilities in Mercia began in 957. Each is accurate in its own way. Moreover, the sources related to B, Æthelwold's account of the establishment of monasteries and the *Life of Dunstan*, reveal how these events, combined with the Church's aversion to joint rule, could be slanted to criticize Eadwig, a slant that provides a context for the 'Sunbury Charter'. Although they will require further study, the charters and coins from the period appear to support this theory as well. Yet one is still left with the impression that the confusion would not have arisen had joint kingship been more common, as it had been previously, in the late Anglo-Saxon period. While politically savvy, Eadwig and Edgar, ruling together between 955 and 959, were out of key with their time.[82]

[82] When I proposed reading on this subject, I was unaware that it had caught the interest of Professor Simon Keynes, who, I now realize, has been gathering information on it for many years. I would like to thank him for his response in Manchester and for improving this paper indirectly through his guide, *Anglo-Saxon England: A Bibliographical Handbook*, 6th ed. (Cambridge, 2005)). Fred A. Cazel, Jr, Andrew M. Pfrenger, Mercedes Salvador and Barbara Yorke are also to be thanked for their help. My own interest grew out of work on *Beowulf*; see 'The Politics of Succession in *Beowulf* and Anglo-Saxon England', *Speculum* 80 (2005), 709–41.

III

Edgar, 959–975

6

The Women in Edgar's Life

BARBARA YORKE

[Cnut] was at Wilton one Pentecost, when, with his customary bloody-mind-edness, he burst into a frightful peal of laughter against the virgin herself [St Edith]: he would never believe that the daughter of King Edgar was a saint, seeing that the king had surrendered himself to his vices and was a complete slave to his lusts, while he ruled his subjects more like a tyrant.[1]

THIS story from William of Malmesbury neatly encapsulates some of the features and problems of studying King Edgar's relationships with women. There are many things that we do not know about the reign of Edgar, but we are relatively well-informed about some of the women who were significant to him. With a shortage of other narrative material, his relations with women were a means through which historians of the Middle Ages sought to elucidate aspects of his reign and find something of his elusive personality. The concentration in more recent years has been on the women themselves. The study of Edgar's kinswomen and wives has had a major role to play in Pauline Stafford's pioneering studies of the political and family roles of Anglo-Saxon royal women that are a major influence behind this paper.[2] However, its main aim is to return to the issue of what we can learn about Edgar himself, and his shifting reputation, through the women associated with him.

The female relatives and wives who played significant roles at different points in Edgar's life can be introduced briefly. Edgar's mother Ælfgifu died in c. 944,[3] that is shortly after, and perhaps therefore as a result of, his own birth. Little is known of her or her paternal background, but her own mother Wynflæd has left

---

[1] William of Malmesbury, *The Deeds of the Bishops of England (Gesta Pontificum Anglorum)*, trans. D. Preest (Woodbridge, 2002), ch. 87, p. 127.

[2] In particular, P. Stafford, 'Sons and Mothers, Family Politics in the Early Middle Ages', *Medieval Women*, ed. D. Baker, Studies in Church History, Subsidia 1 (Oxford, 1978), pp. 79–100; 'The King's Wife in Wessex 800–1066', *Past and Present* 91 (1981), 3–27; *Queens, Concubines and Dowagers: The King's Wife in the Early Middle Ages* (Athens, GA, 1983); *Queen Emma and Queen Edith: Queenship and Women's Power in Eleventh-Century England* (Oxford, 1997).

[3] Campbell, *Æthelweard*, p. 54; for discussion of the date of her death see S. Keynes, 'King Alfred the Great and Shaftesbury Abbey', *Studies in the Early History of Shaftesbury Abbey*, ed. L. Keen (Dorchester, 1999), pp. 17–72, at 65, n. 78.

a more significant imprint in contemporary documentation.[4] She seems to have had particular connections with Shaftesbury abbey, which had been founded by King Alfred, where a cult of her daughter had been established by, or during, the reign of Edgar, for it is referred to by Lantfred of Winchester writing in the early 970s.[5] The dominant female figure of Edgar's early years (both in his life and in the kingdom) was his paternal grandmother Eadgifu, the third wife of King Edward the Elder who was a member of a powerful ealdormanic family from Kent.[6] The women whom Edgar's father and grandfather married cemented ties between the throne and important noble families, and nurtured saints' cults that enhanced the special status of the royal line.[7] One can also mention in this latter context Eadburh, the daughter of Eadgifu and thus Edgar's aunt who was a nun and subsequently a saint at Nunnaminster, which had been founded by her paternal grandmother Ealhswith, wife of King Alfred.[8]

The unravelling of King Edgar's own multiple marriages is a complex matter and is the subject of some controversy. However, from the various sources that are available a case can be made for recognizing three marriages during Edgar's brief life, in addition to other temporary liaisons. Little is known of his first wife, Æthelflæd, known as *candida* (white) or *eneda* (duck) who is only named by William of Malmesbury and John of Worcester.[9] Her father is said to have been Ealdorman Ordmær, although no ealdorman of that name is recorded elsewhere.[10] Æthelflæd may have died *c.* 960 after giving birth to Edgar's eldest known son, Edward (subsequently king and martyr). Goscelin's *Vita S. Edithe* indicates that Edgar's second wife was Wulfthryth.[11] His *Vita* of her cousin

---

4   S 744, and probably S 485 and S 1539 (will); for the probability that these documents all concern the same person and that she was the maternal grandmother of Edgar (as named in S 744), see Keynes, 'King Alfred and Shaftesbury', 43–5; *Shaft*, pp. xxvi–vii and nos. 13 and 26.

5   Lantfred of Winchester, *Translatio et Miracula S. Swithuni*, in *The Cult of St Swithun*, ed. M. Lapidge, Winchester Studies 4.ii (Oxford, 2003), pp. 328–9.

6   B. A. E. Yorke, 'Edward as Ætheling', *Edward the Elder 899–924*, ed. N. J. Higham and D. H. Hill (London, 2001), pp. 25–39, at 32–4. S 562, *Shaft*, 17, seems to suggest that Eadgifu may also have had an association with Shaftesbury.

7   M. A. Meyer, 'Patronage of the West Saxon Royal Nunneries in Late Anglo-Saxon England', *Revue Bénédictine* 91 (1981), 332–58; A. Thacker, 'Dynastic Monasteries and Family Cults: Edward the Elder's Sainted Kindred', *Edward the Elder*, ed. Higham and Hill, pp. 248–63.

8   S. J. Ridyard, *The Royal Saints of Anglo-Saxon England: A Study of West Saxon and East Anglian Cults* (Cambridge, 1988), pp. 96–139.

9   William of Malmesbury, *Gesta Regum Anglorum*, I, ed. R. A. B. Mynors, R. M. Thomson and M. Winterbottom (Oxford, 1998), pp. 260–1; JW, *Chronicon*, II.416–17.

10 A. Williams, *Æthelred the Unready: The Ill-Counselled King* (London, 2003), pp. 2–5, where doubt is expressed about Æthelflæd's very existence and it is suggested that Edward may have been a son of Edgar's second wife Wulfthryth.

11 A. Wilmart, 'La Légende de Ste Édith en prose et vers par le moine Goscelin', *Analecta Bollandiana* 56 (1938), 5–101, 265–307, at 41 (subsequently cited as *Vita Edithe*); 'Goscelin's Legend of Edith', trans. M. Wright and K. Loncar, *Writing the Wilton Women. Goscelin's Legend of Edith and Liber Confortatorius*, ed. S. Hollis (Turnhout, 2004), pp.17–93, at 26.

Wulfhild, whom at one time Edgar had intended to marry, suggests that they were descended from a significant noble house, probably with long-established links with the ealdormanry of Wiltshire and the nunnery of Wilton to which Wulfthryth withdrew as abbess when her marriage was dissolved soon after the birth of Edith in *c.* 963.[12] Edgar was then free to marry his third wife, Ælfthryth, in 964 or 965 (the most secure date we have for any of these unions).[13] The dating is tight to enable Edgar to have had three wives between 961 and 964, but not impossible, particularly when it is appreciated that the date of 964 often cited for the birth of Edith is only an approximate date produced by the first editor of her *Vita*. The date range that can be estimated for Edith's birth is 962 x 965.[14]

Ælfthryth's father Ordgar was appointed ealdorman of the south-west at the time of her marriage to Edgar.[15] She bore the king two sons, Edmund, who died in 971,[16] and Æthelred Unræd. Edith is the only daughter certainly born to Edgar,[17] but when he married Ælfthryth she seems to have been already the step-mother of Ælfflæd, the daughter of the first marriage of her previous husband, Ealdorman Æthelwold of East Anglia. The couple made provision for Ælfflæd by founding the nunnery of Romsey (Hants) (where their son Edmund was to be buried) and Ælfflæd was venerated there as a saint by the early eleventh century.[18]

The study of Edgar through his women is aided by the fact that many of the sources ostensibly referring to them are tacitly writing about Edgar himself. References to women in early medieval sources are sufficiently limited as to raise questions about the reasons behind those that do exist. They may not be a simple reflection of the power of individual women for women could be 'good

---

[12] M. Esposito, 'La Vie de Saint Wulfilda par Goscelin de Cantorbery', *Analecta Bollandiana* 32 (1913), 10–26, at 14 (henceforth cited as *Vita Wulfhilde*). I am grateful to Shashi Jayakumar for pointing out that their grandfather Wihtbrord is probably the man who witnessed charters of Edward the Elder and is mentioned in the Fonthill letter. They may be linked with the family of an earlier Wulfthryth, the wife of King Æthelred I: Yorke, 'Edward as Ætheling', pp. 35–7.

[13] *ASC* D, s.a. 965: Cubbin, *MS D*, p. 46; JW, *Chronicon*, II.416–17; S 725.

[14] For further discussion of the dates, see B. A. E. Yorke, 'The Legitimacy of St. Edith', *Haskins Society Journal* 11 (2003 for 1998), 97–113, at 102–4.

[15] Williams, *Æthelred the Unready*, pp. 2–3; P. Stafford, 'Ælfthryth', *ODNB*.

[16] Edmund was buried at Romsey; see *ASC* 971: Earle and Plummer, I.118–19.

[17] S 1449, a vernacular account 970 x 975 of the adjustment of the boundaries of the three minsters in Winchester that was added to the *Codex Wintoniensis* in the mid-twelfth century, identifies Abbess Eadgifu as the king's daughter. The king in question would presumably have been Edgar, but it is possible that the phrase is a later interpolation by someone who has confused Eadgifu with Edith (Eadgyth); see Rumble, *Property and Piety*, no. 7, pp. 140–3, especially n. 16.

[18] D. Rollason, 'Lists of Saints' Resting-places in Anglo-Saxon England', *ASE* 7 (1978), 61–94, at 92; B. A. E. Yorke, *Nunneries and the Anglo-Saxon Royal Houses* (London, 2003), p. 78; however, the background of Ælfflæd can only be deduced from rather garbled references in her later medieval Lives in BL, Landsdowne 436, fol. 43b and *Acta Sanctorum* 12 October, 918–26 [John Capgrave], and there is some confusion over whether the correct form of her name is Ælfflæd or Æthelflæd.

to think with', a means of saying as much about the men they were associated with as the women themselves.[19] Such an approach is apparent in the quotation from William of Malmesbury's *Gesta Pontificum* cited at the beginning of the paper where a reputed attack by Cnut on the sanctity of Edith has been used to highlight her father's reputation for immorality. The purposes of the sources that look at Edgar's relations with women varied over time and within different genres, and this paper will discuss in different sections the evidence from the tenth, eleventh and twelfth centuries. However, differences between sources may not simply be the result of variations in genre or over time, but a reflection of multiple narratives concerning Edgar that were a by-product of the political tensions of his reign in which his relations with certain women played a major part.

Contemporary Sources from the Reign of Edgar

Documents from the lifetime of Edgar are primarily records of administration or ceremonial which do not so much provide a narrative of his relations with women as opportunities to compare their status with each other and that of Edgar himself. Edgar made his first public appearance in charter witness-lists in the company of his formidable grandmother Eadgifu who seems to have been responsible for the upbringing of himself and his elder brother Eadwig after the early death of their mother.[20] Edgar honoured his grandmother at the start of his reign and restored lands to her that had been confiscated by his brother Eadwig.[21] She must have been quite elderly by this time, and Ælfthryth seems to have taken over as the dominant queen at Edgar's court after her marriage in 964. In the New Minster foundation charter of 966 Eadgifu witnesses after Ælfthryth,[22] and this was probably her last public appearance for she died soon after.[23] Eadgifu and Ælfthryth both seem to have been dominant among the women of the royal court during their lifetimes, eclipsing any other royal wives.[24] The enhanced position of queen in the tenth century, in contrast to the apparently depressed position of queenship in ninth-century Wessex, no doubt owed much to Carolingian practice where the queen had specific ceremonial and other duties as part of the administration of the royal court. But the enhanced position may also have been developed specifically for the widowed Eadgifu as part of an alliance with her stepson Æthelstan in which she supported his position and he recognized her sons as his heirs. Very unusually for a medieval

---

19 J. Nelson, 'Women and the Word in the Earlier Middle Ages', *Women in the Church*, Studies in Church History 27 (Oxford, 1990), 53–78.
20 A. Campbell, *Encomium Emmae Reginae*, Camden 3rd series 72 (London, 1949), appendix 2, pp. 62–5; see also Stafford, *Queen Emma and Queen Edith*, pp. 199–204.
21 S 811, 1211 and 1212.
22 S 745; *WinchNM*, no. 23, pp. 95–111.
23 P. Stafford, 'Eadgifu', *ODNB*.
24 Stafford 'King's Wife'; Stafford, *Queen Emma and Queen Edith*, pp. 162–206.

monarch Æthelstan never married and it is possible that that was part of their agreement. Ælfthryth therefore inherited from Eadgifu a position as dominant queen that had perhaps come to be seen as necessary for the smooth running of the court. Ælfthryth was succeeded in her turn by her daughter-in-law Emma of Normandy under whom the potential for turning queenship into an office was taken further.

Ælfthryth as Edgar's longest-serving wife also had more opportunity to appear in the contemporary documentation from his reign than his two first wives. But it is important not to overemphasize her position during his reign. While Edgar was alive, Ælfthryth witnessed charters less regularly than Eadgifu had done at the height of her powers and in a less prestigious position. She appears to have achieved greater prominence during the minority of her son Æthelred between 979 and 984, and in the 990s where she appears with her grandsons for whom she, like Eadgifu before her, seems to have had responsibility. It was as queen-mothers that both Eadgifu and Ælfthryth enjoyed their highest standing. It was during her regency for her son Æthelred that Ælfthryth was able to bestow favours on her family and other supporters, and intervene effectively in land disputes.[25] She does not appear to have been as influential during Edgar's lifetime.

In reviewing the evidence for Ælfthryth as queen we need to try to distinguish enhancement of the queen's position as part of the wider development of regalian rights and ideology, focused on Edgar himself, from attempts to promote the position of Ælfthryth as a means of manipulating the succession of one of her sons which may have been the aim of a rather more limited factional group. One of the interesting questions is whether Edgar himself supported their preference. The interest of the monastic reformers in developing the Christian context of kingship naturally included enhancement of the position of the queen as consort to the king, a development that owed much to Carolingian and Ottonian precedents. When Edgar was inaugurated as king for the second time in 973 at Bath, the ceremony included the consecration of Ælfthryth as queen that is recorded in the second Anglo-Saxon coronation *ordo*.[26] Like Edgar, Ælfthryth may have been receiving her second consecration in 973 for she may already have been anointed as queen at the time of her marriage to Edgar *c.* 964.[27] She regularly witnesses charters as *regina* from that date, and is the first West Saxon queen to be given such a designation in witness-lists.[28] Rites to enhance the position of the queen in England seem to have been paralleled by an increasing interest in Marian iconography in the reign of Edgar, and particularly in Mary

[25] P. Stafford, 'The Reign of Æthelred II: A Study in the Limitations of Royal Policy and Actions', *Æthelred the Unready: Papers from the Millenary Conference*, ed. D. Hill, BAR 59 (Oxford, 1978), pp. 15–46; Keynes, *Diplomas*, pp. 163–77; Williams, *Æthelred*, pp. 19–42.

[26] J. L. Nelson, 'The Second English *Ordo*', in her *Politics and Ritual in Early Medieval Europe* (London, 1986), pp. 361–74.

[27] J. L. Nelson, 'Inauguration Rituals', *Politics and Ritual*, pp. 83–307, at 300–7.

[28] Stafford, *Queen Emma and Queen Edith*, pp. 61–3.

as queen of heaven.[29] This is particularly marked in the depiction of the death and coronation of the Virgin in the *Benedictional of St Æthelwold* which is the earliest known representation of the latter in a western manuscript.[30] The paralleling of the religious roles of king and queen is also to be found in the *Regularis Concordia* of c. 970 where the king was allotted special oversight of the male religious communities, while the queen was to be the protector of the nunneries.[31] However, as the document explains, this separation was made in order to avoid scandal; a pointed reference to Edgar's priapic interest in nuns that emerges more clearly in later records.

Ælfthryth as queen was far from the equal of her husband Edgar as king. The second coronation *ordo*, and other references to the event, emphasize her role as the king's consort and bed companion rather than granting her any position comparable to the king's.[32] Nor was Mary evoked in the blessing of the queen as occurred in Ottonian coronation ceremonies. Unlike the later *Liber Vitae* of New Minster with its prefatory portraits of Cnut and Emma, the New Minster foundation charter of 966 has a portrait of Edgar alone as its beneficiary on the opening page of the booklet.[33] Ælfthryth and her elder son Edmund are among the witnesses to the charter.[34] Ælfthryth is designated as *legitima prefati regis coniuncx*, and Edmund as *clito legitimus prefati regis filius*. He witnesses before his older half-brother, who is merely described as *eodem rege clito procreatus*. The difference in status is underlined by the fact that the crosses of Edmund and Ælfthryth are filled with gold, while that of Edward has been left as a painted outline.[35] The implication seems to be that Ælfthryth and her son Edmund were 'legitimate' in a way that Edward and his mother were not, probably on the grounds that Ælfthryth had been a consecrated queen when she conceived and gave birth to her son, but Æthelflæd had not. The interesting question is whether the New Minster charter represents what occurred at a major ceremony for the refoundation of New Minster in which the relative status of the two æthelings was made apparent, or whether it depicts an interpretation made at Winchester after the event.[36] If the former it would strongly suggest that Edgar himself was among those who wanted a son of his third marriage to succeed him, whereas the latter might be seen as owing more to the preferences of Bishop Æthelwold of Winchester who was, of course, also closely associated with the production of the *Regularis Concordia* and the Benedictional which bears his name, both of which could be seen as reinforcing the status of Ælfthryth.

---

[29] M. Clayton, *The Cult of the Virgin in Anglo-Saxon England*, CSASE 2 (Cambridge, 1990).

[30] R. Deshman, *The Benedictional of Æthelwold*, Studies in Manuscript Illumination 9 (Princeton, 1995), pp. 124–38, 204–7, pl. 34 (fol. 102v).

[31] Symons, *RC*, p. 2.

[32] Nelson, 'Second English *Ordo*'; Deshman, *Benedictional*, pp. 204–7.

[33] C. E. Karkov, *The Ruler Portraits of Anglo-Saxon England* (Woodbridge, 2004), pp. 111–14, 119–45.

[34] S 745; *WinchNM*, pp. 95–111.

[35] *WinchNM*, pp. 105–6.

[36] *WinchNM*, pp. 110–11.

Æthelwold appears to have been a personal supporter of Ælfthryth, and it is a moot point where his wider ecclesiastical interests ended and his more factional political involvement began. Æthelwold's refoundation of Ely had enjoyed the patronage of Ælfthryth and her first husband, the East Anglian ealdorman Æthelwold, and as queen she continued to be a major supporter of his foundations, usually jointly with Edgar.[37] Bishop Æthelwold appears to have been one of the major advisors with Ælfthryth during the minority of her son Æthelred, and it was only after Æthelwold's death in 984 that the somewhat extenuated minority came to an end.[38] Ælfthryth also had the backing of the powerful family of the ealdormen Ælfhere and Ælfheah.[39] However, the ætheling Edward had his own supporters including Æthelwine of East Anglia, whose brother had been Ælfthryth's first husband.[40] Archbishop Dunstan seems also to have been among them, and a genealogical tract produced at his monastery of Glastonbury in 969 gives Edward precedence over Edmund and Æthelred.[41]

Whether Edgar himself supported the succession of his sons by Ælfthryth over Edward is therefore not clear. He must have been aware of the dangerous factional polarization of some of the major noble families which had erupted around earlier succession crises.[42] For a peaceful reign, it was essential that a balance was kept between the great families, and that he made efforts to achieve this may be suggested by the provisions he made for his second wife Wulfthryth on their separation. The fourteenth-century cartulary of Wilton preserves a grant made by Edgar to Wulfthryth as abbess, and two others from Edgar in favour of Wilton when it would have been under her control.[43] Although these charters are not without their problems, they cannot be dismissed out of hand as having no reliable historical base. The charter of 965 in which a substantial grant made *temporaliter* to Wulfthryth is confirmed in perpetuity as a possession of Wilton may be evidence of a handsome settlement made to Wulfthryth when she separated from Edgar that she had confirmed as the possession of the nunnery soon after.[44] Her family was a distinguished one which may have had a long connection with Wilton and the ealdomanries of Wiltshire and western Wessex.[45] The

---

[37] B. A. E. Yorke, 'Æthelwold and the Politics of the Tenth Century', Yorke, *Æthelwold*, pp. 65–88, at 81–2.

[38] Stafford, 'The Reign of Æthelred II', p. 27; Keynes, *Diplomas*, pp. 176–7.

[39] A. Williams, '*Princeps Merciorum gentis*: The Family, Career and Connections of Ælfhere, Ealdorman of Mercia', *ASE* 10 (1982), 143–72; Yorke, 'Æthelwold and Politics'. The will of Ælfheah also seems to regard only the sons of Ælfthryth as æthelings: S 1485; Whitelock, *Wills*, no. 9, pp. 22–5 and 121–25.

[40] C. R. Hart, 'Athelstan "Half-King" and his Family', *ASE* 2 (1973), 115–44.

[41] Dumville, 'Ætheling', 4–5; Williams, *Æthelred the Unready*, p. 8; for various later sources that gave Dunstan a major role in securing Edward's coronation, see Keynes, *Diplomas*, p. 166, n. 48.

[42] Yorke, 'Politics of Æthelwold'.

[43] S 799; S 766 and S 767; *Registrum Wiltunense*, ed. J. I. Ingram (London, 1827).

[44] S 766; not all of the estates included here were still in Wilton's possession at the time of Domesday Book. M. A. Meyer, 'Patronage of the West Saxon Royal Nunneries in Late Anglo-Saxon England', *Revue Bénédictine* 91 (1981), 332–58, at 353–4.

[45] See n. 12.

dissolution of her marriage to Edgar would have required careful handling especially as it had the potential for major political repercussions. Although Anglo-Saxon custom allowed for remarriage if a spouse entered a religious community, under a stricter application of canon law Edgar could have been barred from legitimately remarrying while Wulfthryth was still alive.[46] Did Dunstan have recourse to such arguments when he prevailed in securing the succession of Edward? Edgar evidently kept a potentially explosive situation revolving around his marriages under control while he was alive, but it erupted after his death with fighting between the two camps.[47] The rivalry of the supporters of Edward and Æthelred was only superficially resolved after the former's death in 978 and ensured that the issue of Edgar's marriages remained a topic of interest.

Eleventh-Century Saints' Lives

Goscelin's *Vita S. Edithe* has not generally been given much credit as a reliable source for Edgar's family life. Susan Ridyard has made the Life more widely known through her discussion of the cult of Edith,[48] which seems to have been first promoted in the reign of her half-brother Æthelred, and a recent translation and discussion of the work will no doubt stimulate further studies.[49] A certain reluctance to accord any historical reliability to the work is understandable. Hagiography had to meet various expectations and conventions of the genre if it was to prove its case for sanctity. Goscelin's *Vita S. Edithe* is a particularly literary, if not florid, example of the form with lengthy digressions on the virtues of Edith and her mother in both prose and verse. Goscelin did not complete the first version of the work until *c.* 1080, although he seems to have begun it sometime before then, and it is dedicated to Archbishop Lanfranc.[50] It therefore belongs to the period in the aftermath of the Norman Conquest when many religious communities felt the need to produce Latin Lives of their Anglo-Saxon saints to ensure continuing respect for them.[51] The inclusion of references to Æthelwold and Dunstan may be a suspicious feature of the *Vita Edithe* designed to meet the expectations of Norman-appointed churchmen such as Lanfranc

---

46 Yorke, 'Legitimacy of St Edith', 108–9.
47 D. V. J. Fisher, 'The Anti-monastic Reaction in the Reign of Edward the Martyr', *Cambridge Historical Journal* 10 (1950–2), 254–70; Keynes, *Diplomas*, pp. 163–76.
48 Ridyard, *Royal Saints*, pp. 140–75.
49 *Writing the Wilton Women*, ed. Hollis.
50 The dedication to Lanfranc is contained in Oxford, Bodleian Library, Rawlinson C.938 fols. 1–29 (early thirteenth century) which Wilmart considered was the earliest version with a subsequent revision being represented by Cardiff, Public Library, 1.381, fols. 81–120 (early twelfth century); Wilmart, 'La Légende de Ste Édith', 8–12; *Writing the Wilton Women*, ed. Hollis, pp. 23–44.
51 S. J. Ridyard, '*Condigna Veneratio*: Post-Conquest Attitudes to the Saints of Anglo-Saxon England', *ANS* 9 (1987), 179–206; Ridyard, *Royal Saints*, pp. 171–5.

that the cult of Edith had had formal episcopal approval.[52] On the other hand, one should not overlook the fact that Goscelin's *Vita* belongs to a relatively rare (especially for women) category of saint's life written close to its subject life-time.[53] Goscelin had had a close association with Wilton for many years, possibly stretching back to soon after the appointment of his patron Herman as bishop of Ramsbury in 1058.[54] He had served as chaplain to the Wilton nuns for a number of years, and though he is unlikely have met people who personally knew Edith, who died between 984 and 987, some of the older nuns would have had memories of her mother Wulfthryth, who probably lived into the early years of the eleventh century.[55] Memories of Wulfthryth and Edith would have been attached to the many objects and buildings associated with them at Wilton to which Goscelin refers.[56] It is therefore not inconceivable that, leaving aside the problem of whether there was any earlier written material on which he could draw, Goscelin was able to utilize oral traditions at Wilton that originated in the lifetime of Wulfthryth.

Much of what Goscelin has to say concerns the promotion of the cult of Edith during the reigns of Æthelred Unræd and subsequent rulers. However, he also throws some light on the reign of Edgar. Goscelin states clearly that Edgar and Wulfthryth had been married, but separated amicably after the birth of Edith.[57] The *Vita* is particularly concerned to emphasize how Edith's status as a legitimate princess was acknowledged by Edgar after the separation. He is said to have appointed two foreign tutors from Trier to oversee her education.[58] She is said to have had regular access to the king who was willing to grant her petitions and foreign ambassadors might call at Wilton in order to visit her.[59] Some of her clothing was preserved at Wilton and demonstrated that she had dressed like a princess.[60] A chapel and other indications of her patronage indicate that she had considerable personal wealth at her disposal, as the survival of her seal also suggests.[61] In her sanctity she is said to have been following in the tradition of other female saints of the royal house, including her grandmother

---

[52] P. A. Hayward, 'Translation-Narratives in Post-Conquest Hagiography and English Resistance to the Norman Conquest', *ANS* 21 (1998), 67–93.

[53] B. A. E. Yorke, 'Writing the Biographies of Anglo-Saxon Female Saints', *Medieval Biography. Essays Presented to Frank Barlow*, ed. D. Bates, J. Crick and S. Hamilton (Woodbridge, 2006), pp. 49–60.

[54] *The Life of King Edward Who Rests at Westminster*, ed. F. Barlow, OMT, 2nd ed. (Oxford, 1992), pp. 133–45; *Writing the Wilton Women*, ed. Hollis, pp. 117–24.

[55] For calculation of dates see Yorke, 'Legitimacy of St. Edith'.

[56] For example, her clothes-chest (ch. 13), alb embroidered by Edith (ch. 16), chapel dedicated to St Denis (ch. 20–1).

[57] Goscelin, *Vita Edithe*, ch. 2.

[58] Yorke, 'Legitimacy of St. Edith', Goscelin, *Vita Edithe*, chs. 5 and 7.

[59] Goscelin, *Vita Edithe*, ch. 11.

[60] Goscelin, *Vita Edithe*, chs. 12–13.

[61] Goscelin, *Vita Edithe*, chs. 20–1; F. Douce, 'Some Remarks on the Original Seal Belonging to the Abbey of Wilton', *Archaeologia* 18 (1817), 40–54; T. A. Heslop, 'English Seals from the Mid-Ninth Century to 1100', *Journal of the British Archaeological Association* 133 (1980), 1–16, at p. 4.

St Ælfgifu of Shaftesbury.[62] The message from Goscelin's Wilton was that Edith was acknowledged as Edgar's legitimate daughter, and that relations between Edgar and both Wulfthryth and Wilton remained cordial after their separation. Ælfthryth is not mentioned by name, but the mother of Æthelred is said to have been responsible for the death of her stepson Edward, at which point a group among the nobility is said to have considered elevating Edith to the throne.[63] Edith naturally declined, and most historians have doubted whether there is any historical validity behind the story, but it remains an intriguing possible addition to our understanding of the disturbed conditions after the death of Edgar. For all the skills that Goscelin brought to the work, a certain tension remains between his attempts to create a plausible picture of Edith as a saint from the Wilton traditions about her as a princess.[64] This stress on the legitimacy of Edith and of the marriage Wulfthryth and Edgar could have been, as we have seen, very relevant in the disputed succession on Edgar's death as it would have been a means through which to question the legitimacy of his marriage to Ælfthryth. Although Goscelin wrote in the eleventh century, it may have been that the case for Edith's legitimacy had been gathered together much closer to the reign of Edgar to be utilized in such an eventuality.

A rather different perspective on both Edgar and Ælfthryth emerges from the *Vita* of Wulfthryth's cousin Wulfhild, abbess of Barking, that was also written by Goscelin. From this we learn that Edgar's original intention had been to marry Wulfhild as, it would appear, part of an alliance with her family.[65] However, Wulfhild was already a professed nun, unlike Wulfthryth, who the *Vita* says, had not taken vows and was merely being educated at Wilton. Wulfhild fought off an attempted seduction by Edgar at the house of her aunt after which he pursued her into the cloisters of Wilton, but eventually agreed to marry Wulfthryth instead. He compensated Wulfhild with the appointment as abbess of Barking and many generous gifts.[66] Although the attempted seduction of Wulfhild provided Goscelin with the opportunity to present Edgar in the commonplace hagiographical role of the powerful man who puts a saint's chastity to the test,[67] the tone in general towards him is approving. He is a *rex strenuissimus* and praised for his generosity.[68] However, there is criticism of Queen Ælfthryth who is said to have conspired with the priests of Barking to have Wulfhild deprived of her position so that she could enjoy possession of Barking herself, and was severely rebuked by St Æthelburh, the foundress of Barking for her

---

62 Goscelin, *Vita Edithe*, ch. 18.
63 Goscelin, *Vita Edithe*, chs. 18–19.
64 Yorke, 'Legitimacy of St. Edith'; *Writing the Wilton Women*, ed. Hollis, pp. 244–56.
65 Esposito, 'La Vie de Sainte Wulfhilde', chs. 2–3.
66 Esposito, 'La Vie de Sainte Wulfhilde', ch. 4.
67 S. Millinger, 'Humility and Power: Anglo-Norman Nuns in Anglo-Norman Hagiography', *Medieval Religious Women*, I: *Distant Echoes*, ed. J. A. Nichols and M. T. Shank (Kalamazoo, MI, 1984), pp. 115–30.
68 Esposito, 'La Vie de Sainte Wulfhilde', ch. 6; *strenuissimus* was much prized by Bede in a king.

presumption.[69] Ælfthryth's actions against Wulfhild are likely to have occurred after the death of Edgar as she is identified in the *Vita* as the mother of Æthelred, and thus provides further confirmation that she enjoyed much greater powers as queen-mother than she had as queen.

The character of Ælfthryth was also blackened in the late eleventh-century *Passio Edwardi*, another work which has sometimes been attributed to Goscelin, but cannot certainly be assigned to him.[70] In this account Ælfthryth is made responsible for arranging the murder of Edward in order to allow for the succession of her own son Æthelred. She does not herself stab the king, as she would do in later versions of the legend, but she is said to have connived at his death. The *Vita Oswaldi* which was written in the reign of Æthelred does not assign her any role in the conspiracy that is said to have arranged the death of Edward, but Edward is said to have been visiting her and Æthelred when his death occurred.[71] Any application of the principle of *cui bono* might reach the conclusion that Ælfthryth must have known what was being planned. However, the role of Ælfthryth in the *Passio* account is likely to have been developed from models provided in the accounts of other young Anglo-Saxon princes, such as the brothers Æthelbert and Æthelred of Kent, King Æthelbert of the East Angles and Kenelm of Mercia who met untimely, violent deaths.[72] There was considerable interest in these cults in late tenth and eleventh centuries, perhaps either as a means of commenting indirectly on the fate of Edward to undermine the position of Æthelred or as a means of preparing the way for the promotion of his cult in ways that would benefit his brother as king.[73] One of the common features that the *Passio Edwardi* shares with the accounts of other royal martyrdoms is the role of a wicked royal woman in encompassing the death of an innocent victim in order to benefit a member of her own family. The crime of Ælfthryth in the *Passio* therefore seems to have been as much derived from a hagiographical stereotype than from any reliable transmission of the events that had led up to Edward's death.[74] But once the precedent had been provided, Ælfthryth's reputation could only sink further as additional bad behaviour was attributed to her in later accounts of Edward's death.[75]

The women of Edgar's family who entered religious communities are ranged

[69] Esposito, 'La Vie de Sainte Wulfhilde', ch. 9.

[70] *Edward King and Martyr*, ed. C. E. Fell, Leeds Texts and Monographs (Leeds, 1971); Barlow, *Life of King Edward*, p. 148.

[71] Raine, pp. 448–52; B. A. E. Yorke, 'Edward, King and Martyr: A Saxon Murder Mystery', in *Studies in the Early History of Shaftesbury Abbey*, ed. L. Keen (Dorchester, 1999), pp. 99–116.

[72] D. Rollason, 'The Cults of Murdered Royal Saints in Anglo-Saxon England', *ASE* 11 (1983), 1–22; P. A. Hayward, 'The Idea of Innocent Martyrdom in Late Tenth- and Eleventh-century English Hagiography', *Studies in Church History* 30 (1993), 81–92.

[73] Keynes, *Diplomas*, pp. 163–76; Ridyard, *Royal Saints*, pp. 154–68.

[74] Williams, *Æthelred the Unready*, pp. 11–17 for the suggestion that the 'murder' could have been an accident, like that of Edward's grandfather King Edmund at Pucklechurch, around which rumours subsequently developed.

[75] Fell, *Edward King and Martyr*, pp. xvi–xx.

in the hagiographies against Ælfthryth. In the *Passio* Edith and Wulfthryth are said to have taken part in the transfer of Edward's remains from Wareham to Shaftesbury once the deed had been discovered,[76] and in Goscelin's *Vita S. Edithe* Edward is said to have been killed through the treachery of his step-mother.[77] Even Ælfthryth's own foundation of Wherwell remembered her as causing the death of Edward and the nunnery is said to have been founded in expiation of the crime.[78] Although she had been a generous patron of Ely, she was accused in the *Liber Eliensis* of witchcraft and causing the death of an abbot.[79] Only in the rather later *Vita* of her stepdaughter Ælfflæd of Romsey is she remembered rather more enthusiastically as a monastic patron.[80]

Anglo-Norman Chronicles

The tenth century was of considerable interest to late eleventh- and twelfth-century writers for in it they could trace the origins of much that was important in their Anglo-Norman world. It was the period from which many religious houses could trace a continuous history as reformed Benedictine communities, and the promoters of this reform, Æthelwold and Dunstan, had also provided criticisms of lay society of which later monastic chroniclers could approve. Important precedents might be provided for the Anglo-Norman world by Anglo-Saxon customs which therefore had to be carefully explored to establish their legitimacy. The precedent for women temporarily withdrawing into Anglo-Saxon nunneries, especially in times of trouble, and then re-emerging into the world was of vital importance for the marriage prospects of certain high-born women in late eleventh and early twelfth centuries.[81] It was Prior Nicholas's careful investigation for Eadmer of whether royal anointings in the reign of Edgar could provide a contemporary precedent that has helped modern understanding on this topic.[82] For other writers the tenth century was the period in which one could find the beginnings of courtly behaviour and suitable ancestors of the Anglo-Norman kings.

In addition to written sources of the tenth and eleventh centuries, it seems likely that various oral traditions circulated about the reign of Edgar, in particular in the major monastic communities. In his section on Wilton, William of Malmesbury reproduces accounts of St Edith's encounters with Dunstan and

---

[76] Fell, *Edward King and Martyr*, pp. 8–9.

[77] Goscelin, *Vita Edithe*, ch. 18.

[78] BL, Egerton 2104a, fols. 43 and 45 (the Wherwell cartulary); Yorke, *Nunneries*, 78–9. See also William of Malmesbury, *Gesta Regum*, pp. 258–9, and discussion below.

[79] *LE*, ch. 56, pp. 127–9; *Liber Eliensis. A History of the Isle of Ely from the Seventh Century to the Twelfth*, trans. J. Fairweather (Woodbridge, 2005), pp. 153–4.

[80] See n. 18; even in these accounts Ælfthryth runs into trouble for not showing sufficient respect to the saint, and the portrait of Edgar as monastic patron is more positive.

[81] E. Searle, 'Women and the Succession at the Norman Conquest', *ANS* 3 (1980), 159–70, at 165–6; Yorke, *Nunneries*, pp. 89–92.

[82] Nelson, 'Inauguration Rituals', 63–9; Williams, *Æthelred*, pp. 3–4.

Æthelwold from Goscelin's *Vita*, but a third story, Cnut's mocking of Edgar's reputation with which this paper opened, has no known written precedent and contrasts with Goscelin's portrayal of Cnut's unqualified respect for the saint.[83] William's account may be what circulated orally about what Cnut had said while Goscelin's version is what he or the Wilton nuns deemed more suitable for wider consumption. It would appear that various rumours about Edgar's sexual predilections for nuns which had reputedly earned him seven years' penance from Dunstan were circulating in the late eleventh and twelfth centuries, but there was some uncertainty about which of Edgar's wives were involved. Osbern believed that one seduced nun was the mother of Edward the Martyr,[84] while Eadmer knew a story of a lay girl being educated at Wilton who snatched a veil from one of the nuns when Edgar came calling to protect herself from his un- wanted attentions.[85] William thought the story referred to Wulfthryth who 'was not actually a nun as popular opinion crazily supposes',[86] but he was uncertain as to the identity of another nun whom Edgar had violently abducted and raped several times.[87] Perhaps there are echoes of Wulfhild's encounters with Edgar here which Goscelin again had turned into something more respectable in which her honour was preserved.

William's investigation of the histories of Anglo-Saxon religious communi- ties threw up other stories of Edgar's lust. One recounted how a noble woman when asked to provide her daughter for the king's bed substituted a slave-girl instead.[88] Another concerned the circumstances in which Edgar came to marry Ælfthryth. According to this account Edgar had heard of the great beauty of Ælfthryth and sent Ealdorman Æthelwold to investigate and woo her on his behalf.[89] Æthelwold was so impressed by her that he decided to marry Ælfthryth himself, but to report to the king that she was nothing special so that he would lose interest. His bluff was called when Edgar eventually met Ælfthryth, who did her best to seduce him, and he was so smitten that he killed Æthelwold under the cover of a hunting trip so that he might marry her himself. A version of this story was also known to Gaimar who gave it a rather different emphasis in order to exploit its romantic possibilities.[90] Æthelwold's villainy is stressed, and he is killed in an ambush on the way to a new appointment. Ælfthryth is much more an innocent beauty whose marriage to Edgar was compromised because Edgar was godfather to her child with Æthelwold (and so earned the condemnation of Dunstan). Gaimar says his story came from Wherwell, while William's places Ealdorman Æthelwold's fatal hunting-trip in Wherwell (Harewood) forest. Both

83 Hamilton, *Gesta*, ch. 87, pp. 188–91.
84 Stubbs, *Dunstan*, pp. 111–12, 114,
85 Stubbs, *Dunstan*, pp. 163, 209–10, 422–4.
86 Hamilton, *Gesta*, ch. 87; trans. Preest, p. 127.
87 Hamilton, *Gesta*, ch. 158, pp. 258–9.
88 Hamilton, *Gesta*, ch. 159, pp. 258–61.
89 Hamilton, *Gesta*, ch. 157, pp. 256–9.
90 A. Bell, 'Gaimar and the Edgar–Ælfthryth Story', *Modern Language Review* 21 (1926), 278–87; *L'Estoire des Engleis by Geffrei Gaimar*, ed. A. Bell (Oxford, 1960), pp. 113–30.

men say that the nunnery of Wherwell was founded to expiate the crime. Wherwell nunnery may have provided both men with their information which they treated differently according to their own attitudes towards women, those of their anticipated audiences and the conventions in which they wrote. William's story of the substitute slave-girl is said to have taken place at Andover which is close to Wherwell and so it may have come from the same source. Are these the type of tales that Anglo-Saxon nuns had recounted about Edgar behind closed doors?

These stories from Wherwell may not all have originated in the same circumstances. Elizabeth Tyler has drawn attention to the role that rumours (*fama*) flying around the court of Harthacnut may have had in stimulating Emma to commission the *Encomium*.[91] It is possible that the gossip still circulating in the twelfth century about Edgar and his wives had its origin in the tensions surrounding his different marriages at his own court and which were to flare up as open hostility between rival noble factions after his death. William's story of the substitute slave-girl ends with him raising her in status to be his favoured bed-fellow before he fell for Ælfthryth. Possibly this is an illusion to Edgar's first wife Æthelflæd *candida* whose relatively lowly status, compared to that of Ælfthryth, was stressed by those who opposed the succession of her son Edward the Martyr. William's second story of the nun abducted from her convent and forced to sleep with Edgar might therefore be an allusion to Wulfthryth from the same source especially as the implication is that Edgar discarded her rather than married her. However, ultimately it was the rumours about Ælfthryth as the seducer of Edgar, dispossessor of Wulfhild and, above all, the murderer of her stepson that would that made most impact. Ælfthryth attracted greater infamy presumably in part because she was the most powerful and politically influential of the wives, especially during the minority of her son Æthelred. But her declining reputation must also be connected with the fact that she stirred up resentment in the nunneries of late Anglo-Saxon England through asserting her role as protectress of nunneries during her regency, as is illustrated by the expulsion of Wulfhild from Barking. Barking, Wilton, Shaftesbury and her own foundation of Wherwell all promoted negative accounts of Ælfthryth that found their way into the written record in the eleventh and twelfth centuries, and are the likely sources of other gossip about her that did the rounds. Stories about the shortcomings of his Anglo-Saxon predecessors would no doubt have been welcome at Cnut's court, and may lay behind the remarks on Edgar's lustfulness which William attributed to him.

---

[91] E. Tyler, 'Talking about History in Eleventh-century England: The *Encomium Emmae Reginae* and the Court of Harthacnut', *Early Medieval Europe* 13 (2005), 359–83, especially 364–7.

Conclusion

Edgar's three marriages and his predatory interest in nuns would have been regarded as normal royal behaviour in most circles in Anglo-Saxon England during his reign. However, the attitudes of reforming churchmen, and the increase in number and type of written records between the tenth and the twelfth centuries, have meant that more was written about them than for many previous reigns. As with his grandfather's and father's plural marriages, Edgar's three unions can be seen as successive alliances with leading noble families in order to keep the balance of power between contending groups. Edgar's eagerness to marry Ælfthryth may not have been the type of romance that Gaimar chose to present so much as a need to placate the powerful noble faction with which she was associated – though as her brother-in-law was apparently one of those who supported the succession of Edward perhaps there was some truth in the rumour that Edgar had begun to court her before she had been widowed. Serial monogamy like Edgar's in part took the place of earlier more polygamous relationships,[92] and the stories that show Edgar expecting to enjoy sexual relations with other daughters of the nobility are all too likely to be true. Nunneries were one of the places in which concentrations of these girls were to be found (without it necessarily being the case that all were vowed to lives of chastity) and Edgar's predatory behaviour towards them recalls that of earlier kings.[93] Bishop Boniface from the safety of Germany rebuked King Æthelbald for sleeping with women from nunneries,[94] and Dunstan may have spoken out against Edgar's similar behaviour.

But not only do we have the critical views of reforming churchmen on Edgar's sex life, albeit preserved via an Anglo-Norman perspective, so may we have something remaining of the opinions of the women who enjoyed – or suffered – his attentions which we do not have for any earlier reign. Perhaps surprisingly, the saints' Lives written closest to his reign give Edgar a generally favourable reference. His generosity to the women he abandoned seems to have countered the potential for bitterness towards him, but naturally did not completely dampen the gossip about his behaviour. Edgar was able to keep resentments in check while he was alive, but the tensions surfaced after his early death to the detriment of the reputation of his widow Ælfthryth and, ultimately, of the image of him as a model Christian king that had been carefully nurtured during his reign.

---

[92] R. Mazo Karras, 'The History of Marriage and the Myth of Friedelehe', *EME* 14 (2006), 119–52.
[93] Yorke, *Nunneries*, pp. 153–9.
[94] *EHD*, no. 177.

7

Edgar, Albion and Insular Dominion

JULIA CRICK

At this time, the name of Britaine, lay forgotten and growne quite out of use among the Inhabitants of this Island: remaining only in books, and not taken up in common speech. And hereupon it is, that Boniface the bishop of Mentz, descended from hence, called this our country, *Saxony beyond the Sea*. Howbeit, K. Eadred, about the yeare of our Lord, 948. used in some charters and Patents the name and title of *King of Great Britain*: like as *Edgar* in the yeare, 970. bare this stile also, *The Monarch of all whole Albion*.[1]

ALBION, that ancient term of British geography, used from the time of Pliny onwards to designate the island of Britain, came of age in the seventeenth century. When James VI of Scotland acceded to the English throne in 1603 and created an island polity, Albion found its political meaning. Indeed, to judge from the output of British presses, it exploded into life. Drayton's *Poly-Olbion*, published in 1612, carried on its title page the personification of Albion, 'th'Oceans Island'. In the following year James Maxwell celebrated in print the genealogy of 'the infanta of Albion', James I's daughter, while his *Carolanna* was published in 1619 'in honour of the immortall memory of our late good queen of Albion and Union'.[2] The personified Albion featured in Jonson's masque for the Court at Twelfth Night 1623, New Albion served as a term for the American colonies and thereafter Albion provided a suitably grandiloquent style for kings, queens and princesses:[3] thus Albion's Tears were shed for Queen

1   William Camden, *Britain, or a Chorographical Description of the most flourishing King-domes, England, Scotland, and Ireland, and the Ilands adioyning, out of the depth of Antiquitie ... translated newly into English by Philemon Holland, Doctour in Physick* (London, 1610), p. 139.

2   Michael Drayton, *Poly-Olbion* ([London, 1612]); James Maxwell, *An English-royall pedegree common to the two most noble princes lately married Friderick ... and ... Elizabeth, Infanta of Albion, Princesse Palatin[] onely daughter of our most gracious King Iames and Queene Anne ...* (London, 1613); James Maxwell, *Carolanna, That is to say, A Poeme in honour of our King, Charles-Iames. Queene Anne, and Prince Charles; But principally in honour of the immortall memory of our late noble & good queene of Albion and Union ...* (London, [1619]).

3   Ben Jonson, *Neptunes triumph for the Returne of Albion, celebrated in a Masque at the Court on the Twelfth Night 1623* (London, 1624); Robert Evelyn, *A Direction for adventurers with small stock to get two for one, and good land freely; And for Gentlemen and*

Mary, Albion's elegy was addressed to Prince James and Albion's Blessing to William III.[4] The currency of the term Albion in the seventeenth century merely heightens the anachronism of Edgar's reported style. Camden's claim that Edgar bore the title 'Monarch of all whole Albion' is no better documented than the notion that Eadwig called himself 'King of Great Britain'.[5] Neither style occurs in any extant charter, genuine or forged, and it is perhaps significant that neither appeared in Camden's Latin original, an Elizabethan artefact of 1586, both entering the text in the first Stuart edition, of 1607, four years after James's accession.[6] So what connects Albion to Edgar? That is the question which drives the following discussion.

As is well known, sixteenth- and seventeenth-century writers recognised Edgar as much more than an English king. John Dee expressed this point of view particularly forcefully in his *General and Rare Memorials pertayning to the Perfect arte of Navigation* published in 1577. He saw Edgar as 'one of the perfect Imperiall Monarchs of the Brytish Impire', and remarked not just on the further flung elements of his dominion but on the political formation which constituted its 'greater portion': Albion.[7] In seven pages filled with patriotic rhetoric, Dee sustained a panegyric to Edgar, praising his ability to create peace and justice 'in all Quarters of this ALBION', writing of his 'Impire of Albion' whose 'Peaceable Possession' was demonstrated 'with the Passing and yeerly Sayling about this Brytish Albion, with all the Lesser Iles, next adiacent, round

all *Servants, Labourers, and Artificers to live plentifully. And the true Description of the healthiest, pleasantest, and richest plantation of new Albion, in North Virginia proved by thirteen witnesses* ... ([London], 1641). Compare George [Abbot], *A Briefe Description of the Whole World* ([London], 1650), p. 293 on Nova Albion.

4   Anon., *Albion's tears on the Death of Her Sacred Majesty Queen Mary. A Pindarick Poem* (London, 1695); M. L. *Albion's Elegie: or, A Poem, Upon the High and Mighty Prince James Duke of Albany and York, his Departure from Scotland.* (Edinburgh, 1680); Thomas D'Urfey, *Albion's Blessing. A Poem Panegyrical On His Sacred Majesty, King William the III. And on His Happy Return, and the Publishing the Late Glorious Peace* (London 1698).

5   Given in Camden's Latin version as *Magnæ Britanniæ Regis* and *Totius Albionis Monarche*: [William] Camden, *Britannia, sive florentissimorum regnorum, Angliæ, Scotiæ, Hiberniæ, et insularum adicentium ex intima antiquitate Chorographica descriptio* (London, 1607), p. 99. On the testimony of acceptable charters Eadwig was styled 'king (or governor) of all (the land of) Britain': *totius britannice telluris rex* (S 595, S 609, S 622); *rex ... tocius Britannie* (S 614, S 629); *totius britannice telluris gubernator et rector* (S 595, S 620, S 641). The closest parallel to Edgar's alleged style occurs in S 779 AD 970 (authenticity disputed: forty-two manuscript-witnesses from s. xi/xii to xviii): Ego Eadgarus basileus dilectæ insulæ **Albionis** subditus nobis sceptri Scotorum . Cumbrorumque. ac Brittonum . et omnium circum circa regionum quiete pacem perfruens ...

6   Compare [William] Camden, *Britannia, sive florentissimorum regnorum, Angliæ, Scotiæ, Hiberniæ, et insularum adicentium ex intima antiquitate Chorographica descriptio* (London, 1600), p. 107, and *ibid.* (London, 1607), p. 99.

7   *General and Rare Memorials pertayning to the Perfect Arte of Navigation* [London, 1577], p. 56, p. 54. On early modern attitudes to Edgar see W. H. Sherman, *John Dee: The Politics of Reading and Writing in the English Renaissance* (Amherst, 1995), pp. 143 and 170–1.

about it'.[8] This rhetoric was largely imposed by Dee on the textual remnants invoked to support his case. Dee, for example, spiralled into flights of imperial fancy on the strength of the famous *Altitonantis* charter which never once mentions Albion.[9] Nevertheless, one of the medieval 'memorials' which he cites in support of his case did use the term Albion. This is the foundation charter of Ely, a creation of disputed authenticity surviving as an immediately post-Conquest single sheet and arguably of pre-Conquest date.[10] Dee excerpted it, putting into upper case three terms: the king's name, that of his realm (Albion) and the nature of his rule (*imperium*): '... Ego ÆDGARUS, Basileus Dilectæ Insulæ ALBIONIS' in the dispositive section and, from the attestations, '... Ego ÆDGARUS, totius ALBIONIS Basileus ...'.[11] Indeed, the form of the attestation resembles in essence the 'Monarch of all whole Albion' style claimed for Edgar by Camden's translator. Camden evidently paraphrased, but something like Dee's source might have encouraged Camden to make the claims he did. Dee and Camden were not alone in discerning a connexion between tenth-century kings and rulership of Albion. Drayton, writing in the preface to his *Poly-Olbion* of 1612, attempted to counter '*Buchanan*'s obiection against our Historians about *Athelstans* being King of all *Albion*'; apparently in reference to a passage in which the Scottish historian, George Buchanan, attempted to debunk contemporary claims about insular dominion.[12] Buchanan cited narrative rather than documentary sources and he described the island as *Britannia* not Albion but Drayton's reaction illustrates the kind of skirmishing which could be conducted on the far-distant terrain of tenth-century precedent.

This is not the place to investigate Elizabethan and Stuart polemic but this episode serves to redirect the discussion. In the sixteenth and seventeenth centuries, antiquaries and polemicists saw and, more importantly, attempted to document a connexion between post-Alfredian kings and rule of Albion; this was a connexion made for Edgar in particular and Dee at least found some

---

8   Dee, *General and Rare Memorials*, pp. 54–60 at 58, 60.
9   *General and Rare Memorials*, pp. 58–60. Dee's citation discussed by J. Crick, 'The Art of the Unprinted: Transcription and English Antiquity in the Age of Print', *The Uses of Script and Print, 1300–1700*, ed. J. Crick and A. Walsham (Cambridge, 2004), pp. 116–34, at 124–5. On *Altitonantis* see J. Barrow, 'How the Twelfth-Century Monks of Worcester Perceived their Past', *The Perception of the Past in Twelfth-Century Europe*, ed. P. Magdalino (London, 1992), pp. 53–74, at 69–71.
10   S 779. On the date see J. Pope, 'Ælfric and the Old English Version of the Ely Privilege', *England before the Conquest: Studies in Primary Sources presented to Dorothy Whitelock*, ed. P. Clemoes and K. Hughes (Cambridge, 1971), pp. 85–113.   .
11   Dee, *General and Rare Memorials*, p. 59.
12   Drayton, *Poly-Olbion*, p. A 3. His jibe apparently refers to Buchanan's prologue: *Rerum Scoticarum historia auctore Georgio Buchanano Scoto* (Edinburgh, 1582), fol. 3v. In the posthumous English translation the passage is rendered: 'That Alured, Athelstan, and some other of the Saxon kings did sometimes Reign over the whole Island, when yet, 'tis clear, they never passed beyond the Wall of Severus. For when they Read, That they held the Empire of all Britain, they presently thought, that the whole Island was possessed by them.' *The history of Scotland. Written in Latin by George Buchanan. Faithfully rendered into English.* (London, 1690), p. 8.

documentary evidence to support it. Returning to the Middle Ages, where this paper belongs, we find a series of striking facts. 151 purported pre-Conquest charters contain mentions of Albion, of which one third bear Edgar's name.[13] Of the fifty-one Edgarian charters only eight survive in pre-Conquest form, the rest being preserved as cartulary copies or as late single sheets. More than a dozen appear to be post-Conquest confections which reflect the development of Edgar's posthumous reputation, but leaving these aside we find a substantial residue of authentic material.[14] Even confining the search to evidence surviving in pre-Conquest form, we find a broadly comparable pattern. Twenty-one extant pre-Conquest charters credit tenth- and eleventh-century kings with rule of Albion (see Table 7.1). One survives for each of the reigns of Eadwig, Cnut and Harthacnut; two so style Eadred, Edward, and Æthelstan (these last are retrospective and spurious), three commemorate Æthelred, but nine survive in the name of Edgar, that is three times as many occurrences as for any other king. Charters surviving in tenth-, eleventh- and twelfth-century form indeed describe royal power in terms of Albion, then, as early modern commentators observed, and getting on for half of these name Edgar as king.[15]

Despite this accumulation of evidence, the connexion between Edgar and Albion has attracted very little comment.[16] Janet Nelson saw Edgar 'in his later years as ruler of a British Empire, tenth-century style' and she detected in a variety of late tenth-century contexts 'the authentic voices of a hegemonial imperialism'.[17] Eric John's uncannily prescient papers on 'hegemonic' themes in

---

[13] Edgar (52 instances), rivalled by Æthelred (26), Eadwig (19), Eadred (18), Æthelstan (11), Edward (10), Cnut (7), Edmund and Edward the Martyr (2), Harthacnut (1). For comments on their authenticity see the 'Electronic Sawyer' (details at p. 60, n.2, above).

[14] Of the later copies S 682, 689, 692, 732–4, 741, 776, 779, 787, 792, 796–7, 814–15, 818, 825 have been deemed spurious. On Edgar's posthumous reputation see R. R. Davies, *The First English Empire: Power and Identities in the British Isles 1093–1343* (Oxford, 2000), pp. 9–10; D. E. Thornton, 'Edgar and the Eight Kings, AD 973: *Textus et Dramatis Personae*', *EME* 10.1 (2001), 49–79; J. Barrow, 'Chester's Earliest Regatta? Edgar's Dee-Rowing Revisited', *EME* 10.1 (2001), 81–93.

[15] In textual and palaeographical terms the early charters betray a connexion with his reign. None of the Albion-charters issued in the names of Edgar's precedessors, Æthelstan, Eadred and Eadwig, survives in contemporary form. Indeed, two of the Eadred charters are linked to Archbishop Dunstan, one a notoriously complicated text, the Reculver charter S 546, discussed by N. Brooks, *The Early History of the Church of Canterbury: Christ Church from 597 to 1066* (Leicester, 1984), pp. 232–6; *idem*, 'The Career of St Dunstan', *St Dunstan: His Life, Times and Cult*, ed. N. Ramsay *et al.* (Woodbridge, 1992), pp. 1–23, at 17–8.

[16] Michael Lapidge identified three occurrences of the term Albion in the later tenth century: M. Lapidge *et al.*, *The Cult of St Swithun*, Winchester Studies 4.ii, The Anglo-Saxon Minsters of Winchester (Oxford, 2003), pp. 258–9, n. 34. Discussions of claims to insular dominion have been conducted in general terms or have focused on *Britannia*: see below, nn. 17–18. Wendy Davies noted the use of Albion as a synonym for Britain: *Patterns of Power in Early Wales* (Oxford, 1990), p. 62.

[17] J. L. Nelson, 'Inauguration Rituals', in her *Politics and Ritual in Early Medieval Europe* (London, 1986), pp. 283–307 (originally ptd *Early Medieval Kingship*, ed. P. H. Sawyer and I. N. Wood [Leeds, 1977], pp. 50–71), at 302–3, see also pp. 296–304.

Table 7.1. Kings of Albion: royal styles in charters extant in pre-Conquest form

Face date	Reference	Date of copy	King	Style	Archive
929	S 401	s. xi¹, xi²	Æthelstan	*regnum totius Albionis … dispensans*	Worcester
933	S 421	s. x/xi	Æthelstan	*apice totius Albionis sublimatus*	Exeter
949	S 546	s. x²	Eadred	*totius Albionis monarchus*	Christ Church Canterbury
955	S 563	s. x *med.*	Eadred	*primicherius tocius Albionis*	Glastonbury
956	S 618	s. x²	Eadwig	*primicerius totius Albionis*	Abingdon
951 for 959	S 670	s. x²	Edgar	*primicerius totius Albionis*	Westminster
951 for 959	S 1450	s. x²	Edgar	*primicerius totius Albionis*	Westminster
961	S 697	s. x²	Edgar	*rex totius Albionis insulae*	Winchester, Old Minster
963	S 717	s. x²	Edgar	*imperio totius Albionis*	Christ Church Canterbury
965	S 736	s. x²	Edgar	*totius Albionis rex*	Abbotsbury
966	S 745	s. x²	Edgar	*totius Albionis basileus*	Winchester, New Minster
967	S 753	s. x²	Edgar	*primicerius totius Albionis*	Westminster
968	S 1215	s. x²	Edgar	*rex Albionis* (attestation)	Christ Church Canterbury
969	S 772	s. x², xi¹	Edgar	*totius Albionis rex*	Worcester
995	S 884	s. x²	Æthelred	*primicerius totius Albionis*	Muchelney
997	S 890	s. x/xi	Æthelred	*totius Albionis rex*	Exeter
1007	S 916	s. xi*in.*	Æthelred	*totius Albionis … basileus*	St Albans
1031	S 963	s. xi¹	Cnut	*rex totius Albionis*	Exeter
1042	S 994	s. xi *med.*	Harthacnut	*rex Anglorum aeque totius Albionis*	Winchester, Old Minster
1045	S 1008	s. xi *med.*	Edward	*rex Anglorum et aeque totius Albionis*	Winchester, Old Minster
1049	S 1019	s. xi *med.*	Edward	*Angol-Saxonum et aeque totius Albionis rex*	Christ Church Canterbury

tenth-century charters – this is a truly Mancunian topic – pursue questions of imperial style (*basileus, imperator*) and dominion in Britain (*Britannia*). He examined the sources, and he was confident enough to proclaim that 'Certainly the reign of Edgar marks the apogee of the "empire of Britain" after the fashioning of the Anglo-Saxons', but he never once commented on the term Albion, nor does it feature in his index, although *Britannia* does: nine times.[18] He cited a number of charters employing the term Albion, but he made no comment on Albion itself as a geographical term; indeed, he courted notoriety by defending the tenth-century origins of a number of purportedly Edgarian charters claimed as post-Conquest productions by many other scholars, among them the Ely charter, but again he made no comment on the geographical terminology.[19] I conclude that John silently took Albion as a poetic synonym for *Britannia*, a pairing which Patrick Wormald accepted in print. If so, on these grounds alone, it merits discussion. Island dominion was no idle ambition in the tenth century.[20]

Nelson, and John before her, found imperial rhetoric not simply in charters but in a variety of texts connected with Edgar. John himself drew attention to the hegemonic vocabulary in the *Vita Oswaldi*, now attributed to Byrhtferth of Ramsey, including the description of Edgar's death.[21] His conclusions were arresting: 'The earlier saints' lives and Bede's *History*, if they all have their virtuous and successful kings, are nothing like so much in love with their empire and their power as the *Vita Oswaldi*.'[22] In other words tenth-century *imperium* finds expression not just in charters but, as in the eighth century, in prescriptive literature, at the heart of the English church. The cluster of later tenth-century imperial references noted by John and Nelson point straight to the rhetoric of Albion. In the *Vita Oswaldi* we find Edgar styled 'emperor of all Albion' (*et totius **Albionis** imperator*) while his immediate subordinates, guided by Dunstan, 'prince of bishops' and Æthelwold, the holy prelate, constitute the nobility of all Albion (*omnisque dignitas totius Albionis*).[23] Michael Lapidge, in his recent edition of another source close to the heart of the reforming faction, Lantfred's *Translatio et miracula S. Swithuni*, written *c.* 975, observed similar kind of rhetoric and discussed in a footnote Lantfred's use of the term Albion, locating a single comparandum in a charter of Æthelred of 982.[24] Two further occurrences

---

[18] E. John, *Orbis Britanniae and Other Studies* (Leicester, 1966), pp. 1–63, esp. pp. 5–10, 44–60, also pp. 56 and 298. See further Davies, *The First English Empire*, pp. 8–10, 36–8.

[19] John, *Orbis*, pp. 51, 58–9.

[20] P. Wormald, *The Making of English Law: King Alfred to the Twelfth Century, I: Legislation and its Limits* (Oxford, 1999), p. 445. As Professor Keynes pointed out to me, the rhetoric of *Britannia* was far from spent. The charter evidence is indeed striking, although less strongly skewed towards Edgar's reign, but note his extraordinary style *monarchiam totius Britanniae insulae ... obtinens* attested in a tenth-century single sheet (S 736).

[21] John, *Orbis*, pp. 53, 58. See also Nelson, 'Inauguration Rituals', pp. 301–2.

[22] John, *Orbis*, p. 60.

[23] Raine, *York*, I.399–475, at 448 and 425.

[24] Lapidge, *The Cult of St Swithun*, pp. 258–9, n. 34.

both attach themselves to Edgar's reign in the person of his archbishop, Dunstan
(959–88). B's *Life* of Dunstan, written at much the same time as Byrhtferth's
Life of Oswald in the pontificate of Ælfric of Canterbury (995–1005), recounts
the conversion of the English in new terms: 'therefore the people of Albion [lit.
the Albions, i.e. the English], who before him [Augustine] had scorned the Lord,
believed and were joined to his God through recognition of the true faith'.[25] In a
prayer to Dunstan entered in the prayerbook BL, Cotton Nero A.ii in or before
the second quarter of the eleventh century, Albion is directly subordinated to
Dunstan's influence: 'O celebrated confessor of Christ, O light and teacher [to]
the English people, O good shepherd Dunstan, foster-father of all Albion'.[26] And
here is something surely significant. The 'hegemonic' themes so prominent in
the charters of tenth-century kings project ecclesiastical as much as royal ideology. Insular ambition characterizes both.

   The dual nature of Albion, as the locus of royal and clerical power, should
occasion little surprise. It illustrates one of the best known characteristics of
Edgar's regime, what Eric John dubbed its 'caesaropapism'.[27] Less expected,
perhaps, is the extraordinary proximity between territorial aspiration and reforming ideology: reforming rhetoric is arguably ventriloquized in diplomatic
references to Albion.[28] Simon Keynes has assembled a collection of mid-tenth-
century charters directly connected with Dunstan, beginning at Glastonbury
during his abbatiate but whose diplomatic reverberations continue into his pontificate.[29] It happens that the great majority of the so-called 'Dunstan B' charters
and all the charters allegedly written by Dunstan himself project the king's
authority on an insular plane as rulership of Albion.[30] If Albion was deployed
not just in Dunstan's circle, as liturgical and hagiographical usage indicates,

---

25 'Itaque qui ante eum spreuerat crediderit uniuersus **Albionum** populus Domino, et adi-
    unctus est per uerae fidei agnitionem Deo suo': Stubbs, *Dunstan*, p. 6. For other instances
    of Albion in the plural see W. J. Watson, *The History of the Celtic Place-Names of Scot-
    land* (London, 1926), p. 10. On the text see M. Lapidge, 'B. and the *Vita S. Dunstani*',
    in his *Anglo-Latin Literature 900–1066* (London, 1993), pp. 279–91 (originally ptd *St
    Dunstan*, ed. Ramsay *et al.*, pp. 247–59).
26 *Oratio ad Dunstanum* (addressing Dunstan): O inclite confessor Christi, O candelabra
    doctorque Angligena gente, O bone pastor Dunstane, altorque totius Albionis (ed. Stubbs,
    Dunstan, p. 440). From BL, Cotton Nero A.ii c.1029–46 (on the date see R. Rushforth,
    An Atlas of Saints in Anglo-Saxon Calendars [Cambridge, 2002], p. 26).
27 John, *Orbis*, p. 60. See also R. Deshman, '*Christus rex et magi reges*: Kingship and
    Christology in Ottonian and Anglo-Saxon Art', *Frühmittelalterliche Studien* 10 (1976),
    367–405.
28 Highly pertinent discussion of tenth-century territorial claims can be found in D. Bethell,
    'English Monks and Irish Reform in the Eleventh and Twelfth Centuries', *Historical
    Studies VIII: Papers Read before the Irish Conference of Historians, Dublin, 27–30 May,
    1969*, ed. T. D. Williams (Dublin, 1971), pp.111–35, at 130–2, and Wormald, *The Making
    of English Law*, pp. 444–8.
29 S. Keynes, 'The "Dunstan B" Charters', *ASE* 23 (1994), 165–93, *idem*, *Diplomas*, pp.
    46–8.
30 In twenty-five of the thirty-two 'Dunstan B' charters identified by Keynes the king's power
    is expressed in terms of dominion of Albion: listed by Keynes, 'The "Dunstan B" Char-
    ters', pp. 173–9. The exceptions are S 579 of Eadred, S 676, 676a, 678 and 750 of Edgar,

but in his lifetime and possibly through his agency, as the charters suggest, then this explains why references to Albion antedate Edgar's reign but reach fruition under Edgar when Dunstan reached the apex of his influence. A final occurrence, not closely datable, demonstrates the centrality of insular rhetoric to the reforming cause. According to an English coronation rite in existence by 986 at the latest, at the point of consecration of the king, the celebrant sought blessing 'for Thy servant, whom we elect with humble devotion in the kingdom N. of all Albion or equally of the Franks' and charged the new king 'that he should so nourish, instruct, defend and prepare the church of all Albion, with the peoples annexed to it'.[31] The text, usually known as the second English coronation *ordo*, survives in a liturgical collection copied in France for Ratoldus, abbot of Corbie (ob. 986). The form of the consecration prayer in particular clearly betrays hybrid origins, but scholars are in agreement that an English source lay behind the text.[32] Opinions vary about the date of the text and whether the rite was used in England, if at all. Robinson saw the *ordo* as the work of Dunstan; Hohler was emphatic that the *ordo* was 'Certainly used at the coronation of King Edgar in 973'; Nelson saw the text as fitting more closely the circumstances of Edward the Elder or Æthelstan; most recently, Orchard refrained from venturing an opinion on the grounds of lack of evidence.[33]

Leaving aside the Ratoldus sacramentary, then, we have enough to suggest a significant cluster of associations between Edgar and Albion. Albion appears as a royal style, in descriptions of Edgar's dominions in hagiographical texts, twice describing ecclesiastical authority in Britain in texts connected with Dunstan. Totted up crudely we have: nine charters in Edgar's name, one translation-narrative written at the end of Edgar's reign, two saints' lives written after his death about his reforming bishops, a further prayer to one of these bishops. The tally rises impressively if we admit post-Conquest evidence: forty-one further

---

S 854 and 862 issued under Æthelred. On Dunstan's autograph charters see Brooks, *Early History*, p. 235 and *idem*, 'The Career of St. Dunstan', pp. 17–18.

[31] '... et super hunc famulum tuum, quem supplici deuotione in regnum N. **Albionis** totius uidelicet Francorum pariter eligimus, benedictionum tuarum dona multiplica ... Et totius **Albionis** ecclesiam deinceps cum plebibus sibi annexis ita enutriat, ac doceat, muniat, et instruat ...': *The Sacramentary of Ratoldus (Paris, Bibliothèque nationale de France, lat. 12052)*, ed. N. Orchard, HBS 116 (London, 2005), no. 138, p. 49.

[32] On the manuscript see C. Hohler, 'Some Service-Books of the Later Saxon Church', *Tenth-Century Studies: Essays in Commemoration of the Millennium of the Council of Winchester and Regularis Concordia*, ed. D. Parsons (London, 1975), pp. 60–83 and 217–27, at 64–9; *The Sacramentary*, ed. Orchard, pp. xiii–cxciii. On the *ordo* see J. A. Robinson, 'The Coronation Order in the Tenth Century', *Journal of Theological Studies* 19 (1918), 56–72, at 70–2; Hohler, 'Some Service-Books', pp. 67–9; Nelson, 'Inauguration Rituals', pp. 299–304; Nelson, 'The Second English *Ordo*', in her *Politics and Ritual*, pp. 361–74; R. A. Jackson, 'Manuscripts, Texts, and Enigmas of Medieval French Coronation Ordines', *Viator* 23 (1992), pp. 35–71, at 44–9 (I owe this last reference to the kindness of Dr Sarah Hamilton); *The Sacramentary*, ed. Orchard, pp. cxxix–cxxxvi.

[33] Robinson, 'The Coronation Order', pp. 68–72; Hohler, 'Some Service-Books', p. 68; Nelson, 'The Second English *Ordo*', pp. 365–6; *The Sacramentary*, ed. Orchard, p. cxxxiv.

Edgarian charters mentioning Albion surviving as post-Conquest copies only.[34] Camden would have found plenty of medieval evidence to support his contention about Edgar's style. But we need to explain the bulge in the evidence. Even taking Albion as nothing more than elegant variation for Britannia, we still need to explain the explosion in the tenth century. The next stage is to look at the longer history of the term Albion.

Albion

Classical geographers termed this island Albion, and Ptolemy, Pliny, Avienus all gave their authority to the usage.[35] Bede was the first English writer to show knowledge of the term, thanks to his acquaintance with Pliny, and it lent erudition to his description of the island of Britain in the *Historia ecclesiastica*.[36] The translator of the Old English Bede repeated the statement,[37] but Bede's status and wide readership did not immediately popularize the use of Albion as a synonym for Britain or even as a historic name for the island, and Albion goes unmentioned in the work of Boniface, Alcuin, and all other Insular writers before the tenth century, as it had earlier in the work of Aldhelm. When the term does reappear, it does so at a time when Bede was being read with renewed enthusiasm[38] and Lapidge attributed Lantfred's use to acquaintance with Bede.[39] Thus far the story is unproblematic: dormancy followed by interest just when we might expect it, at the moment when reformers rediscovered the early English church and its writers. Furthermore, in the era of hermeneutic Latin when recondite vocabulary carried its own aesthetic rewards, taste enters into consideration: why choose to write *Britannia* when on excellent authority it is established that ancient geographers supplied an altogether more interesting term?

But viewed in a wider perspective still, this tenth-century eruption of interest looks more striking. Dormancy before the tenth century is followed by

---

[34] Contrast with *Britannia*: sixteen only (one of these contemporary: S 690).

[35] Pliny (AD 23–79), *Historia naturalis*, 14.1–3: **Albion** ipsi nomen fuit, cum Britanniae uocarentur omnes de quibus mox paulo dicemus. For Avienus and Ptolemy see Watson, *The History*, pp. 10–13. The etymology of Albion has been discussed by W. Meid, 'Über Albion, elfydd, Albiorix und andere Indikatoren eines keltischen Weltbildes', *Celtic Linguistics Ieithyddiaeth Geltaidd: Readings in the Brythonic Languages. Festschrift for T. Arwyn Watkins*, ed. M. J. Ball, *et al.* (Amsterdam, 1990), pp. 435–9; E. P. Hamp, 'Welsh *elfydd* and *albio-*', *Zeitschrift für Celtische Philologie* 45 (1992), 87–9.

[36] 'Britannia Oceani insula, cui quondam **Albion** nomen fuit': *Historia ecclesiastica*, I.i, *Bede's Ecclesiastical History of the English People*, ed. B. Colgrave and R. A. B. Mynors, rev. ed. (Oxford, 1992), pp. 14–15, quoting Pliny, *Historia naturalis*, 14.1–3 (K. Scarfe Beckett, 'Sources of Beda, *Historia ecclesiastica gentis Anglorum*', *Fontes Anglo-Saxonici: World Wide Web Register*, http://fontes.english.ox.ac.uk/ accessed July 2004).

[37] *Breoton ist garsecges ealond, þæt wæs iu geara **Albion** haten, The Old English Version of Bede's Ecclesiastical History of the English People*, ed. T. Miller, EETS 95, 110, 111 (London 1890–8), I.24.

[38] J. Hill, *Bede and the Benedictine Reform*, Jarrow Lecture 1998 (Jarrow, 1999).

[39] As above, n. 24.

a return to dormancy after it, or at least after the first half of the eleventh century. In the century after the Norman Conquest, when Bede's history circulated with renewed vigour, Anglo-Norman writers in general failed to respond to the undoubted resonances of the term Albion. William of Malmesbury did not exploit its possibilities in his rewriting of the life of Dunstan and neither he nor Henry of Huntingdon used the term except in direct citation of pre-Conquest authority.[40] Orderic Vitalis, however. constitutes an exception. He used Albion repeatedly, always inflected, adopting it as a term for the English inheritance of the Anglo-Norman kings.[41] Harold usurped it, William I's sons disputed it, its stability was threatened by rebellion, William Rufus was its king. The *regnum Albionis* denotes the kingdom of Albion, occasionally as a description of royal power (William Rufus as king of Albion), and also as a term for collective representation within its borders: William I's consecration in the presence of the prelates, abbots and magnates of all the kingdom of Albion; the monks of all Albion at the council of Windsor in 1070. But Orderic appears to be alone in finding in this formulation a synonym for the Anglo-Norman realm, despite the opportunities which it might have presented. His position of relative obscurity among Anglo-Norman historians – his work circulated very modestly indeed – means that this is an isolated exception to a general rule.[42]

In the tenth century, by contrast, Albion did have currency both as a geographical and as a political term and it is to both aspects that we must now turn. Classical geographers agreed that Albion was an island.[43] Edgar's style as king of Albion and Dunstan's spiritual stewardship of its people carried territorial implications, therefore. Britannic claims were famously advertised in the charters of Mercian and West Saxon kings: evidence which John knitted together into his 'empire of Britain' thesis.[44] Without needing to subscribe to his particular interpretation, we might usefully pursue his discussion into a footnote devoted to apparently parallel claims being pressed for the metropolitan at Canterbury. John noted that the *Vita Wilfridi* proclaimed Berhtwald (archbishop of Canterbury 692–731) as archbishop 'Cantuariorum ecclesiae et totius Brittannie' ('of the church of the Kentishmen and of all Britain') and that that claim for Britannic authority of Canterbury was coincidentally matched by Frank Barlow's

---

[40] William of Malmesbury, *Gesta Pontificum*, c. 252, citing S 796 (a purported diploma of AD 974): Hamilton, *Gesta*, p. 404. Henry of Huntingdon, *Historia Anglorum*, i.2, citing Bede's *Historia*: *Henry, Archdeacon of Huntingdon, Historia Anglorum: The History of the English People*, ed. and trans. D. Greenway (Oxford, 1996), pp. 12–13. On the twelfth-century reception of Bede's History see A. Gransden, 'Bede's Reputation as an Historian in Medieval England', *Legends, Traditions and History in Medieval England* (London, 1990), pp. 1–29, originally ptd *Journal of Ecclesiastical History* 32.4 (1981), 397–425.

[41] He used it twenty-six times, including in connexion with eight different rebellions: *The Ecclesiastical History of Orderic Vitalis*, ed. M. Chibnall, 6 vols. (Oxford, 1969–81).

[42] Davies observed the contraction of insular ambitions in the church at precisely this time: *The First English Empire*, pp. 11–12, 38–9.

[43] See n. 35 above.

[44] See n. 18 above.

assertion of the 'natural primacy' of Canterbury in the 'Anglo-Saxon period'.[45] Davies took these claims beyond the Conquest, when Canterbury professions after the Norman Conquest repeated the claims made in the seventh of Augustine's questions to Gregory, but they resurface periodically during the earlier lifetime of the see, a point which Bethell placed beyond doubt.[46] This discussion, like his, has returned to the tenth century when Dunstan, 'the foster-father of all Albion' apparently acted as an agency in the proliferation of the term. To use the term Albion was to reassert the insular authority anciently accorded to the metropolitan. To do so in the later tenth century was to reinforce claims being made for the king.[47]

Albion also had a second meaning, at least in the tenth century, one which did not have to be excavated from texts: as a *political* expression. Albion lies at the root of Irish *Alba* or *Albu*, which before the tenth century denoted much the same as Albion (i.e. the island of Britain).[48] The term has occasioned some disagreement among students of Irish philology, not least about the etymology of the word, but O'Rahilly has traced a clear transition, from Cormac's glossary *c.* 900, in which Alba is used in its older and wider sense, denoting Britain, to the Annals of Ulster s.a. 899, in which a *rí Alban* appears for the first time. O'Rahilly is clear that this term was applied retrospectively as a royal style for earlier kings and that 'It was the conquest of Pictland by Cinaed mac Alpín († 858) that caused *Alba* to be narrowed down to mean "North Britain" '.[49] In other words, Alba acquired political meaning in the later ninth century and began to be used as a political designation in texts in the first half of the tenth, a generation or so before the English efflorescence which we have been observing.[50] What remains unclear is the relationship between the two: the extent to which

---

[45] *Orbis*, pp. 15–16, n. 2 citing F. Barlow, *The English Church 1000–1066* (London, 1963), p. 235; see also *ibid.*, 2nd ed. (London, 1979), pp. 232–8; *Vita Wilfridi*, c. 53, *The Life of Bishop Wilfrid by Eddius Stephanus*, ed. B. Colgrave (Cambridge, 1927), pp. 110–11.

[46] 'We commit to you, my brother, all the bishops of Britain that the unlearned may be instructed, the weak strengthened by your counsel, and the perverse corrected by your authority', *Historia ecclesiastica* I.27.VII: *Bede's Ecclesiastical History*, ed. Colgrave and Mynors, pp. 86–9. From 1072 onwards, suffragan bishops swore allegiance to the archbishop of Canterbury as *Britanniarum primas* (with occasional variants such as *totius Britannice regionis primas*, *primas totius Britannice insule*): *Canterbury Professions*, ed. M. Richter, Canterbury and York Society 67 (1973), see, for example, nos. 35–41, 44, 47, 50a–53, 60. See Davies, *The First English Empire*, pp. 37–9 and Bethell, 'English Monks', pp. 129–35. For a ninth-century resurgence see S. Keynes, 'Between Bede and the Chronicle: London, BL, Cotton Vespasian B.vi, fols. 104–9', *Latin Learning and English Lore: Studies in Anglo-Saxon Literature for Michael Lapidge, I*, ed. K. O'Brien O'Keeffe and A. Orchard (Toronto, 2005), pp. 47–67, at 59–61.

[47] See n. 22 above.

[48] *Dictionary of the Irish Language based mainly on Old and Middle Irish Materials*, Royal Irish Academy, Dublin (Dublin, 1913–76), I.284.

[49] T. F. O'Rahilly, *Early Irish History and Mythology* (Dublin, 1946), p. 386.

[50] On the political context and early usage see M. Herbert, 'Sea-divided Gaels? Constructing Relationships between Irish and Scots c. 800–1169', *Britain and Ireland 900–1300: Insular Responses to Medieval European Change*, ed. B. Smith (Cambridge, 1999), pp. 87–97. See also D. N. Dumville, 'Ireland and North Britain in the Earlier Middle Ages:

Edgar's propagandists were goaded by north British politics into reconsideration of their own terminology and the extent to which they worked in deliberate ignorance. Either way, developments in north and south Britain reflect undoubted experimentation with political vocabulary seen elsewhere in the British Isles: the obsolescence of *Brytaniaid* in the twelfth century prefigured by the creation of Alba and England in the ninth and tenth.[51]

One further wonders what became of both terms. Albion fell into disuse as an active political term but so, for the most part, did *Albania*, the Latinisation of the Irish *Alba*. Both were rescued from oblivion by Geoffrey of Monmouth – Albion as the aboriginal state of the Island, *Albania* via Albanactus, his eponym for Scotland – but both had been deprived of their political valency.[52] Indeed, the Angevin kings outgrew it. Henry II's empire crossed the Irish sea and so encompassed more than Albion. Albion hardly described rule in Britain, either, despite Henry II's temporary mastery of Albion after his capture of William the Lion in 1173/4. Edgar *rex totius Albionis* was remembered not for his contribution to political vocabulary but for raw power: Eadmer's Worcester informant, Nicholas, writing perhaps half a century before Henry II's expedition to Ireland, remembered Edgar as the king who not only ruled all England, Scotland and the surrounding islands, but who had subdued Dublin.[53]

Conclusion

So early modern antiquaries correctly observed a connection between Edgar and Albion, even though they may have put their trust in non-contemporary and inauthentic supporting evidence. For writers in Edgar's day and in the generation afterwards, no less than for seventeenth-century writers, the term Albion encapsulated aspirations of insular dominion. Edgarian writers used Bede, father of the English church, and their usage perhaps gained extra resonance from competition from the northern kings, from the *rí Alban*. Although much of the imperial rhetoric (and by extension, the allusions to Albion), clearly attaches to the figure of Edgar, some dates from after his death. Indeed, Julia Barrow has recently argued that Edgar's immediately posthumous reputation as an imperial figure was an effort of retrospection, a conscious aggrandizement of the stature of Edgar in the hands of reformers.[54] For the purposes of this argument,

Contexts for *Míniugud Senchasa Fher nAlban'*, *Rannsachadh na Gàidhlig 2000: Scottish Gaelic Studies 2000* (Aberdeen, 2002), pp. 185–211.

[51] On *Brytaniaid* for Wales see R. R. Davies, *Conquest, Coexistence and Change: Wales 1063–1415* (Oxford, 1987), p. 16.

[52] *The Historia Regum Britannie of Geoffrey of Monmouth, I: Bern, Burgerbibliothek, MS. 568*, ed. N. Wright (Cambridge, 1985), §21 on Albion, §§23–4 on Albanactus and *passim* on *Albania*.

[53] Nicholas, monk of Worcester, letter to Eadmer: Stubbs, *Dunstan*, pp. 422–4, at 422–3. See Barrow, 'How the Monks of Worcester Perceived their Past', p. 70 and Thornton, 'Edgar', pp. 56–7.

[54] Barrow, 'Chester's Earliest Regatta?', pp. 91–3.

however, the chronology operates rather differently. The reforming connexion may have caused the reformers to anticipate Edgar's claims to Albion as much as to create them retrospectively: reformers were generating the rhetoric of Albion throughout, before as well as after Edgar, in the language of charters, in hagiography, in ritual, and the mode of expression which they chose went beyond the double historical reference of *imperium*.[55]

Some modern writers have come to describe England before the Norman Conquest in terms of the *gens Anglorum*, as 'an ethnically conceived polity', a notion propagated by the church, developed in the rhetoric of tenth-century kingship and brought to fruition by the historians of the twelfth century and their assertion of Englishness in the face of Norman domination.[56] It is well known that tenth-century English kings had their imperial credentials proclaimed in the rhetoric of their royal diplomas and that twelfth-century writers, proponents of Englishness like William of Malmesbury, knew and exploited this. When Early Modern antiquaries, habitually grazing on medieval precedent, encountered the same material, they saw something else. Besides reference to imperial authority and pan-British rule proclaimed therein, they correctly identified a sense of dominion unbounded by ethnic history – English and British. They discerned a geographical aspect to the language of early English empire and before them opened up a clear prospect of wider dominion.[57] Albion thus lurks in the shadows of the wider history of the making of England which Patrick Wormald laid out with such devastating logic a decade ago. Like that story, it had Bedan roots, it emerged in the context of the national church, and a united *gens Anglorum* came into its inheritance in the reign of Edgar. When hagiographers, poets and the draftsmen of charters chose Albion to describe the jurisdiction of Edgar or that of his archbishop, we see a new prophecy.[58]

---

[55] That is, to the Bedan *imperium* of the eighth century and to Roman rule. See, for example, Nelson, 'Inauguration Rituals', p. 302. On Bede in the tenth century see P. Wormald, 'The Making of England', *History Today* 45.2 (1995), 26–32.

[56] Davies, *The First English Empire*; Wormald, 'The Making of England'; S. Foot, 'The Making of *Angelcynn*: English Identity before the Norman Conquest', *TRHS*, 6th series 6 (1996), 25–49; J. Gillingham, *The English in the Twelfth Century: Imperialism, National Identity, and Political Values* (Woodbridge, 2000). The quotation is from Davies, *The First English Empire*, p. 196. For a significantly different perspective see D. N. Dumville, *The Mediaeval Foundations of England?* G. O. Sayles Memorial Lectures on Mediaeval History (Aberdeen, 2006).

[57] Here, my interpretation parts company from that of Davies, who saw claims to insular dominion in British terms, as obsolete in the tenth century and displaced by a new rhetoric of Englishness: *The First English Empire*, pp. 50–3.

[58] I am indebted to Donald Scragg for his forebearance as editor and to Simon Keynes for his great kindness in commenting on a draft. This paper draws in part on material presented at the Leeds International Medieval Congress on 15 July 2004.

8

King Edgar and the Men of the Danelaw

LESLEY ABRAMS

IN 1976, in a provocative and influential article, Niels Lund asserted that in
the competitive political environment of the late 950s Edgar was made king
of the Mercians and Northumbrians by important northern laymen, who in 957
withdrew their allegiance from his brother, King Eadwig.[1] These magnates, he
argued, saw an opportunity to use Edgar's need for their support to further their
own, separatist, purposes in those parts of England later called the Danelaw. In
particular, Lund claimed that the magnates of these regions were motivated by
the desire to resist the penetration of royal interference into their domain. In
support of this argument he cited the surviving laws referred to as IV Edgar,
dated by Dorothy Whitelock to 962–3, in which the king sanctioned the legal
autonomy of the region:

> Þonne wille ic þæt stande mid Denum swa gode laga swa hy betste geceosen; ⁊
> ic heom á geþafode ⁊ geðafian wille, swa lange swa me lif gelæst, for eowrum
> hyldum þe ge me symble cyddon.

> I will that such good laws be in force among the Danes as they best prefer,
> and I have always granted them (this), and will grant (it) as long as my life
> endures, for your obedience which you have ever manifested to me.[2]

Lund concluded that Edgar's actions represented a setback to the unification of
England: by holding back from imposing royal rights and encroaching on customary law, this concession to Scandinavian ways of doing things was virtually
equivalent to granting domestic self-government to the Danelaw. That Edgar
was known (at least to some) for his tolerance of Danish ways is demonstrated
by Wulfstan's judgement in the king's obituary in *ASC*:

> Ane misdæde he dyde þeah to swyðe, þæt he elðeodige unsida lufode, ⁊ heþene
> þeawas innan þysan lande gebrohte to fæste, ⁊ utlændisce hider in tihte, ⁊
> deriende leoda bespeon to þysan earde.

---

[1] N. Lund, 'King Edgar and the Danelaw', *MScand* 9 (1976), 181–95.

[2] IV Edgar §12; text and translation in *The Laws of the Kings of England from Edmund to
Henry I*, ed. and trans. A. J. Robertson (Cambridge, 1925), pp. 28–39, at 36–7; also in
EHD, pp. 434–7; translation here from P. Wormald, *The Making of English Law: King
Alfred to the Twelfth Century. Legislation and its Limits* (Oxford, 1999), pp. 318–19.

Yet he did one ill-deed too greatly: he loved evil foreign customs and brought
too firmly heathen manners within this land, and attracted hither foreigners
and enticed harmful people to this country.[3]

Thirty years after Lund stimulated discussion on Edgar's relations with the
Danelaw, I should like to reconsider the king's position.

The world of the Danelaw is complex, varied, and obscure.[4] Little evidence
survives on which to base what is essentially an exercise in speculation. IV
Edgar and the *ASC* D, s.a. 959, therefore loom large in any investigation of
the dynamic between West Saxons and those living north and east of Watling
Street in Edgar's reign. Southern kings since Edward the Elder had had to fight
to impose themselves outside Wessex, but Edgar began his kingship there and
retained authority in those regions throughout his reign. However, the nature of
this authority and the extent of royal rights outside the South remain unclear,
especially in northern England, where West Saxon rule had been so recently
imposed and so intermittently in force in preceding decades. Although IV
Edgar articulated a recognition of legal autonomy, as emphasised by Lund, it
also insisted that the king 'possess my royal prerogatives as my father did' and
explicitly imposed some 'English' law on 'Danish' regions. Measures for the
organisation of sworn witnesses to supervise buying and selling were to 'be
common to the whole people, whether Englishmen or Danes or Britons, in every
part of my dominion'.[5] Therefore, although Edgar's legislation accepted that
'Danish' law was different, it also marked a movement away from local distinctiveness towards common English practice. Later kings clearly approved.
Patrick Wormald pointed out that Edgar's laws acquired symbolic significance
in the eleventh century, remarking that the king may have been seen as 'a suitable patron for an Anglo-Danish *entente*' and his laws as 'a basis for the rec-
onciliation of Englishman and Dane'.[6] Simon Keynes has suggested that Edgar
'regarded the act of acknowledging the diversity of established customs among
different peoples as the best way of maintaining the appearance of overall unity',
and that IV Edgar constituted an admission that the king was not in a position to

---

3   *ASC* 959 D; Cubbin, *MS D*, p. 45; trans. *EHD*, p. 225.
4   Major studies include Stenton's in Stenton, *ASE*, pp. 502–25, and *Preparatory to Anglo-*
    Saxon England, ed. D. M. Stenton (Oxford, 1970), pp. 136–65, 298–313, and 335–45;
    C. R. Hart, *The Danelaw* (London, 1992); *Vikings and the Danelaw. Select Papers from*
    the Proceedings of the Thirteenth Viking Congress, ed. J. Graham-Campbell, R. Hall,
    J. Jesch, and D. N. Parsons (Oxford, 2001); *Cultures in Contact. Scandinavian Settle-*
    ment in England in the Ninth and Tenth Centuries, ed. D. M. Hadley and J. D. Richards
    (Turnhout, 2000); D. M. Hadley, *The Vikings in England: Settlement, Society and Culture*
    (Manchester, 2006).
5   *Sy þeahhwæðere þes ræd gemæne eallum leodscype, ægðer ge Englum ge Denum ge*
    Bryttum, on ælcum ende mines anwealdes; IV Edgar §2a.2; *The Laws*, ed. Robertson,
    p. 32; trans. Wormald, *The Making*, p. 318. Despite the imposition of a common practice,
    the Danes were left free to decide the penalty for transgression (§13).
6   Wormald, *The Making*, pp. 129–33; Cnut harked back to Edgar's laws in his own and in
    his letter of 1019–20.

legislate for the 'Danish' part of his kingdom.[7] I would add that while previous regime changes (and there had been many, especially north of the Humber, in the previous decades) may have confused the issue of legal practice, IV Edgar's provisions may have been a recognition of the viability of local custom in a region where mixed custom was the norm.

Lund's thesis depends on the existence of a certain dynamic between king and northern magnates: Edgar aspiring to power, non-West Saxons defensive of their previous legal independence working to engineer his accession, and a subsequent perception of debt and payback. However, there is no sense in the surviving written evidence that 'Danes' had a factional voice in 957, though our sources are admittedly tight-lipped. Wormald's redating of IV Edgar to the 970s,[8] Edgar's most imperial years, provides an alternative context for its composition, a time when early weaknesses might have been an increasingly distant memory. Nevertheless, even if the hypothetical debt of gratitude is set aside, Edgar was doubtless significantly reliant on local support in the 950s, and Lund's argument has usefully drawn attention to the issue of regional political culture. Edgar would have needed a strong Mercian-Danish power base to take up his share of the divided kingdom with confidence in 957.[9] He may have been especially reliant on the networks of his foster-family, Æthelstan Half-King, ealdorman of East Anglia (and much of the east midlands), and his sons.[10] Unfortunately, there are no surviving documents from that year in Edgar's name to throw light on the king's circle, but a group of charters dated 958 and 959, issued during the period of shared kingship, does survive.

Before turning to discussion of these charters, some general consideration of the Danelaw may be useful. Views on its nature have been diverse: while Frank Stenton focused on its distinctiveness and envisaged a transformative mass migration from Scandinavia, Peter Sawyer minimised the numbers of settlers, interpreting the signs of influence as reflecting not a Scandinavian society but the disproportionate power of a Scandinavian elite.[11] More recently, Dawn Hadley has argued against the discredited idea that in the society of the Danelaw,

---

[7] S. Keynes, 'The Vikings in England, *c*. 790–1016', *The Oxford Illustrated History of the Vikings*, ed. P. Sawyer (Oxford, 1997), pp. 48–82, at 72.

[8] *The Making*, pp. 182 and 442; see also Hart, *The Danelaw*, p. 591, n. 92.

[9] For suggestions that Edgar had in fact become subking in 955, when Eadwig came to power in Wessex, see B. Yorke, 'Æthelwold and the Politics of the Tenth Century', Yorke, *Æthelwold*, pp. 65–88, at 78; on the division of 957 as a political settlement, not the result of civil war, see S. Keynes, 'England, *c*. 900–1016', *The New Cambridge Medieval History, Volume III, c. 900–c. 1024*, ed. T. Reuter (Cambridge, 1999), pp. 456–84, at 477–9. John of Worcester, who portrays the division as a result of revolt in 957, says that Edgar was chosen by the Mercians and Northumbrians, but refers to him only as 'king of the Mercians'; JW, *Chronicon*, II.406.

[10] Hart, *The Danelaw*, pp. 569–604, esp. 575. If Hart's suggestion (p. 576) that Æthelstan's household was based in Huntingdonshire is correct, Edgar's knowledge of the east midlands could have begun at an early age.

[11] See, for example, P. H. Sawyer, 'The Two Viking Ages of Britain', *MScand* 2 (1969), 163–207; for Stenton, see above, n. 4.

'political and military allegiances were ... formed solely along "ethnic" lines'.[12] Following Sawyer and Susan Reynolds, Hadley has downplayed the 'Danishness' of the Danelaw,[13] making the valuable point that some regional peculiarities pre-dated the Scandinavian settlement, and that political allegiance thereafter was likely to be motivated by complex regional rather than simply ethnic considerations. It is easy to imagine that the interests of kings based in the south could have threatened those of all non-West Saxons, and under those circumstances opposition to the southern regime may have inspired more political solidarity than did shared language, heritage, and custom.[14]

It is therefore possible to see the distinctiveness of the Danelaw as regional particularism, and to dispense with the idea that there was a very significant Scandinavian element to society beyond Watling Street in the tenth century. From this perspective, peculiarly Danish characteristics of law and administration in northern and eastern society – mainly visible in documents of the late Anglo-Saxon or post-Conquest periods – have been taken to represent differences of vocabulary rather than substance.[15] It is also possible, however, to take a different view of the original impact of the Scandinavian takeover, an impact which the eventual assimilation of the immigrants into English society may have helped to disguise. Unfortunately, the nature of the written sources means that the Scandinavian perspective of the conquest and settlement periods is largely unrepresented, although there are many physical signs of Scandinavian cultural identity in the form of monumental sculpture and metalwork, especially in the north,[16]

---

[12] D. M. Hadley, ' "Hamlet and the Princes of Denmark": Lordship in the Danelaw, c. 860–954', Cultures in Contact, ed. Hadley and Richards, pp. 107–32, at 114.

[13] D. M. Hadley, 'In Search of the Vikings: The Problems and the Possibilities of Interdisciplinary Approaches', Vikings and the Danelaw, ed. Graham-Campbell et al., pp. 13–30, esp. 25, and 'Viking and Native: Re-Thinking Identity in the Danelaw', EME 11 (2002), 45–70, esp. 50–2; S. Reynolds, 'What Do We Mean by "Anglo-Saxon" and "Anglo-Saxons"?', Jnl Brit. Stud. 24 (1985), 395–414, esp. 406–13; see also P. Stafford, The East Midlands in the Early Middle Ages (Leicester, 1985), pp. 109–21.

[14] William of Malmesbury saw such political solidarity in the reign of Edward the Elder: the West Saxon king 'defeated in battle and subjected the West and East Angles and the Northumbrians, who had already grown into one nation with the Danes' (qui cum Danis iam in unam gentem coaluerant); WM, Gesta Regum, ii.125 (I. 196–7). John of Worcester, on the other hand, explained the collapse of resistance to a viking army on the Humber in 993, which was precipitated by the flight of Frana, Frithogist, and Goduuinus, by the fact that 'they were Danish on their father's side' (ex paterno genere Danici); JW, Chronicon, II.442–3.

[15] Sawyer, The Age, p. 152; D. M. Hadley, The Northern Danelaw: Its Social Structure, c. 800–1100 (London, 2000), p. 300.

[16] R. Cramp, County Durham and Northumberland, 2 vols. (Oxford, 1984), Corpus of Anglo-Saxon Stone Sculpture 1 (hereafter CASSS); R. N. Bailey and R. Cramp, Cumberland and Westmorland, CASSS 2 (Oxford, 1988); J. T. Lang, York and Eastern Yorkshire, CASSS 3 (Oxford, 1991); P. Everson and D. Stocker, Lincolnshire, CASSS 5 (Oxford, 1999); J. Lang, Northern Yorkshire, CASSS 6 (Oxford, 2002); see also R. N. Bailey, Viking Age Sculpture in Northern England (London, 1980). On metalwork, see K. Leahy and C.Patterson, 'New Light on the Viking Presence in Lincolnshire: The Artefactual Evidence', Vikings and the Danelaw, ed. Graham-Campbell et al., pp. 181–202. Thanks to the activities of

and a mass of place-names formed by Norse-speakers.[17] Scandinavian material culture was available to all, of course, but the substantial linguistic footprint is arguably more solid testimony to a significant, specifically Scandinavian, presence. While we now see that Stenton's image of a mass migration of pioneering freedom-loving Danes was far too unsubtle, the evidence in some regions can nonetheless support what the *ASC* only tersely (and summarily) notes, the division and settlement of Northumbria, half of Mercia, and East Anglia by viking armies.[18] And although the sources do not say so, it may be that settlers continued to arrive from Scandinavia during the tenth century. The density of settlement probably varied significantly, according to local circumstance.

The distinctive social and legal practice of the mid-tenth century, to which IV Edgar refers, could therefore reflect a Scandinavian way of doing things, built up over the century since settlement began and combined with English regional custom. From this perspective, the Scandinavian terminology in IV Edgar – according to Patrick Wormald the first English code to use Norse vocabulary to any degree – can be taken to reflect actual Scandinavian practice as well as real Norse speech.[19] Scandinavian control of social regulation in conquered areas before their absorption by the West Saxons is reflected in the treaty of Alfred and Guthrum and also in a law of Edward the Elder:

> *Gif hine hwa feormige syððan, bete swa seo domboc sæcge, ⁊ se scyle ðe flyman feormige, gif hit sy herinne; gif hit sy east inne, gif hit sy norð inne, bete be ðam þe þa friðgewritu sæcgan.*

> If anyone subsequently harbours [a criminal], let him pay as the lawbook says, and as he should who harbours a fugitive, if the offence is committed here [in my kingdom]; but if in the East or North, compensation shall be paid according to what the peace-treaties say.[20]

---

metal-detectorists, discoveries are ongoing; the Portable Antiquities Scheme database at http://www.finds.org.uk provides an up-to-date record of metal-detected finds.

[17] For a review of past scholarship and suggested reinterpretations, see L. Abrams and D. N. Parsons, 'Place-Names and the History of Scandinavian Settlement in England', *Land, Sea and Home. Proceedings of a Conference on Viking-Period Settlement*, ed. J. Hines, A. Lane and M. Redknap (Leeds, 2004), pp. 379–431. A. H. Smith's classic map of 'the Scandinavian Settlement' is reproduced there on p. 383. On other issues of linguistic influence, see J. Hines, 'Scandinavian English: A Creole in Context', *Language Contact in the British Isles*, ed. P. S. Ureland and G. Broderick (Tübingen, 1991), pp. 403–27, and M. Townend, *Language and History in Viking Age England. Linguistic Relations between Speakers of Old Norse and Old English* (Turnhout, 2002).

[18] *ASC* 876, 877 and 880; the word used is *here*.

[19] *The Making*, p. 319. *Lagu* occurs in the plural, as in Norse, for example, and only later becomes singular (in Æthelred's time); see *The Laws*, ed. Robertson, pp. 307–8.

[20] II Edward §5.2 (my translation); *The Laws of the Earliest English Kings*, ed. F. L. Attenborough (Cambridge, 1922), pp. 120–1; Wormald (*The Making*, pp. 438–9) suggested that II Edward preceded the submission of East Anglia to the king in 916–17; for the treaty of Alfred and Guthrum, see S. Keynes and M. Lapidge, *Alfred the Great. Asser's Life of King Alfred and Other Contemporary Sources* (Harmondsworth, 1983), pp. 171–2 and 311–13.

Successive events must have regularly reconfigured the dynamic of interaction between native and immigrant north and east of Watling Street, as viking conquest and independent rule, migration from Scandinavian settlements in Ireland, takeover by the West Saxons, the revival of viking attacks in the 980s, and the Danish conquests of the early eleventh century in turn affected the social and political mix.

It is not difficult to imagine that the interests of the indigenous population merged with that of the Scandinavian community over time, especially, perhaps, after conquest by the West Saxons. How long it took to achieve this convergence is unclear, however, as the immediate and medium-term impact of viking takeover is more elusive than its longer-term result. Members of the indigenous elite could, of course, submit and co-operate in the first instance as well as fight or flee, and from the earliest stages there is evidence of power-sharing and collaboration between English and Scandinavian at the highest level – Ceolwulf in Mercia, for example, Æthelwold in Northumbria, and native East Anglian successors after the death of King Edmund.[21] But it seems unlikely that the new Scandinavian lords slipped quietly into power on the ground as a matter of course, turning conquest into settlement with a friendly handshake. Some native landholders may have been able to retain their estates, but the new rulers had followers to reward, and the establishment of regimes in the ninth century presumably involved some dispossession, competition, and negotiation as well as continuity – felt more in some regions than others. Hadley has recently pointed out that the upheavals may have played a part in weakening patterns of rural organisation and tenurial control, allowing rural populations to move in far greater numbers to towns and stimulating the urban growth that came to be such a feature of the region.[22] Further disruption must have been caused in the North by the transition to Hiberno-Scandinavian rule in the second decade of the tenth century (as exemplified by the seizures of land later condemned by the community of St Cuthbert),[23] and throughout the Danelaw by the West Saxon conquest. In the area around Peterborough, English political control had been applied for more than a generation (approximately forty years) before Edgar's accession. Around York, on the other hand, it had only been three years since a Norse-speaking king had been in charge. In 957, the strength of Scandinavian feeling among descendants of the settlers, and the degree of identification between 'English' and 'Dane', must have varied considerably across the regions settled.

Under these circumstances, 'Danes' are unlikely to have been a single sectarian pressure-group; nor, of course, was ethnic identity exclusively genetic. It has long been recognised that 'Danes' in Anglo-Saxon texts meant more than just 'people from Denmark'; the connotations of the term in the English context

---

[21] *ASC* 877; *ASC* 900; Hart, *The Danelaw*, p. 41.

[22] Hadley, *The Vikings*, pp. 181–2.

[23] *Historia de Sancto Cuthberto. A History of Saint Cuthbert and a Record of his Patrimony*, ed. and trans. T. Johnson South (Woodbridge, 2002), pp. 60–2.

doubtless underwent complex changes throughout the tenth and eleventh centuries.[24] After Edgar's reign, for example, first the revival of viking attacks and
then Cnut's conquest must have given new meaning to the difference between
'Danes' and 'English'. Æthelweard, probably writing in the late 970s or early
980s (before the resumption of viking raids), spoke of *Dani* and *pagani* inter-
changeably in relating ninth-century conflicts and drew attention to the fact that
Dani spoke a different language.[25] Here at least 'Danes' must mean Danes (or at
least an essentially Scandinavian conglomeration). The 'Danes' in tenth-century
texts such as IV Edgar, on the other hand, have been taken to mean 'not West
Saxons' by those scholars of the Danelaw who see little ethnic reality behind the
label, taking the term to refer to Mercian or Northumbrian regionality under a
Danish label of convenience.[26] While we should definitely not assume that the
settlers' descendants 'remained a self-consciously different ethnic group within
the society of the Danelaw' in political terms,[27] as Hadley has warned, other
evidence suggests that a self-conscious Scandinavian culture did continue to be
articulated in some parts of the Danelaw in the tenth century. So who were the
'Danes' and the 'English' in Edgar's reign?

According to the instructions for its circulation, IV Edgar applied to Northumbria, Mercia, and East Anglia. It ends with the injunction that Oslac should
promote its observance among the people of his Northumbrian earldom, and that
'many documents are to be made about this, and to be sent both to Ealdorman
Ælfhere and to Ealdorman Æthelwine, and by them in all directions, that this
measure be known to both poor and rich'.[28] Ælfhere and Æthelwine were the

---

24 A. P. Smyth, 'The Emergence of English Identity, 700–1000', in *Medieval Europeans.
    Studies in Ethnic Identity and National Perspectives in Medieval Europe*, ed. A. P. Smyth
    (Basingstoke, 1998), pp. 24–52.
25 When the ealdorman of Mercia was killed, his body was taken to 'the place called *North-
    uuorthige*, but in the Danish language (*iuxta Danaam linguam*) Deoraby'; Campbell,
    Æthelweard, p. 37; for the date see p. xiii, n. 2, and S. Miller, 'Æthelweard', *Blackwell
    Encycl.*, p. 18. *Dani* alternates with *pagani* and *barbari* in Æthelweard's accounts of
    eighth- and ninth-century viking activity, but he seems to prefer other terms for settled
    Scandinavians: the vikings based in East Anglia in the 890s are described as *plebs
    immunda* (foul people) or *lues* (a pest) (pp. 44, 46). Æthelweard's only reference to the
    Hiberno-Scandinavian kings of York is to 'traitors' (*desertores*) (p. 54). For Æthelweard's
    viking vocabulary, see R. I. Page, '"A Most Vile People": Early English Historians on the
    Vikings', Dorothea Coke Memorial Lecture (London, 1987), esp. pp. 11–14.
26 For example, Hadley, *The Northern Danelaw*, pp. 340–1.
27 *Ibid.*, pp. 307–8; see also M. Innes, 'Danelaw Identities: Ethnicity, Regionalism, and
    Political Allegiance', *Cultures in Contact*, ed. Hadley and Richards, pp. 65–88.
28 *Oslac eorl ꝺ eall here þe on his ealdordome wunað, þæt ðis stande ...; ꝺ write man manega
    gewrita be ðisum ꝺ sende ægðer ge to Ælfere ealdormen ge to Æþelwine ealdormen, ꝺ hi
    gehwyder*: IV Edgar §15, *The Laws*, ed. Robertson, p. 38. These instructions may suggest
    that the meeting at *Wihtbordesstan* (still unidentified) took place in the North, or at least
    in the presence of the northern ealdorman; the reference in §6 (p. 34) to selling 'either
    in a borough or in a wapentake' (*oððe burge oððe wæpengetace*) may link the text to the
    particular areas that used ON *vápnatak* for their internal divisions. According to Stenton
    (*ASE*, p. 504), this is the first English appearance of the ON word. There is no recognition

ealdormen of Mercia and East Anglia, respectively, but the frame of reference
of the law is not entirely clear.[29] Ælfhere's earldom presumably consisted of the
reunited (ex-)kingdom of Mercia, not simply the part to the north and east of
Watling Street which had been taken by vikings in the 870s.[30] Mercia on the
English side had come under West Saxon control in the late ninth century, and
no draftsman would have described it as 'Danish'. 'English' in IV Edgar, if it
did not refer to Edgar's southern subjects, could thus have meant English Mercia
(and indeed Bernicia), its practice contrasted with the custom of those regions
of the three former kingdoms which had once been under Scandinavian rule.
On the other hand, no one is suggesting that Scandinavians wiped out the native
inhabitants of the conquered lands; they need to be included in the picture. Like
all English territory, the land beyond Watling Street was divided into small units
of governance, ruled from local centres. Other forms of evidence, such as place-
names, personal names, sculpture, pottery, and coinage display a regionality
which the more strident ideology of Anglo-Saxon unification can overshadow.[31]
Is it inconceivable that in the mid-tenth century the operation of these units of
local power varied according to local custom, which itself varied according to
the density of Scandinavian settlement and lordly influence? In one district,

here that Northumbria was divided between two earls. The date of the division is uncertain, but it had probably occurred by 966. Late sources (such as the *Libellus de primo
Saxonum uel Normannorum aduentu*; *Symeonis monachi opera omnia*, ed. T. Arnold,
2 vols. (London, 1882–5), II.382) suggest a division when Oslac was appointed. See
D. Whitelock, 'The Dealings of the Kings of England with Northumbria', *The Anglo-
Saxons. Studies in Some Aspects of their History and Culture Presented to Bruce Dickins*,
ed. P. Clemoes (Cambridge, 1959), pp. 70–88, at 77.

29 The later division of England into three law zones – West Saxon, Mercian, and Danish
    – in twelfth- and thirteenth-century legal texts (linked with the text known as the County
    Hidage, possibly originally written in the eleventh century) complicates the issue; see
    H. M. Chadwick, *Studies in Anglo-Saxon Institutions* (Cambridge, 1905), pp. 198–201.

30 According to B., author of the Life of Saint Dunstan, and John of Worcester, Edgar
    acceded to England north of the Thames, not simply north of Watling Street; Stubbs,
    Dunstan, p. 36; JW, *Chronicon*, II.406.

31 On names, see Abrams and Parsons, 'Place-Names', and D. N. Parsons, '*Anna, Dot, Thorir
    ... Counting Domesday Personal Names*', *Nomina* 25 (2002), 29–52, esp. 46–51. On
    regional sculptural zones, see D. Stocker and P. Evison, 'Five Towns Funerals: Decoding
    Diversity in Danelaw Stone Sculpture', *Vikings and the Danelaw*, ed. Graham-Campbell
    et al., pp. 223–43, and on pottery, Hadley, *The Vikings*, pp. 178–9. On coinage, see
    K. Jonsson, 'The Pre-Reform Coinage of Edgar – the Legacy of the Anglo-Saxon King-
    doms', *Coinage and History in the North Sea World, c. AD 500–1250. Essays in Honour of
    Marion Archibald*, ed. B. Cook and G. Williams (Leiden, 2006), pp. 325–46. In Æthelred's
    reign, the region of the Five Boroughs had its own law code (III Æthelred), and older ad-
    ministrative units, such as the Magonsæte, Wreocensæte, and Pecsæte, are cited in a group
    of Edgar's charters, suggesting that local administration was not yet always organised on
    the basis of the West Saxon arrangement of shires and boroughs; see S 677, 723, and
    712a, M. Gelling, *The West Midlands in the Early Middle Ages* (Leicester, 1992), p. 145,
    and Williams, '*Princeps Merciorum Gentis*', pp. 162–3; Hart (*The Danelaw*, p. 451) dis-
    missed this feature as a symptom of the 'antiquarian interests' of the scribe. For the text
    of S 712a, see N. Brooks, M. Gelling, and D. Johnson, 'A New Charter of King Edgar',
    ASE 13 (1984), 137–55.

might 'Danish' lords have regulated society according to their law, whereas other, more English, areas continued to be ruled by English custom? The lands of those who were killed, exiled, or otherwise defeated were most likely to have been given to viking followers and put under Scandinavian lordship, while other districts, such as those where native landholders had submitted and collaborated with the invaders, could have remained more 'English'. There could have been greater continuity of local custom where English lords bought lands inside Scandinavian-controlled territory,[32] and where West Saxon placemen were put in charge when the area submitted to their king. This is not to suggest that law was applied to individuals according to their ethnic identity, but rather that labels might have applied to the type of law that had become customary in a locality: a 'Danish' hundred might have contained many English men and women, to whom law heavily influenced by the immigrant settlers would have applied, and vice versa. 'English' and 'Danish' regions could have sat side-by-side. The clusters of Scandinavian place-names on the map of northern England and the east midlands might provide the geographical context for such areas of 'Danish' law, as might the many Scandinavian hundred-names,[33] or administrative names derived from ON *thing*, such as Thingoe ('assembly mound') in Suffolk, and Thingwall ('assembly field') in Cheshire and Lancashire. Such regional variety may have been in decline by the mid-tenth century, as the two cultures converged, and would have been threatened by the increasing impulse towards uniformity which accompanied the intrusion of royal rights;[34] but it could explain why Edgar, when he had the instructions in IV Edgar recorded for the ealdormen of Northumbria, Mercia, and East Anglia, included provisions for regulations 'among the English' as well as 'among the Danes'.

The men of the *Myrcna witan* of 957–9 presumably reflected the multi-cultural identity of the region.[35] The earls and thegns who witnessed Edgar's charters in 958 and 959 bore a mixture of personal names, English and Norse, showing the proportionate importance at a local level of men with sufficient

---

[32] See S 396 and 397, for lands in Bedfordshire and Derbyshire, respectively, purchased during the reign of Edward the Elder.

[33] There are potentially ten in East Anglia alone: see the map in Abrams and Parsons, 'Place-Names', p. 416.

[34] The laws of both Æthelred and Cnut nevertheless continued to acknowledge the distinction between English and Dane; how this related to the contemporary influx of Danes into areas not previously settled by Scandinavians is an interesting question. On this second phase of immigration, see A. Williams, '"Cockles Amongst the Wheat": Danes and English in the Western Midlands in the First Half of the Eleventh Century', *Midland History* 11 (1986), 1–22, esp. 1–2 and 12–15; Wormald (*The Making*, pp. 129–33) argued that Cnut's declaration in 1018 of commitment to the good old law of King Edgar meant a return to royal respect for regional peculiarities and a withdrawal from Æthelred's level of interventionism.

[35] The *Myrcna witan* is mentioned in a case involving an estate in Middlesex, brought to the court after 'the Mercians chose Edgar as king and gave him control of all royal prerogatives (*cyneriht*)' (S 1447): Robertson, *Charters*, p. 90.

Scandinavian affinity to affect their names.[36] A Norse name does not of course have to indicate a person born in Scandinavia or with Scandinavian parents or grandparents. Mixed marriages doubtless produced bicultural naming, as did baptismal relationships – Guthrum famously becoming Æthelstan in 878.[37] It has been argued that Norse names were widely adopted by the English in the tenth and eleventh centuries in fashionable imitation of the Scandinavian elite,[38] and the *Liber Eliensis* clearly shows late tenth-century families in the eastern Danelaw choosing names from both traditions. More recently, however, the origins of a vigorous naming tradition among the Scandinavians in England have been located in a predominantly Norse linguistic context,[39] and it therefore seems possible that some Scandinavian roots lay close behind the Thurcytels and Hroalds of the witness-lists of the 950s. Equally, a Dunstan or Ælwine could have had a parent or other relative with a Scandinavian background. In any case, it seems that Scandinavian names declared a regional identity, never gaining the same popularity outside the Danelaw.

Edgar's charters rarely record the occasion or place of issue,[40] but royal councils may have taken place several times a year. Wherever he himself happened to be, the king's authority was everpresent through his representatives, his ealdormen and bishops, who exercised their authority in person as a matter of routine. Much of the responsibility for government, however, was carried by thegns, who performed important military, social, and legal functions, sometimes at the king's side, sometimes on their own in the localities. A trend towards the local organisation of legal initiatives in the tenth century is indicated by texts such as the Hundred Ordinance, *Dunsæte*, and IV Edgar itself: 'it is my will that every man be under surety, whether he live in a borough or in the country, and a body of standing witnesses shall be appointed for every borough and hundred'; thirty-six persons were to be chosen as witnesses for every borough (twelve for a small borough and for a hundred).[41] Hundred-courts were supposed to meet every four weeks; borough-courts three times a year, shire-courts twice.[42] Other meetings also took place – of grouped hundreds, for example – which are not mentioned in extant law codes.[43]

Early medieval political action may have been focussed on the royal household

---

[36] I am grateful to David Parsons for his specialist advice on the personal names discussed in this paper. We hope to undertake a study of these names in the future.

[37] *ASC* 890; cf. Hadley, ' "Hamlet" ', pp. 123–4.

[38] Sawyer, *The Age*, pp. 158–61.

[39] Revealed particularly in the many place-names formed with personal names; see Parsons, 'Anna, Dot, Thorir', and M. Townend, *Scandinavian Culture in Eleventh-Century Yorkshire* (Kirkdale, 2007).

[40] An exception is S 667, issued at Penkridge, Staffordshire, in 958.

[41] Wormald, *The Making*, pp. 378–84; IV Edgar §§3–5: *Þæt þonne his þæt ic wille, þæt ælc mann sy under borge ge binnan burgum ge buton burgum. 7 gewitnes sý geset to ælcere byrig 7 to ælcum hundrode.*

[42] I Edgar §1; III Edgar §5.1: *The Laws*, ed. Robertson, pp. 16 and 26.

[43] A. Kennedy, 'Law and Litigation in the *Libellus Æthelwoldi episcopi*', *ASE* 24 (1995), 131–83, at 140.

and the person of the king, but it also operated through this local elite. Study of interpersonal relationships within the ruling classes can suggest much about how society worked before the operation of a full-blown bureaucratic machine. Political leadership was exercised through social relationships – a personal, intimate, context which (as Ann Williams has pointed out) concentration on the development of centralised government can sometimes obscure.[44] Matthew Innes has described local power at work in the Rhine Valley: '[it] was dependent on the ability to carry a public meeting, to exert influence, to cajole support. ... The exercise of local power was rooted in the everyday, in the give-and-take of face-to-face relationships of co-operation, patronage, and mutual back-scratching.'[45] In England, important men acted as both royal and local agents, and it is one of the triumphs of Anglo-Saxon kingship that these roles did not conflict more often. While the creation of a new allegiance to the kingdom of England may have been of primary concern to the West Saxons throughout the tenth century, it had to proceed alongside the operation of regional identities – shaped, in the Danelaw, by the Scandinavian heritage. To understand the Danelaw in Edgar's day, we must consider not just what royal rights the king managed to impose, but who exercised leadership there on a day-to-day basis.

The operation of lordship in the second half of the tenth century is difficult to observe, however, thanks to the nature of the sources. The anecdotal record of property disputes involving Ely in the *Libellus Æthelwoldi* provides only glimpses of courts in action, as do some discursive charters (S 1447, for example), or occasional documents, including Peterborough's list of fes-termen (ON *festumaðr*, 'surety').[46] Wulfstan of Dalham, clearly no ordinary thegn, presided over hundred- and shire-courts at Ely and Cambridge;[47] twenty-four *iudices* gathered near Cambridge to pass judgement on a case;[48] *Sexferth, Oschetel, Osuui, Uvi*, and many other *fideles uiri* witnessed an exchange of land, probably at Cambridge;[49] many *legales uiri* went to Fen Ditton to support a case against a dishonest priest.[50] In a York inquest of 1106, *legislator uel iudex* glosses the Norse term *lagaman*.[51] According to Alan Kennedy, 'lawmen' are

---

[44] A. Williams, '*Princeps Merciorum Gentis*: The Family, Career and Connections of Ælfhere, Ealdorman of Mercia', *ASE* 10 (1982), 143–72, at 143.

[45] M. Innes, *State and Society in the Early Middle Ages: The Middle Rhine Valley, 400–1000* (Cambridge, 2000), p. 139.

[46] The *Libellus* exists as an independent text (unedited) but is also incorporated into Book II of the *Liber Eliensis*, ed. E. O. Blake (London 1962), and now translated by J. Fairweather, *Liber Eliensis. A History of the Isle of Ely from the Seventh Century to the Twelfth* (Woodbridge, 2005); for S 1447 see above, n. 35; for Peterborough's *festermen*, see S 1448 and S 1148a, Robertson, *Charters*, pp. 72–83. On the operation of courts, see Kennedy, 'Law and Litigation', pp. 141–9, and Wormald, *The Making*, pp. 153–8.

[47] *LE*, ii.18; trans. Fairweather, p. 117.

[48] *LE*, ii.11, trans. Fairweather, p. 111; this represented two-thirds the number prescribed by IV Edgar for a major borough (see above, p. 180).

[49] *LE*, ii.11, trans. Fairweather, pp. 107–8.

[50] *LE*, ii.33, trans. Fairweather, p. 131.

[51] *English Lawsuits from William to Stephen*, ed. R. C. van Caenegem, Selden Soc. 106–7 (1990–1), no. 172, I.138–9. I owe this reference – and the reminder that lawmen also

recorded at Cambridge, Lincoln, Stamford, and York and hinted at in Norwich, Thetford, and Ipswich. Although the word is Norse, the role was not exclusive to Scandinavian society, and Kennedy has suggested that *lagaman* was a Danelaw honorific applied to 'prominent borough personages'.[52] What, if anything, distinguished their role from witnessing and standing surety, as described in written law, is unclear. Men such as the Fen Ditton lawmen, Cambridge's borough-witnesses, and Peterborough's festermen may have been among the thegns who gathered to meet the king and witness his charters.[53] Whether or not all thegns did a stint at court, as claimed in King Alfred's time,[54] assemblies and other meetings brought the king's entourage together with these local men. Their witness to royal generosity would have been essential if there was trouble down the road and a grant in the region was challenged.

Witness-lists are not straightforward evidence. Whose names were recorded? Some of Æthelstan's charters were attested by crowds of witnesses, implying very large gatherings. But smaller witness-lists need not mean that fewer people were in attendance when the grant was made (although that might indeed have been the case). Lists were often abbreviated when copied into cartularies. Furthermore, some kind of selection clearly governed the original record. Occasionally, charters from the same meeting survive with different witness-lists.[55] Perhaps different scribes recorded the transaction and chose to write down different names, or scribes noted only those people who could actually be useful to the beneficiary, or only those who were willing to step forward and be officially accountable. Considerations of space, style, and lay-out are also likely to have affected the lists.[56] Some were written later than the body of the charter: the witness-list of a surviving single-sheet grant of Edgar to Abingdon was added by a second scribe after folding.[57] Given these variables, witness-lists cannot represent exactly who was present, or important, when a grant was made. But they do throw some light on the dimly lit world of local power – in the case of England north and east of Watling Street, a world even less lit than most.

In Æthelstan's reign, attestations by numerous earls with Scandinavian names reflect the extension of the king's power northwards. Representation was not

---

appear in the Ordinance of the Dunsaete – to George Molyneaux; for the Dunsaete text, see *Die Gesetze der Angelsachsen*, ed. F. Liebermann, 3 vols. (Halle, 1903–16), I.374–9.

52 Kennedy, 'Law and Litigation', pp. 158–61; for Iceland's Lawspeaker and lawmen, see J. L. Byock, *Medieval Iceland. Society, Sagas, and Power* (Enfield Lock, 1993), p. 64.

53 The *legales uiri Leofricus* and *Siverthus* who acted in a case involving Leofric of Brandon (*LE*, ii.8, trans. Fairweather, p. 105) may potentially be identified with witnesses of the same name in charters with Danelaw associations (S 779 and S 681, respectively).

54 Asser referred to 'noble thegns who lived at the royal court in turns'; *Asser's Life of King Alfred*, ed. and trans. W. H. Stevenson (Oxford, 1959), ch. 100, p. 86; Keynes and Lapidge, *Alfred the Great*, p. 106.

55 S 422 and S 423, for example, both (if genuine) issued at a meeting at Chippenham on 26 January 933.

56 The witnesses of S 681 are grouped in sixes, for example; see below, p. 184.

57 S 690 (961); I am grateful to Simon Keynes for drawing my attention to this charter; for a study of assemblies and the production of witness-lists, see his forthcoming paper in the Manchester *Kingship* volume.

limited to northern occasions. *Scule* and *Halfdene*, for example, witnessed not just charters issued in the Danelaw, i.e. at Nottingham, but also in the heart of Wessex, at Winchester, for example.[58] Such men may have been subordinates of the defeated Scandinavian regime who kept their titles and positions under Æthelstan. They do not appear in Æthelstan's later (non-Æthelstan A) charters, but some of these northern *duces* continued to witness during the reigns of his successors Edmund and Eadred. When the kingdom was divided in 957, however, surviving texts suggest that ealdormen (and bishops) with responsibilities in the North or South generally attested charters of the relevant king.[59] Before 958, few if any thegns with Norse names appear in surviving witness-lists. But substantial numbers occur in several of Edgar's early diplomas.

About a dozen charters issued by Edgar as king of the Mercians in 958 and 959 survive.[60] They relate to lands on both sides of Watling Street and are preserved in the archives of Burton, Chester, Coventry, Peterborough, Wells, Winchester, and York. They differ somewhat from contemporary West Saxon charters in various ways, and some appear to represent a distinctive Mercian diplomatic convention.[61] The locations of the meetings they record are largely unidentified. The majority of witness-lists include thegns with only English names, apart from a distinctive group of three charters, two from Peterborough and one from the York archive. In S 674 (dated 958), Edgar granted an estate probably in Huntingdonshire to Ælfheah *minister*, in the presence of a reasonable-sized gathering that included some northern *duces* and, among the nineteen *ministri*, two or three with Scandinavian names.[62] S 679 (also issued in 958), a grant of land at Sutton, Nottinghamshire, to Oscytel, archbishop of York, records a substantial gathering of six bishops, thirteen *duces*, and twenty-

---

[58] i.e. S 407 (930 for 934) to the church of York for Amounderness, and S 425 (934), a contemporary single sheet from the archive of Christ Church Canterbury.

[59] Only one surviving charter of Eadwig, a large grant of land in Nottinghamshire to the archbishop of York (S 659, dated 958 for 956), includes Scandinavian ealdormen as witnesses.

[60] S 667, 674, 675, 676, 676a, 677, 678, 679, 681; S 576 appears to be a genuine charter of Edgar from 958 in which the name of Eadred has been substituted; S 579 may also have begun as a diploma of Edgar from 957 or 958 but it has been seriously tampered with; Hart has discussed these charters as a group (*The Danelaw*, pp. 449–53). Most describe Edgar as king of the Mercians, although the royal style of S 677 (much like that of the alliterative charters) adds the Northumbrians and Britons in the witness-list. S 679 and S 681, however, call Edgar *rex Anglorum*; see Keynes, *Diplomas*, esp. pp. 69–70, and above, pp. 64–5.

[61] On the distinctive diplomatic of S 712a, 667, 677, and 723, see Brooks *et al.*, 'A New Charter', pp. 145–6, and *Wells*, no. 31. Keynes (*Diplomas*, pp. 75–6) has argued that Edgar established his own centralised production of diplomas as king of the Mercians, suggesting that whoever was responsible for the 'Edgar A' diplomas had started his career with Edgar before he became king of England. For Susan Kelly's association of Edgar A with Abingdon and Æthelwold, see *Abing, Part 1*, pp. lxxxiv–xcii. I should like to thank Susan Kelly for supplying me with her unpublished texts and commentaries and much general expertise.

[62] *Thurkytel*, *Thurmod*, and *Ufa* (potentially a shortened form of the Ulfcytel known elsewhere; see below, p. 184).

eight *ministri*. At least five of the *duces* and over a third of the thegns bear Norse names,[63] including a very early (perhaps the earliest written) example of Somerled (ON *Sumarliði*, 'summer-traveller', 'viking') as a personal name. S 681 (959), a grant of Howden and Drax in Yorkshire to a woman called *Quen*, has a shorter witness-list, but it includes the Danelaw bishops of Chester-le-Street, Lichfield, and Elmham, six *duces*, and twelve *ministri*, five or six with Norse names.[64] A fuller study of Edgar's diplomas would put these men properly into context. *Thurmod* appears in two of these charters and in no other extant diploma. Others with Scandinavian names – *Thurfrith, Cytelbearn, Thurkytel, Thur, Ulfkytel, Rold/Hrowald, Forno*, and *Frana* – make occasional appearances as witnesses elsewhere, usually in charters of the 970s involving the lands of Peterborough, Thorney, or Ely.[65] Other attestations in S 679 and S 681 – by *Dragmel, Arkitel, Ourde*, and *Soca* – seem to be unique charter appearances in this reign. A *Thorð, Thurverðus, Turkitellus*, and *Uvius/Uva* occur in tenth-century contexts in the *Liber Eliensis*.[66] The absence of some of these names from Edgar's subsequent charters, and the overwhelming association of the others with the east midlands, may indicate that they represent local men whose interests were limited to the region. The witness-lists appear to identify a wide range of individuals from a relatively restricted political world who were drawn into Edgar's royal business in the days before his brother's death put him on a wider stage.

The grouping of witnesses in these three charters offers hints about social networks north and east of Watling Street. Thegns of the king's household and other thegns are not explicitly distinguished, but the order of appearance may provide a clue. Especially in the longer lists in S 679 and S 681, the Scandinavian names are found in clusters at or towards the end, and it may not be too fanciful to suggest that this arrangement indicates that the men sat together. Certainly the scribe appears to have seen them as forming an identifiable group, never in primary position. The order of the names – whether recording a seating arrangement on the day or deriving from a pre-prepared list[67] – was presumably

---

63 The thegns include *Þurkitel, Þurmod, Ulfketel, Hrowald, Sumerled, Arkitel, Dor, Ourde, Soca, Cytelbearn*, and *Forno*.

64 *Ulfkytel, Rold, Dragmel, Sigeferð* (possibly OE), *Thurferð*, and *Thurkytel*.

65 Several names recur in S 779 (issued in 970 at an assembly in Kent, confirming Æthelwold's establishment of Ely), S 781 and S 782 (dated 970 and 971, for Ely and Peterborough respectively), S 787 (a confirmation of Peterborough's lands, dated 972), S 792 (a confirmation of Thorney's lands, dated 973), and S 1448a (a list of Peterborough sureties, 963 x 992); a *Cytelbearn*, on the other hand, witnesses S 716 from York (a grant to Earl Gunnar dated 963) as *dux*, and a *Sigeferth/Siferth* appears more widely – in S 586, S 660 and S 680, for example. A meeting of the king and local *sapientes* (including *Thurverðus*) that is recorded in the *LE* (ii.46; trans. Fairweather, p. 138) may have been the occasion on which S 781 was issued.

66 *LE*, ii.32, ii.42–3 and 46, ii.22 and 31 (but as abbot), and ii.11, 18, 33, 35, and 66, respectively; trans. Fairweather, pp. 129, 137–8, 119 and 127, and 107–8, 117, 131, 133, 165.

67 One such list written by two different scribes survives attached to S 298, a ninth-century single sheet. It provides the names of witnesses from the royal entourage in one hand and the archiepiscopal witnesses in another; illustrated in *The Making of England. Anglo-*

determined by status, though regional representation and family or other close relationships could also have influenced the grouping. *Thurketel* and *Thurmod* are paired in both S 674 and S 679, for example. In S 679, the longest list, they are followed by three English names (*Alfere, Alfsi,* and *Alfnod*), then another Scandinavian pair familiar from S 681 (*Ulfkytel* and *Hroald*), a *Duntan,* then a bloc of seven Scandinavian names, with a *Dunstan* bringing up the rear. The positioning of *Alfere, Alfsi, Alfnod, Duntan,* and *Dunstan* in S 679 – all English names,[68] sandwiched in or interleaved with the Scandinavians – may suggest that they also represented local interests. As much as it is possible to identify individuals with common Old English names, it seems that the first three reappear as witnesses only in a charter for York (S 712, dated 963); a *Dunstan minister* attests in an Ely diploma (S 779, dated 970), and *Duntan* appears nowhere else in the surviving charter record of Edgar's reign.

Once Edgar became king of all England, his inner circle naturally reformed. Only charters preserved at Peterborough and York continue to list *Gunner,* his son *Durre* (Thored), and *Myrdah* among the ealdormen, with the addition of *Cytelbearn,*[69] and only diplomas preserved in the archives of east midlands houses include thegns with Scandinavian names.[70] Some of these charters are distinctly disreputable in terms of the transactions they purport to have recorded, but if we risk the assumption that the dubious nature of the contents is less relevant than the apparent authenticity of the names of the witnesses (some known from other records),[71] the smallish number of charters in which these names appear and their restriction to archives and transactions outside Wessex might suggest that the contingents from the North and the eastern midlands had less contact with the king after 959. It could appear that these local men did not move on from regional to national importance, and potential explanations could be found for their being less often at the centre of power around the king: for example, representatives of the Danelaw might have been less likely (or useful) participants at royal councils dealing with legal business after the unification of the kingdom if they had their own way of doing things. Such a conclusion can be challenged, however, by the fact that recording conventions, not to mention the

Saxon Art and Culture AD 600–900, ed. L. Webster and J. Backhouse (London, 1991), p. 257; see also S. Keynes, 'The Control of Kent in the Ninth Century', *EME* 2 (1993), 111–31, at 126–7.

[68] With the possible exception of *Duntan,* an uncertain form (*recte Dunstan?*).

[69] S 712 and S 716 (963); *Myrdah* may have been Hiberno-Scandinavian, to judge from his name (OI Muiredach); cf. also S 712a (unprovenanced though probably from Burton); on northern earls, see L. N. Banton, 'Ealdormen and Earls in England from the Reign of King Alfred to the Reign of King Æthelred II', unpublished D.Phil. dissertation, Univ. of Oxford, 1981, pp. 225–60; he argued (pp. 240–3) that the attesting earls were associated with Northumbria alone, ceasing to witness after Oslac's appointment in 966. On this appointment, see Whitelock, 'The Dealings', pp. 77–9.

[70] See above, n. 65.

[71] The forgers of S 792 for Thorney, for example, obviously worked from a list which included many such names; S 779, for Ely, includes several Scandinavian names which recur in the *Liber Eliensis* (*Oscytel, Thurcytel, Thurstan, Ulf,* and *Uvi*) and in Edgar's early charters.

very limited survival of charters from north of the Thames, hopelessly skew the evidence. The Burton Abbey cartularist only occasionally preserved the names of lay witnesses,[72] for example, and the charter record of northern and eastern religious houses, including the big establishments at York and Chester-le-Street, is extremely poor.[73] Cyril Hart has observed that Edgar (like Eadwig) appears to have granted out estates north of the Thames at a higher rate than Æthelstan and Edmund, suggesting that this reflected his greater hold over these regions.[74] If gifts of land in Mercia and Northumbria were made in exchange for support, it might be expected that the process would continue with some urgency after 959. IV Edgar specifically refers to the king's gratitude for the loyalty of the region.[75] The vast majority of Edgar's surviving charters relate to lands outside the Danelaw, however, and we can only assume that if charters were issued at the same rate to record transactions north and east of Watling Street, they have been lost in very significant numbers. On the other hand, we cannot be certain that landholding in the Danelaw ever mirrored West Saxon practice to the extent that documentation by charter was required or desired. Scandinavian immigrants might have seen little value in buying into an English system of written validation of their ownership of land, and the practice may never have been habitual outside Wessex. Perhaps the kind of oral transactions which lay behind S 1448a – a list of sureties provided by a series of individuals selling their lands to Peterborough Abbey – represented the routine of land transfer.[76] When the Northumbrian Priests' Law, an eleventh-century text associated with Wulfstan, says *we willað þæt landceap J lahceap J witword J getrywe gewitnes J riht dom ... stande* ('and it is our will that the purchase of land and the purchase of legal rights and agreements and trustworthy witness and just judgment ... are to remain valid'),[77] it may be that *landceap* was understood as a customary transaction with a formal, but charter-free, ritual of transfer.

There are other difficulties, most of which cannot be pursued here. For example, what do we conclude from the fact that the three post-unification charters of Edgar most likely to have been granted at an assembly in the North (S 712, S 712a, and S 716, all dated 963),[78] have only English names among the witnessing thegns? At least two *duces* with northern associations continued

---

72 *Charters of Burton Abbey*, ed. P. H. Sawyer, (London, 1979).

73 Susan Kelly has suggested to me that the relative lack of reformed monasteries may have played a role in this absence of documentation.

74 *The Danelaw*, p. 452.

75 IV Edgar §12; see above, p. 171.

76 S 1448a (963 x 992), Robertson, *Charters*, pp. 74–81; cf. Stenton, *ASE*, p. 512.

77 *Councils & Synods*, pp. 449–68, at 467; cf. III Æthelred §3; *The Laws*, ed. Robertson, pp. 64–5 and 319.

78 S 712 to Oslac for Sherburn (Yorkshire), S 712a to Æthelferth for Ballidon (Derbyshire), and S 716 to Gunnar for Newbald (Yorkshire); S 712a preserves 'a record of an important meeting of the king's witan with a particularly strong Mercian and northern element', according to Brooks *et al.*, 'A New Charter', p. 145; see also S. Keynes, 'The Additions in Old English', *The York Gospels. A Facsimile with Introductory Essays*, ed. N. Barker (London, 1986), p. 87. One or all of these charters may confirm the reference in a thirteenth-century St Alban's chronicle to an (undated) royal council convened by Edgar

to witness after 959, though they have been described as 'rare visitors'.[79] Did royal grants of northern lands take place in the South with primarily southern witnesses? Or locally, but with witnessing thegns drawn from regions with a stronger English identity than S 674, S 679, and S 681? Were lists more vigorously pruned after 959? Or might Edgar's charters of 958–9 reflect a different sort of royal lordship, with an intimate involvement in the meetings that handled legal matters, which after 959 more commonly occurred without royal participation, the men of the Danelaw being left to their own devices? Unfortunately, we cannot assume that witness-lists represent complete and unaltered records, and their reflection of Danelaw life is intermittent; but if they offer any accurate reflection, the king's court after 959 was less well populated by men with names declaring a Danelaw identity. Looking forward, only a handful of charters of King Æthelred from Danelaw archives survive with complete witness-lists, but two from Burton Abbey (S 906 and S 922) show the same kind of English-Scandinavian demographic as in S 674, S 679, and S 681.[80] On the other hand, Æthelred's charters from southern archives also preserve a sprinkling of Scandinavian names among the thegns. A fuller prosopographical analysis would be required to investigate whether this simply represents the spread of these names outside the Danelaw or can serve to indicate greater regional representation at the king's side than in Edgar's reign.

The boundary-clause of S 681, preserved only in Peterborough's mid-twelfth-century cartulary (but with few apparent alterations) is also of interest in that the bounds exhibit substantial signs of Scandinavian influence.

Þis sind þa landgemære to `H'æafuddene Of Usan up on wilbaldes fleote . of wilbaldes fleote on þa dic . andlang dices on Deorwentan . of Deorwentan on gerihtne on cærholm . of cærholme andlang dices eal ombutan þane wuda on Fulanea . ꝺ lang Fulanea on ealdan Deorwentan . ꝺ lang ealde Deorwentan þ eft on Usan .

Þa sind þa tunas þa hærað to Heafoddene mid sace ꝺ mid socne . Cnyllingatun . Beornhyll . Cafeld . Þorp . Hyðe . Eastringatun . Belleby . Celpene .

Þis sindon ða landgemære æt Ealdedrege. Of Yr on `h'rodlafes holm . of hrodlafes holme to se mære on sigeres ac. of sigeres ac on Usan ꝺ lang Usan þ eft up on Yr .[81]

Norse elements include *kjarr*, 'brushwood', and *holmr*, 'raised ground in marsh or river meadow', in the place-name Caerholm, and a second *holmr* in *Hrodlafes holme*; *Belleby* is a characteristically Scandinavian place-name in *-by*; and

---

in York: *The Chronicle Attributed to John of Wallingford*, ed. R. Vaughan, Camden Soc. 3rd ser. 90 (1958), pp. 54–5.

[79] Brooks *et al.*, 'A New Charter', p. 145; Banton, 'Ealdormen', pp. 241–9; see above, n. 69.

[80] The *ministri* in the only surviving charter of Cnut in the York archive S 968 (1033) are almost all Scandinavian (arguably 'new' Danes as well as 'old').

[81] The text is taken from Susan Kelly's forthcoming edition of the Peterborough archive.

Thorp could be English or Norse.[82] That this may be one of the earliest extant references to sake and soke is of great interest.[83] The bounds of S 679 similarly include a place-name in *-by* (*Þuresby*) and another *thorp*.[84] These boundary clauses may preserve echoes of the speech of the men who had interests in *Caerholm, Belleby* and *Þuresby* in the 950s and who witnessed Edgar's grants – some of the 'Danes', in other words, whom the king expected to bear the responsibility of decision-making in IV Edgar.

Whether or not there were fewer of these men at Edgar's side after 959, throughout his reign all kinds of men (and potentially women) with Scandinavian connections moved in his circle or operated in his name. This is not the place to consider Edgar's diplomatic relations with Scandinavian polities in the Irish Sea (including Dublin, with which he was associated in later Worcester tradition),[85] or his potential interaction with the regime of the Haraldssons and the kingdom of the Isles.[86] Shashi Jayakumar has suggested that Edgar brought substantial numbers of Scandinavians into England to man his fleet,[87] and many of his mints seem to have been run by Scandinavians: half of the names of moneyers of the Reform issue from York are Norse.[88] Merchants from the North may also have mixed in royal circles. The *ASC* notes that Edgar ordered the ravaging of Kent in retribution for an attack at Thanet on merchants from York;[89] this may simply represent royal fierceness against lawbreakers, but it does indicate the king's protection of men who could have been the occupants of those workshops and houses now excavated and reconstructed at York's Jorvik Centre.[90]

While Edgar's court is of course particularly known for its interest in ecclesiastical reform, nothing survives to link him – or the reform circle – with a special interest in the absorption of Scandinavians into the Church. Oda – the only archbishop of Canterbury known to have been the son of a viking – died in June 958, not long after Edgar came to power in Mercia, but reflections of a possible meeting between the two exist in a diploma of 956 (S 633), preserved at

---

82 I am grateful to David Parsons for comments on these bounds; for names in *-by*, see Abrams and Parsons, 'Place-Names'.

83 Cf. S 659 (958 for 956), preserved in a fourteenth-century cartulary from York.

84 S 674 has no extant bounds.

85 See Stubbs, *Dunstan*, pp. 422–3, and S 731, the controversial 'Altitonantis' charter, dated 964.

86 D. E. Thornton, 'Edgar and the Eight Kings, A.D. 973: *textus et dramatis personae*', *EME* 10 (2001), 49–79, esp. 70–4; A. Williams, 'An Outing on the Dee: King Edgar at Chester, A.D. 973', *MScand.* 14 (2004), 229–43; and S. Jayakumar, 'The "Foreign Policies" of Edgar "the Peaceable"', *HSJ* 10 (2001), 17–37, esp. 31–5.

87 Jayakumar, 'The "Foreign Policies"', pp. 27–37.

88 V. Smart, 'Scandinavians, Celts, and Germans in Anglo-Saxon England: The Evidence of Moneyers' Names', *Anglo-Saxon Monetary History*, [ed. M. A. S. Blackburn] (Leicester, 1986), pp. 171–84, at 178; for earlier names, including Edgar's pre-Reform moneyers, see V. Smart, '"Not the Oldest Known List": Scandinavian Moneyers' Names on the Tenth-Century English Coinage', *Coinage and History*, ed. Cook and Williams, pp. 297–324.

89 *ASC* DE, s.a. 969.

90 Illustrated in R. Hall, *English Heritage Book of Viking Age York* (London, 1994), pp. 55–81 and accompanying plates.

Worcester, and a forged charter (S 337), preserved in the archive of St Paul's.[91] After the sidelining of the treacherous Wulfstan I, Oscytel, a kinsman of Oda, became archbishop of York in 956. Edgar gave him generous grants of land, probably to shore up West Saxon influence in Northumbria. Oscytel was followed by Oda's nephew, the reformer Oswald. Whitelock suggested that it was policy to install men of Scandinavian ancestry from the eastern Danelaw to ecclesiastical office in York.[92] While the criticisms by Wulfstan II, archbishop from 1002, of the feeble state of Christianity in his diocese have been seen by some as a reflection of the negative impact of Scandinavian immigration on northern society,[93] nothing survives to indicate what Edgar's churchmen of Scandinavian extraction thought about or aspired to when it came to integrating their communities into English Christian society. Oda's *Constitutiones*, addressed to the king and society at large in the 940s, relied heavily on the legatine council of 786, offering familiar instructions on good kingship and displaying a concern with traditional faults of ecclesiastical discipline and pastoral care.[94]

Whatever his interactions – domestic or diplomatic – with people with Scandinavian connections might have been, Edgar is largely absent from Scandinavian historical tradition. One route into that tradition was skaldic poetry, and two Icelandic poets – Egill Skallagrímsson and Gunnlaugr 'Snake-tongue' – are said to have addressed verses to Anglo-Saxon kings: Æthelstan and Æthelred, respectively.[95] Fragments of praise-poems to these kings (and to Eric, king of York, and Cnut as king of England)[96] have been preserved in later sagas. But no poetry

---

91 S 337 (dated 867) is modelled on a charter of Æthelred, king of the West Saxons, granting land in Essex, but the names of Edgar and Oda have been added at the beginning of the ninth-century witness-list. For Oda's ancestry, see Raine, *York*, I.404–5.

92 Whitelock, 'The Dealings', pp. 75–6.

93 For a recent study questioning this view, see A. L. Meaney, '"And we forbeodað eornostlice ælcne hæðenscipe": Wulfstan and Late Anglo-Saxon and Norse "Heathenism"', *Wulfstan, Archbishop of York*, ed. M. Townend (Turnhout, 2004), pp. 461–500, esp. 486–99.

94 *Councils & Synods*, pp. 67–74.

95 Preserved in *Egils saga* and *Gunnlaugs saga*; see J. Jesch, 'Skaldic Verse in Scandinavian England', *Vikings and the Danelaw*, ed. Graham-Campbell *et al.*, pp. 313–25, esp. 313–17. I am grateful to Judith Jesch for much useful discussion on the issue of literary transmission.

96 On Eric, see J. Hines, 'Egill's *Hofuðlausn* in Time and Place', *Saga-Book of the Viking Soc.* 24 (1994–7), 83–104, and on Cnut, R. Frank, 'King Cnut in the Verse of his Skalds', *The Reign of Cnut: King of England, Denmark and Norway*, ed. A. R. Rumble (London, 1994), pp. 106–24, and R. Poole, 'Skaldic Verse and Anglo-Saxon History: Some Aspects of the Period 1009–1016', *Speculum* 62 (1987), 265–98. See M. Townend, 'Whatever Happened to York Viking Poetry? Memory, Tradition and the Transmission of Skaldic Verse', *Saga-Book of the Viking Soc.* 27 (2003), 48–90, for the near-absence of surviving literary commemoration in Old Norse of the great kings of York and Dublin from the first half of the tenth century (with the exception of Eric). In contrast, the Hiberno-Scandinavian king of York, Olaf Cuaran, may have entered English vernacular tradition: some have argued that the story of Havelok the Dane, known from Geoffrey Gaimar's *Estoire des Engleis* (c. 1135–40) and the thirteenth-century Middle English poem, *Havelok*, despite the evident fictionality of its plot, goes back to stories about Olaf that circulated in northern England; see *Havelok*, ed. G. V. Smithers (Oxford, 1987), pp. lv–lvi, and S. Kleinman,

composed for Edgar survives. As Judith Jesch has pointed out, however, conditions for the preservation of Anglo-Scandinavian verse were unpromising, and
the surviving corpus probably represents only a small percentage of what once
existed.[97] Edgar's name appears as emblematic of English royalty in *Knútsdrápa*,
when Cnut's poet Óttar svarti complimented his patron on defeating 'the race
of Edgar';[98] but England was far more often represented in surviving Norse
verse as the 'inheritance of King Ælle', reference to the period of ninth-century
conquest, not tenth-century assimilation.[99] In the prose sagas of the later medieval period, the concentration of attention appears to be on those English kings
with whom Danes and Norwegians fought wars – Alfred, Æthelstan, Edmund,
Æthelred, Edmund Ironside – or who became saints: Oswald and Edward the
Confessor acquired their own sagas.[100] Edgar is not unknown: Æthelred is called
Iátgeirssynir, son of Edgar, in one version of *Olafs saga Tryggvasonar*,[101] and
other versions of this saga and *Olafs saga helga* show knowledge of the names of
the entire West Saxon royal line.[102] The stories transmitted in English vernacular
tradition, however – the rowing on the Dee, for example, the altercation with
Kenneth, king of the Scots, or Edgar's sexual adventures[103] – are not featured in
surviving Scandinavian literature, where Edgar has only the smallest of parts to
play. In one saga, for example, he is named as the father of an English exile in
Norway who needs the help of the hero, Göngu-Hrólf, to reclaim England; in
another he is credited with the appointment of Dunstan (the saga's protagonist)
to Worcester and Canterbury.[104] It is a meagre tally for the *rex admirabilis*[105]
whose fleets commanded the seas, who kept a tight grip on a vastly expanded
kingdom, and who claimed authority over the kings of Britain. Such uneven
representation of Anglo-Saxon history raises questions about the transmission
of historical lore from England to Scandinavia and Iceland. The trade routes and
other peaceful channels of communication which we have assumed were active
during the tenth and eleventh centuries may have kept friendly links between

'The Legend of Havelock the Dane and the Historiography of East Anglia', *Studies in
   Philology* 100 (2003), 245–77.
97   Jesch, 'Skaldic Verse', p. 323.
98   *English and Norse Documents Relating to the Reign of Ethelred the Unready*, ed. and
   trans. M. Ashdown (Cambridge, 1930), pp. 136–7.
99   M. Townend, '*Ella*: an Old English Name in Old Norse Poetry', *Nomina* 20 (1997),
   23–35. A. P. Smyth has argued that traditions of Ragnar Loðbrok and the ninth-century
   conquests were kept alive in England by descendants of the Scandinavian invaders; see
   Scandinavian Kings in the British Isles 850–880 (Oxford, 1977).
100 M. Fjalldal, *Anglo-Saxon England in Icelandic Medieval Texts* (Toronto, 2005), pp. 87–
   90 and 94–100; King Edward the Martyr also features prominently in *Dunstanus saga*.
101 *Text by Snorri Sturluson in 'Óláfs Saga Tryggvasonar en Mesta'*, ed. Ó. Halldórsson
   (London, 2001), p. 8.
102 I am grateful to Elizabeth Rowe for advice on this point.
103 C. E. Wright, *The Cultivation of Saga in Anglo-Saxon England* (London, 1939), esp. pp.
   146–57.
104 *Göngu-Hrólfs saga* and *Dunstanus saga*; Fjalldal, *Anglo-Saxon England*, pp. 92–4 and
   118.
105 Campbell, *Chronicle*, p. 55.

England, Iceland, and the homelands alive, but in the process some memories were absorbed into tradition while others were forgotten.

Edgar does appear with the rest of the West Saxon kings in the Icelandic annals (the earliest of the collections being from the end of the thirteenth century).[106] These were likely to have been transmitted through ecclesiastical channels, just as the sagas of English saints depended on service-books, compilations of excerpted texts, and *vitae* that travelled to Iceland in the later medieval period.[107] If there were contemporary links with Norway through English reformers of the tenth century, we might expect Edgar to have had a higher overseas profile. In contrast, the death of Edmund of East Anglia was important enough to supply the date used by Ari Thorgilsson in the early twelfth century to anchor the first history of Iceland.[108]

Edgar seems to have had surprisingly little impact on the historical consciousness of Viking-Age and medieval Scandinavians. Although in domestic terms he may have had crucial relationships with the Scandinavian community of the Danelaw, his low profile outside England suggests that Anglo-Scandinavian business was of less than compelling interest to the wider Scandinavian world. No history of the English *landnám* (land-taking) was preserved for posterity, and no saga tells of how the men of the *Dena lagu* served their English king. If the foreigners that Edgar was thought to have overfavoured included poets, their verses have been lost. Edgar's Danelaw charters, on the other hand, provide a rare slice of life in the 950s. As a contribution to our understanding of the social composition of the region, they offer potentially far earlier evidence than Domesday Book and the other post-Conquest documents on which so much analysis has rested. Although IV Edgar is well known, these other documents of Edgar's reign, modest though they may be, offer a significant reflection of Danelaw society in the tenth century, providing glimpses into the world of local power and insight into the regional diversity of the Anglo-Saxon kingdom.

---

[106] *Islandske Annaler indtil 1578*, ed. G. Storm (Christiania, 1888).

[107] C. E. Fell, 'Anglo-Saxon Saints in Old Norse Sources and Vice Versa', *Proceedings of the Eighth Viking Congress*, ed. H. Bekker-Nielsen, P. Foote, and O. Olsen (Odense, 1981), pp. 95–106, at 101–4.

[108] *The Book of the Icelanders (Íslendingabók) by Ari Thorgilsson*, ed. H. Hermannson (London, 1930), p. 48; Ari gives the date of Edmund's death as 870, 'according to what is written in his saga' (which could refer to a Latin or vernacular work, and which does not survive). See *Íslendingabók. Kristni saga. The Book of the Icelanders. The Story of the Conversion*, trans. S. Grønlie (London, 2006), for a new translation (esp. pp. 3 and 16).

9

The Pre-Reform Coinage of Edgar

HUGH PAGAN

IT is universally accepted by numismatists that a reform of the coinage was put in hand at a national level at some date not very far from the end of Edgar's reign, whether in 973, as was strongly urged by the late Professor Michael Dolley,[1] or just a little later. The result was a coinage of Reform Small Cross type, in which all the coins struck throughout Edgar's kingdom were of a uniform design carrying the king's name and bust on the obverse, and a small cross in the centre of the reverse surrounded by an inscription which provided the name of every coin's moneyer and mint. Design uniformity was further enforced by a new administrative framework under which coin dies were manufactured centrally, initially perhaps at Winchester only. The issue of coins of this Reform Small Cross type continued under Edward the Martyr and into the first years of the reign of Æthelred II, and the coins of the type as a whole received full discussion by Kenneth Jonsson in 1987.[2] It is not therefore necessary to review the Reform Small Cross type as such within the limits of the present paper, but it is proper to note that the evidence that surviving coins of the type provide for the location of mints and moneyers in the reform period is often material in considering the coinage struck earlier in Edgar's reign.

In the period up to the reform any understanding of Edgar's surviving coin types from English mints generally is made difficult by the fact that many of the coins carry the name of a moneyer but not that of a mint town, and it was only with the publication in 1989 of Blunt, Stewart and Lyon's *CTCE*[3] that the extant numismatic material for the pre-reform portion of Edgar's reign was set

---

[1] M. Dolley, 'Roger of Wendover's Date for Eadgar's Coinage Reform', *BNJ* 49 (1979), 1–11, offers the most considered presentation of Dolley's opinions on the date of Edgar's reform.

[2] K. Jonsson, *The New Era, the Reformation of the Late Anglo-Saxon Coinage*, (Stockholm and London, 1987). Jonsson's book also includes an extensive discussion of the pre-Reform period of Edgar's coinage, and he has revisited this period, from a different approach to that of the present paper, in a recent article, 'The pre-Reform Coinage of Edgar – the Legacy of the Anglo-Saxon Kingdoms', *Coinage and History in the North Sea World c.500–1250*, ed. Barrie Cook and Gareth Williams (Leiden and Boston, 2006), pp. 325–46.

[3] I am grateful to Stewart Lyon for supplying me with information about a number of more recently discovered coins of Edgar's reign, and for much other helpful comment.

out with sufficient clarity to interpret the underlying structure of the coinage. The authors of *CTCE* chose to discuss the numismatic evidence for the period in separate chapters devoted to individual coin types, and were thus able to successfully relate the pattern of coin types struck in Edgar's reign to the pattern of coin types struck in the preceding reigns of Edmund, Eadred and Eadwig. What seems desirable for the purposes of the present paper is to set out the same numismatic evidence, amplified where necessary in the light of post-1989 discoveries, on a region-by-region basis.

For southern England and the south-east Midlands the authors of *CTCE* were able to record seventy-five surviving coins of Edgar's Circumscription Cross type (with small crosses as the central feature of the design on obverse and reverse, surrounded by circumscriptional inscriptions), identified by the coins' reverse inscriptions as having been struck by the following moneyers:

five at Bath (Æthelferth, Æthelric, Æthelsige, Burnferth, Wulfbald)
one at Bedford (Grim)
one at Buckingham (Tunulf)
one at Canterbury (Boia)
two at Chichester (Cynsige, Flodvin)
three at Exeter (Eadælfstan, Mangod, R[.]old)
four at London (Ælfnoth, Æthelred, Æthelsige, Athelwold)
one at Malmesbury (Wulfric)
one at an unidentified mint **MI** (Richtmund)
one at **NIPANPO** [Newport Pagnell ?] (Ælfsige)
five at Oxford (Æthelwine, Leofsige, Selewold, Wulfsan/Wulfstan, Wynnelm)
one at Shaftesbury (Leofstan)
one at Southampton (Burhstan)
one at Totnes (Dunstan)
three at Wallingford (Beorhtric, Eadwine, Heremod)
five at Wilton (Boia, Eadstan, Leofsige, Leofwold, Osbearn)
nine at Winchester (Ælfsige, Æthestan, Deal, Eatstan, Frithemund, Rodbriht, Wihtsige, Wulfsige, Wynsige)
one known only from a fragmentary coin from which the mint name is missing ([O?]swine)
three known from coins stylistically similar to those struck at Exeter and Totnes but without intelligible mint signatures (Borhtnoth, Brrehtferth, Wynstan).[4]

From the same approximate geographical area they were aware additionally of some forty-five coins of Bust Crowned type (with a crowned bust of Edgar on the obverse), identified by reverse inscriptions as having been struck by the following moneyers:

4   *CTCE*, pp. 181–3 (providing a corpus of the extant coins of the type).

one at Bath (Biorhtulf)
four at Bedford (Ælfsig, Forthgar, Grim, Liofstan)
one probably at Exeter (Wnebirht, with mint signature **EA**)
three at Hertford (Abenel, Ma[ ], Wulfmær)
two at Huntingdon (Dudinc, Pirim)
six at London (Ælfnoth, Æthelferth, Æthered, Athulf, Bircsige, Hiltwine)
one at Totnes (Burhstan)
twelve known from coins without mint signatures (Ælfsig/Ælfsige,
    Æthelbrand, Albe[rt?], Baldwin, Byrnferth, Eadmer, Liofstan, Mantat,
    Siferth, Tunolf, Wulfmær, Wul(e)stan)[5]

A southern English or south-east Midlands origin may also be presumed
for some at least of the twenty or so extant coins of Horizontal Trefoil type
(with moneyer's name only, set out in two horizontal lines divided by a line
of crosses, and with trefoils of pellets above and below), which the authors of
CTCE deemed to be of 'uncertain location, including Midlands'.[6] These are
of a very miscellaneous character, but of those listed in *CTCE* the coins by
the moneyers Ælfsige (SCBI BM 874), Æthelstan (Manx Museum), Æthered
(Duke of Argyll collection), Brother/Brothar (SCBI BM 897, 898), Godeferth
(Carlisle Museum), Grim(es) (SCBI BM 921, 922), Martin (Grosvenor Museum,
Chester), Sigefreth (Grosvenor Museum, Chester), and Wulfstan (Lockett sale,
1955, lot 614) seem the most likely to have been struck in the region. Among
these the coins of Brother/Brothar were most probably struck by the Bedford
moneyer of this name, now recorded for a coin of Edgar's Bust Crowned type
(below), and the same may be true of the coins in the name of Grim(es), while
the coin of Martin may be presumed to be of Winchester, for which a moneyer
Martin is also now recorded in the Circumscription Cross type (below).

A more definite southern English origin may be presumed for a small
grouping of coins of Horizontal Cross and Horizontal Cross Trefoil types (as
the Horizontal Trefoil type, but with a cross or crosses in place of the trefoils),
numbering four coins only but all of seemingly southern style and carrying
the names of well-recorded southern moneyers (Beorhtric, Biorhtulf, Byrnferth,
Sedeman). Of these individuals Biorhtulf and Byrnferth are recorded in the pre-
Reform period of Edgar's reign for mint-signed coins of Bath (above); Beorhtric
for mint-signed coins of Wallingford (above), as well as for post-Reform coins

---

5   *CTCE*, pp. 199–200 (providing a summary list of the extant coins of this type rather than
a corpus, but the number of known coins is not significantly in excess of those that they
itemise). Of the coins of this type that do not carry mint signatures, that by the moneyer
Tunolf is almost certainly by the Buckingham moneyer Tunulf recorded for the Circumscription Cross type; that by the moneyer Wulfmaer may well be by the Hertford moneyer
of that name known in the Circumscription Cross type; and that by Mantat is doubtless
by the moneyer of that name known at Northampton in the Circumscription Cross type
(Northampton coins of Circumscription Cross type form a distinct grouping and are separately categorised in the present paper).

6   *CTCE*, pp. 161, 164.

of Lymne and Wareham; and Sedeman for post-Reform coins of Chichester and Rochester.[7]

Lastly, there exist a few coins in Edgar's name of 'exceptional types'. Of the eight such coins listed in *CTCE*, two, round halfpennies respectively carrying across their reverses the London monogram and the inscription PIN, may be presumed to have been manufactured at London and Winchester. Two coins essentially of Circumscription Cross type, but with branch-shaped ornaments as a major feature of their obverse design, carry reverse inscriptions respectively identifying them as a coin of the moneyer Byrhtnoth struck at a mint **LIHA** and as a coin of a moneyer [.]bold (the coin is a fragment and the rest of the inscription is missing); the authors of *CTCE* tentatively attribute the first coin to Leicester, a mint a little outside this geographical region, but the identification is not a certain one and it may be that both these coins were struck somewhat further south. The other four coins of 'exceptional types', by the moneyers Ælfsige, Hildulf, Oswald and Oswine, can be attributed with greater confidence to somewhere in the Midlands, but probably again a little outside this region.[8]

The coins attributable to southern England and the south-east Midlands during the first fifteen years of Edgar's reign known to the authors of *CTCE* thus numbered not much more than 140, which is a quite remarkably small total having regard to the fact that the region included London and Winchester, both major centres of coin production throughout the tenth century, as well as Bath, Bedford, Canterbury, Exeter, Oxford and Wallingford, in all of which there were well-established local coining operations. The explanation clearly lies in the uneven incidence of discovery, for no coin hoards deposited between 959 and the date of Edgar's reform appear to have come to light before 1989 either south of the Thames or in the southern Midlands, and coin hoards deposited further north, whether in the north-east Midlands, the north-west Midlands or in Scotland, Ireland or the Isle of Man, have produced no great number of coins of southern English manufacture. The authors of *CTCE* were nonetheless able to set out a chronology under which the earliest coins from the region were likely to have been of Horizontal Trefoil type, the type struck in the area in Eadwig's reign.[9] These would have given way almost immediately to an issue of coins of Bust Crowned type, a type which one surviving coin indicates was introduced into the region under Eadwig, but the authors were aware that no mint-signed coins of Bust Crowned type were known for Winchester or for some other significant southern mints and they concluded that the type was 'relatively short-lived'.[10] There then followed a issue of coins of Circumscription Cross type,

---

[7]   *CTCE*, pp. 161–2 and 167. As they note, Sedeman is also known for coins of Horizontal Trefoil type of North-East Midland styles (NE I and NE V), and is recorded at York in the Reform Small Cross type, but his coin of Horizontal Cross type is of evident Southern style.

[8]   *CTCE*, pp. 203–6.

[9]   *CTCE*, p. 276.

[10] *CTCE*, p. 274.

evidently on a more substantial scale than currently attested by the surviving numismatic material, and this was to continue until the date of the reform.

The most important post-1989 development has been the discovery of a southern English hoard predominantly of coins of Circumscription Cross type. Regrettably, the hoard was not disclosed to the authorities on its discovery, and a published reconstruction of it by Marvin Lessen is necessarily inferential, but the first coins attributable to the hoard appeared on the market in the early 1990s, and it seems to have been predominantly comprised of mint-signed coins by Winchester and Southampton moneyers.[11] Of the twenty-five coins associated with the hoard by Lessen, nineteen are of Winchester and evidence between them seven previously known moneyers for the type and four that are new (Burhelm, Man, Martin, Rægenulf), while five others are of Southampton and are all by moneyers previously unrecorded for the type (Eadgild, Landbriht, Osulf, Wistan).[12] Lessen lists one other coin only, a possibly unrelated coin of Circumscription Cross type by the York moneyer Herolf, but it is believed that the hoard may also have been the source for a coin of Circumscription Cross type by the Bath moneyer Æthelferth and coins of the same type by the Lewes moneyer Hyldic and the Oxford moneyer Selewold, all of which have appeared on the market in recent years without provenance.[13] The Lewes coin adds both a new mint and a new moneyer for the type. There is also a more distant possibility that the hoard may have included a handful of coins of Bust Crowned type, for a few new specimens of that type also emerged on the market in the early 1990s. Other relevant discoveries include single finds of coins of Circumscription Cross type of Wallingford, moneyer Beorhtric; Wilton, moneyer Leofwold; and Winchester, moneyers Ælfsige and Frithemund.[14] Another single find has produced a new moneyer, Brother, for Bedford in the Bust Crowned type.[15] It is not possible on the evidence available to go much beyond the conclusions about the types' relative chronology reached by the authors of *CTCE*, but if the coin of Horizontal Trefoil type by the moneyer Martin is now to be assigned to

---

[11] M. Lessen, 'A Presumed "Hampshire" Hoard of Eadgar CC Type', *Numismatic Circular* (April 2003), 61–2.

[12] The coin of the Southampton moneyer Osulf had previously been published in the *BNJ*'s Coin Register as one of a group of single finds made near Winchester before May 1991 (*BNJ* 62 (1992), coin no. 267 on p. 222).

[13] Private information.

[14] Three of these coins have been published in the Coin Register: Wallingford, Beorhtric, a grave find from excavations at Ty Newydd, Bardsey Island, Gwynedd in 1996 (*BNJ* 68 (1998), coin no. 120, on p. 172); Wilton, Leofwold, found on Bullock Down Farm, Beachy Head, East Sussex (*BNJ* 58 (1988), coin no. 166 on p. 155); and Winchester, Aelfsige, found near Crawley, Hampshire on 8 March 2003 (*BNJ* 74 (2004), coin no. 175 on p. 215). Two finds of coins of the Winchester moneyer Frithemund have been featured in issues of the periodical *The Searcher* for 2006 (information from Stewart Lyon), but await more formal publication.

[15] This coin, found in North Essex in or before 1987, was initially published in the Coin Register without mint attribution (*BNJ* 57 (1987), coin no. 127 on p. 138), but has subsequently been identified by Lord Stewartby as a coin of the Bedford mint (Lord Stewartby, 'Brother, a Bedford moneyer of Edgar', *Numismatic Circular* (Oct. 1994), 357).

Winchester, this is the first clear evidence that the Horizontal Trefoil type was struck under Edgar at his principal mint town in England south of the Thames. The present writer also suspects that the issue of the type may have extended a little further into Edgar's reign than has as yet been supposed, but more evidence on that point is necessary.

Moving to a neighbouring region, it is convenient to record here that the theoretical possibility that a few of the 'uncertain location' coins of Horizontal Trefoil type mentioned above may have been struck in the central or southern parts of the West Midlands is the only suggestion that can be made to plug what is virtually a complete numismatic void in the pre-reform period of Edgar's reign. No coins exist of any type that can clearly be associated as the production of moneyers working at such towns as Gloucester, Hereford and Worcester, and the only coins potentially attributable to this part of the country are a fragment of a coin of Circumscription Cross type with a Warwick mint signature and the two extant coins of Circumscription Cross type of the mint **PEARDBV**, one by a moneyer Æthelferth and one by a moneyer Ælfstan.[16] This is evidently the West Midlands borough *Weardburh* recorded as having been built by Æthelflæd in *ASC*, s.a. 915, but it has not as yet been successfully located geographically either by documentary historians or by numismatists. What can however be recorded from a more central part of the Midlands is one significant outlying group of coins of Circumscription Cross type, struck by eight moneyers whose coins carry the Northampton mint signature (Baldric, Eadulf, Ginard, Hardbrit, Mantat, Oswald, Thurferth, Wærin), and by a further six moneyers whose coins are of similar style but do not carry mint signatures (Dudeman, Eaferard, Leofhelm, Rathulf, Wine, Wulftan). At least thirty-three coins of this nature were known to the authors of *CTCE*.[17]

From East Anglia coins exist of Bust Crowned type only. Regrettably, none of the twenty or so specimens recorded in *CTCE* carry an unquestionable mint signature, but all are clearly identifiable by style as being of East Anglian origin, and three of the eleven moneyers involved appear to have worked at Norwich in earlier reigns. Post-1989 discoveries have added three probable new East Anglian moneyers for the type (Erhembald, Sib[.], and Swa[.]), of whom Erhembald may be equated with Erconbold, a moneyer in Edgar's Reform Small Cross type at Norwich, and also further specimens by the known moneyers Bruninc, Folchard, Norbert and Saydtinc.[18] For other parts of England the surviving numismatic

---

[16] *CTCE*, pp. 177, 183.

[17] *CTCE*, pp. 175–6, 183.

[18] The following single finds of East Anglian coins of this type have been published in the Coin Register: Bruninc, found at Congham, Norfolk June 1994 (*BNJ* 64 (1994), coin no. 199 on p. 151); Bruninc, found at Colkirk, Norfolk April 1996 (*BNJ* 66 (1996), coin no. 214 on p. 160); Bruninc, found at Kelsale, Suffolk, 1997 (*BNJ* 67 (1997), coin no. 128 on p. 138); Bruninc, found near Sevenoaks, Kent, by 2005 (*BNJ* 76 (2006), coin no. 211 on pp. 381–2); Folchard, found at Gayton, Norfolk, Sep. 1993 (*BNJ* 63 (1993), coin no. 211 on p. 150); Folchard, found in Essex 2000 (*BNJ* 70 (2000), coin no. 94 on p. 164); Folchard, found at Hindringham, Norfolk, by 2005 (*BNJ* 76, coin no. 212 on p. 382); and

material is much more extensive. From York the initial coinage of the reign was a substantial coinage of Horizontal Trefoil type by the three moneyers Æsculf, Durand and Heriger, and both this and an equally large successor coinage of Circumscription Cross type, the great bulk of which is in the names of the moneyers Durand, Fastolf and Herolf, are well represented in coin hoards of the period from Scotland, Ireland and the Isle of Man.[19] The attribution of these coins to York is securely based on the style of the coins and on the evidence provided by the production of the moneyers Æsculf and Heriger in previous reigns. The authors of *CTCE* also showed that shortly before the reform there was an issue from York of coins of Horizontal Pellet type (as the Horizontal Trefoil type, but with single pellets rather than trefoils of pellets). They were able to record just five coins of this type, but these were by five different moneyers (Ælfstan, Colgrim, Herulf, Serclos and Sumerleda), of whom two, Colgrim and Serclos, were to reappear as York moneyers in the Reform Small Cross type. A very recent discovery has added a coin by a sixth moneyer, Asmund.[20]

Further to the south, there is another very substantial coinage of Horizontal Trefoil type, also well represented in coin hoards, which was struck by some sixty moneyers who may be presumed to have been based in the north-east Midlands. Three of these moneyers, Adelaver, Eanulf and Levic, recur at Lincoln in the Reform Small Cross type, while five, Cnapa, Elfwald, Hild, Levic again and Ricolf recur at Stamford in the same type. As it happens, this is sufficient to associate a rather larger number of moneyers with one or other of these mint towns, for the great majority of the coins involved belong to a single obvious stylistic grouping, classified in *CTCE* as NE V, and within this stylistic grouping there are coins evidently of Lincoln by the moneyers Adelaver and Eanulf which share obverse dies with coins of the moneyers Farthe(i)n, Grid, Isembert, Ive, and Unbein.[21] Further die-links connecting the production of other moneyers within

Sib[.], found at Soham, Cambridgeshire, March 1993 (*BNJ* 63 (1993), coin no. 212 on p. 150). A coin of Folchard of this type has also been found in Cambridge, in 1998 or earlier. The coins of the new moneyers Erhembald and Swa[.], the latter a cut halfpenny, were acquired by Stewart Lyon from the Spink firm in 1990 and 2002 respectively, while the coins of Norbert and Saydtinc have also passed through the Spink firm's hands (*Numismatic Circular* (Feb. 1993), 124 and *ibid.* (Sep. 1993), 6141).

19 Other York-attributable coins of Circumscription Cross type include a number on which Fastolf's name is joined with those of Boiga, Oda or Rafn, divinably the names of junior partners in his coinage operation; a single coin of the moneyer Heriger; and a newly discovered coin of the moneyer [Tho?]rstan, found at Middleton on the Wolds, Yorkshire, in 2002, which is the only coin of the type yet recorded to carry an actual York mint signature (S. Lyon and S. Holmes, 'The Circumscription Cross Penny of Eadgar from Middleton on the Wolds', *Numismatic Circular* (Aug. 2002), 192; the coin was also listed in the Coin Register, *BNJ* 72 (2002), coin no. 177 on p. 206).

20 Now published in the Coin Register, *BNJ* 76 (2006), coin no. 210 on p. 381. The coin was found in the Barton-on-Humber area of North Lincolnshire in December 2004.

21 The die-links involving coins of Farthe(i)n (as 'Carthen'), Eanulf, Grid, Isembert and Ive are noted by *CTCE*, p. 159. The further die-link involving Unbein is a more recent discovery by Stewart Lyon.

the NE V grouping have also been recorded.[22] The only coins that are clearly of a distinct character are a group of seven coins in a die-cutting style carried over from the reign of Eadwig; of the seven moneyers whose names appear on them just one, Umbein, is also known, as Unbein, as a moneyer of coins of NE V style, and it seems clear that the coins date from early in Edgar's reign. It should however be noted as a complicating factor that among the coins of the NE V grouping there are coins by eight moneyers – Andreas, Bernferth, Harcer, Hildo(lf ?), Isembert, Macus, Mamolet, Ranuwin and Wiferth[23] – involved in die-chains linking their issues to obverse dies originally produced for use by the York moneyers Æsculf, Durand and Heriger. It would seem distinctly unlikely that any of these moneyers ever worked at York itself, where coin production between the early 940s and early 970s seems to have been concentrated in the hands of no more than three or four moneyers at any one time, but it may yet turn out that some at least of these eight moneyers were based at a town in the region rather closer to York than to Lincoln or Stamford.

The twenty-eight coins of Edgar's reign in a hoard of thirty-nine coins found in 1997 at Warlaby, North Yorkshire, were all of this type and stylistic grouping, by eight different moneyers (Æsculf, Benediht, Durand, Eanulf, Hacuf, Harcer, Heriger and Mamolet), but each of these moneyers was already known for the type and it would seem likely that our knowledge of the issues struck in the north-east Midlands in Edgar's reign is relatively complete, were it not for the fact that a recent single find from Caistor, Lincolnshire, has produced the first recorded coin of Circumscription Cross type with a Lincoln mint-signature, by a moneyer Æthelverth.[24] It joins a handful of coins of the same type by the moneyers Asferd, Grid, Igolferth(es) and Leofinc(es) which do not carry mint signatures but which may nonetheless be presumed to have been struck in the north-east Midlands. Those of the moneyers Asferd and Grid include coins struck from obverse dies which are also found paired with reverse dies of HT1 type of NE V style, and these moneyers may therefore have been operating at Lincoln as well. It is relevant here that a moneyer whose name is spelled Grind is known for mint-signed Lincoln coins of Edgar's Reform Small Cross type and it is a reasonable conjecture that Grid and Grind were the same individual. The coins of Igolferth(es) and Leofinc(es) are of slightly different appearance and may be the product of a smaller mint in the region.

That leaves for discussion the surviving coins known to have been struck in the north-west Midlands and north-central Midlands. It is appropriate to review these at rather greater length, for the position here is rather more clear cut

---

[22] A number of these die-links are recent discoveries by Stewart Lyon, and details of them and of other die-links referred to here are recorded in an unpublished compendium of inter-moneyer die-links maintained by him for the period Æthelstan–Edgar.

[23] The die-links involving coins of Andreas, Isembert and Mamolet are recent discoveries by Stewart Lyon.

[24] The content of the Warlaby hoard is summarized *Numismatic Chronicle* 158 (1998), 299. The Circumscription Cross type coin of Lincoln, moneyer Æthelverth, has been recorded in a note by M. Blackburn and K. Leahy, 'A Lincoln Mint-signed Coin from the Reign of Edgar', *Numismatic Chronicle* 156 (1996), 239–41.

than in most other English regions, in that coins of Circumscription type, with obverse and reverse inscriptions arranged in an outer circle round a central cross or rosette, were struck in the region from the very beginning of Edgar's reign, as explained below, and the production of moneyers at Chester, Derby, Stafford and Tamworth, the region's principal mints, includes a number of dies on which the mint town is specifically named. More helpfully still, the reverse design of the last type struck in this region before Edgar's reform, the Horizontal Rosette 3 (HR3) type, is set out so as to provide three parallel lines of inscription across the back of the coin, of which the top and bottom lines give the name of the coin's moneyer and the central line is intended to identify the coin's place of manufacture. This has enabled numismatists to associate least nineteen moneyers of this type with Chester, identified on the coins by the letters **LE**, and two moneyers of this type with Derby, identified on the coins by the letters **DE**. Beyond this, the presence of the initials **TE** in the same position have been used by scholars to associate four moneyers with Tamworth, and this seems on other grounds to be a correct conclusion, notwithstanding the fact that an **E** does not follow the **T** in contemporary forms of Tamworth's town name. The two remaining known coins of this type, by the moneyers Ælfred and Siulf, carry the initials **NE** in the same position, and their place of minting may therefore be Newark-on-Trent, but it is to be noted that the moneyer Siulf is known at Stafford, quite some distance away, in the Reform Small Cross type, and it may be that in this instance the letters **NE** are simply the final letters of the word **MONE**(tarius). Alternatively, analogy with the **TE** coins might suggest that it is only the letter **N** that is the important one and that we need not necessarily be looking for a mint town the name of which begins **NE**.

We can thus see that in the early 970s coins of this HR3 type were being issued across the region, with Chester as the predominant mint town and with lesser minting operations at Derby, at Tamworth and perhaps at Newark. The dating of the HR3 type to this period is made certain by the fact that the type was entirely absent from the Chester (1950) hoard, deposited in the mid 960s, and was represented by one specimen only in the Chester (1857) hoard, deposited around 970. As to whether the surviving coins provide a fair representation of the scale of the type's production, and of the relative size of coinage operations at each mint, the evidence for coin production at Chester and Tamworth in this type is reasonably extensive, and it is legitimate to conclude that the hundred or so coins of Chester moneyers and twenty or so coins of Tamworth moneyers of this type known today reflect contemporary levels of activity. The production of the two Derby moneyers and the two **NE** moneyers, by contrast, is evidenced today by one coin only of each moneyer, and this is probably a fair reflection of these moneyers' output, for Derby coins of this type have not occurred in contemporary coin hoards from Scotland and Isle of Man in which coins by Chester and Tamworth moneyers of the same type occur quite regularly. The volume of coinage produced by Derby moneyers at this date must thus have been indeed small. Working backwards, the Chester (1857) hoard, which, as we have just seen, contained one coin only of HR3 type, contained in all some sixty-one coins of which a description is available. Of these, fifty-two were of Horizontal Rosette 2 (HR2) type, on which the reverse inscription records the moneyer's name only, set out in two lines above and below a central line formed by a cross between two annulets, and this must evidently have been the type struck in the north-west Midlands between the coins of Circumscription type struck at the beginning of Edgar's reign and the coins of HR3 type struck in the early 970s.

Some 175 coins of this type are known today, in the names of twenty or twenty-one moneyers – it is not clear whether the moneyers Ælfsig and Ealfsige are separate individuals – and of these, eleven or twelve recur as moneyers of coins of HR3 type carrying the letters **LE** and can therefore be certainly associated with Chester. Of the remaining moneyers, three, Siferth, Teothred and Werstan, are known from Chester-style coins of preceding types, and this leaves six moneyers only, Ælfred, Alhmund, Gunar, Hrodulf, Othelriht and Thurferth, who are not associable with Chester on the evidence of past or future production. As it happens, the known coins of Ælfred and Alhmund of HR2 type are struck from dies indistinguishable in style from those of the moneyers who are definitely of Chester, so these moneyers are likely to be of Chester also. That reduces the potential number of non-Chester moneyers known for the type to four, known for five coins between them. It has been suggested that Gunar is the moneyer of that name known for Derby-style coins of earlier types, and that Othelriht may be the same individual as Othelric, another moneyer known for Derby-style coins of earlier types,[25] but if that is the case, the participation of Derby moneyers in the HR2 type is as minimal as in the HR3 type, while there is no evidence at all for the participation of Tamworth moneyers in the HR2 type.

The Chester (1950) hoard, deposited in the mid 960s and containing some 545 coins in all, had a content drawn from mints all over England, with the result that a relatively small proportion of the hoard was the production of moneyers working at Chester itself. Of 136 coins of Edgar present in the hoard, 39 only are likely to have been struck at Chester, of which 18 were of Circumscription Rosette type, 9 were of Circumscription Cross type, 1 was a Circumscription Rosette/Circumscription Cross mule, and 11 were of HR2 type. The coins of HR2 type are by seven moneyers, of whom six, Ælfsig, Eadmund, Eoroth, Freothric, Thurmod and Werstan, had been active at Chester in earlier types, and only one, Ælfred, was new, and it may be concluded from this and from the fact that the coins of HR2 type are outnumbered by those of Circumscription type that the HR2 type had not been in issue for very long at the time of the hoard's deposit.

As for the coins of Circumscription types struck by Chester moneyers, those of Circumscription Rosette type can be placed at the start of the Edgar series, as mules exist struck from a Chester obverse die produced for Eadwig's HR3 type (the substantive Chester type of Eadwig's reign) and a Chester reverse die of Circumscription Rosette type intended for use with an obverse die carrying

<hr>

[25] *CTCE*, p. 163.

Edgar's name. Twelve moneyers of coins of this type are securely associable with Chester, in two cases in the light of the presence of the letters **LE** at the end of the coins' obverse inscriptions, and in the other cases from the evidence of style and of the moneyers' known production in other types. Alongside these coins of Circumscription Rosette type, of which about seventy-five are known, there exist some fifteen coins of Circumscription Cross type, struck by four moneyers, all of whom are also known for coins of Circumscription Rosette type, and three of whom are clearly identified as Chester moneyers by the presence of an abbreviated Chester mint name on their coins. Finally there exist eight coins that mule Circumscription Cross and Circumscription Rosette designs, but these do not add to the tally of known Chester moneyers for the period, as the two moneyers of the coins concerned are known from true coins of both Circumscription types.

What however differentiates this earliest phase of coin production under Edgar is that the extant coins attributable to Chester by no means dominate the surviving coins issued over the north-west Midlands and north-central Midlands as a whole. At Derby there had been a very substantial coinage in Eadred's reign of Horizontal Rosette 1 (HR1) type (with the moneyer's name on the reverse in two lines above and below a line of three crosses, and rosettes of pellets above and below), and coins of this type continued to be struck there by at least eight moneyers under Eadwig and by perhaps as many as twelve moneyers in the reign of Edgar (Ælfred(es), Æthelulf(es), Berenard/Bernard, Boiga(es), Frethic(es), Gunar(es), Iol(es), Mani(es), Othelric(es), Regther(es), Sigar(es), Wulfgar(es)). It is worth explaining in this context that it is rather more difficult to attribute moneyers to Derby at this date than it is to attribute moneyers to Chester, for coins of HR1 type seem to have struck in the reigns of Eadred, Eadwig and Edgar not merely at Derby itself but at other so far unidentifiable towns in a stretch of territory extending south from Derby into the central East Midlands. A small group of coins of minor variants of HR1 type, described by the authors of *CTCE* as R/HR4 (moneyers Britfert, Loandferth, Manin, Winem(es)), R/HC4 (moneyers Æthered, Manin, Osferth, Oslac, Ugelberd) and R/HR1 (moneyers Ethelwine, Lefinc(es) and Meinard), seem likely to have been struck within this territory, as do related coins of HR1 type by such moneyers as Æthered, Grimter, Landferth, Lefinc(es), Mane(es), Manin, Osferth, Ugelberd, Winem(es), Wulstan, and perhaps also Osward(es).[26] Further coins of HR1 type by such moneyers as Elfstan, Demence, Eofermund, Ingelberd, Ingelri(es), Lefman(es), Leofhelm, Leofstan, Manna, Osulf(es), Redwine and Wulfwerd are not as obviously placeable; some of the moneyers concerned may be additional Derby moneyers, but for others a Derby base is less likely.

From elsewhere in the region there exist coins of Circumscription Rosette type struck by one moneyer, Amund, at Stafford; by two moneyers, Deorulf and Eofermund, at Tamworth; and by three moneyers not certainly locateable,

---

[26] To the coins of these minor variants of HR1 type listed by *CTCE*, p. 169, there can be added a coin of R/HR4 type of the moneyer Manin, Gantz sale, 1941, lot 1058.

Daniel, Frothald and Hildulf. The Tamworth moneyers Deorulf and Eofermund are also known for a few coins of Circumscription Cross type. Although these coins might date from any point in the earlier Edgar series, it is not necessary to assume that coin production at smaller mints in the region began immediately, and the present writer's feeling is that production at Stafford, Tamworth and elsewhere may not have begun until after an important and regrettably not easily dateable event in coinage operations at Derby. Moneyers at Derby had in fact been producing coins of HR1 type continuously since shortly after Eadmund's recovery of the Five Boroughs from Anlaf Guthfrithsson in 942, and although this coinage seems to have peaked in the reign of Eadred, there is ample evidence for coinage of HR1 type by up to a dozen Derby moneyers into the 960s. As this coinage was of HR1 type it was distinct in physical appearance from coins of HR2 type and HR3 type struck at Chester in the reigns of Eadred and Eadwig, and indeed from the coins of Circumscription type initially struck at Chester under Edgar, and although Chester and Derby have been discussed up to this point as mint towns within a single region, the likelihood is that before the 960s the north-west Midlands and north-central Midlands were divided by an invisible monetary frontier which may also have been an administrative one.

The authors of *CTCE* took the view that the extant coins of Circumscription type by Derby moneyers should be dated to the beginning of Edgar's reign, and that Derby moneyers reverted thereafter to striking coins of their customary HR1 type, but it is not clear on what evidence this view was founded, other than an unstated assumption that the Circumscription types were introduced simultaneously at each mint in the region.[27] An alternative and perhaps more plausible scenario is that the moneyers at Derby continued to strike coins of HR1 type into the early 960s but then opted to produce, or were ordered to produce, coins of Circumscription Rosette and Circumscription Cross type similar to those already being produced at Chester. Six Derby moneyers – Boiga, Frethic, Iole, Man, Osulf and Othelric – have so far been recorded for Circumscription Rosette coins, and four Derby moneyers – Berenard, Boi(g)a, Frethic and Gunar – are known for coins of Circumscription Cross type. The coins are struck from well-cut dies evidently prepared by a local die-cutter, so the Derby moneyers had not as yet been assimilated into the orbit of coinage operations at Chester, but the fact that the coins produced at Derby were now of the same type as those being produced at Chester, for the first time since very early in Eadred's reign, must have mattered at the time, and it can be seen as the first step in a downgrading of coinage production at Derby which led to minimal participation by Derby moneyers in the coinage of the later 960s and early 970s. A decision that Derby should switch to the production of coins of Circumscription type in the 960s may also have been related to the introduction of the Circumscription Cross type at mints in southern England and in the southerly East Midlands.

One important question to decide is whether or not any coins were struck either in this region or elsewhere in the Midlands in the name of Edgar during

----

[27] *CTCE*, p. 275.

the two years between 957 and 959 during which Edgar reigned as king in Mercia and apparently in the rest of England north of the Thames, while his brother Eadwig reigned in England south of the Thames. The authors of *CTCE* concluded that there was no numismatic evidence to show that Edgar went as far as having coins struck in his name, although they accepted that Edgar 'may well have taken the profits from the mints under his control'.[28] In the course of their remarks they did however draw attention to the fact that Eadwig's reign saw unexpectedly substantial issues of coins from mints in southern Mercia, i.e. in the south-east Midlands, the manufacture of which would have to be concentrated into the first two years of Eadwig's reign if he was unable to have coins struck in his name at mints in Mercia thereafter. They do not expand on this statement, but the situation is exemplified by the content of the Chester 1950 hoard, in which there was a substantial group of mint-signed coins of Eadwig of Horizontal Trefoil 3 (HT3) type (with a three-line inscription on the reverse, of which the central line gives the mint name), struck at Bedford, Northampton and a mint which may have been Newport Pagnell, and there were also almost as many coins of Eadwig of the normal Horizontal Trefoil type originating from the same general area, without mint signatures but struck by several of the same moneyers as those of HT3 type.

Two substantive types were therefore produced in this part of southern Mercia under Eadwig, and it would certainly seem rather hard to have to concentrate the issue of both types into a two-year period. It can also be noted that although mules exist between coins of Eadred and Eadwig, and between coins of Eadwig and Edgar, no mule has yet been recorded between Mercian coins of Eadred and Edgar, as might have occurred had there been only a two-year gap between their respective issues. That said, no coins at all are known that are likely to have been struck for Eadwig at East Anglian mints, despite the fact that such coins should certainly exist for the period 955–7, if not for 957–9 as well, and any new hoard deposited in Wessex, Mercia or East Anglia between 955 and 960 is likely to be extremely informative.

Finally, it has been common ground among numismatists since the discovery of the Chester 1950 hoard that coins of the second and third quarters of the tenth century which carry rosettes as part of their design – whether as a central feature, as on coins of Circumscription type, or above, below and between the lines of the reverse inscription, as on coins of Horizontal Rosette type – were all struck within the frontiers of the historic kingdom of Mercia. It can be established from coins of Circumscription Rosette type struck under Æthelstan that at that period coins with rosettes on were struck by moneyers at Chester, Hereford, Shrewsbury, Stafford, and at a mint that may have been Warwick, and not elsewhere. In the reign of Edmund, a coinage of Horizontal Rosette type was initially struck at the same range of mints, but after Edmund's recovery of the Five Boroughs in 942 coins of Horizontal Rosette type were also produced at Derby and perhaps at Nottingham and elsewhere in the more northerly ter-

---

[28] *CTCE*, pp. 278–80.

ritories of the Five Boroughs as well. In the reigns of Eadred and Eadwig the area within which coins of Rosette types were manufactured seems to have been broadly the same, although it looks as if Hereford no longer fell within its boundaries. In the pre-Reform period of Edgar's reign Warwick seems also to have fallen outside the relevant area and there is no certain evidence for coin production at Shrewsbury. Tamworth however emerges as an additional identifiable mint where Rosette coins were produced, although moneyers there may in fact already have been producing Rosette coins without mint signatures in the reigns of Edgar's immediate predecessors.

We can thus see that there was a defined area in the north-west Midlands where coins with Rosette designs were the customary currency between Æthelstan's reign and Edgar's reform, and that there was a parallel area in the north-central Midlands where coins with Rosette designs were the customary currency between 942 and Edgar's reform. It is a matter for historians to decide if these areas corresponded with administrative areas, but a major priority for numismatists is to determine the geographical extent of the area in the north-central Midlands in which coins of Horizontal Rosette type and Circumscription Rosette type were manufactured and circulated. It does seem probable on general grounds that it extended to cover Nottingham, a mint town to which no coins of non-Rosette types can be plausibly attributed, but it is still worryingly uncertain to what extent coins of Rosette type may have been struck at other places within the former territory of the Five Boroughs. Indeed, it has been pointed out in this context that Iole, a Derby moneyer in Edgar's Circumscription Rosette type, may be the same individual who recurs as a Stamford moneyer after Edgar's reform,[29] and it cannot as yet be claimed that we know where the monetary frontiers between the north-central Midlands, the north-east Midlands and the south-east Midlands lay.

---

[29] *CTCE*, p. 162.

Table 9.1: Moneyers working at Chester between 946 and 979

The tabulation of moneyers for the Reform Small Cross type includes moneyers who struck coins of this design in the reigns of Edward the Martyr and Æthelred II.

EADRED HR2	EADWIG HR3	CC and CR	EDGAR HR2	HR3	RSC
Ælfsig(e)	Ælfsig(e)	Ælfsig(e)	Ælfsig	Ælfsig	
Ælfstan		Elfstan	Ælfstan	Ælfstan	
Deorulf	Deorulf		Deorulf	Deorlaf	Deorlaf
Duran				Duran	
Eadmund	Eadmund	Eadmund	Eadmund	Eadmund	
Eoferard	Eoferard	Eoferard			
Eoroth	Eoroth	Eoroth	Eoroth	Eoroth	
Frard	Frard				
Frothric	Freotheric	Freotheric	Freotheric	Frothric	
Gilles	Gilys	Gilys	Gillys	Gillys	
Mærten			Martin	Martin	
Siferth		Siferth	Siferth		
Sunu					
Teothred			Teothred		
Theodulf					
Thurmod	Thurmod	Thurmod	Thurmod	Thurmod	Thurmod
Werstan	Werstan	Werstan	Werstan		
Wilaf					
Wilsig	Wilsig	Wilsig			
Wulfstan					
	Ethelstan				
		Aldewine	Aldewine	Aldewine	
			Ælfred		
			Æthelm	Ethelm	
			Alhmund		
			Leofstan	Leofstan	
			Teothuc	Teothuc	
				Boia	Bogea
				Flodger	
				Mælsuthan	Mælsuthan
				Monna	
				Wulgar	

Table 9.2: Moneyers working at Derby, 'NE', Stafford and Tamworth between the mid 960s and 979

The tabulation of moneyers for the Reform Small Cross type includes moneyers who struck coins of this design in the reigns of Edward the Martyr and Æthelred II.

CC and CR	HR2	HR3	RSC
Amund (S)			
Ber(e)nard (D)			
Boiga (D)		Boia (D)	
Deorulf (T)		Deorulf (T)	Deorulf (T)
Eofermund (T)			
Frethic (D)			
Gunar (D)	Gunar		Gunar (D)
Iole (D)			
Man (D)			
Osulf (D)			Osulf (D)
Othelric (D)	Othelriht		
		Ælfred (NE)	
		Eofrlf (T)	
		Grim (D)	Grim (D)
		Leofwine (T)	Lefwine (T)
		Monna (T)	Mana (T)
		Siulf (NE)	Siulf (S)
			Ælfsie (S)

IV

Edgar and the Monastic Revival

VI

The Monastic Revival

10

The Chronology of the Benedictine 'Reform'

JULIA BARROW

THE process which saw the foundation of the great medieval English Benedictine monasteries in the tenth century was, if not necessarily the most important development within the English church of the time, certainly the best recorded.[1] Many aspects of the process – including the use of the term 'reform' – have been undergoing re-evaluation recently.[2] However, mapping out the chronology of the Benedictine movement overall has not been attempted since David Farmer sketched it out in the early 1970s, summarising the account in David Knowles' *Monastic Order*, so it is high time to re-attempt it.[3] Chronology matters because establishing the sequence of events is a necessary step before working out causation and influence. It also allows us to observe which group of people was operating in any particular context. This paper will deal with the chronology of the Benedictine movement in Edgar's reign not only because Edgar is the subject of the volume, but also because his reign was the most dynamic period of the process.[4] Part of the key to working out the chronology of the Benedictine movement under Edgar is the identification of a satisfactory date for *Regularis Concordia*, the set of uniform monastic customs commissioned by Edgar and written by Æthelwold of Winchester to be followed by all inmates of Benedictine communities in England. *Regularis Concordia* became necessary once there were several houses in existence following slightly dif-

---

[1] Blair, *Church*, pp. 346–54, esp. 351; a numerically far more significant phenomenon of the same period, though very poorly recorded, was the growth of parish churches: Blair, *Church*, pp. 368–425.

[2] On the use of the term 'reform' to describe the phenomenon, see Julia Barrow, 'The Ideas and Application of Reform', *The Cambridge History of Christianity*, III, *600–1100*, ed. T. F. X. Noble and J. M. H. Smith (forthcoming, 2008), and Julia Barrow, 'The Ideology of the Tenth-century English Benedictine "Reform"', *Challenging the Boundaries of Medieval History*, ed. Patricia Skinner (forthcoming).

[3] D. H. Farmer, 'The Progress of the Monastic Revival', *Tenth-Century Studies: Essays in Commemoration of the Council of Winchester and Regularis Concordia*, ed. David Parsons (Chichester, 1975); David Knowles, *The Monastic Order in England*, 2nd ed. (Cambridge, 1963), pp. 31–56. Cf. also comments by Eric John, 'Some Latin Charters of the Tenth-century Reformation in England', *Revue bénédictine* 70 (1960), 333–59, and Sarah Foot, *Veiled Women*, 2 vols. (Aldershot, 2000), I.95 and n. 38.

[4] Blair, *Church*, pp. 350–1, and literature there cited.

ferent variations of the Benedictine routine, which Edgar viewed as a worrying development. He wished to impose a unified observance on all monks and nuns in his kingdom.

Regularis Concordia *in Traditional Chronology*

The dating of *Regularis Concordia* is uncertain, though it must precede Edgar's death on 8 July 975 and cannot be earlier than his marriage to Ælfthryth in 964 (or, at the latest, 965), since she is given a major responsibility in the text, being put in charge of all the nunneries in the kingdom. Over the last half-century historians have usually placed the work late in Edgar's reign, *c.* 970 or in 973, in the year when Edgar was crowned in Bath.[5] Symons, the editor of *Regularis Concordia*, thought that the meeting at Winchester could not have been held until after each of the three major ecclesiastical figures in the process, Archbishop Dunstan of Canterbury, Bishop Æthelwold of Winchester and Bishop Oswald of Worcester, had begun to found, or run, monasteries.[6] Dunstan's Glastonbury and Æthelwold's Abingdon had both existed before Edgar became king,[7] but Oswald only set up his first monastery after he became bishop of Worcester (961). This was a small community of clerks and children which was gathered together by Oswald and which he housed in the church at Westbury on Trym near Bristol; Byrhtferth in his *Vita Oswaldi* does not supply a date for the coming together of this group but places it in his narrative immediately after his account of how Oswald became bishop. He also says that because Westbury was a *parochia* Oswald was unable to promise it permanently to the monks, since he feared

---

5   For discussion of the date of Edgar and Ælfthryth's marriage, see n. 38 below. For views on the dating of *Regularis Concordia*, see Symons, *RC*, p. xxiv: 'The exact date is uncertain, but may be placed between the years 965 when Ælfthryth became Edgar's queen and 975, the year of Edgar's death, say 970'; Thomas Symons, 'The *Regularis Concordia* and the Council of Winchester', *Downside Review* 80 (1962), 140–156, at 153–6 (972 or 973); Knowles, *Monastic Order*, 42: 'in the neighbourhood of the year 972'; Stenton, *ASE*, p. 452, kept his options open: 'between 963 and 975'; Thomas Symons, '*Regularis Concordia*: History and Derivation', *Tenth-Century Studies*, ed. Parsons, pp. 37–59 at 41–2 (973, the year of Edgar's coronation at Bath); *Councils & Synods*, I.135 (unlikely to be before 970, probably 973); Pauline Stafford, *Unification and Conquest* (London, 1989), p. 184 ('c.970'); Lucia Kornexl, *Die Regularis Concordia und ihre altenglische Interlinear-version*, Texte und Untersuchungen zur englischen Philologie 17 (Munich, 1993), p. xxv (between 964/5 and 975, probably 972 or 973); Lucia Kornexl, '*Regularis Concordia*', in *Blackwell Encycl.*, p. 389 ('c.973'); Mechthild Gretsch, *The Intellectual Foundations of the English Benedictine Reform*, CSASE 25 (Cambridge, 1999), p. 240 ('c.973').
6   Symons, '*Regularis Concordia*: History and Derivation', 39–42.
7   For Glastonbury, see Nicholas Brooks, 'The Career of St Dunstan', *St Dunstan: His Life, Times and Cult*, ed. Nigel Ramsay, Margaret Sparks and Tim Tatton-Brown (Woodbridge, 1992), pp. 1–23, at 11–14, and Lesley Abrams, *Anglo-Saxon Glastonbury: Church and Endowment* (Woodbridge, 1996), pp. 343–6; for Abingdon, see *Vita Æthelwoldi* in Lapidge and Winterbottom, *WulfstW*, chs. 11, 13, and Alan Thacker, 'Æthelwold and Abingdon', Yorke, *Æthelwold*, pp. 43–64, esp. 54–8.

that his successors would take it back into their control.[8] Later, Oswald moved the community to a new site at Ramsey in the Fens.[9] The dating of Ramsey's foundation is not clearly stated in any contemporary source, but is given as 969 in some post-Conquest Ramsey sources.[10] In Symons' eyes, Westbury, which was impermanent, was too unimportant to count as a fully-fledged Oswaldian monastic foundation. Therefore he took the foundation of Ramsey Abbey as the *terminus post quem* for the council which Edgar urged Dunstan, Oswald and Æthelwold to hold in order to draw up a common set of customs for their monasteries. This was the council at Winchester at which *Regularis Concordia* was promulgated. Symons began with a foundation date for Ramsey of 968 x 970 and thus proposed 970 as the date for the council in his 1953 edition of *Regularis Concordia*, but later, in the *Tenth Century Studies* volume published in 1975, he suggested that Ramsey could have been founded as late as *c.* 971, and chose 973 as the date for the council, linking it with Edgar's coronation at Bath in that year.[11] Symons based his dating for religious houses on Knowles' *Monastic Order* and Knowles and Hadcock's *Medieval Religious Houses of England and Wales*, both of which works were largely based, as far as the pre-Conquest period was concerned, on the early nineteenth century re-edition of Dugdale's *Monasticon Anglicanum*.[12] In particular Symons did not himself re-assess the evidence of the date of foundation for Ramsey abbey, and therefore there is good reason to open up the dating of the entire Benedictine movement in Edgar's reign and in particular that of the Winchester Council.

---

[8] Raine, *York*, I.423–4. Byrhtferth, who would have been influenced by continental practice thanks to Abbo of Fleury, seems to be using the term *parochia* (in *in quadam parochia sui episcopatus quae Westbyrig dicitur*) to mean 'parish church'; Blair, *Church*, pp. 427–8, overlooks this reference when he says that no genuine Anglo-Saxon document uses the term *parochia* to mean a parish, but his general thesis, that *parochia* was not normally used in England to mean parish until the twelfth century, is right. On the further history of Westbury see n. 25 below.

[9] Raine, *York*, I.430–1 and 433–4 on the move to Ramsey and see also below.

[10] The principal Ramsey sources with the 969 foundation date are a forged charter of Edgar and a list of abbots: *Cartularium monasterii de Rameseia*, ed. W. H. Hart and P. A. Lyons, 3 vols., RS (London, 1884–93), II.51–9 (S 798) and III.170–89, at 170. The Edgar forgery (S 798), the earliest manuscript evidence for which is thirteenth-century, bears the date 28 December 974 and says the abbey had been established 5 years and 18 days earlier than 8 November 974, when the church was consecrated. The marginal note giving the date 969 for the construction of stone buildings at Ramsey in the *Ramsey Chronicle* does not occur in the earliest manuscript of the *Chronicle*: cf. *Chronicon Abbatiae Rameseiensis*, ed. W. D. Macray, RS 83 (London, 1886), 40. *The Chronicle of John of Worcester*, ed. R. R. Darlington and Patrick McGurk, 2 vols. to date (II, III) (Oxford, 1995–8), II.418–19, says a monk of Ramsey became dean of Worcester cathedral in 969: John's *Chronicle* may have been used by Ramsey monks as a source for the foundation date.

[11] Symons, *RC*, p. xxiii; Symons, '*Regularis Concordia*: History and Derivation', 42; on the council of Winchester see below.

[12] Symons, '*Regularis Concordia*: History and Derivation', 40, n. 20; David Knowles and R. N. Hadcock, *Medieval Religious Houses: England and Wales*, 2nd ed. (London, 1971); William Dugdale, *Monasticon Anglicanum*, rev. ed. by Bulkeley Bandinel, John Caley and Henry Ellis, 6 vols. in 8 (London, 1817–30).

Factors to take Note of in Revising the Chronology

The sequence of events in the Benedictine movement under Edgar is hard to
work out because the chronology of Edgar's reign itself is full of gaps. At the
root of this are the limitations of *ASC* A, which, since it was contemporary, is
precisely the source we would most expect to rely on.[13] Its very scrappiness may
be the consequence of Æthelwold's actions in removing clergy from Old Minster
and New Minster and replacing them with monks. Malcolm Parkes argued that
in the later tenth century it appeared to have been owned and maintained not by
a community but by a succession of individual scribes.[14] This may open the possibility that it belonged to one of the dispossessed Winchester clergy, and that it
was not taken over by the monks at Old Minster or New Minster. If it had been,
one would expect it to have been fuller on Edgar's reign and the Benedictine
movement; Æthelwold was after all interested in writing up monastic history,
as *Edgar's Establishment of Monasteries* makes clear.[15]

For the rest, we must rely principally on Wulfstan of Winchester's *Life of
Æthelwold*, Byrhtferth of Ramsey's *Life of St Oswald* and the evidence of
charter witness lists.[16] Additionally, some later sources can be drawn on with
caution.[17] The charters, though helpful, can only provide *termini ad quem* for
the appointments of abbots; they do not always name the monastic houses
governed by them, and it is not always clear whether the abbots are new-look
Benedictines or old-fashioned heads of minsters, although the ones who were
Æthelwold's protégés were clearly the former. Wulfstan's *Vita Æthelwoldi* is
straightforward and useful to those seeking a chronology of events. It has three
explicit dates, and for the events which it does not date precisely it has a strict
relative chronology, analysed by Michael Lapidge and Michael Winterbottom

---

13 Bately, *MS A*, esp. pp. xiii–xxxviii; M. B. Parkes, 'The Palaeography of the Parker Manu-
    script of the *Chronicle*, Laws and Sedulius, and Historiography at Winchester in the Late
    Ninth and Tenth Centuries', *ASE* 5 (1976), 149–71, at 169–70. David Dumville disagreed
    with Parkes about Winchester, but on the earlier tenth century, not the later tenth century:
    Dumville, *Wessex and England from Alfred to Edgar* (Woodbridge, 1992), 134. Patrick
    Wormald, *The Making of English Law: King Alfred to the Twelfth Century*, I, *Legislation
    and its Limits* (Oxford, 1999), 164–72, esp. 171, reconsidered the question and was not
    unhappy about the idea of A being a Winchester product.
14 Parkes, 'The Palaeography', 170–2.
15 For Æthelwold's interest in history, see 'An Account of King Edgar's Establishment of
    Monasteries', *Councils & Synods*, I.i.142–54.
16 *Vita Aethelwoldi*; Raine, *York*; Keynes, *Attestations*.
17 E.g. *Chronicle of John of Worcester*, of the first half of the twelfth century, and the early
    thirteenth-century Thomas of Marlborough, *History of the Abbey of Evesham*, ed. Jane
    Sayers and Leslie Watkiss (Oxford, 2003). John of Worcester is not wholly trustworthy
    on events in Worcester itself in the 960s, since he wished to project a particular view
    of Benedictine reform there (see Julia Barrow, 'How the Twelfth-century Monks of
    Worcester Perceived their Past', *The Perception of the Past in Twelfth-Century Europe*,
    ed. Paul Magdalino (London, 1992), pp. 53–74), but he is in general a valuable source
    for late Anglo-Saxon history, and often has material on south-western England not found
    elsewhere.

in their edition. Lapidge and Winterbottom show that once further precise dates are furnished from other sources, for example the dates of the deaths of kings from *ASC*, the other events in the work can be dated to within five or six years, sometimes less.[18] Byrhtferth's *Vita Sancti Oswaldi* – alas – has not yet been edited by Lapidge and Winterbottom. Byrhtferth, like Wulfstan of Winchester, relates events in his hagiography in chronological relationship to each other, as we shall shortly observe, but hitherto, his chronology has usually been treated rather dismissively.[19] Yes, it isn't easy to argue for the internal chronological coherence of a text which places the Battle of Maldon (991) before the death of Dunstan (988), but – bearing in mind that Byrhtferth was an expert on computation and that Dunstan's death was peripheral to his interests – I am going to try to do so. (I have done so before, when trying to work out the dating of Oswald's activities at Ramsey and Worcester, but there is a little more that can be gleaned from the text.)[20]

One final point to note before mapping out the chronology is the question of how it was possible to take over minsters to turn them into Benedictine foundations. Most of the new Benedictine foundations of Edgar's reign were converted former minsters, previously (at least since the later ninth century) served by clerics, and in the ninth century and earlier often by a mixture of clerics and religious.[21] It would have been possible to take over a minster on the death or resignation of the abbot, or nominal abbot, who held it. Many minsters were under royal authority, and kings from at least the reign of Alfred onwards used the post of abbot in each one to benefit favoured clerics, often bishops or future bishops (Asser, for example),[22] in a pattern which we see most clearly in the eleventh century in the careers of Duduc, Regenbald, Stigand and Spirites.[23]

---

[18] See comments on the chronology of *Vita Æthelwoldi* in Lapidge and Winterbottom, *WulfstW*, pp. xxxix–xlii.

[19] Dorothy Whitelock commented: 'He (Byrhtferth) is a florid and sometimes obscure writer, with little sense of arrangement, and is weak on chronology. Like many writers of saints' lives, he is not interested in exact or relative chronology' (*Councils & Synods*, I.113). Cf. Michael Lapidge, 'Byrhtferth and Oswald', *St Oswald of Worcester: Life and Influence*, ed. Nicholas Brooks and Catherine Cubitt (London, 1996), pp. 64–83, at 66: 'It will also be clear that the broad outline of Byrhtferth's narrative is chronological. I say "broad", because Byrhtferth was very little concerned with precise details of chronology', and p. 68: 'My impression is that Byrhtferth was sublimely unconcerned about the details of mere chronology, because he had his eyes on a higher goal.'

[20] Julia Barrow, 'The Community of Worcester, 961–c.1100', *St Oswald of Worcester*, ed. Brooks and Cubitt, pp. 84–99, at 93–6.

[21] For full and recent discussion of this point, see Blair, *Church*, pp. 82, 112–13, 124–5, 164–5, 294 and 342–9.

[22] *Asser's Life of King Alfred*, ed. W. H. Stevenson, new impression with an article on recent work on Asser's Life of Alfred by Dorothy Whitelock (Oxford, 1905; repr. 1959), 68 (c. 81); trans. by Simon Keynes and Michael Lapidge, *Alfred the Great* (Harmondsworth, 1983), 97. A slightly earlier example is Ealhstan, bishop of Sherborne, who controlled Malmesbury abbey in the mid-ninth century: *Malm*, 14.

[23] On Duduc and then Stigand at St Oswald's in Gloucester, see Michael Hare, 'The Documentary Evidence to 1086', *The Golden Minster: the Anglo-Saxon Minster and Later Medieval Priory of St Oswald at Gloucester*, ed. Carolyn Heighway and Richard Bryant,

Where kings gave the office of abbot to a bishop, they usually seem to have avoided giving it to the bishop of the diocese in which the minster was sited, probably to avoid the possibility of the minster being incorporated into the endowments of the see and thus being removed from royal patronage.[24] These figures would normally have been absentees from the minsters of which they were the superiors, leaving the services to be performed by the remaining clergy of the community. We can probably assume that, in each case of a Benedictine takeover of a minster under royal patronage, the abbot would have been a high-ranking cleric, perhaps a bishop.[25] Some minsters were under the authority of nobles, and a similar pattern doubtless operated in these. However, as the example of Oswald's Westbury shows us, minsters under the control of the diocesan could not be alienated by an individual bishop, but had to be retained with the episcopal estates for future successors.[26]

Council for British Archaeology Research Report 117 (York, 1999), pp. 32–45, at 39; on Regenbald, see Simon Keynes, 'Regenbald the Chancellor (sic)', *ANS* 10 (1988), 185–222, at 195, 212; on Stigand, see M. F. Smith, 'Archbishop Stigand and the Eye of the Needle', *ANS* 16 (1994), 199–219; on Spirites, see Frank Barlow, *The English Church 1000–1066*, 2nd ed. (London, 1979), pp. 131–2, 135; on the use of minster churches by kings to reward high-flying clergy, see Julia Barrow, 'Wulfstan and Worcester: Bishop and Clergy in the Early Eleventh Century', *Wulfstan, Archbishop of York*, ed. Matthew Townend (Turnhout, 2004), pp. 141–59, at 157–8, and Julia Barrow, 'The Clergy in English Dioceses c. 900–1066', *Pastoral Care in Late Anglo-Saxon England*, ed. Francesca Tinti (Woodbridge, 2005), pp. 17–26, at 21. Bampton minster in Oxfordshire was held by Leofric, bishop of Exeter TRE and then, after the Conquest, by Bishop Robert of Hereford from Leofric's successor Osbern, who held 'from the king': *Domesday Book*, 14: *Oxfordshire*, ed. Clare Caldwell (Chichester, 1978), 5.1 (Domesday Book, I, fol. 155a). Might perhaps Oundle, where Archbishop Wulfstan I of York was buried 956 (*ASC*, DE), have been in Wulfstan's charge?

24 For what Anglo-Saxon bishops were capable of doing with minster churches in their control and within their dioceses, see Francesca Tinti, 'The "Costs" of Pastoral Care: Church Dues in Late Anglo-Saxon England', *Pastoral Care*, ed. Tinti, pp. 27–51, at 46–7.

25 Cf. text below at n. 64.

26 Westbury remained in the patronage of the bishops of Worcester; although Bishop Wulfstan II (1062–95) granted it to the monks of Worcester cathedral priory in a charter of 1093 (for a text of which see *Hemingi Chartularium Ecclesiae Wigorniensis*, ed. Thomas Hearne, 2 vols. (Oxford, 1723), II.421–4), his successor, Bishop Samson (1096–1112), ejected the monks from Westbury and destroyed the charter (Hamilton, *Gesta*, p. 290). An attempt by the monks of Worcester to forge a charter supposedly datable 1149 x 1150 of Bishop Simon (*The Cartulary of Worcester Cathedral Priory (Register I)*, ed. R. R. Darlington, Pipe Roll Society n.s. 38 (London, 1968), pp. 37–8, no. 62), was ineffective: see H. J. Wilkins, *Westbury College from a. 1194 to 1544 A.D.* (Bristol and London, 1917), and *English Episcopal Acta*, 33, *Worcester 1062–1179*, ed. Mary Cheney, David Smith, Christopher Brooke and Philippa M. Hoskin (Oxford, 2007), no. 109. I am very grateful to Christopher Brooke for allowing me to see the edition ahead of publication.

A Proposal for a Revised Chronology

Already before 957 there were at least three communities which could have some claim to being Benedictine: Bath,[27] Glastonbury,[28] and Abingdon.[29] The early years of Edgar's reign are likely to have seen the takeover of Westminster by Dunstan (probably when he was bishop of London 957–9).[30] The early twelfth-century chronicler John of Worcester places the establishment of Tavistock, by Ordgar, shortly to be Edgar's father-in-law, in 961: since this information was entered in the margin of John's chronicle, and since John was writing nearly two hundred years after the event, this date may not be reliable, but the alternative version of the circumstances of the foundation of Tavistock, preserved in a charter of Æthelred of 981, is not above question either.[31] Oswald became bishop of Worcester in 961 (perhaps as early as Christmas 960) and gathered a group of clerks and children around him to teach them the Rule of St Benedict. When the number of adults reached twelve Oswald set them up in the church of Westbury on Trym; this was not a church which he could grant to them permanently, and he worried about their future.[32] In 963 it is probable that an abbot of Muchelney witnesses one of Edgar's charters for the first time,[33] and at the end of the year, on 29 November, Æthelwold was consecrated bishop of Winchester.[34] On 19 February 964 Æthelwold, with help from Edgar, drove the clerks out of Old Minster, Winchester, and replaced them with monks drawn from Abingdon.[35]

---

[27] John Nightingale, 'Oswald, Fleury and Continental Reform' *St Oswald of Worcester*, ed. Brooks and Cubitt, pp. 23–45, at 26–7.

[28] See n. 7 above.

[29] See n. 7 above.

[30] Julia Barrow, 'Wulfsige [St Wulfsige], d. 1002', *ODNB*; Simon Keynes, 'Wulfsige, Monk of Glastonbury, Abbot of Westminster (*c*. 990–3), and Bishop of Sherborne (*c*. 993–1002)', *St Wulfsige and Sherborne: Essays to Celebrate the Millennium of the Benedictine Abbey, 998–1998*, ed. Katherine Barker, David A. Hinton and Alan Hunt (Oxford, 2005), pp. 53–94, at 56–9.

[31] *The Chronicle of John of Worcester*, II.414–15; see also pp. 420–1 for a mention of Ordgar's death s.a. 971. According to S 838, a charter of Æthelred for Tavistock dated 981, the monastery was in fact founded by Ordgar's son Ordulf, presumably after Ordgar's death; the authenticity of S 838 is disputed by Keynes, *Diplomas*, pp. 97n, 101n, 180n, 239, who thinks it is spurious, and Susan Kelly (*Abing*, I.xci–xcii), who sees no reason to question its validity; see also Christopher Holdsworth, 'Tavistock Abbey in its Late Tenth Century Context', *Report and Transactions of the Devon Association for the Advancement of Science* 135 (2003), 31–58, for further discussion and for a translation of S 838. At all events, Tavistock evidently became a Benedictine house thanks to one of Ælfthryth's close kin in the later tenth century.

[32] Raine, *York*, I.423–4.

[33] Keynes, *Attestations*, table LV (2), with a query to show that Muchelney is not a definite identification.

[34] *Vita Æthelwoldi*, Lapidge and Winterbottom, *WulfstW*, ch. 16.

[35] *Vita Æthelwoldi*, Lapidge and Winterbottom, *WulfstW*, chs. 17–18. It should be noted that the bull of Pope John (XII or XIII) which is supposed to have given permission for this action is a forgery of the late eleventh or early twelfth century: see Julia Barrow, 'English Cathedral Communities and Reform in the Late Tenth and the Eleventh Centuries', *Anglo-*

The A version of *ASC* says that in 964 Edgar drove out the priests from Old Minster and New Minster and out of Chertsey and Milton Abbas, and replaced them with monks.[36] If Chertsey and Milton had fallen vacant as the result of the death of a senior cleric, that cleric might perhaps have been Bishop Byrhthelm of Winchester, Æthelwold's predecessor.[37] Wulfstan's *Vita Æthelwoldi* puts the introduction of the Benedictine Rule into Winchester's Nunnaminster soon after the upheaval in Old Minster and New Minster, so perhaps also in 964.[38] 964 is the likeliest date for Edgar's marriage to Ælfthryth, who was to play an active role in the Benedictine movement. She came, as we have seen, from a family which supported Benedictine monasticism through its support of Tavistock abbey; she was an ally of Æthelwold, and her attestation to the 966 New Minster refoundation charter states that she had instituted monks in New Minster with the king's approval.[39]

Since Byrhtferth of Ramsey says that Oswald's small community at Westbury stayed there for four years or slightly longer before moving on, 965 is the likeliest date for the meeting at which Oswald tried to sort out their future.[40] This was an Easter meeting, but not the synod which launched *Regularis Concordia*, since, according to Byrhtferth's *Vita S. Oswaldi*, Edgar was present at the former, at which he presided, whereas the prologue to *Regularis Concordia* shows that he was absent from the latter, which he arranged by letter to Dunstan.[41] The Easter meeting attended by Edgar is recorded only by Byrhtferth, but was evidently of importance to the whole Benedictinizing process, since it was there that Edgar

---

Norman Durham, 1093–1193, ed. David Rollason, Margaret Harvey and Michael Prestwich (Woodbridge, 1994), pp. 25–39, at 37–8. Another point which should be noted in the context of Æthelwold's expulsion of the clergy from Old Minster is the mention in *ASC* A, s.a. 963, of the deaths of two clerics, Wulfstan the deacon on 28 December 962 and Gyric the priest in 963: if these had been senior members of the community at Old Minster their decease might well have left the remaining clerics less able to defend their interests.

36 *ASC* s.a. 964; cf. *Vita Æthelwoldi*, Lapidge and Winterbottom, *WulfstW*, ch. 20.
37 Byrhthelm last occurs witnessing charters in 963: Keynes, *Attestations*, table LIV (2).
38 *Vita Æthelwoldi*, Lapidge and Winterbottom, *WulfstW*, ch. 22.
39 On Ælfthryth, see Pauline Stafford, 'Ælfthryth', *ODNB*, and see n. 74 below. The marriage had taken place by 965 when Edgar issued a charter granting dower to Ælfthryth, S 725; *ASC* D dates the marriage to 965, but Ælfthryth's involvement in the monasticisation of New Minster (see text below at n. 58) suggests that she was already married to Edgar in 964. Barbara Yorke ('The Legitimacy of St Edith', *HSJ* 11 (2003 for 1998), 97–113, at 103–4) argues for 964 as the probable date of the marriage, partly because John of Worcester dates the marriage to 964 (*The Chronicle of John of Worcester*, II, 416–17).
40 Barrow, 'The Community', 94–5; note also that according to Raine, *York*, I.425–35, the meeting occurred at least a year before the foundation of Winchcombe, which another source suggests is likely to have occurred in 966 (see n. 55 below).
41 See Raine, *York*, I.425–30 for the meeting over which Edgar presided. By contrast, Edgar sent instructions in writing to Dunstan for the *Regularis Concordia* meeting: see Symons, *RC*, pp. 2–3 and cf. also Byrhtferth's comment about Edgar's order to Dunstan that he should make Æthelwold and Oswald place monks or nuns in all *monasterii loca*, Raine, *York*, I.434.

ordered more than forty monasteries to be founded.[42] Edgar also offered Oswald a choice of three sites for his flock of monks: the two great shrines of Ely and St Albans and a former Viking fortress, Benfleet, at the head of a coastal inlet in Essex.[43] This suggests that Ely and St Albans were still 'ripe for development' in Benedictine terms in 965; later, by 971, Ely was to be taken over by Æthelwold and Benedictinized, while events at St Albans are much less certain.[44] Benfleet did not in the end become a monastery, but it is worth comparing it with Sudborne in Suffolk, granted by Edgar and Ælfthryth, evidently after their marriage in 964/5, to Æthelwold in return for translating the Rule of St Benedict into Old English.[45] Sudborne also controlled an inlet. Similarly, Ælfthryth gave Æthelwold Holland-on-Sea, in Essex, another coastal site. Both Sudborne and Holland eventually formed part of Ely's endowments.[46] Could Edgar have been hoping that the Benedictines would assist in maintaining coastal defences, or was he trying to improve their trading prospects?[47] Oswald rejected all three of Edgar's choices in favour of Ramsey, which was given to him at the same Easter meeting by the ealdorman Æthelwine.[48]

The site at Ramsey was made ready in the summer of the same year (presumably 965) and in March or April of the following year ('while the sun was beginning to climb in the sign of Aries', according to Byrhtferth) building in stone began.[49] 'At the same time' (*eadem tempestate*), evidently therefore at about Easter, which, in 966, fell on 15 April, Edgar ordered Dunstan to see that Æthelwold and Oswald established monks or nuns in all minsters (or, as Byrhtferth puts it, 'all places of minster' (*omnia monasterii loca*)).[50] Æthelwold and Oswald would have been particularly singled out to act because they alone controlled sufficient pools of monk-power. Edgar's command to restore monasteries is also noted in Thomas of Marlborough's *History of Evesham*, written in the early thirteenth century, where it is placed some time before the refoundation of

[42] Raine, *York*, I.426.
[43] Raine, *York*, I.427. On Benfleet, see *ASC* A, s.a. 893, mentioning the fort which Hasten built there in Alfred's reign.
[44] On Ely, see *Vita Æthelwoldi*, Lapidge and Winterbottom, *WulfstW*, pp. xli, xlviii, 38–40 (ch. 23), n. 61 below, and Simon Keynes, 'Ely Abbey 672–1109', *A History of Ely Cathedral*, ed. Peter Meadows and Nigel Ramsay (Woodbridge, 2003), pp. 3–58, at 20–3; St Albans was probably brought under the Benedictine rule under Abbot Ælfric, at some point between 965 and 991, and more probably between *c.* 969 and 990: see *StAlb*, pp. 18–23.
[45] *LE*, 111 (Bk II, ch. 37).
[46] *LE*, 105 (Bk II, ch. 31); this is a grant by Ælftreth, *matrona*, of property given to her by King Edgar's grandmother (*avia*) Eadgiva. The identification with Ælfthryth the queen is very probable.
[47] For discussion of earlier Anglo-Saxon churches being established in places favourable for trade, see Blair, *Church*, pp. 257–60.
[48] Raine, *York*, I.429–30; Barrow, 'The Community', 94–5.
[49] Raine, *York*, I.433–4; Barrow, 'The Community', 95 and n. 58.
[50] Raine, *York*, I.434.

Evesham,[51] which probably happened in 970, as we shall see shortly. Thomas of Marlborough refers to Oswald at the time of the synod as archbishop of York, an office which he did not hold until 971, but this may well be an authorial glance into the future, since Thomas dates the synod to a point before Osweard became abbot, and Osweard first witnesses Edgar's charters as abbot in 970.[52] Edgar's command – here with the comment that Edgar had ordered the expulsion of clerks as well – also occurs in John of Worcester's Chronicle, under the year 969.[53] It is likely that the command of Edgar to which Byrhtferth, Thomas and John refer was the letter which the king sent to Dunstan and the other bishops to order them to draw up *Regularis Concordia*. John of Worcester's proposed date of 969 cannot be relied on, for he was reworking history to claim that Oswald drove clerks out of Worcester cathedral in that very year to replace them with monks, and in the autograph version of his chronicle the 969 entry has been erased and rewritten.[54] Contemporary charter evidence and Byrhtferth's *Vita Sancti Oswaldi*, however, both disprove John's claim about Worcester, since they show that Oswald set up a group of monks in addition to the community of clerks, with a new church of St Mary for the monks.[55] Byrhtferth places Oswald's creation of his new *monasterium* at Worcester and his refoundation of Winchcombe immediately after Edgar's command to Dunstan.[56] This fits in well with the Winchcombe Annals' statement that Germanus, Oswald's protégé, became abbot there in 966[57] and with the earliest evidence for the church of St Mary in the cathedral precinct at Worcester – also 966.[58] Finally, 966 works better than 969 as a date for *Regularis Concordia* because of the latter's close textual links with Edgar's 966 New Minster refoundation charter; both were, it is generally agreed, the work of Æthelwold, and it is surely possible that they were written in close succession to each other.[59] The New Minster refoundation charter was another of the many Benedictine achievements of the year 966; it contains an elaborate theological justification for the process of expelling clergy from churches and replacing them with monks, and its numerous witnesses include five Benedictine abbots, mostly pupils of Æthelwold's, and, of course, Ælfthryth and also her baby son Edmund, described as *clito legitimus*

---

51 Thomas of Marlborough, 142: after the council summoned by Dunstan, Æthelwold, who had been visiting various sites, came 'at last' (*tandem*) to Evesham and installed Osweard as abbot.
52 Thomas of Marlborough, 140–2.
53 *The Chronicle of John of Worcester*, II.418–19, s.a. 969.
54 Barrow, 'How the Twelfth-century Monks', 59–60.
55 Barrow, 'How the Twelfth-century Monks', 55–7; Barrow, 'The Community', 86–92; Raine, *York*, I.472 says a 'crowd of monks and a multitude of clerks' attended Oswald's funeral.
56 Raine, *York*, I.435.
57 BL, Cotton Tiberius E.iv, fol. 17v, s.a. 966.
58 Barrow, 'The Community', 89.
59 Michael Lapidge, 'Æthelwold as Scholar and Teacher', in his *Anglo-Latin Literature, 900–1066* (London, 1993), pp. 183–211, at 189–96; see also comments by Dorothy Whitelock, *Councils & Synods*, I.i,119, 135.

and placed ahead of his older half-brother Edward, who is termed simply *clito*.[60] 966 is also the date of a charter of Edgar for Shaftesbury, containing the phrase *ad usus monialium*. This does not necessarily refer to Benedictine nuns, since *moniales* might be canonesses.[61] On the other hand Æthelwold may have been less worried about the form of women's religious life than he was about religious life for men, since canonesses were more likely to be celibate than canons were.

John of Worcester tells us that Edgar installed nuns under Abbess Merewenna in Romsey Abbey in 967 and collected monks at Exeter under Sideman in 968.[62] Edgar's charter for Wilton of 968 refers to 'the common use of the nuns (or canonesses) living in Wilton'.[63] Goscelin in his *Life of St Edith* says that Edgar imported a monk from St-Rémi in Rheims and a canon of St Paulinus in Trier to act as priests for the nuns of Wilton, so the latter had mixed monastic and clerical influences.[64] Sideman began to attest Edgar's charters as abbot in 970, which was also the first year in which the abbots of Ely, Pershore and Evesham are recorded witnessing Edgar's charters.[65] In addition it was the year in which Bishop Oswulf of Ramsbury died, after witnessing Edgar's charter S 780 of 970 for Ely. Oswulf had held Evesham, presumably up to his death.[66] He may have been typical of Anglo-Saxon bishops in being abbot of an ancient minster church at the same time as being bishop. Other forms of pluralism, such as holding sees jointly, or sees and Benedictine abbacies, were not uncommon in the tenth and eleventh centuries.[67] Clergy favoured by kings probably received several of these abbacies, as we have seen in the case of Asser, and would not necessarily have given them up once they became bishop. Throughout the tenth

---

[60] New edition with full commentary by Rumble, *Property and Piety*, pp. 65–97, esp. 93–5; see also David F. Johnson, 'The Fall of Lucifer in *Genesis A* and Two Anglo-Latin Royal Charters', *JEGP* 97 (1998), 500–21, and Barrow, 'The Ideology'.

[61] S 744; on canonesses, see Rohini Jayatilaka, 'The Old English Benedictine Rule: Writing for Women and Men', *ASE* 32 (2003), 147–87, at 186–7; see also comments by Yorke, 'The Legitimacy', 109–10, on the possibility of inmates of Wilton leaving to marry – which would be feasible for canonesses, though forbidden to Benedictine nuns.

[62] *The Chronicle of John of Worcester*, II.416–18, s.a. 967, 968.

[63] S 767.

[64] André Wilmart, 'La légende de Ste Edith en prose et vers par le moine Goscelin', *Analecta Bollandiana* 56 (1938), 5–101, 265–307, at 50 (Radbod of St-Rémi and Benna (presumably Benno) of St Paulinus).

[65] Keynes, *Attestations*, table LV (4).

[66] For Oswulf's death, see *The Chronicle of John of Worcester*, II.420–1, s.a. 970; for his last charter attestations see Keynes, *Attestations*, table LIV (4); Thomas of Marlborough, 140, says he held Evesham.

[67] For examples of sees being held in plurality, see D. Whitelock, 'The Dealings of the Kings of England with Northumbria in the Tenth and Eleventh Centuries', *The Anglo-Saxons: Studies in Some Aspects of their History and Culture Presented to Bruce Dickins*, ed. P. A. M. Clemoes (London, 1959), pp. 70–88, at 73–6, and Janet Cooper, *The Last Four Anglo-Saxon Archbishops of York*, Borthwick Papers 38 (York, 1970), pp. 1–2; for Archbishop Dunstan of Canterbury and then Bishop Wulfsige of Sherborne holding Westminster abbey, see Barrow, 'Wulfsige', 556; for Ælfward bishop of London (1035–44) being simultaneously abbot of Evesham see Barrow, 'How the Twelfth-century Monks', 63.

century and for much of the eleventh the death of any bishop might have opened
up several priest-abbot positions in ancient minster churches. Very probably,
Æthelwold and his colleagues had to wait for such vacancies before taking over
old minsters to convert them into houses of Benedictine monks; in addition, of
course, Benedictine houses required very generous funding, which – together
with the relative unsuitability of Benedictine monks for the provision of pastoral
care – helps to explain why the vast majority of old minsters simply carried on
as they were.[68]

At Evesham Oswulf was succeeded by Osweard, a protégé of Æthelwold.[69]
Meanwhile another of Æthelwold's followers, Foldbriht, became abbot of Pershore.[70] The *Vita Æthelwoldi* shows that Ely was refounded between 964 and
971; we have seen that it was probably refounded after 965. The likeliest date
is probably 970, since it would have taken Æthelwold some time to build up the
necessary endowments.[71] In the *Vita Æthelwoldi* the foundations of Peterborough and then of Thorney come after Ely, but before the Translation of Swithun
15 July 971, and Peterborough is mentioned in a charter of 971.[72] If the twelfth-
century Peterborough historian Hugh Candidus is correct, Æthelwold tried to
refound Oundle before Peterborough, only moving to the latter after being
warned by Christ in a vision, but it is possible that this sequence may simply be
designed to give Peterborough extra significance. Hugh also places the founding
of Thorney after that of Peterborough.[73] Probably in 972 Æthelwold was trying
to revive another ancient shrine church at Breedon on the Hill in Leicestershire,
for which he was granted land by Edgar.[74] This project, however, did not get off
the ground properly, and Breedon had to become a satellite of Peterborough.

Conclusions

Revisiting the chronology puts three features into sharper perspective:
(1) The timing of Æthelwold's activities. This revisitation suggests that *Regularis Concordia* may well belong in the big surge of monasticising activity in
the middle of the 960s, rather than near the end of Edgar's reign.[75]
(2) Ælfthryth's role in the proceedings. She too was hyperactive in the years

---

68 On minster survival, see Blair, *Church*, pp. 354–67.
69 Thomas of Marlborough, 142, c. 133; Keynes, *Attestations*, table LV (4), for Osweard's
    first occurrence as abbot in 970.
70 Raine, *York*, I.439; Keynes, *Attestations*, table LV (4): Foldbriht, too, first occurs as abbot
    in 970.
71 *Vita Æthelwoldi*, Lapidge and Winterbottom, *WulfstW*, pp. xli, 38–40 (ch. 23); cf. also
    Keynes, 'Ely Abbey', 21–3.
72 *Vita Æthelwoldi*, Lapidge and Winterbottom, *WulfstW*, pp. xli, 40–2 (ch. 24); S 782.
73 *The Chronicle of Hugh Candidus, a Monk of Peterborough*, ed. W. T. Mellows (Oxford,
    1949), pp. 27–8 (Oundle), 28–31 (Peterborough) and 42–3 (Thorney).
74 S 749, dated 967 for 972.
75 Note also that Gretsch, *Intellectual Foundations*, pp. 233–41, argues for rather earlier
    dating of Æthelwold's major Old English works than has previously been proposed.

964–966, which saw her marriage to Edgar, her production of an heir and her assistance with the monastic takeover at New Minster. Ælfthryth belonged to a family which was interested in monasticism, she supported Æthelwold, and her reward, a very valuable one, was to be put in charge of all the nunneries (and thus of their assets, which, as Pauline Stafford has recently reminded us, were considerable).[76]

(3) The opportunities that opened up on the deaths of individual bishops. Before minsters were refounded as Benedictine monasteries they were probably communities of secular clerics under the leadership of a senior cleric. This leading clerk could often be a bishop, for minsters were not infrequently given to bishops or to bishops-to-be, like Asser and Oswulf. Quite probably each of the bishops in tenth-century England held at least one such minster, possibly several. Deaths of bishops may have been just as necessary for the Benedictines as getting together sufficient funds, and the small number of episcopal deaths in the final five years of Edgar's reign may help to explain why the rate of conversion of old minsters into Benedictine houses slowed down so noticeably after 971.[77]

---

[76] Pauline Stafford, '*Cherchez la femme*. Queens, Queens' Lands and Nunneries: Missing Links in the Foundation of Reading Abbey', *History* 85 (2000), 4–27, at 10–13; Yorke, 'The Legitimacy', 110, points out that Ælfthryth's exploitation of nunneries was partly at the expense of nuns with royal connections.

[77] A vacancy at Wells came too late for Edgar to exploit; a vacancy at Crediton in 972 could have opened possibilities. I am very grateful to Chris Lewis for this explanation of why the final years of Edgar's reign are so short of Benedictine takeovers.

11

The Frontispiece to the New Minster Charter and the King's Two Bodies

CATHERINE E. KARKOV

THE New Minster Charter (BL, Cotton Vespasian A.viii) was produced in Winchester in 966 to commemorate the refoundation of the New Minster two years earlier by King Edgar with the assistance of his new bishop, Æthelwold. The famous frontispiece (frontis. to this book) has been understood largely as a political statement: a visualization of the ideals of the monastic reform, of Edgar's exalted vision of kingship (or Æthelwold's exalted vision of Edgar's kingship), and of the united concerns of king and bishop, specifically as they are conveyed in the text of the charter the miniature prefaces.[1] The iconography of the frontispiece has been associated most frequently with that of the Ascension of Christ,[2] as represented by, for example, the Ascension miniature in the Galba Psalter of ca. 925–39 (BL, Cotton Galba A.xviii),[3] or the slightly later Benedictional of Æthelwold (BL, Add. 49598),[4] the date of which will be considered in more detail below. The manuscript's assimilation to a liturgical book is also well-remarked, both as regards its lavish format and materials, and as regards its probable display on the altar of the church.[5] It is written on parchment of a very high quality and light colour, which is showcased by the ample margins that surround the text. It is also the only illuminated charter and the only manuscript written entirely in gold to survive from the Anglo-Saxon period. These are aspects of the image that have received a great deal of attention from art historians and historians alike, and ones which I in no way wish to refute. What I wish to propose in this paper, however, is that the frontispiece may also have

---

[1] C. E. Karkov, *The Ruler Portraits of Anglo-Saxon England* (Woodbridge, 2004); R. Gameson, *The Role of Art in the Late Anglo-Saxon Church* (Oxford, 1995); S. Keynes, *The Liber Vitae of the New Minster and Hyde Abbey, Winchester, British Library, Stowe 944* (Copenhagen, 1996); S. Miller, *Charters of the New Minster, Winchester* (Oxford, 2001); R. Deshman, *The Benedictional of Æthelwold* (Princeton, 1995).

[2] See ultimately, K. Mildenberger, 'The Unity of Cynewulf's *Christ* in Light of Iconography', *Speculum* 23 (1948), 431.

[3] Illustrated in T. Ohlgren, *Anglo-Saxon Textual Illustration* (Kalamazoo, MI, 1992), p. 145.

[4] Illustrated in Deshman, *Benedictional*, pl. 25.

[5] See e.g. Gameson, *Role of Art*, p. 6; Keynes, *Liber Vitae*, p. 29.

had a liturgical meaning, indeed that it may have been as important for its liturgical references as it was for its political ones. More specifically, I suggest that
it may have been intended to function as a symbolic evocation of the dedication
of the church, a ceremony traditionally associated with the issuing of foundation
charters on the continent.[6] I am not saying that the image is to be understood
as a record of a specific historical ceremony, though that may well be the case.
There is nothing to rule out such a ceremony having taken place between 964
and 966, especially if the dedication to Mary (and perhaps Peter) was added at
this time.[7] Liturgically, such an addition to the dedication would have required a
rededication ceremony. John of Worcester's *Chronicon* records that in 972 Edgar
'ordered the church of the New Minster, begun by his father King Edmund,
but completed by himself, to be solemnly dedicated',[8] and it may be that the
rededication ceremony was delayed until that date. What I am suggesting here
is firstly that the image functions not as a record, but as a visual evocation of a
dedication ceremony, created, perhaps with an eye toward the dedication which
eventually took place in 972. As such it furthers the message of purification
and renewal conveyed in the text of the charter itself, serving as a sign of the
reform-era renewal of the church, its eternal purification, and the eternal presence of Christ within the New Minster, his house on earth. Secondly, I will
suggest that the figure of the king serves a dual function within the miniature,
standing for both Edgar and his royal authority, and for the corporate body of
the New Minster comprised not of its land and architecture but of its community
and congregation.

The frontispiece is divided into two unequal levels, the uppermost being
devoted to Christ in Majesty, one hand raised in blessing and the other holding
the book of judgement. He is surrounded by a mandorla supported by four
angels. Below him stands King Edgar flanked by Mary and Peter, the patron
saints of the New Minster. Mary holds a golden palm branch and cross, and
Peter holds his golden cross-key, while Edgar offers the golden charter to Christ
in his outstretched arms. Mary and Peter are also depicted as representatives of
the church rather than members of the kingdom of heaven to whom the church is
being offered. The charter is not being offered to them and they make no gesture

---

6 Amy G. Remensnyder, *Remembering Kings Past: Monastic Foundation Legends in Medieval Southern France* (Ithaca and London, 1995), pp. 19–22.

7 Miller, *Charters of the New Minster*, p. 39, notes that there is no evidence of the dedication to Mary prior to the reform. Similarly, there is no evidence for the Trinity being
added to the dedication until the 980s. Ch. VIII of the charter states that the re-established
monastery is dedicated to the Saviour, Mary and all the apostles (Rumble, *Property and
Piety*, p. 82).

8 Keynes, *Liber Vitae*, p. 29; Miller, *Charters of the New Minster*, p. xxxi and note 35.
Edmund's rebuilding is also mentioned in the brief history of the abbey included in the
New Minster Liber Vitae, though it does not reveal which parts of the church or monastery were rebuilt. It is most likely that the dedication commemorated on 10 June in the
calendar of Ælfwine's Prayerbook (BL, Cotton Titus D.xxvii, fol. 5v) refers to the early
tenth-century dedication as the church is identified only as St Saviour's with no mention
of Mary, Peter or the Trinity.

of acceptance,[9] rather they hold out their cross and cross-key in the manner of offerings and symbols of judgement and salvation.[10] Chapter VIII of the charter makes it clear that it is to the Saviour, made present in the miniature, that the grant is made and the charter offered.[11] In addition the palm held by Mary and the key held by Peter are *adventus* symbols: the palm of Palm Sunday, the Entry into Jerusalem, and the entry into paradise; and the key the entry into heaven.[12] It is also possible to understand the two figures as symbols of the larger Church: Peter as the rock upon which the Church was built, and Mary as Ecclesia. Her pose with the palm and cross is very like that of the figure of Ecclesia in the initial to Psalm 51 in the Bury Psalter (Vatican, Biblioteca Apostolica, Reg. lat. 12, fol. 62r) from the first half of the eleventh century.[13]

It is Edgar's body that unites the figures on both levels: we read him as si-multaneously part of the horizontal group of Mary, Edgar, Peter, and as part of the inverted triangle formed by the bodies of the angels. This latter shape also serves to create the impression that the angels and Christ are in the process of descending towards earth, while the king is in the process of ascending towards heaven. There is, in other words, a mutual coming together. The composition of the page as a whole certainly suggests a balance between the heavenly and earthly realms, as well as the oft-noted assimilation of Edgar to Christ as both king and judge.[14] This is mirrored in the wording, arrangement, and perhaps even the metre of the couplet on the facing page (Fig. 11.1):

SIC CELSO RESIDET SOLIO QUI CONDIDIT ASTRA
REX VENERANS EADGAR PRONUS ADORAT EUM[15]

But the king's body is also enlarged. He is bigger than Mary, Peter, and even Christ, and it is possible to understand his inflated size, along with his pivotal place in the spatial hierarchy of the page, as an indication that he may stand for something bigger than just himself.

The purple background of the page and its acanthus border are also symbolic.

---

9   A point noted by Deshman, *Benedictional*, p. 87.
10 Karkov, *Ruler Portraits*, p. 87.
11 The monastery is identified as the 'Lord's property' (*possessionem Domini*).
12 Deshman, *Benedictional*, pp. 88, 198–200.
13 Illustrated in Ohlgren, *Anglo-Saxon Textual Illustration*, p. 265.
14 Deshman, *Benedictional*, p. 196; Karkov, *Ruler Portraits*, pp. 86–93.
15 'Thus he who created the stars sits on a lofty throne; King Edgar, inclined in venera-tion, adores him.' Translation based on Rumble, *Property and Piety*, p. 70. While some scholars have translated *pronus* as 'prostrate' rather than 'inclined', a search of the various dictionaries has turned up no reason why this should be the case. Rather than wondering why there is a discrepancy between the upright stance of the king in the portrait, and the description of him as 'inclined', or 'bowing', or 'prostrate' in the couplet, it might be useful to think of the the portrait as complementing rather than illustrating the text. On the one page, Edgar is upright, and the nadir of a V shape formed by the king and the angels that surrounds Christ; on the other he is humbled beneath the throne of God.
    It is noteworthy that hexameter is used in the first line of the couplet and pentameter in the second, perhaps to distinguish the celestial from the earthly realm; see further M. Lapidge, 'Æthelwold as Scholar and Teacher', Yorke, *Æthelwold*, pp. 89–117, at 96.

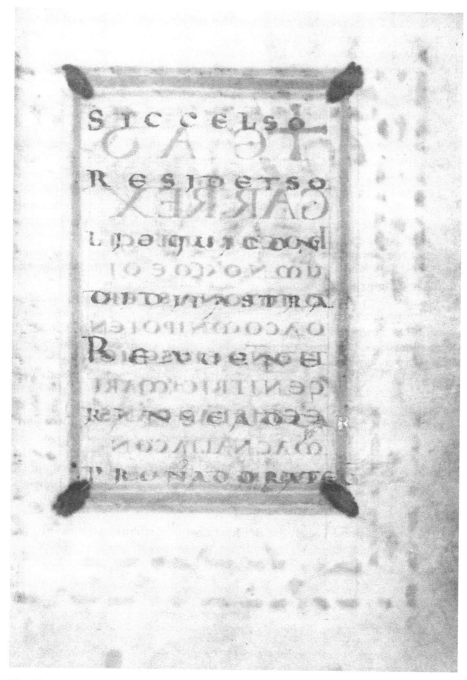

Fig. 11.1 London, British Library, Cotton Vespasian A.viii, fol. 3r.

Traditionally, purple is symbolic of kingship, both earthly and celestial; and of the blood of Christ eternally present within the church in the form of the wine of the mass. It had been used by both the Byzantines and Carolingians to figure royal patronage, the sacrifice of Christ, and the mystery of the transformation of the Eucharist on the altar,[16] in images with which the Anglo-Saxons were certainly familiar – such as the manuscripts associated with the courts of Louis the Pious and Charles the Bald. The purple background of the New Minster frontispiece is an abstract space that contains no architectural specifics such as are present in, for example, the earlier image of Æthelstan offering his book to St Cuthbert (Cambridge, Corpus Christi College, 183, fol. 1v), or the later image of Ælfgifu/Emma and Cnut offering their cross to the New Minster (London, BL, Stowe 944, fol. 6r),[17] or even the image accompanying the blessing for the dedication of a church on folio 118 verso of the roughly contemporary Benedictional of Æthelwold (Fig. 11.2). This abstract, eternal, sacred and royal setting suggests that the figures have been brought together in the same space, a space that is at one and the same time both yet neither of this world and the next – a space of transformation. The acanthus vine that frames that space was a symbol of the redemption of sin, and was used frequently throughout the Middle Ages as a device to indicate the joining of heaven and earth.[18]

It is just such a transformative setting that was created in the rite of dedication. During that ceremony the barrier between the secular and the sacred worlds was broken down and the church was elevated from the secular to the sacred, removing it from the here and now and placing it within the eternal space of heaven as *domus Dei* and establishing the assembled celebrants as a covenant people of God.[19] This is expressed verbally in the ordo through repeated references to the Lord as present in the church during its dedication, and by the convening of Christ, Mary, the angels and saints as witnesses to the rite.[20] The foundation legends of a number of continental royal churches and monasteries go so far as to picture Christ and the angels descending from heaven and performing the dedication or consecration themselves.[21] As far as I know we have nothing quite so literal surviving from the Anglo-Saxon world, although the *Vita* of St Edith of Wilton does describe Christ 'crowned with glory and honour', watching with approval Dunstan's dedication of the church Edith had built at Wilton.[22]

The ordo as preserved in the Benedictional of Archbishop Robert (Rouen, Bibliothèque municipale, Y.7) is prefaced by a homily of Cesarius of Arles (no.

---

16 Herbert L. Kessler, *Seeing Medieval Art* (Peterborough, Ont., 2004), pp. 29 and 33.
17 Illustrated in Karkov, *Ruler Portraits*, figs. 4 and 17.
18 Kessler, *Seeing Medieval Art*, p. 75 (citing the apse mosaic at S. Clemente, Rome).
19 See further B. Repsher, *The Rite of Church Dedication in the Early Medieval Era* (Lewiston, NY, 1998), pp. 6–7.
20 Repsher, *Church Dedication*, pp. 41, 45–6.
21 Remensnyder, *Remembering Kings Past*, pp. 80–1.
22 'The *Vita* of Edith', ed. and trans. Michael Wright and Kathleen Loncar, *Writing the Wilton Women: Goscelin's Legend of Edith and the Liber confortatorius*, ed. Stephanie Hollis, *et al.* (Turnhout, 2004), p. 53.

229) which equates the baptized who constitute the body of Christ with the dedicated church.[23] In both the Benedictional of Archbishop Robert and the Egbert Pontifical (Paris, Bibliothèque nationale de France, lat. 10575) the ordo opens with a prayer uniting the participants with the Lord, and beseeching the Lord that all their good works begin and end in him:

Actiones nostras quaesumus domine aspirando preueni et adiuuando prosequere ut cuncta nostra operatio a te semper incipiant et per te certa finiantur. per.[24]

The antiphon that follows unites the spaces of heaven and earth in the church

Zache festina descende quia hodie in domo tua oportet me manere. at ille festinans descendit et suscepit illum gaudens in domo suo. hodie huic domui salus ad nos facta est. Alleluia[25]

The litany, recited during the bishop's circuit of the church, then summons the presence of Christ, the angels and saints – Mary and Peter foremost among the latter.

Kyrieleison
Christe eleison
Christe audi nos
Sancta maria ora
Sancte Michael ora
Sancte Gabriel ora
Sancte Raphael ora
Omnes sancti angeli orate
Sancte Petre ora ...[26]

This is followed by the bishop knocking on the door of the church and his repetition of 'tollite portas principes uestras et eleuamini porte aeternales et introibit

---

[23] 'Omnes enim nos frartes karissimi ante baptismum fana diaboli fuimus . post baptismum templa christi esse meruimus ... Quomodo multa membra christi faciunt corpus unum.' *The Benedictional of Archbishop Robert*, ed. H. A. Wilson, HBS 24 (London, 1903), p. 69 (hereafter *Robert*).

[24] 'Deign to direct all our actions towards you, Lord, we beseech you, through your holy inspiration and carry them on through your assistance so that all of our works may always begin from you and through you be happily ended.' *Robert*, p. 73; *Two Anglo-Saxon Pontificals (the Egbert and Sidney Susex Pontificals)*, ed. H. M. J. Banting, HBS 104 (London, 1989), p. 32 (hereafter *Egbert*).

[25] 'Zacheus, make haste and come down for this day I must abide in thy house. And he made haste and came down, and received him with joy in his house. This day is salvation come to this our house. Alleluia' (Luke 19:5–6, 19:9), *Egbert*, p. 32; *Robert*, p. 73.

[26] 'Lord have mercy. Christ have mercy. Christ hear us. Holy Mary pray. Holy Michael pray. Holy Gabriel pray. Holy Raphael pray. All the holy angels pray. Holy Peter pray.' The text quoted here is from *Egbert*. The litany in Robert puts St John before Peter, but then repeats the name of John after Andrew (*Robert*, p. 74).

rex gloriae',[27] and 'Quis est iste rex gloriae'.[28] The Benedictional of Robert includes the prayer 'Ascendant ad te domine preces nostrae et ab eclesia tua cunctam repelle nequitiam.'[29] The bishop then enters the church and a second litany is recited at the altar. The Lord is implored to be present in the church once again in the prayer 'Magnificare domine deus noster in sanctis tuis et hoc in templo aedificationis appare',[30] and later in the antiphon 'Ingredere, bendicte domine: preparata est habitatio sedis tue'.[31]As the ceremony progresses the bishop moves around, into and through the body of the church, tracing, purifying and blessing each of its parts. The description of similarly traced (though not purified or blessed) bounds is a normal part of a charter, though not, curiously, of this charter. What this charter provides instead is a presentation of the community as a chosen people united to both Edgar and Christ through faith and duty. That they are a people united in Christ and in the king is made clear in Chapter VIII in which Edgar beseeches the Lord that what Edgar has done for His (the Lord's) people, 'He do for those collected together by Himself under me'.[32] Elsewhere Edgar refers to his people as his 'flock' ('gregi').[33]

In the dedication ordo the church is also treated consistently as a living being and equated with its congregation, the chosen people of God.[34] The equation is present in the earliest commentaries on the rite of dedication, and was well established in liturgical texts long before the tenth century. Bede, for example, wrote in his sermon *in dedicatione ecclesia*:

> Domus solummodo in qua ad orandum vel ad mysteria celebranda convenimus templum sit domini ... appellemur et simus cum manifeste dicat apostolous: Vos estis templum Dei vivi sicut dicit Deus, in habitabo in eis et inter illus ambulato. Si ergo templum Dei simus curemus solerter et bonis satagemus actibus ut in eodem suo templo saepius ipse et venire et missionem facere dignetur.[35]

---

27 'Raise up your gates princes and rise eternal gates that the Lord of glory may enter.'
28 'Who is the king of glory?'
29 *Robert*, p. 75. 'We beseech you, O Lord, grant that our prayers may ascend to you and that your church may be defended against all the assaults of iniquity.'
30 'Be magnified Lord our God, in your holy ones and appear in this temple built for you' (*Egbert*, p. 38; *Robert*, p. 77).
31 *Robert*, p. 96. 'Enter, blessed Lord, the dwelling of your home is prepared.'
32 'Hoc subnixe efflagitans deposco . ut quod suis egi . hoc agat in mihi ab ipso conlatis ...'
33 Rumble, *Property and Piety*, p. 80; see also n. 98.
34 Repsher, *Church Dedication*, pp. 66, 121.
35 *Homiliae evangelii*, ed. D. Hurst, CCSL 122 (Turnhout, 1955), p. 359; trans. in Repsher, *Church Dedication*, p. 30: 'This house alone in which we gather in order to pray and celebrate the mysteries is the temple of the Lord ... we are called and we are his temple, since the Apostle says clearly: You are the temple of the living God, just as God said, I will dwell in you and I will walk among you. If therefore we are the temple of God, let us shrewdly take care and busy ourselves with good works so that in this place, his temple, he himself frequently deigns to come and make his abode.'

The equation is at the very heart of the ordo and is reflected in specific passages far too numerous to document here. It is evoked in the prayer in which the Lord is magnified in his 'holy ones' as his presence within the church is invoked ('Magnificare domine deus noster in sanctis tuis ...'), and in antiphons and prayers that request the Lord to bless or bring peace to the church and all who dwell in it.[36] It is also evoked by the various texts which treat the building, its furnishings, vessels, vestments, and so on, as if they were people in need of purification – as for example in the exorcism and blessing of salt, water and ashes. The result is that the building is effectively baptized as though it were one of the congregation.

The phenomenon has been analyzed at great length by Brian Repsher in his book on church dedication in the early Middle Ages.[37] Repsher was dealing exclusively with the Romano German Pontifical and the dedication ordo as developed during the Carolingian reform, but the passage from Bede quoted above, and the adoption of many of the prayers, blessings and other texts found in the rites in use on the continent by the compilers of the earliest surviving Anglo-Saxon pontificals and related manuscripts demonstrates that exactly the same set of associations was current in Anglo-Saxon England. Admittedly, there is no Anglo-Saxon pontifical containing the ordo for the dedication of a church that predates the Benedictine reform. The Dunstan Pontifical (Paris, BN, lat. 943) is seemingly the earliest, and is tentatively dated after 960 and possibly before 973;[38] it is followed by the Egbert Pontifical, which has been dated variously between the mid tenth and early eleventh century.[39] Dumville believes that the Benedictional of Archbishop Robert could not have been written before c. 1020. He agrees with the view that the manuscript was produced at the New Minster – it is partially dependent on the Benedictional of Æthelwold – but he points out

---

[36] 'Benedic domine domum istum et omnes habitantes', *Egbert*, p. 36; 'Pax huic domui et omnibus habitantibus in ea', *Egbert*, p. 36 and *Robert*, p. 76.

[37] Repsher, *Church Dedication*, esp. pp. 33 and 115–20.

[38] J. L. Nelson and R. W. Pfaff, 'Pontificals and Benedictionals', *The Liturgical Books of Anglo-Saxon England*, ed. R. W. Pfaff, *OEN Subsidia* 23 (Kalamazoo, MI, 1995), pp. 87–98, at 89; N. P. Brooks, *The Early History of the Church of Canterbury* (Leicester, 1984), p. 248.

[39] Banting, the manuscript's editor, dated it to the mid tenth century on palaeographic grounds and the evidence of its contents, especially the *Cena Domini* and coronation ordos (*Egbert*, pp. xiv, xxiv–xxv). He also noted that the litany at the beginning of the dedication ordo includes early English (in addition to Flemish and Northern French) saints – such as Guthlac, Cuthbert, Omer, Bertin, Vigor, Paternus and Justus (whose head was given to the Old Minster by King Æthelstan in 924) – but not later English saints such as Æthelwold, Swithun or Dunstan, as one might expect of a later manuscript. Dumville, on the other hand, preferred a date of c. 1000 on palaeographic grounds (D. N. Dumville, *Liturgy and the Ecclesiastical History of Later Anglo-Saxon England* (Woodbridge, 1992), pp. 85–6; D. N. Dumville, 'On the Dating of Some Late Anglo-Saxon Liturgical Manuscripts', *Trans. Cambridge Bibliographical Soc.* 10 (1991), 40–58, at 51). Both were uncertain as to provenance, but Banting tentatively proposed Wessex. Nicholas Orchard has recently suggested a late tenth- or early eleventh-century date and a 'southern' provenance (*The Leofric Missal*, HBS 113, 2 vols. (London, 2002), I.262).

Fig. 11.2 London, British Library, Additional 49598, fol. 118v.
© British Library Board. All Rights Reserved.

that this does not mean that it was necessarily used at the New Minster.[40] Nevertheless, it does suggest that the dedication ordo as preserved in Robert, and the closely related Egbert, is not likely to be significantly different from that in use in Winchester in the late tenth century. (Clearly, churches were dedicated and consecrated, and it was assumed by the time of the Council of Chelsea in 816 that every bishop had a book containing the consecration ordo.[41]) Moreover, the blessing for the dedication of a church on folio 118 verso of the Benedictional of Æthelwold contains the same essential symbolism as that of the ordo. The date of this manuscript, traditionally 973, has been implicitly, and somewhat reluctantly, questioned by Michael Lapidge who points out that the manuscript contains no blessing for the feast of the translation of Swithun, which took place on 15 July 971.[42] It is odd, to say the least, that an event so important to the history and development of the Old Minster, Æthelwold's own church, would not have been commemorated in his personal Benedictional, and the omission opens the possibility that the manuscript might be datable to the 960s (or at least before 971). Whatever its date, the blessing for the dedication of a church with which the manuscript ends reads:[43]

Benedicat et custodiat uos omnipotens deus domumque hanc sui muneris praesentia illustrare atque suae pietatis oculos super eam die ac nocte dignetur aperire. Amen.

Concedatque propitius, ut omnes qui ad dedicationem huius basilicae deuote conuenistis, intercedente beato, illo, et ceteris sanctis suis, quorum reliquiae hic pio uenerantur amore, uobiscum hinc ueniam peccatorum uestrorum reportare ualeatis. Amen.

Quatinus eorum interuentu, ipsi templum sancti spiritus, in quo sancta deus trinitas iugiter habitare dignetur, efficiamini et, post huius uitae labentis excursam, ad gaudia aeterna feliciter peruenire mereamini. Amen.[44]

---

[40] Dumville, 'Dating,' 53.

[41] Nelson and Pfaff, 'Pontificals', p. 88; Brooks, *Canterbury*, p. 164. The texts for the consecration and dedicaton of a church are basically the same. Compare the texts for consecration in Robert to those for dedication in Egbert.

[42] M. Lapidge, *The Cult of St. Swithun*, Winchester Studies 4.ii (Oxford, 2003), p. 23. It does contain the blessing for the deposition of St Swithun on 2 July. Lapidge suggests that the texts for the Benedictional may have been assembled before 971, and presumably that the illustrations were completed afterwards. The Benedictional is dated 973 only because its royal iconography has been tied to Edgar's second coronation in that same year (Deshman, pp. 212–14). There is no reason to assume, however, that the iconography had not been developed earlier in Edgar's reign, especially because of the paralleling of Edgar and Christ, King of Heaven, in the New Minster Charter.

[43] The text is ordo XLI in the Romano German Pontifical.

[44] 'May the omnipotent God bless and keep you and this house [and] may he deign to illuminate you and this house by the presence of his gift, and deign to open the eyes of his kindness over it day and night. Amen.

'And may he beneficently grant that all you who devoutly gather at the dedication of this basilica might be worthy, through the blessed intervention of N. [the saint to whom the church is dedicated] and those other saints, whose relics here are devoutly venerated with love, to obtain the forgiveness of your sins. Amen.

'Since with their intervention, you yourselves might be made the temple of the Holy

In the miniature accompanying the benediction (Fig. 11.2) the use of outline drawing to depict both the church and the congregation conveys the identification of the one with the other, albeit in a way different from that used in the New Minster Charter frontispiece.[45]

Before turning once again to the iconography of the frontispiece, it should be noted that there are some significant similarities between the texts of the ordo and that of the charter that would certainly not have been lost on Æthelwold. The idea that Christ is present in the church and the congregation expressed in the ordo and the blessing in the Benedictional is also very much a part of the charter. The charter records the granting of the New Minster to Christ by Edgar. Christ is present in figural form in the frontispiece, where he is shown receiving his newly cleansed church. He is present symbolically in the large chi-rho which prefaces the words 'Omnipotens totius machinae conditor'[46] on folio 4 recto. His presence is invoked a final time in the dating clause that appears directly above the king's subscription on folio 30 recto,[47] and by the sign of the Holy Cross that accompanies the names of most of the witnesses. A number of these crosses, most importantly the large cross preceding Edgar's subscription, are filled in with gold ink and, like the gold letters of the text of the charter, they function as signs of the light of heaven infusing both the book and the earthly world of which it is a part. The golden crosses, chrismons and letters, in the words of Herbert Kessler, negotiate the space 'between the world of matter and the world of spirit',[48] as do the sacred texts in which they are usually found and the liturgical ceremonies to which those texts are usually connected.

The dedication ordo was also, as we have seen, centred on the process of cleansing or baptism. The purification and exorcisms enacted in the ordo are as concerned with expulsion and judgement as they are with entrance and the blessing of the newly cleansed church and everything associated with it. Take, for example, one of the texts for the cleansing of salt:

> Exorcizo te creatura salis . per deum uiuum . per deum uerum . per deum sanctum . per deum qui te per eliseum prophetam in aquam mitti iussit ut sanaretur sterelitas aque . ut effeciaris sal exorcizatum in salutem credentium . ut sis omnibus te sumentibus sanitas anime et corporis et effugeat atque discedat ab eo loco quo aspersus fueris omnis fantasia et nequitia uel uersutia

---

Spirit, in which God, the Holy Trinity, might deign to dwell continuously, and after the running out of the excursion of this life of labouring, you might merit to come successfully to eternal joy. Amen.' Prescott, p. 19, quoting Deshman, *Benedictional*, p. 141.

45 Deshman, *Benedictional*, pp. 142–5, has explored the baptismal symbolism of both the blessing and the miniature.

46 'Almighty creator of the whole order of creation'.

47 'Anno incarnationis dominicę .dcccclxvi. scripta est h'u'ius priuilegii singrapha his testibus consentientibus quorum inferius nomina ordinatim caraxantur.' ('The document of this privilege was written in the year of the Lord's incarnation 966, with these witnesses in agreement whose names are written below'.)

48 Kessler, *Seeing Medieval Art*, p. 29.

diabolice fraudis omnisque spiritus immundus adiuratus per eum qui uentures est iudicare uiuos et mortuos et saeculum per ignem.[49]

Or the antiphon 'Asperges me domine ysop et mundabor lauabis me et super niuem dealbabor.'[50]

The emphasis in the ordo on the purification of the church and the driving out of evil from everything associated with it is paralleled in the frontispiece by the symbolism of Mary's palm[51] and Peter's key, and in the text of the charter by the latter's repeated references to the cleansing of the New Minster by the driving out of the secular canons. The expulsion of the canons is commemorated symbolically in the prologue and first four chapters of the charter in the lengthy account of the fall of the rebel angels and the fall of Adam and Eve.[52] Here, as in the ordo, the community is portrayed as the Lord's chosen people. Men replaced angels, grew corrupt, and are now replaced by the reformed community. Chapter VI, the chapter that provides a transition from the proem to the dispositive section of the charter begins with the words 'hinc ego Eadgar' ('hence I Edgar') signalling the direct and causal relationship between the events. The expulsion of the canons is also recorded literally in chapter VII, where Edgar is described as 'vicarius christi' ('the vicar of Christ'), a term used later in the charter for the abbot.[53] Rumble suggests that it is as vicar of Christ that Edgar is depicted in the charter's frontispiece.[54] But the dual use of the term also suggests that Edgar is to be associated with the Minster itself, that his figure may literally negotiate the space between the monastery under the rule of the abbot, and the kingdom of heaven under the rule of Christ. This is further suggested in the charter by the equation of the monastery with heaven as earthly and heavenly paradises respectively,[55] an equation that is perhaps furthered by the lush acanthus orna-ment and golden bars of the frame of the frontispiece. This is not the sort of language one usually finds in a charter, but it is an important part of dedication and consecration ceremonies in which the cleansing of the monastery revealed it to be a type of paradise.

---

[49] *Egbert*, p. 39: 'I *exorcize* you creature of salt through the living God, through the true God, through holy God, through the God who commended you through the prophet Elijah to be thrown into the water so that the sterility of the water might be cured, so you, ex-orcized salt, might bring about the salvation of those believing and so you might be for everyone who partakes of you health of the soul and body and so that every phantom and evil and craftiness of diabolical fraud and every impure spirit having been adjured may flee and depart from this place where you will have been sprinkled. Through he who is about to come to judge the living and the dead through fire.'

[50] *Egbert*, p. 41. 'Thou shalt sprinkle me, Lord, with hyssop and I shall be cleansed, thou shalt wash me and I shall be made whiter than snow' (Ps. 50:9).

[51] See Deshman, *Benedictional*, p. 199 on the complex symbolism of the palm.

[52] On the fall of the angels see D. F. Johnson, 'The Fall of Lucifer in *Genesis A* and Two Anglo-Latin Royal Charters', *JEGP* 7 (1998), 500–21.

[53] Ch. 14; Rumble, *Property and Piety*, p. 88.

[54] Rumble, *Property and Piety*, p. 81, n. 46; see also p. 70.

[55] In Chapter VI the monastery is identified as the Lord's ploughland ('Domini cultura'), and in Chapter XVIII as Christ's ploughland ('Christi cultura').

From its original foundation in the early tenth century, the New Minster was a uniquely royal church. Possibly the vision of King Alfred,[56] the forerunner of the tenth-century minster is likely to have been the *monasteriolum* given to Grimbald of Saint-Bertin, who arrived in England in 887 and died in 901 prior to the completion of the new foundation.[57] The relics of Grimbald and St Judoc (a Breton prince who became a priest and hermit) became the principle relics of the early church. The earliest grant of land to the new foundation may be preserved in a charter of 901 (S 1443; Miller no. 2) which records the granting by Bishop Derewulf and the Old Minster community of a 'pind circan' ('wind church') and stone dormitory to Edward the Elder in exchange for the church of St Andrew and its worthy. I mention the grant because of the possibility that the wind church might have been an abandoned church (as opposed to a 'thatched' or 'wattled' church),[58] a motif that occurs regularly in legends of foundation or refoundation on the continent,[59] and one which interestingly prefigures the abandoning of the church by the secular canons prior to the 964 refoundation. In both instances we are dealing with spaces that, while neglected, are already 'intrinsically and essentially sacred'.[60] According to the charter, Edward acquired the new land in order to build a church for the salvation of his soul and that of his venerable father, King Alfred.[61] A second charter of the same year (S 365; Miller no. 4) calls for prayers of intercession to be said daily for Edward, the venerable Alfred and their ancestors.[62] The New Minster very quickly became a dynastic mausoleum with the translation of Alfred's body to the new church shortly after its construction,[63] and the subsequent burial there of Ealhswith in 902, Æthelweard in the early 920s and Edward and his son Ælfweard in 924. Eadwig, Edgar's brother (d. 959), was the last of the West Saxon kings to be buried there. Edgar, like his father Edmund, would eventually be buried at Glastonbury, possibly due to the politics of succession rather than his own wishes – although obviously we have no way of knowing this for certain.[64] The New

---

[56] M. Biddle. '*Felix Urbs Winthonia*: Winchester in the Age of Monastic Reform', *Tenth-Century Studies*, ed. D. Parsons (London and Chichester, 1975), pp. 123–40, at 128–31; Keynes, *Liber Vitae*, pp. 16–18; M. Hare, 'The Documentary Evidence in 1086', *The Golden Minster: The Anglo-Saxon Minster and Later Medieval Priory of St Oswald at Gloucester*, ed. C. Heighway and R. Bryant (York, 1999), pp. 33–46, at 34; but see also Miller, *Charters of the New Minster*, p. xxv.

[57] Keynes, *Liber Vitae*, p. 17, describes the identification of the *monasteriolum* as a forerunner of the New Minster as having been made 'in retrospect'.

[58] *WinchNM*, p. 6, citing P. R. Kitson, *A Guide to Anglo-Saxon Charter Boundaries*, forthcoming.

[59] Remensnyder, *Remembering Kings Past*, pp. 40, 47, 48.

[60] See the discussion by Remensnyder, *Remembering Kings Past*, p. 44.

[61] *For mine saule haelo ꝺ mines þæs arwyrðan fader.*

[62] *Pro me et venerabilis patre et auibus meus cotidie orations fiant et intercessiones.*

[63] As *WinchNM* points out, S 365 implies that Alfred's body might already have been buried in the 'wind-church'.

[64] One wonders why he was not buried at Æthelwold's Winchester since the two had worked so closely together in life. It may be simply that he wanted to be buried near his father and in one of the houses associated with the origins of the reform. It could also be that

Minster was clearly by Edgar's day a church associated with the bodies of the West Saxon royal family that it had come to house. The history of the abbey contained in the later Liber Vitae shows that the community was very aware of its royal foundations and its royal burials. It is highly unlikely that Edgar would have been unaware of how his actions of refoundation paralleled those of the original founders.

Burial was something that seems to have set the New Minster apart from the Old Minster. While royal burials had taken place in the cemetery of the Old Minster, they were not contained within the body of the church prior to the construction of the west-work, which was not begun until 971.[65] The people of Winchester also seem to have had the right of burial in the New Minster cemetery. That right is not recorded until the move to Hyde Abbey in 1110, but by then it was understood as having been of long-standing tradition.[66] In contrast to the Old Minster, the bishop's church, the New Minster was identified not only with the bodies it contained, but also with the king and the people of the city.[67] There is certainly a distinct difference in the plans of the two churches. The New Minster was over twice as long as the Old Minster, with a wide nave flanked by side aisles and a spacious eastern transept.[68] It was intended from the start to hold a large congregation. The Old Minster, prior to the rebuilding in the 980s, was small and crowded, with a nave only about forty feet long and small eastern porticus rather than a transept. Even after its rebuilding it remained a very narrow church, its entire body only about as wide as the nave of the New Minster (without its side aisles). The latter thus seems to have been from the first intimately associated with its congregation, the people of the royal burh which was itself intimately associated with the rise of the West Saxon dynasty; just as it was intimately associated with the bodies of the West Saxon kings and princes. All churches are equated with the congregations they house, but in the case of the New Minster the associations seem to have been made particularly apparent. No other Anglo-Saxon church contained so many royal bodies, presumably in marked graves,[69] and this was as much a part of the original conception of what the church should be as was its impressive size. To see the impressive body of Edgar in the New Minster charter as a sign of this royal foundation with its royal burials and its large congregation is perfectly in keeping with the purpose and symbolism of the New Minster itself, especially as he is flanked by the Minster's new patron saints.

This type of symbolism is in no way exclusive to the New Minster Charter.

Glastonbury was chosen by his eldest son Edward, who would have organized the burial, because Æthelwold supported the cause of his brother Æthelred. I thank the late Patrick Wormald for this last suggestion.

[65] The west-work was built above the cemetery, and after its construction burials are known to have taken place within it. Biddle, 'Felix Urbs Winthonia', p. 138.

[66] M. Biddle, *Winchester in the Early Middle Ages* (Oxford, 1976), p. 314.

[67] *WinchNM*, p. xxvii.

[68] See the plan in Biddle, 'Felix Urbs Winthonia', p. 130.

[69] The Liber Vitae (fol. 5), for example, records that Edward's burial was to the right of the high altar (Keynes, *Liber Vitae*, p. 19), implying that it must have been marked visually.

Fig. 11.3 London, British Library, Cotton Tiberius A.iii, fol. 2v.

The visualization of the church as a living body is generally an important part of the art associated with the reform, especially art produced under the patronage of, or in association with, Bishop Æthelwold. It is conveyed by the use of outline drawing to suggest the unity of church and congregation in the miniature for the blessing of a church in his Benedictional (Fig. 11.2).[70] It is evident in the depiction of St Swithun on folio 97 verso of the same manuscript,[71] in which Swithun is literally a human column, a living part of the architecture. It is evident also in the story of St Æthelthryth and the refoundation of Ely, in which the legal possession of the saint's body and her church were one.[72] This took material form in the creation and display of the golden statues of Æthelthryth and the Ely virgins donated to the church at Ely by abbot Byrhtnoth sometime before his death in 999 – a literal making visible of the bodies of the women, the human foundations on which the refoundation rested.

For Æthelwold, Edgar's body might have come to stand in a similar way not just for the man himself, but for the body of the church he refounded. Eventually it came to stand for the reform itself. Edgar is depicted as a co-author of the reform in the miniature that prefaces the *Regularis Concordia* in the Tiberius A.iii manuscript (Fig. 11.3). The manuscript was produced at Christ Church Canterbury in the middle of the eleventh century, but it is believed by some art historians to be a copy of a reform period original,[73] possibly designed by Æthelwold himself.[74] It depicts King Edgar enthroned between two figures usually identified as Bishop Æthelwold and Archbishop Dunstan.[75] Their bodies are united by the scroll which may represent the Rule and/or the process of its production.[76] Below them is a monk who has girded his loins with the 'faith and good works' described in the text.[77] All eyes are on Edgar who stares fixedly out at us like Christ in majesty, or like the imperial portraits of Otto III. Recently I compared this image of Edgar to the famous portrait of Otto on folio 16 recto of

---

[70] In a talk delivered to a meeting of the Society of Antiquaries in Oxford (October, 2004), the Biddles commented on how closely the depiction of the church in the miniature accords with what is known of the architecture of the Old Minster.

[71] Illustrated in Deshman, *Benedictional*, pl. 32.

[72] S. Ridyard, *The Royal Saints of Anglo-Saxon England: A Study of West Saxon and East Anglian Cults* (Cambridge, 1988), ch. 6; C. E. Karkov, 'The Body of St Æthelthryth: Desire, Conversion and Reform in Anglo-Saxon England', *The Cross Goes North: Processes of Conversion in Northern Europe, AD 300–1300*, ed. M. Carver (York, 2002), pp. 398–411.

[73] See, e.g. J. J. G. Alexander, 'The Benedictional of St Æthelwold and Anglo-Saxon Illumination in the Reform Period', *Tenth-Century Studies*, ed. D. Parsons (London and Chichester, 1975), pp. 169–83, at 183; R. Deshman, '*Benedictus Monarcha et Monarchus*: Early Medieval Ruler Theology and the Anglo-Saxon Reform', *FS* 22 (1988), 204–40, at 207–10 and 219.

[74] Deshman, '*Benedictus*', 210.

[75] But see B. Withers, 'Interaction of Word and Image in Anglo-Saxon Art, II: Scrolls and Codex in the Frontispiece to the *Regularis Concordia*', *OEN* 31.1 (1997), 38–40 for alternative possibilities.

[76] Withers, 'Interaction of Word and Image'. Withers goes further and suggests that the scroll is a sign of oral rather than written production (p. 39).

[77] Deshman, '*Benedictus*', 205.

the Aachen (or Liuthar) Gospels (Aachen, Cathedral Treasury), in which a scroll carried by symbols of the four evangelists divides the emperors head from his body.[78] The portrait was central to Kantorowicz's thesis of the king's two bodies: the body itself representing the mortal king and the staring frontal head crowned by the hand of God, his eternal and divinely granted authority.[79] I argued that the scroll in the Edgar portrait functioned much the same way, marking the two natures of Edgar's kingship: the human and the sacral. I now think, however, that that interpretation is in some need of modification. I do think that the scroll does indicate that Edgar has two bodies, but I would suggest that they are not human and sacral, so much as individual and corporate. We should note that the same scroll that separates Edgar's head from his body also separates the heads of Æthelwold and Dunstan from their bodies. It serves, I would argue, to identify them as both the individuals who initiated and oversaw the reform and who produced the *Regularis Concordia*, and as the corporate body of the reformed church itself, a church comprised in this monastic agreement of the king, bishop, archbishop and the monastic community – the latter represented by the monk in the lower half of the page. There is, of course, an eternal nature to the symbolism, but in this manuscript it is connected with the eternal authority of the Rule and the reformed church rather than with sacral kingship. This image has a very different manuscript context than the gospelbook portrait of Otto III.

The portrait of Edgar in the New Minster charter prefaces a charter, a manuscript that maps and describes not the topography or structure of the New Minster, but its purification, one that lays out the interdependence of the monastery and the king, and one that likens the king's relationship to Christ to the abbot's relationship to Christ. Like the Tiberius A.iii drawing, it is not just about Edgar's exalted position, but about his relationship to the living bodies that make up the community for whom the charter was written and decorated, and the living bodies of the congregation for whom the church was built, and who, at least on special occasions, would likely have seen the charter displayed on the altar. For both groups the frontispiece would have visualized their own dual history as a royal foundation and as a covenant people with God. Edgar's body was one with which they could all identify in offering up themselves to Christ. The descent of the divine towards Edgar's body was also one with which they could identify, both in terms of their desire to be united with Christ in the future, and in their experience of baptism, the moment at which they too would have been touched by the Holy Spirit. In baptism, Christ was not just himself, but 'his members baptized into his ecclesiastical body'.[80] For the New Minster faithful looking at the frontispiece Edgar too was visually and symbolically a

---

78 Illustrated in Karkov, *Ruler Portraits*, fig. 15.
79 E. Kantorowicz, *The King's Two Bodies: A Study in Medieval Political Theology* (Princeton, NJ, 1957), pp. 61–78.
80 The quotation is from Deshman, *Benedictional*, p. 145. For the ways in which this symbolism is brought out in the Benedictional's miniatures of the Baptism of Christ and the dedication of a church see *ibid.*, pp. 142–5.

type of ecclesiastical body, a corporate body representing this particular church in which they were all united and in which they had all been made 'as living stones built up, a spiritual house, a holy priesthood, to offer up spiritual sacrifices' (I Peter 2:5). The image was a perpetual reminder that they were just what the words of the charter said they were, a people 'collected together' by God under Edgar.

12

The Laity and the Monastic Reform in the Reign of Edgar

ALEXANDER R. RUMBLE

O F the two main divisions within Anglo-Saxon society, ecclesiastical and lay, the latter made up the vast majority of the population. However, because of the purpose and bias of the surviving written sources relating to the tenth-century monastic reform, lay people were only very selectively mentioned in them, mainly as either benefactors or despoilers of the endowment. We should not think from this that the rest of the lay population were unaware of, or impervious to, the events and consequences of the reform and there are clear indications that some individuals, families, and groups were greatly affected in one way or another.

The reform could not have succeeded without the power and authority of the king and his officials. There is documentary evidence that other members of the laity gave support of a physical as well as a financial nature to the process of re-establishing the monastic life. Some of these may have been merely obeying orders from their superiors, but others may have been genuinely moved by religious sentiment to help the monks and nuns in their pursuit of a form of monastic life closer to the *Regula S. Benedicti*.

According to Wulfstan the Cantor's *Vita S. Æthelwoldi*, the important king's thegn Wulfstan of Dalham was sent by Edgar [in 964] to supervise the expulsion of the secular priests from the Old Minster, Winchester and their replacement by monks:

> The king also sent there with the bishop one of his agents, the well-known Wulfstan of Dalham (*quendam ministrorum suorum famosissimum, cui nomen erat Wulfstan æt Delham*), who used the royal authority to order the canons to choose one of two courses: either to give place to the monks without delay or to take the habit of the monastic order. Stricken with terror, and detesting the monastic life, they left as soon as the monks entered ...[1]

Wulfstan of Dalham was described in the *Liber Eliensis* as *sequipedus* 'close companion' of King Eadred, and so by the reign of Edgar was already an expe-

---

[1] Wulfstan, *Vita S. Æthelwoldi*, ch. 18. See Lapidge and Winterbottom, *WulfstW*, pp. 32–3.

rienced official.[2] He was a royal reeve and probably the steward in East Anglia of the estates of the queen mother Eadgifu.[3] His locational byname could be either from Dalham in Suffolk or Dalham in Kent, as he appears to have had connections with both shires.[4] He was given the Latin designation *discifer* in S 768 (AD 968) – equivalent to OE *disc-þegn*, and was called *prefectus* in S 796 (AD 974).[5] Although he would have been obliged to act in accordance with royal commands, it is also significant that later he was personally recorded as a benefactor of the monasteries at both Ely and Bury St Edmunds.[6] He subscribed to documents 958 x 974, probably including the hugely important New Minster Refoundation Charter of 966.[7]

It is very probable that the physical expulsion of the secular clergy from the New Minster was also effected by lay royal officials, but on that occasion by those employed by the queen, Ælfthryth, if her subscription to the Refoundation Charter is to be taken literally.

+ I, Ælfthryth, the legitimate wife of the aforementioned king. with the king's approval establishing the monks in the same place, by the sending of my ambassador (*mea legatione monachos eodem loco rege annuente constituens*), have made the mark of the Cross.[8]

The date of this action was probably between 964 and 966, that is, after Ælfthryth became queen by her marriage to Edgar and the date of this witness-list.[9] Although *ASC* A refers to the expulsion of the secular priests from the New Minster s.a. 964, in the same annal as its reference to the reform of the Old Minster and Chertsey and Milton, its account should probably be seen as an over-simplification of an extended process.[10]

Some of Edgar's ealdormen and their families were also recorded as patrons of the reform. Æthelwine 'Dei Amicus', ealdorman of East Anglia, was the founder of Ramsey (in 966).[11] Æthelmær, the son of Ealdorman Æthelweard of the Western Provinces who succeeded his father *c.* 1012, founded Cerne

---

[2] *LE*, II.xxviii, p.102.
[3] Lapidge and Winterbottom, *WulfstW*, p. 32, n. 2.
[4] C. R. Hart, *The Early Charters of Northern England and the North Midlands* (Leicester, 1975), p. 379. See respectively A. D. Mills, *A Dictionary of British Place-Names* (Oxford, 2003), p. 147 and J. K. Wallenberg, *The Place-Names of Kent* (Uppsala, 1934), p. 119.
[5] *Burt*, no. 23; and *Malm*, no. 28 (which records the restoration of an alienated monastic estate).
[6] Hart, *Early Charters of Northern England and the North Midlands*, p. 379.
[7] Rumble, *Property and Piety*, no. 4, at p. 97, n. 164.
[8] Rumble, *Property and Piety*, no. 4, at pp. 93–4.
[9] For an apparently genuine diploma issued in 964 by King Edgar in favour of his queen Ælfthryth, see S 725; *Abing*, no. 101. For the credibility of the Refoundation Charter's witness-list, see Rumble, *Property and Piety*, p. 92, n. 125 and p. 93, n. 128.
[10] Bately, *MS A*, pp. 75–6.
[11] On Æthelwine, see C. Hart, 'Athelstan Half-King and his Family', in his *The Danelaw* (London, 1992), pp. 569–604, at 591–7. For the date 966, see Julia Barrow, 'The Community of Worcester, 961–c.1100', in *St Oswald of Worcester: Life and Influence*, ed. Nicholas Brooks and Catherine Cubitt (London, 1996), pp. 84–99, at 93–5.

(987) and Eynsham (1005).[12] Ealdorman Byrhtnoth of Essex is recorded as a benefactor and a defender of the rights of Ely.[13]

Some ealdormen themselves later became monks after a life of secular business: thus Æthelstan 'Half-King' retired to Glastonbury in 957 and was buried there.[14] Such late entrants into the monastery were among the intended audience of Æthelwold's translation of the Benedictine Rule, as he himself stated in the vernacular tract on 'King Edgar's Establishment of Monasteries':

> Although keen-witted scholars who understand clearly the two-fold wisdom – that is, the wisdom of things actual and spiritual – ... do not require this English translation, it is nevertheless necessary for unlearned laymen (*niedbehefe ungelæredum woroldmonnum*) who for fear of hell-torment and for love of Christ abandon this wretched life and turn to their Lord and choose the holy service of this rule; lest any unconverted layman (*ænig [u]ngecyrred woroldman*) should in ignorance and stupidity break the precepts of the rule and employ the excuse that he erred on that day because he knew no better.[15]

Bequests are recorded of lands and money to reformed churches by rich laypersons, who often had a royal connection. There was a close nexus of noble supporters of the reform at this time. This is exemplified by the will of Ælfgifu, 966 x 975, who was probably the divorced wife of King Eadwig.[16] She was described as a kinswoman of King Edgar in S 737–8 and in her will made bequests to him and to the queen and to 'the ætheling' (probably he who as king became known as Edward the Martyr).[17] She also bequeathed estates to the monasteries of the Old Minster, Winchester, where she was to be buried, to the New Minster, Winchester, and to Romsey, Abingdon and Bath, as well as to Bishop Æthelwold personally. She gave money too for the repair of monasteries and the relief of the poor. Her sister Ælfwaru was also a benefactor of the Old Minster, giving the estates of Alverstoke, East Woodhay and Exton, Hants.[18]

Not all of the nobility were always so helpful to the monastic cause, although some opposition amongst the nobility to monastic churches seems to have been selective rather than general, and to have had a political or personal rather than a theological cause. Ealdorman Ælfhere of Mercia was described, in *ASC* DE 975 and the *Vita Oswaldi*,[19] as a despoiler of Ramsey after the death of King Edgar

---

12 Keynes, *Diplomas*, pp. 192 and 197, n. 163.
13 Janet M. Pope, 'Monks and Nobles in the Anglo-Saxon Monastic Reform', *ANS* 17 (1995), 165–80, at 170, 177–8; *LE*, II.27, 62.
14 Lesley Abrams, *Anglo-Saxon Glastonbury: Church and Endowment*, Studies in Anglo-Saxon History 8 (Woodbridge, 1996), 344, n. 129 and 346.
15 *Councils & Synods*, i, no. 33; *c*. 970 – 984.
16 S 1484; Whitelock, *Wills*, no. 8, and pp. 118–19; for an updated commentary, see Cyril Hart, 'The Will of Ælfgifu', in *The Danelaw*, pp. 455–65, with map.
17 Whitelock, *Wills*, p. 120.
18 Winchester, Hampshire Record Office, Episc. 1 (Reg. Pontissara), fol. 160v.
19 Cubbin, *MS D*, pp. 46–7; Irvine, *MS E*, p. 59; *EHD*, no. 236.

but he was elsewhere recorded as a benefactor of Glastonbury and Abingdon.[20] His actions against Ramsey and Ealdorman Æthelwine's against Ely have been thought to have had more to do with their mutual rivalry over control of south-east Mercia than any general anti-monastic feeling.[21] It has also been noted that some noble families bequeathed estates to both monastic and secular churches alike.[22]

Perhaps the laymen who had greatest cause to fundamentally oppose the reform were those belonging to families whose members lost land and influence as a consequence of it, including the families (and heirs) of some of the secular priests who had lost their quasi-hereditary livings and did not choose to convert to monasticism.[23]

There were also those individuals or families who had been forced to give up church land previously held on a lease or to return alienated estates. Some estates and title-deeds may have been surrendered unwillingly at this time. The forced denial of such an event in the testimony of (Queen) Ælfthryth, by then the widow of King Edgar, given 995 x 1002 concerning her and Bishop Æthelwold's past actions relating to the estate of Ruishton, Somerset, does not mean that such actions did not occur elsewhere:

> Ælfthryth ... bear[s] witness that Archbishop Dunstan assigned Taunton to Bishop Æthelwold, in conformity with the bishop's charters. And King Edgar then relinquished it ... and moreover he put Ruishton under the bishop's control. And then Wulfgyth rode to me at Combe and sought me. And I, then, because she was my kinswoman, and Ælfswith because he [i.e. Leofric] was her brother, obtained from Bishop Æthelwold that they [i.e. Wulfgyth and Leofric] might enjoy the land for their lifetime, and after their death the land should go to Taunton ... And with great difficulty we two brought matters to this conclusion. Now I have been told that Bishop Æthelwold and I must have obtained the title-deed (*boc*) from Leofric by force. Now I, who am alive, am not aware of any force any more than he would be, if he were alive. For Leofric had a new title-deed (*boc*); when he gave it up he thereby manifested that he would engage in no false dealings in the matter. Then Bishop Æthelwold told him that none of his successors could dispossess him. He then commanded two documents (*twa gewritu*) to be written, one he kept himself, the other he gave to Leofric.[24]

Although in the diplomatic form of a letter, this document was, according to Pierre Chaplais, probably the written record of a lawsuit held in the presence of

---

[20] Ann Williams, '*Princeps Merciorum Gentis*: The Family, Career and Connections of Ælfhere, Ealdorman of Mercia, 956–83', *ASE* 10 (1982), 143–72, at 166–7.

[21] Williams, '*Princeps Merciorum Gentis*', pp. 161, 164–6; Abrams, *Anglo-Saxon Glaston-bury*, pp. 346–7; Pope, 'Monks and Nobles', pp. 179–80.

[22] Pope, 'Monks and Nobles', pp. 176–7.

[23] For three priests who did convert, see Lapidge and Winterbottom, *WulfstW*, ch. 18, p. 33, nn. 3–5. For a suggestion that in churches away from Æthelwold's influence monks and secular priests managed to live side by side, see Blair, *Church*, p. 352.

[24] S 1242; F. E. Harmer, *Anglo-Saxon Writs* (Manchester, 1952), no. 108.

Archbishop Ælfric of Canterbury, one of the addressees of the text.[25] That a lay person felt able to challenge at the highest level the (monastic) bishop of Winchester's tenure of Ruishton and to question the actions of the queen mother, a notable supporter of the reform, being directly involved in the changes at the New Minster[26] and having been designated by the *Regularis Concordia* as the protrectress of the nuns,[27] seems indicative of a general lessening of monastic power after the deaths of Æthelwold, Dunstan and Oswold.[28]

Before that time, however, the revival of monasticism caused physical changes to the landscape which would have affected its appearance to all sections of the population. New churches and buildings were constructed at the monastic centres themselves,[29] and some improvements were probably made on the outlying estates too. Within the city of Winchester, four adjacent walled or hedged precincts were constructed, probably in 970, one each for the Old Minster, the New Minster and Nunnaminster and one around the bishop's palace at Wolvesey.[30] A permanent consequence of this was that streets were closed, streams diverted and houses demolished. Some citizens were forced to move from their dwellings, while others were pressurised to exchange one piece of land for another or for money. The construction of these monastic enclosures was in accordance with the *Regula S. Benedicti*, cap. 66. 6–7:

> Monasterium autem, si possit fieri, ita debet constitui ut omnia necessaria, id est aqua, molendinum, hortum, vel artes diversas intra monasterium exerceantur, ut non sit necessitas monachis vagandi foris, quia omnino non expedit animabus eorum.[31]

It was following this precept that King Edgar ordered each of the three monasteries to be surrounded with a 'space' (*spacium*), marked by walls or hedges, where each community might be 'removed from the bustle of the citizens' (*á ciuium tumultu remoti*):

25 'The Anglo-Saxon Chancery: From the Diploma to the Writ', *Journal of the Society of Archivists* 3 (1965–9), 160–76, at 173, reprinted in *Prisca Munimenta: Studies in Archival and Administrative History presented to Dr A. E. J. Hollaender*, ed. Felicity Ranger (London, 1973), pp. 43–62, at 57–8.

26 See above, p. 243.

27 Symons, *RC*, p. 2.

28 Respectively in 988, 984 and 992, see *Handbook of British Chronology, Third Edition*, ed. E. B. Fryde, D. E. Greenway, S. Porter and I. Roy, Royal Historical Society Guides and Handbooks 2 (London, 1986), 214, 223, 224. For the immediate political effects of the death of Æthelwold, see Keynes, *Diplomas*, pp. 176–86.

29 Margaret Deanesly, *Sidelights on the Anglo-Saxon Church* (London, 1962), pp. 93–102.

30 Rumble, *Property and Piety*, pp. 23–5, fig. 4, and nos. 6–8.

31 'The monastery should, if possible, be so constructed that within it all necessities, such as water, mill and garden are contained, and the various crafts are practiced. Then there will be no need for the monks to roam outside, because this is not at all good for their souls.' *RB 1980: The Rule of St Benedict in Latin and English with Notes*, ed. Timothy Fry with Imogene Baker, Timothy Horner, Augusta Raabe and Mark Sheridan (Collegeville, MN, 1981), pp. 288–9.

ut cenobite inibi degentes á ciuium tumultu remoti tranquillius Deo seruirent honorifice magna dilataui cautela. spaciumque omne prefatis cenobiis contiguum dissipatis secularium domunculis ... spacium omne muris uel sepibus complexum ...[32]

The building of the ecclesiastical precincts at this time entailed the 'expulsion' of the laity from most of the south-east quarter of the walled city, a process which has left its mark on the topography of Winchester to the present day.

It is clear from cap. xii of the New Minster Refoundation Charter that the purpose of such a precinct was to prevent monks and nuns mixing with the laity for the good of their souls as much as to keep the citizens from encroaching on monastic property:

> Let regular monks therefore, not seculars, dwelling in the aforementioned monastery in company with Christ, conform to the practices of a rule ... Let them blush with shame – under perpetual interdict – at being made table-companions of the citizens within the city. (*Ciuium conuiuae intra urbem perpetuo interdictu fieri erubescant.*) Let charitable people who dwell in the city employ permitted foods in the refectory, rejecting, like melancholy, the showy and lascivious delights of the worldly ... Let them entertain most warily guests of a sacred, or of the highest, rank, if reason requires it, and well-ordered pilgrims coming from far-distant lands, at the abbot's table in the refectory. Let seemly kindness be shown to laymen in the guest-house; And let none of the monks be allowed to eat or drink with them, in accordance with the decrees of the Fathers; Moreover let [laymen] not be brought into the refectory to eat or drink ...[33]

The phrase *ciuium conuiuae* is an echo of *secularium conuiuia* in the *Regularis Concordia* which in the mid eleventh-century manuscript is glossed in OE by the more graphic phrase *poruldmanna gebeorscypas*.[34]

The construction of the precincts appears to have taken a long time and some land and water was still being acquired by Bishop Æthelwold in the reign of Edgar's successor Edward the Martyr. According to a document of 975 x 978, one Ælfwine exchanged two acres and an adjacent stream within the city with the bishop and the community of the Old Minster for twelve hides of land *Æt Mordune* (unidentified):[35]

---

[32] 'so that the monks and nuns living therein might serve God more peacefully, removed from the bustle of the citizens ... all the space adjacent to the aforesaid monasteries when the small houses of the secular have been demolished ... the whole space, encompassed by walls or hedges ...' S 807; Rumble, *Property and Piety*, no. 6.

[33] S 745; Rumble, *Property and Piety*, no. 4, at pp. 85–7.

[34] *Regularis Concordia*, ch. 11; in BL, Cotton Tiberius A.iii, fol. 5v, see W. S. Logeman, 'De consuetudine monachorum [Cod. Cotton Tib. A. III]', *Anglia* 13 (1891), 365–454, at 375, line 133.

[35] For a discussion of the difficulties of identifying this place, see Rumble, *Property and Piety*, p. 145, n. 5.

he ... has granted ... land amounting to 2 acres within Winchester and the stream which runs next to it, within the space (*binnan þæm rymette*) which the bishop has enclosed into the monastery ...[36]

Among the witnesses to the exchange were the citizens of Winchester (*seo burhwaru*) the first record of them acting as a corporate body. The document is, however, chiefly of interest to the present paper because Ælfwine was a member of a local family which had been associated with the Old Minster for several generations. He states that his forefathers had previously granted to the community an annual food-rent from the estate *Æt Mordune* and that they are all buried at the Old Minster (*þær eal his forðfædren rest*). His father Ælfsige had increased the family's gift by granting the same estate to the clergy for their subsistence. This rural estate was thus in 975 x 978 being returned by the Old Minster to its previous lay owners, in exchange for the strategically placed land in the city. In view of the family's long association with the Old Minster, we cannot take it for granted that Ælfwine was necessarily a supporter of the monastic reform, but may merely have been continuing a long tradition of supporting the community attached to the local cathedral. His family is said to have held the urban property by virtue of a diploma issued by King Alfred, which Ælfwine handed over, so from the time of that king's refortification and replanning of the city in the late ninth century.[37]

The leading role apparently played by Æthelwold in the exchange of mills and the diversion of watercourses between the three reformed Winchester monasteries is recorded in another document from the end of Edgar's reign, datable to ?970 x 975.[38] This, together with a statement by Wulfstan the Cantor about Æthelwold's provision of fresh running water for the Old Minster,[39] and Æthelwold's earlier diversion of part of the River Thames for the mill of Abingdon Abbey *c.* 960,[40] reflects an interest in civil engineering to be placed besides his other skills.

Such major works on the landscape would only have been possible through effective management of the estates within an endowment, including the movement of servile labourers (*geburas*) between estates, as may have occurred between the Ely Abbey estates of Hatfield, Walden, Munden, Datchworth, etc. in Hertfordshire.[41] Some serious disruption, at least temporary, would have been made to the personal lives of the peasant families involved in these schemes.

---

[36] S 1376, OE version; Rumble, *Property and Piety*, no. 8(i).
[37] *Winchester in the Early Middle Ages: An Edition and Discussion of The Winton Domesday*, ed. Martin Biddle, Winchester Studies 1 (Oxford, 1976), 450–3.
[38] S 1449; Rumble, *Property and Piety*, no. 7.
[39] Wulfstan, *Narratio metrica, epistola specialis*, lines 41–4; Lapidge, *Cult of St Swithun*, pp. 374–5 and n. 42.
[40] C. J. Bond, 'The Reconstruction of the Medieval Landscape: The Estates of Abingdon Abbey', *Landscape History* 1 (1979), 59–75, at 69.
[41] David A. E. Pelteret, 'Two Old English Lists of Serfs', *Mediaeval Studies* 48 (1986), 470–513, especially 480–3. See also Rosamond Faith, *The English Peasantry and the Growth of Lordship* (London and Washington, 1997), pp. 81–4.

The construction programmes associated with the re-establishment of the monastic churches would also have had repercussions on nearby estates, whether royal, ecclesiastical or thegnly. There would have been a large demand for raw materials such as timber and stone, as well as an initial need for food and livestock. On one occasion at least a local estate seems to have been used as the location of a workshop for lay craftsmen involved in making religious artefacts. An estate or *villa* more than three miles to the west of Winchester[42] was referred to by Wulfstan the Cantor as the place where the silver, gold and jewelled reliquary-shrine of St Swithun was made on the orders of King Edgar between 971 and 974.[43] In Michael Lapidge's collection of written materials relating to *The Cult of St Swithun*, the text and translation appear as follows:

> Conueniunt uillam fabri properanter ad illam
> quam 'magnam' uocitare solent, opus eximiumque
> certatim fabricare student atque ocius explent,
> auxilio comitante Dei …[44]

> The goldsmiths hastily convene at that royal estate which people are accustomed to call the 'Great' … and they strive eagerly to fashion the excellent work, and quickly bring it to completion with God's assistance

As can be seen, although no word for 'royal' actually occurs in the Latin text, Lapidge translated *villa* as 'royal estate'. Like Biddle, Dodwell and Crook before him,[45] he assumed that such precious metalworking would take place at a royal residence. Because of this and its position seven miles west of Winchester, he like the others went on to identify the *villa* as Kings Somborne, Hants, which belonged to the king in 1066.[46]

There are two reasons to question this identification. Firstly, the Latin word *villa* in later Anglo-Saxon texts, unless qualified by another word such as *regis*, *regia* or *regalis*, did not necessarily designate a major royal estate or residence.[47] Although in Bede, *Historia ecclesiastica*, and in charters before 800 it seems that *villa* may usually be equated with a royal 'central place',[48] this usage need

---

[42] The citizens walked three miles from the city to meet the reliquary; Wulfstan, *Narratio metrica*, Bk ii, lines 28–30; Lapidge, *Cult of St Swithun*, pp. 494–5. Lapidge, p. 493, n. on lines 9–10, asserts that the reliquary had been brought an equal distance to meet the citizens but this is not in the text.

[43] Lapidge, *Cult of St Swithun*, pp. 18–19, 35.

[44] Wulfstan, *Narratio metrica*, Bk ii, lines 9–12; Lapidge, *Cult of St Swithun*, pp. 492–3.

[45] Biddle, *Winchester in the Early Middle Ages*, p. 466; C. R. Dodwell, *Anglo-Saxon Art* (Manchester, 1982), p. 67; John Crook, 'King Edgar's Reliquary of St Swithun', *ASE* 21 (1992), 177–202, at 198, n. 84.

[46] London, The National Archives, E 31/2 (Great Domesday Book), fol. 39v: *Domesday Book, 4: Hampshire*, ed. Julian Munby (Chichester, 1982), 1: 47

[47] Compare the various non-royal habitative usages of the vernacular word OE *tūn*, with which *villa* is often equated; A. H. Smith, *English Place-Name Elements*, 2 vols., EPNS 25–6 (Cambridge, 1956), II.188–98, especially 189–91.

[48] J. Campbell, 'Bede's Words for Places', *Names, Words, and Graves: Early Medieval Settlement, Lectures Delivered in the University of Leeds, May 1978*, ed. P. H. Sawyer (Leeds, 1979), pp. 34–54, at 43–50.

not have been so strictly applied in the more varied administrative geography of the later tenth century. We may note that in the same text Wulfstan the Cantor used a more precise term *uicus regis* to refer to Andover, Hants, the site of meetings of the *witan* in 980 and earlier.[49] Secondly, it seems that workshops for working with precious metals were sometimes set up on non-royal estates, belonging to a church or a member of the nobility, some of whom employed their own goldsmiths.[50]

I suggest that a more probable location on onomastic evidence is the manor of 'Michelton' in Broughton, Hants. This appeared as *MVLCELTONE* in Great Domesday Book, where 2 virgates were held by the thegn Edmund *Tempore Regis Willelmi*. One of these 2 virgates had been held by Edmund's father from King Edward, but there is no surviving evidence of royal possession in the previous century.[51] The Great Domesday spelling is corrupt (with the intrusive *L* in *MVLC-* borrowed from the subsequent *-LT-*) and stands for *MVCELTONE*. A better form is *Michelton* 1207, etc.[52] This name, meaning 'large estate', from OE *micel* and *tūn*, would be the exact vernacular equivalent of the Latin *villa ... magna* of Wulfstan's text.[53]

'Michelton' is later associated in documents, from the thirteenth to the eighteenth centuries, with the manor of Roake in Broughton, represented on the Ordnance Survey map as Roake Farm.[54] This has an unrelated name from ME *atte oke* 'at the oak tree', but is useful as giving a rough location for 'Michelton' which is not shown on modern maps. Both Roake and King's Somborne are settlements just off the same Roman road (Margary 45a) leading from Winchester to Old Sarum,[55] but on opposite banks of the River Test; Roake being about three miles further west. If 'Michelton' is nearby, its location would fit the text as well as that of King's Somborne and would have the onomastic credibility that the latter lacks. Its position might have been chosen as being equally accessible for craftsmen or smiths from the mints of Winchester, Wilton and

---

49 Wulfstan, *Narratio metrica*, Bk i, lines 81–2 (*uico regis in Andeferan*); Lapidge, *Cult of St Swithun*, pp. 378–9. Andover was also the place where a lawcode of Edgar (probably 'II and III Edgar') was promulgated, see Peter Sawyer, 'The Royal *Tun* in Pre-Conquest England', *Ideal and Reality in Frankish and Anglo-Saxon Society: Studies Presented to J. M. Wallace-Hadrill*, ed. Patrick Wormald, with Donald Bullough and Roger Collins (Oxford, 1983), pp. 273–99, at 290.

50 Elizabeth Coatsworth and Michael Pinder, *The Art of the Anglo-Saxon Goldsmith* (Woodbridge, 2002), pp. 213–14.

51 London, The National Archives, E 31/2 (Great Domesday Book), fol. 50r; *Domesday Book, 4: Hampshire*, ed. Munby, 69: 20.

52 Richard Coates, *The Place-Names of Hampshire* (London, 1989), p. 139.

53 For *tūn*, see Smith, *English Place-Name Elements*, II.188–98.

54 *The Victoria History of the County of Hampshire*, ed. William Page (London, 1911), IV. 495; Winchester, Hampshire Record Office 2M29/1 (manor court book of Roake and Michelton 1598–9); 2M59/32 (lease of messuage etc. in Michelton and Broughton, 1780). Nicholas de Michelton witnessed a charter relating to Broughton and Meonstoke inspected in 1246, see *Calendar of Charter Rolls*, I: *1226–1257* (London, 1903), p. 310.

55 Ivan D.Margary, *Roman Roads in Britain*, 3rd ed. (London, 1973), pp. 100–101.

Southampton.[56] Unfortunately as yet no Anglo-Saxon archaeological finds have been made at Roake, although there is evidence of some Roman activity in the area.[57]

The carrying of the reliquary from *villa magna / micel tūn* to the city was accompanied by an outpouring of religious fervour. On the orders of the king, a mixed crowd of the city's inhabitants – men and women of all ages and 'whether slave or nobly born' – proceeded barefoot three miles westwards to meet the reliquary coming from its place of manufacture and then travelled with it, singing and clapping, to the west gate of the city. The first person coming out from within the city to greet the shrine, a blind girl, was immediately cured of her blindness.[58] This occurrence accords well with the blindness (and also poverty) of many of those cured in miracles attributed to the powers of St Swithun.[59]

In a modern and increasingly secular world, we should beware of being too cynical about the effect of religious cults on the lives of the poor or disabled. Stories of miracles were an expected ingredient of the literary genre of saints' lives because they were (and still are) necessary for the process of canonisation. Nevertheless, this is not to say that all of the claims made in them were wholly fictional or literary in origin and that many of the miracle stories were not based on claims believed at the time by a large number of people. The Benedictine reformers deliberately fostered the cults of local saints whose relics they collected and held in their rebuilt churches.[60] There is no doubt however that such cults provoked a great deal of genuine religious excitement amongst the laity of the region and we should not underestimate the spiritual depth of such fervour and its effect on the lives of individuals.

There were thus a variety of ways in which the monastic reform was affected by, and in turn impinged upon, the laity. It was a lasting paradox that, although the New Minster Refoundation Charter and other documents urged the monks and nuns to shun lay people and their behaviour, they could not in fact follow the exclusive monastic life to which they aspired without the patronage, protection and sympathy of both those in authority and the general population living around their monasteries.

---

[56] For their location and dates, see David Hill, *An Atlas of Anglo-Saxon England* (Oxford, 1981), figs. 217, 225. For connections between goldsmiths and minting, see Coatsworth and Pinder, *The Art of the Anglo-Saxon Goldsmith*, pp. 87, 237.

[57] *Ex inf.* Andy Puls, Assistant Archaeologist, Hampshire County Council, 14 March 2005.

[58] Wulfstan, *Narratio metrica*, Bk ii, lines 54–8; Lapidge, *Cult of St Swithun*, pp. 494–5.

[59] For accounts (composed 972–974) of various blind people being cured through the saint's relics, see Lantfred of Winchester, *Translatio et miracula S. Swithuni*, chs. 5, 8, 12, 15, 16, 18, 21, 22, 26, 28, 29 and 36; Lapidge, *Cult of St Swithun*, pp. 289–331, *passim*.

[60] Blair, *Church*, p. 353; David Rollason, *Saints and Relics in Anglo-Saxon England* (Oxford, 1989), pp. 177–82; cf. Pope, 'Monks and Nobles', pp. 171–2.

13

The Edgar Panegyrics in the *Anglo-Saxon Chronicle*

MERCEDES SALVADOR-BELLO

W HILE rhetorically and stylistically less brilliant than *The Battle of Brunanburh*, two other poems from the *ASC*, known as *The Coronation of Edgar* (in the entry for 973) and *The Death of Edgar* (975), deserve attention because of what they reveal about the politics and culture of Edgar's period.[1] These poems have much in common with *The Battle of Brunanburh* and another of the *Chronicle*'s panegyrics, *The Capture of the Five Boroughs* and, taken together, they celebrate three tenth-century kings, Æthelstan, Edmund and Edgar, distinguishing them from the monarchs that are only mentioned in non-poetic entries. Thus they eulogize the kings who were actively involved in the process of the Benedictine reform,[2] probably a particularly relevant event to the tenth- and eleventh-century chroniclers.

Yet within this group, the poems about Edgar are distinct because they focus not on single battles against heathens, but on particular moments in the king's reign that allow for elaboration on his strengths as a monarch, setting Edgar above the others. By focusing solely on the two Edgar poems of the *Chronicle*, in this article I intend to demonstrate that the two pieces are probably literary

---

[1] Jayne Carroll, 'Engla Waldend, rex admirabilis: poetic representations of King Edgar', *RES* 59 (2007), 113–32, was published too late to be taken account of here. There is also an on-line essay which deals with the Edgar poems separately, see J. C. Weale, 'The Canonicity of two Edgar Poems', *The Heroic Age* 3 (Summer 2000), at http://www.mun.ca/mst/heroicage/issues/3/weale.html. Combined with the analysis of other *Chronicle* poems, studies of *The Coronation of Edgar* (henceforth *The Coronation*) and *The Death of Edgar* (henceforth *The Death*) can be found in Daniel Abegg, *Zur Entwicklung der historischen Dichtung bei den Angelsachsen* (Strassburg, 1894), pp. 42–53, Katherine O'Brien O'Keeffe, 'Poems of the *Anglo-Saxon Chronicle*' in her *Visible Song: Transitional Literacy in Old English Verse* (Cambridge, 1990), pp. 108–37, Matthew Townend, 'Pre-Cnut Praise-Poetry in Viking Age England', *RES* 51 (2000), 349–70, and Janet Thormann, 'The Anglo-Saxon Chronicle Poems and the Making of the English Nation', *Anglo-Saxonism and the Construction of Social Identity*, ed. Allen J. Frantzen and John D. Niles (Gainesville, 1997), pp. 60–85.

[2] Both Æthelwold and Dunstan, the leaders of the movement, were closely related to Æthelstan's court; Edmund in turn appointed Dunstan as abbot of Glastonbury, a fact that may be said to have planted the seeds of the reform. As for Edgar, his key role as patron of the monastic revival most likely gave rise to the insertion in the *Chronicle* of two poems that – if not the best in terms of poetic skill – clearly make him stand out among the other monarchs.

products created to propagandize reformist ideas. From this, it might be inferred that these poems were viewed by their author(s) and contemporary audiences as pro-reform panegyrics.[3] A comparative analysis of the diction, imagery, and themes offered by the two texts not only suggests that they could be read as interrelated eulogistic pieces but also that they might illustrate the existence of a well-established tradition of praise-poetry running parallel to the development of the Benedictine reform.[4]

The Coronation of Edgar

       Her Eadgar wæs,   Engla waldend,
       corðre micelre   to cyninge gehalgod
       on ðære ealdan byrig,   Acemannesceastre;
       eac hi igbuend   oðre worde
  5   beornas Baðan nemnaþ.   Þær wæs blis micel
       on þam eadgan dæge   eallum geworden,
       þon(n)e niða bearn   nemnað ⁊ cigað
       Pentecostenes dæg.   Þær wæs preosta heap,
       micel muneca ðreat,   mine gefrege,
  10   gleawra gegaderod.   ⁊ ða agangen wæs
       tyn hund wintra   geteled rimes
       fram gebyrdtide   bremes cyninges,
       leohta hyrdes,   buton ðær to lafe þa (a)g<e>n
       wæs wintergeteles,   þæs ðe gewritu secgað,
  15   seofon ⁊ twentig;   swa neah wæs sigora frean
       ðusend aurnen,   ða þa ðis gelamp.
       ⁊ him Eadmundes   eafora hæfde
       nigon ⁊ .xx.,   niðweorca heard,
       wintra on worulde,   <þa> þis geworden wæs,
  20   ⁊ þa on þam .xxx. wæs   ðeoden gehalgod.[5]

---

[3] As is shown below, p. 265, the allusion to the so-called 'anti-monastic reaction' in *The Death* has cast doubts on the poem's structural unity and its possible ascription to the panegyric genre.

[4] From a different standpoint, Townend, 'Pre-Cnut Praise-Poetry' (see especially pp. 353–5), has argued that the two Edgar poems, together with *The Battle of Brunanburh* and *The Capture of the Five Boroughs*, could be considered as evidence of the existence of an Anglo-Saxon eulogistic trend deriving from contemporary Norse encomiastic tradition. For a thoroughgoing analysis of praise-poetry and invective in Anglo-Saxon, Celtic and Norse tradition, see Frederick M. Biggs, 'Deor's Threatened "Blame Poem,"' *Studies in Philology* 94.3 (1997), 297–320.

[5] 'In this year Edgar, ruler of the English, with a great company, was consecrated king in the ancient borough, *Acemannesceaster* – the men who dwell in this island also call it by another name, Bath. There great joy had come to all on that blessed day which the children of men call and name the day of Pentecost. There was assembled a crowd of priests, a great throng of learned monks, as I have heard tell. And then had passed from the birth of the glorious King, the Guardian of Light, ten hundred years reckoned in numbers, except that there yet remained, by what documents say, seven and twenty of the number of years, so nearly had passed away a thousand years of the Lord of Victories, when this took place.

There are some aspects that clearly distinguish *The Coronation* from *Brunanburh* and *The Capture*. This text is, for example, remarkable for the insistence on Edgar's being consecrated, in the opening and again in the conclusion. Even though there are precedents of Anglo-Saxon royal anointing before the tenth century, the emphatic mention of Edgar as being *gehalgod* (2b and 20b) dramatically sets him apart from the other kings eulogized in the *Chronicle*.[6] Furthermore, the figure of the king is deliberately likened to that of a priest when Edgar is said to be aged thirty (20a), the minimum age for sacerdotal consecration. Also, the text mentions that the coronation took place on Whitsun (8a), a traditional date for baptism ceremonies and episcopal ordination.

By the same token, the poem stands out from the other *Chronicle* panegyrics in its conspicuous use of ambivalent terms applying to Christ and Edgar. For example, Christ is styled as *bremes cyninges* (12b) – which might equally designate the earthly king – and *leohta hyrdes* (13a) – a phrase which could refer either to the pastoral role of a monarch or to that of the abbot in the monastic context of the time. Similarly, Edgar is said to be *Engla waldend* (1b), a typically ambivalent reference that is also suggestive of the celestial king.[7] Also importantly, the coronation ceremony is associated with Christ's Second Coming (10–16b). In addition to this, the location where the event took place, is intriguingly mentioned twice – *Acemannesceastre* (3b) and *Baðan* (5a).

All these peculiarities may be explained if we tentatively assume that *The Coronation* is charged with contemporary overtones, a hypothesis that might be first backed up by manuscript evidence. To begin with, the poem is extant in *ASC* B (BL, Cotton Tiberius A.vi, fols. 1–35), which has been dated by most scholars to the second half of the tenth century.[8] Interestingly, this copy of *ASC* ends at annal 977. Besides, the accompanying genealogical regnal table reaches up to Edward the Martyr's reign although it does not mention his death occurring in 978.[9] These two aspects have suggested a more precise date between 977 and

---

And Edmund's son, bold in battle, had spent 29 years in the world when this came about, and then in the thirtieth was consecrated king.' Here and elsewhere quotations from *ASC* are from the A version (Cambridge, Corpus Christi College, 173), Bately, *MS A*, and translations from *EHD*.

6 There are only a few references to royal consecrations that have been recorded in the *Chronicle* and these are but poor terse allusions in comparison with the 973 entry. Notably, Æthelstan's consecration at Kingston is only reported by the CD versions of the *Chronicle* (in the entry for 924): '] Æðelstan wæs gecoren to cynge of Myrcum,] æt Cyngestune gehalgod.' Similar laconic references are recorded for Æthelred II, Edward the Confessor, and Harold II.

7 Karkov has also pointed out the possible punning effect of *Engla waldend* in this poem. She has compared the employment of this stylistic device to the paronomastic pair *angelorum/anglorum*, referring to both the angels and Edgar, in the 'New Minster Refoundation Charter' (966, S745). See Catherine E. Karkov, *The Ruler Portraits of Anglo-Saxon England* (Woodbridge, 2004), p. 88.

8 The are only a few unimportant spelling divergences between the versions of *The Coronation* in A and B. According to Bately, the scribe who copied annals 973–1001 (Hand 5) in A is of the early eleventh century. See Bately, *MS A*, p. xxxvii.

9 The B *Chronicle* was complemented by a genealogy that was detached from the original

979.[10] Thus, according to O'Brien O'Keeffe, 'Of the manuscripts transmitting the tenth-century poems, B, with a date close to 977/79, is nearest in time to the coronation and death of Edgar (973 and 975 respectively). For this reason, it is unlikely that B is many copies away from the original compositions chronicling the events of 973 and 975.'[11] Seen in this light, it is quite likely that *The Coronation* might be roughly contemporary with the crowning of Edgar proper.

The chronological proximity of *The Coronation* to the events described may also be supported by the presence of a poem commemorating both Edgar's coronation and death in Æthelweard's *Chronicon*. This text, which follows closely *ASC* A, is dated to 978–88 by Campbell.[12] Interestingly, Æthelweard's *Chronicon* is a well-known illustration of the so-called 'hermeneutic style,'[13] which has been associated by several scholars with the school of Æthelwold and the intellectual concerns of the reform.[14] Being the only poetic piece included in this work, the occurrence of Edgar's panegyric right at the end of Æthelweard's historical account similarly points to the probable contemporary character of the poem, since the author's intention was most likely to honour either the ongoing

---

manuscript and is currently found in BL, Cotton Tiberius A.iii (fol. 178). The genealogy was initially separated from the *Chronicle*'s end by two blank leaves.

[10] On paleographical grounds Ker dates this manuscript between 977 and 979. N. R. Ker, *Catalogue of Manuscripts Containing Anglo-Saxon* (Oxford, 1957), p. 249 (no. 188). Taylor in turn offers 977–1000 although he defends an earlier date in that time span: see Taylor, *MS B*.

[11] O'Brien O'Keeffe, *Visible Song*, p. 125. It has also been suggested that *ASC* B's provenance is Abingdon, a well-known Benedictine centre in the late tenth century. Edgar granted Æthelwold the monastery of Abingdon, from which reformed monks were sent to other monastic houses in England. Also, Abingdon monks were supplied to replace the clerics that were expelled from the New Minster. See Wulfstan Cantor's account of this in his *Vita S. Æthelwoldi*, Lapidge and Winterbottom, *WulfstW*, chs. 16 and 18, pp. 30–1 and 32–3.

[12] Campbell, *Æthelweard*, p. xiii, n. 2.

[13] In his introduction to *The Chronicle of Æthelweard*, p. xlv, Campbell employs the term *hermeneutic* to refer to the literary trend whose greatest exponent is Aldhelm. He then describes hermeneutic composition as indulging in 'recondite vocabulary derived from glossaries'. Michael Lapidge, 'The Hermeneutic Style in Tenth-Century Anglo-Latin Literature', *ASE* 4 (1975), 67–111, at 67, defines it as 'a style whose most striking feature is the ostentatious parade of unusual, often very arcane and apparently learned vocabulary'. See also Mechthild Gretsch, *The Intellectual Foundations of the English Benedictine Reform* (Cambridge, 1999), and Michael D. C. Drout, *How Tradition Works: A Meme-Based Cultural Poetics of the Anglo-Saxon Tenth Century* (Tempe, AZ, 2006), esp. pp. 187–92.

[14] Æthelwold himself was a practitioner of hermeneutic composition. Cf. Gretsch's argument that Æthelwold might be the author of the gloss corpora contained in the Royal Psalter (BL, Royal 2.B.V) and in Aldhelm's *De virginitate*. Also, see Lapidge's 'The Hermeneutic Style', for an analysis of hermeneutic features in the *Benedictional of St Æthelwold* and Lantfred's *Translatio et Miracula S. Swithuni*, both of which were most likely commissioned and possibly supervised by Æthelwold. Lapidge has stated that Æthelwold's Latin, 'particularly in the preface to the *Regularis Concordia*, is a flamboyant example of the "hermeneutic" style which was practised by Latin authors in tenth-century England', *Blackwell Encycl.*, s.v. Æthelwold.

monarch or a recently deceased one.[15] The existence of this encomium in a collection of annals that is roughly contemporary with Edgar's reign thus supports the contention that the Edgar poems contained in the *Chronicle* may likewise be a product of the Benedictine period.

A possible obstacle to accepting the contemporary background of the Edgar poems is the fact that the initial *Her* in both *The Coronation* and *The Death* is necessary for the correct scansion of the first verse.[16] This has prompted the idea that the two poems were composed by the chronicler.[17] By contrast, *Brunanburh* and *The Capture*, clearly offer *Her* as an extra-metrical syllable, so that it has been argued that they were produced as autonomous pieces which were eventually added in order to highlight particular episodes of the *Chronicle*. The metrical argument however does not preclude the possibility that the Edgar poems might have been created independently of the *Chronicle* and later incorporated to the annalistic sequence. In Campbell's words 'The Old English chronicles, which we possess, were put together in monasteries, but the creative forces which gave rise to their most important parts were independent of those monasteries.'[18] Outstanding entries like *The Coronation* and *The Death* might have therefore had their origin as separate pieces that were at some point inserted in the *Chronicle*. The compiler(s) of the *Chronicle* probably decided to emphasize the centrality of Edgar's reign by substituting the typical prose account for a flamboyant poetic piece that was available at a moment when the major patron of monasticism was probably frequently honoured in that way. This assumption implies that the adaptation of both *The Coronation* and *The Death* to the annalistic style would only require the substitution of *Her* for an originally monosyllabic word.[19] No doubt any poet could do that.

---

15 By contrast, Æthelstan and Edmund are both allotted prose chapters. Even the battle of Brunanburh is a prose account in this work. Significantly, there is a short, though favourable, reference to Eadwig, a probable relative of Æthelweard.

16 In the case of *The Death*, there is a slight possibility that the first line (*Her geendode eorðan dreamas*) might have functioned as a metrically regular verse. However, as pointed out by Scragg, 'Technically *geendode* might form a complete half-line but of a rare type, but in view of the opening of *Coronation* it seems more likely that we are to regard *her* as integral to the verse.' See Donald Scragg, 'A Reading of *Brunanburh*', *Unlocking the Wordhord: Anglo-Saxon Studies in Memory of Edward B. Irving, Jr.*, ed. Mark C. Amodio and Katherine O'Brien O'Keeffe (Toronto, 2003), pp. 109–22, at 121, n. 27.

17 Abegg, for example, states that the introductory *Her* in both *The Coronation* and *The Death* is metrically inherent. Accordingly, he concludes that the two poems were specifically composed by the annalist to be included in the Anglo-Saxon *Chronicle*. See Abegg, *Zur Entwicklung der historischen Dichtung bei den Angelsachsen*, p. 53.

18 Alistair Campbell, *The Battle of Brunanburh* (London, 1938), p. 34.

19 As with *Brunanburh* and *The Capture*, Campbell envisaged the possibility that the inclusion of *The Coronation* and *The Death* might respond to the compiler's interest in improving an otherwise terse account of the reigns of the monarchs implied. Thus, he states that 'assuming they were not written for their places in the *Chronicle*, [*The Coronation* and *The Death*] must be slightly modified at their beginnings, for in the first the initial half-line will not scan without the introductory *her* and in the second it is necessary for the sense', Campbell, *Brunanburh*, p. 36, fn. 2. In the case of *The Death*, however, he considers that only the first twelve lines would correspond to that hypothetical original

The association of *The Coronation* with the reform can be supported by the presence of certain stylistic features in the poem. Notably, there is evidence that the poem's diction and imagery conjure up late tenth-century royalist propaganda that seems to be connected with the political aims of Anglo-Saxon Benedictinism. As suggested above, *The Coronation* is significant in that the figure of the king is likened to that of a priest. Deshman has stated that a similar emphasis on Edgar's role as *rex et sacerdos* is found in late tenth-century works, whose affinities with Benedictine ideology are evident.[20] In this sense, Byrhtferth's *Vita S. Oswaldi*, the composition of which is dated *c.* 997, is one of the extant accounts of the event that is closer in time to the coronation date.[21] A passage from this hagiography describes Edgar's coronation ceremony as being similar to an ordination rite taking place at Pentecost. Even though this passage is far from offering an eye-witness account,[22] the meticulously detailed narrative suits an ecclesiastical author concerned with stressing the sacerdotal colouring of the coronation ritual:

Acceperunt dehinc duo episcopi manus regis, qui eum deduxerunt ad ecclesiam, cunctis alta et modulata concinentibus voce hanc antiphonam, *Firmetur manus tua, et exaltetur dextera tua; justitia et judicium præparatio sedis tuæ, misericordia et veritas præcedant faciem tuam.* Hac finita antiphona, *Gloria Patri, et Filio, et Spiritui Sancto* adjunxerunt. Cumque pervenissent in ecclesiam, et rex ante altare se prosterneret, deponendo prius diademam de capite,

poem whereas the remaining section, more conventional in general, would be the work of the chronicler (*ibid.*, pp. 36–7).

20 Specifically, he has demonstrated that various iconographic motifs found in Æthelwold's *Benedictional*, whose compilation was probably supervised by Bishop Æthelwold himself, were possibly designed to function as propagandistic elements intended to favour both the monarchy and the monastic reform. For example, the double role of Christ as *rex et sacerdos* is reflected in the miniature of Christ's Baptism (fol. 25a) in the *Benedictional*. As explained by Deshman, the emphasis on Christ's royal and priestly character in this picture has to do with the double role assigned to Edgar on his Coronation ceremony: 'Edgar evidently scheduled his coronation on Whitsun in 973 to liken it to the baptismal investiture of Christ as *rex et sacerdos*. ... The ceremony might also have been timed to liken Edgar's inauguration to a monk's profession, for this monastic rite was considered a second baptism.' Robert Deshman, *The Benedictional of Æthelwold* (Princeton, 1995), p. 213 and plate 19; see also pp. 45–50. For Deshman's comments on the characterization of Edgar as *rex et sacerdos* in *The Coronation*, see pp. 213–14. See also his '*Christus rex et magi reges*: Kingship and Christology in Ottonian and Anglo-Saxon Art', *FS* 10 (1976), 367–405.

21 According to Lapidge, the *Vita S. Oswaldi* 'was composed between 997 and 1002, perhaps within five or so years of Oswald's death [occurred in 992]', Michael Lapidge, 'Byrhtferth and Oswald', *St Oswald of Worcester: Life and Influence*, ed. Nicholas Brooks and Catherine Cubitt (London, 1996), pp. 64–83, at 65.

22 As demonstrated by Lapidge, Byrhtferth's account lacks originality as it is mainly based on the 'Second Anglo-Saxon Ordo' or 'B-version'. See his 'Byrhtferth and Oswald', esp. pp. 70–73. Also, see Janet L. Nelson, 'The Second English *ordo*', in her *Politics and Ritual in Early Medieval Europe* (London, 1986), pp. 361–74.

incept princeps episcoporum Dunstanus hymnum glorificum excelsa voce: *Te Deum laudamus, Te Dominum confitemur.*[23]

This passage clearly presents Edgar conducting himself as someone to be ordained, as the escorting by the two bishops, the prostration and the lavish report of the antiphons and hymns sung on that occasion all suggest. Besides, this hagiography notes that the coronation took place at Pentecost.[24] Æthelweard's *Chronicon* not only mentions Pentecost as the date of the coronation but also establishes a parallel between Edgar and Moses' priestly role.[25] The sacerdotal characterization of Edgar and the preoccupation with the date of the coronation observed in these excerpts therefore echo the emphasis placed on the king being *gehalgod* and the reference to Pentecost in *The Coronation*.

A further distinctive feature of the *Chronicle* poem is the conspicuous insistence on the place where Edgar was crowned.[26] The poet took pains to make clear the exact name of the place as *Acemannesceastre* (3a), which seems to be a Latinate version of *Baðan* (5a).[27] Æthelweard's *Chronicon* similarly offers the Latin and vernacular name of the city.[28] Different hypotheses have been put forward to explain the choice of Bath instead of Kingston, the traditional coronation site of English kings in the tenth century. It has been argued that the Latinate name *Acemannesceastre* in the *Chronicle* poem – or *Akimannis castrum* in Æthelweard's work – would bring up imperial connotations as the town was renowned in Roman times. Similarly, it has been suggested that the site might have been chosen by analogy with Charlemagne's consecration at Aix-la-chapelle, also a spa town. The deliberate comparison with Charlemagne would therefore set Edgar in the role of imperial champion of the Christian faith. Yet the author's emphasis on the location of the ceremony may similarly point to the prominence of Bath during the reform period. B's biography of Dunstan, for instance, records the archbishop's visits to this town's monastery: 'Venit etiam ex hac salubri consuetudine ad locum thermarum, ubi calida lympha de abyssi latibulis guttatim vaporando ebullit, quem incolæ locum sub paterna lingua Bathum soliti sunt appellare.'[29] During one of his (apparently frequent) stays at

---

23 Text from Raine, *York*, I.437. Italics in the text are Raine's. My translation: 'The two bishops then took the king's hands and led him to the church, while everyone was singing in high and melodious voice the following antiphon: "Let your hand be strengthened and your right hand exalted; may justice and judgement be the threshold of your throne; may grace and truth precede your face." When the antiphon was ended, they added: "Glory to the Father, the Son and the Holy Ghost." When they had arrived in the church and the king, having taken off the crown from the head, had prostrated himself before the altar, Dunstan, the first among bishops, with his magnificent voice started a hymn of glorification: "We praise you, God, and believe you, Lord."'

24 Raine, *York*, I.436.

25 Campbell, *Æthelweard*, p. 55.

26 As pointed out by Thormann, *The Anglo-Saxon Chronicle Poems*, p. 70.

27 With regard to *Acemannesceastre* Plummer notes that 'It is possible that the first part of the name contains the Latin *aquae*.' Earle and Plummer, II.161.

28 Campbell, *Æthelweard*, p. 55.

29 My translation: 'Because of this healthy custom he [Dunstan] used to come to the places

Bath, Dunstan is said to have had a premonition of a boy's death in Glastonbury, which is subsequently confirmed. The reference to one of Dunstan's miracles taking place as he visits the community at Bath is thus indicative of the relevance that this location might have had in the late tenth century.

The Coronation still reveals more aspects that can be linked to the reform context. For example, a significant portion of the poem (lines 10b–16) is devoted to associating the date of this event with the approaching end of the first millennium. A similar insistence on the chronological setting of the event and its association with the impending millennium is found in Æthelweard's *Chronicle*.[30] Apart from an evident concern with the exact reckoning of time, this feature again connects to the ideological frame of the reform. As Frank Stenton, Eric John and others have pointed out, after his imperial coronation, Edgar started to be explicitly propagandized as *Christus domini* (Christ's anointed) or as an earthly counterpart of the king of heaven.[31] Accordingly, the concept of the Second Coming became specially relevant in the monastic agenda, since it served reformist aims to secure Edgar's position as undisputed authority in his realm. In doing so, the reformers publicized Edgar's reign as a new era characterized by order and justice while they guaranteed for themselves a successful development of the reform process.

By linking the coronation to the Second Coming, the *Chronicle* poem also indirectly conjures up the conventional image of Christ as a dispenser of justice, a role that is in turn implicitly associated with Edgar. The identification of the king with the Supreme Judge is, for example, attested to in the New Minster Refoundation Charter (966, S 745):

> Timens ne eternam incurrerem miseriam si adepta potestate non facerem quod ipse qui operatur omnia quae in celo uult et in terra suis exemplis iustus examinator innotuit . uitiosorum cuneos canonicorum . e diuersis nostri regminis coenobiis Christi uicarius eliminaui.[32]

By presenting Christ as *iustus examinator* and Edgar himself as *Christi uicarius*, the king is thus characterized as a fair judge expelling the licentious canons from the monasteries.[33]

---

of the hot baths – where drop by drop, vapouring hot water is sent out from the hidden bowels of the earth, a site which the inhabitants are used to call 'Bath' in their native tongue.' Text from Stubbs, *Dunstan*, ch. 34, p. 46. This reference is also in William of Malmesbury's *Vita S. Dunstani*, Stubbs, *Dunstan*, ch. 16, p. 305.

[30] Campbell, *Æthelweard*, p. 55.

[31] See Stenton, *ASE*, p. 368, and Eric John's chapter 'The Age of Edgar' in *The Anglo-Saxons*, ed. James Campbell (Harmondsworth, 1982), esp. pp. 188–9.

[32] 'Fearing lest I should incur eternal misery if I, on the acquisition of power, should not do what He wishes who Himself administers everything in Heaven and [who] has become known on earth as a Righteous Judge from His warning punishments, I, the vicar of Christ, have expelled the crowds of depraved canons from the various monasteries of our kingdom.' Text and translation from Rumble, *Property and Piety*, ch. vii, p. 81.

[33] Deshman has likewise studied the relevance of the Second Coming in Æthelwold's *Benedictional* and other texts related to the reform. Notably, the miniature of the Second

As pointed out above, the poem is also particularly remarkable for the ambivalent use of several terms denoting royalty, which could apply to either Edgar or Christ, as is the case of *bremes cyninges* (12b) and *leohta hyrdes* (13a). Incidentally, in the preface to the *Regularis Concordia* (*c.* 973), the paramount document of the reform, Edgar is praised as *gloriosus* and *egregius* – equivalent to *bremes* in the poem.

> Gloriosus etenim Eadgar, Christi opitulante gratia Anglorum ceterarumque gentium intra ambitum Britannicae insulae degentium rex egregius. . . . Regali utique functus officio ueluti Pastorum Pastor sollicitus a rabidis perfidorum rictibus, uti hiantibus luporum faucibus, oues quas Domini largiente gratia studiosus collegerat muniendo eripuit.[34]

In this passage, Edgar is also significantly compared to Christ as the Good Shepherd (*Pastorum Pastor*), an image which was closely related to the Benedictine ideological conception of kingship.[35]

The identification of Christ with a shepherd is of course a conventional image that was used throughout the Middle Ages but, at the moment *The Coronation* was composed (probably shortly after this event took place), pastoral imagery was undoubtedly akin to reformist ideology. Indeed, the pastoral metaphor pervasively occurs in *St Benedict's Rule*, as the role of the abbot is frequently compared to that of Christ as the shepherd of the flock.[36] Owing to the influence exerted by the *Rule*, the pastoral analogy started to be frequently used in

---

Coming (fol. 9v) introduces the liturgical section of the manuscript, thus confirming the pre-eminence granted to this concept in reform-oriented texts. See Deshman's comments on this topos in *The Benedictional*, pp. 64–9 and pl. 10.

[34] 'Edgar the glorious, by the grace of Christ illustrious King of the English and of the other peoples dwelling within the bounds of the island of Britain. ... Thus, in fulfilment of his royal office, even as the Good Shepherd, he carefully rescued and defended from the savage open mouths of the wicked – as it were the gaping jaws of wolves – those sheep which by God's grace he had diligently gathered together.' Text and translation from Symons, *RC*, ch. 3. Note that *breme* is usually glossed as *celeber, clarus, illustris, famosus, notus, cognitus*, see BT(S). The first entry for *breme* reads *celebrated, renowned; illustrious, glorious* in the *DOE*.

[35] The pastoral metaphor applying to the monarch in turn derives from the Carolingian conception of kingship. See Oswyn Murray, 'The Idea of the Shepherd King from Cyrus to Charlemagne', *Latin Poetry and the Classical Tradition: Essays in Medieval and Renaissance Literature*, ed. Peter Godman and Oswyn Murray (Oxford, 1990), pp. 1–14.

[36] The image is drawn from John 10:11–17; see Deshman, *The Benedictional*, p. 206. Deshman also has a full discussion of this image in '*Benedictus Monarcha et Monachus*: Early Medieval Ruler Theology and the Anglo-Saxon Reform', *Learning and Literature in Anglo-Saxon England: Studies Presented to Peter Clemoes on the Occasion of his Sixty-Fifth Birthday*, ed. Michael Lapidge and Helmut Gneuss (Cambridge, 1985), pp. 204–40, especially 225–28, and in *The Benedictional*, pp. 205–6. See also Karkov, *The Ruler Portraits*, pp. 100–1. I have elsewhere discussed the pastoral metaphor, the relevance of the sacerdotal role of Christ and the Second-Coming motif in the Advent Lyrics and other pro-reform texts in 'Architectural Metaphors and Christological Imagery in the Advent Lyrics: Benedictine Propaganda in the Exeter Book?' *Conversion and Colonization in Anglo-Saxon England*, ed. Catherine E. Karkov and Nicholas Howe (Tempe, AZ, 2006), pp. 169–211, especially 188–210.

other texts. For example, the image is present in the New Minster Refoundation Charter:

> Si autem qualibet ocasione diabolo instigante contigeret ut fastu superbientes arrogantię deiecti canonici monachorum gregem quem ego uenerans cum pastore in Dei constitui possessione . deicere insidiando uoluerint . agatur de eis et de omnibus qui quolibet munere cecati iuuamen eis impenderint ...[37]

Here, the abbot is clearly said to be installed by Edgar as the shepherd (*pastore*) of his flock (*gregem*, the monks). The topos was also widely employed in pro-reform texts, applying to the king and the leading reformers in liturgical pieces, hagiographies and other works. Thus, Æthelwold is portrayed as a shepherd to his monks in Wulfstan's *Vita S. Æthelwoldi*,[38] while in the hymn known as *Ave Dunstane*, Dunstan is also typically characterized as a pastoral figure protecting the community from its enemies.[39] The use of the pastoral cliché in these texts corroborates the special prominence that this image had in the monastic context.

A further favourite topos of pro-reform works was the image of either the reformers or the king as effective guarantors of communal unity and order. Significantly, *The Coronation* openly stresses the general agreement as regards the acceptance of the king as supreme ruler and leader of the reform. On closer examination, it seems the poet's intention is to highlight the fact that the consensus reached all major ranks of society. There is a reference to a numerous group of priests (*preosta heap*, 8b); a multitude of monks (*micel muneca þreat*, 9a), and then, a large gathering of wise men (*gleawra gegaderod*, 10a).[40] The poet's concern is not only to highlight the great amount of people witnessing the event (cf. *heap*, *micel*, *þreat*, and *gegaderod*) but also to offer a significant representation of contemporary society. The terms *preosta* and *muneca* thus suggest a ceremony in which a massive delegation of priests and monks underscores the church's solid back-up of this event. The poet's main aim is probably to transmit the image of a unified church unanimously welcoming the king's anointment, which points to the probable Benedictine affiliation of the text.

The term *gleawra* in the poem could simply be read as a variation on the preceding *muneca þreat*. Indeed, *gleawra* seems to be an appositional complement of *þreat*, so that it is a 'multitude of wise men gathered there' that the poet

---

[37] 'If moreover it should happen on any occasion, at the Devil's instigation, that, glorying in the arrogance of presumption, the cast-down canons should wish to plot to cast down the flock of monks which I [Edgar] have respectfully established with a shepherd in God's property, let it be done with them, and with everyone who might give them aid, blinded by some kind of bribe ...' Text and translation by Rumble, *Property and Piety*, IV.ix, p. 83.

[38] See Lapidge and Winterbottom, *WulfstW*, ch. 28.

[39] See Inge B. Milfull, *The Hymns of the Anglo-Saxon Church: A Study and Edition of the 'Durham Hymnal'* (Cambridge, 1996), no. 82, pp. 318–19.

[40] Thormann, 'The *Anglo-Saxon Chronicle* Poems', p. 69, points out that this passage is reminiscent of heroic poetry, where 'Monks take the place of thegns to compose a sort of ecclesiastical comitatus to function as witnesses for the spectacle.'

is alluding to.[41] But the group of wise men might also be pointing to a different social rank, either noblemen in general or those who form part of the king's council. I am not alone in reading *gleawra* in *The Coronation* as a possible reference to lay representatives attending the ceremony, since, as Thormann has stated 'the *þreat*, the crowd, is made up of monks and wise men in attendance'.[42] Likewise Magennis has concluded that in this poem 'the congregation is of ecclesiastics and wise men, a fact which emphasizes the coincidence of religious and secular in Edgar's rule'.[43] Æthelweard's *Chronicon* offers a clearcut distinction of the crowd of lay men and that of ecclesiastics, which supports the social contrast suggested in the *Chronicle* poem: 'Aduenit et populus pariter sine nomine turmæ,/ Quin etiam ferro syncipite rasi corona' (13–14).[44] The passage thus openly differentiates between the anonymous throng of secular people and the easily recognizable tonsured ones. In this light, with a similar two-fold reference to the group of wise men and the monks, the *Chronicle* poem is therefore probably revealing the author's monastic bias, since this passage illustrates the notion of 'the concord of court and cloister', as Deshman calls it, that is so typical of pro-reform works.[45]

The image of an idyllic England unified as a result of the general acceptance of Benedictinism is a well-known cliché in late tenth-century texts. There is no room for doubt that the reformers took considerable pains to propagandize the monarch's notable contribution to national unification. The proem to the *Regularis Concordia* famously presents Edgar as a monarch urging the strict adherence to *St Benedict's Rule* in order to achieve monastic and national unity: 'monuit ut concordes aequali consuetudinis usu, sanctos probatosque imitando patres, regularia praecepta tenaci mentis ancora seruantes, nullo modo dissentiendo discordarent; ne impar ac uarius unius regulae ac unius patriae usus probrose uituperium sanctae conuersationi irrogaret'.[46] In the preface to the *Translatio et Miracula S. Swithuni*, composed between 972 and 974,[47] Lantfred offers a eulogistic digression on Edgar which similarly stresses the unity achieved during his reign: 'Eadgaro regnante, basileo insigni atque inuictissimo, prepotente ac clementissimo necnon gloriosissimo sceptrigera ditione et feliciter gentibus imperante compluribus habitu distantibus, uoce atque moribus, diffuse in insula

---

[41] That is, for example, Whitelock's interpretation, as observed in her translation of the poem in *EHD*.

[42] 'The *Anglo-Saxon Chronicle* Poems', p. 69.

[43] Hugh Magennis, *Images of Community in Old English Poetry* (Cambridge, 1996), p. 196.

[44] 'The people came too, both crowds without name, and a troop shaven upon their heads with steel', Campbell, *Æthelweard*, p. 55.

[45] Deshman, '*Benedictus Monarcha et Monachus*', p. 210.

[46] 'He [Edgar] urged all to be of one mind as regards monastic usage, to follow the holy and approved fathers and so, with their minds anchored firmly on the ordinances of the Rule, to avoid all dissension, lest differing ways of observing the customs of one Rule and one country should bring their holy conversation into disrepute', Symons, *RC*, ch. 4.

[47] For the dating, see *The Cult of St Swithun*, ed. Michael Lapidge (Oxford, 2003), pp. 235–37.

commorantibus ...'.[48] In the tract known as King Edgar's Establishment of the Monasteries[49] Edgar's predecessor, Eadwig is precisely criticized for having provoked the division of his kingdom and the scattering of ecclesiastical possessions.[50] Further, in the same document Edgar is conversely praised for having amended the disasters of Eadwig's reign and for having reunited the kingdom.[51] In these two excerpts the repetition of the term *annesse* and the occurrence of words such as *tostencte, todælde* (twice) and *twislunge*, all of them denoting division, highlight the necessity of unity and the dangers of national fragmentation.

So far, this analysis has shown that *The Coronation* evinces a consistent employment of the imagery and diction which parallels the stylistic and rhetorical features of late tenth- and early eleventh-century texts that are closely related to the Benedictine reform. All this suggests that the poem was most likely composed not much later than 973 – when the cult of Edgar as champion of the reform was at its peak – by an author with a possible monastic affiliation. The presence of this poem in the *ASC* ABC – especially in B which is close in time to the event described – supports the contention that the poem is charged with contemporary overtones. In this sense, *The Coronation* is probably an example of praise-poetry connected to one of the monastic centres in which propagandistic hymns and liturgy were also encouraged to honour the Benedictine pantheon in which the king was possibly granted a prominent position.[52]

[48] 'With Edgar reigning, that renowned and unconquerable king, powerful and most merciful and fully glorious in his sceptre-bearing sovereignity, blessedly commanding several peoples distinct in appearance, speech and custom, dwelling widely scattered in the island ...' Text and translation from Lapidge, *The Cult*, pp. 258–59. Also, for a parallel version of this passage, see Wulfstan Cantor's *Narratio Metrica de S. Swithuno* in Lapidge, *ibid.*, lines 161–67, pp. 408–9.

[49] Whitelock maintains that this document was most likely drafted by Æthelwold as a preface to the Old English translation of *St Benedict's Rule*, see Dorothy Whitelock, 'The Authorship of the Account of King Edgar's Establishment of Monasteries', *Philological Essays: Studies in Old and Middle English Language and Literature in Honour of Herbert Dean Meritt*, ed. James L. Rosier (The Hague, 1970), pp. 125–36.

[50] Text and translation in *Councils & Synods*, pp. 142–54, at 146, and quoted in Biggs' essay, above, p. 134.

[51] *Councils & Synods*, pp. 146.

[52] Note that the *Regularis Concordia* prescribed prayers for the royal couple. Also, Edgar's mother Ælfgifu was venerated as a saint at her burial place in Shaftesbury. A reference to this is found in Lantfred's *Translatio et Miracula S. Swithuni*. See Lapidge's *The Cult*, ch. 36, pp. 328–9. It is also possible that Edgar himself was honoured as a saint after his death. Plummer, for example, states that he 'was buried at Glastonbury, where he seems to have been treated very much as a saint, undergoing translation and working a miracle in 1052 ...', see Earle and Plummer, II.162, for this citation and historical references to Edgar's saintly status, as the miracle is recorded by William of Malmesbury and other chroniclers.

The Death of Edgar

Her geendode   eorðan dreamas
Eadgar, Engla cyning,   ceas him oðer leoht,
wlitig ꝥ wynsum,   ꝥ þis wace forlet,
lif þis læne.   Nemnað leoda bearn,
5   men on moldan,   þæne monað gehwær
in ðisse eðeltyrf,   þa þe ær wæran
on rimcræfte   rihte getogene,
Iulius monoð,   þæt se geonga gewat
on þone eahteðan dæg   Eadgar of life,
10   beorna beahgyfa,   ꝥ feng his bearn syððan
to cynerice,   cild unweaxen,
eorla ealdor,   þam wæs Eadweard nama.
ꝥ him tirfæst hæleð   tyn nihtum ær
of Brytene gewat,   bisceop se goda,
15   þurh gecyndne cræft,   ðam wæs Cyneweard nama.
þa wæs on Myrceon,   mine gefræge,
wide ꝥ welhwær   Waldendes lof
afylled on foldan.   Fela wearð todræfed
gleawra Godes ðeowa;   þæt wæs gnornung micel
20   þam þe on breostum wæg   byrnende lufan
Metodes on mode.   Þa wæs mærða Fruma
to swiðe forsewen,   sigora Waldend,
rodera Rædend,   þa man his riht tobræc.
ꝥ þa wearð eac adræfed,   deormod hæleð,
25   Oslac of earde   ofer yða gewealc,
ofer ganotes bæð,   gamolfeax hæleð,
wis ꝥ wordsnotor,   ofer wætera geðring,
ofer hwæles eðel,   hama bereafod,
ꝥ þa wearð ætywed   uppe on roderum
30   steorra on staðole,   þone stiðferhþe,
hæleð higegleawe,   hatað wide
cometa be naman,   cræftgleawe men,
wise soðboran.   Wæs geond werðeode,
Waldendes wracu   wide gefrege,
35   hungor ofer hrusan;   þæt eft heofona Weard
gebette, Brego engla,   geaf eft blisse gehwæm
egbuendra   þurh eorðan westm.[53]

---

[53] 'In this year Edgar, king of the English, reached the end of earthly joys, chose for him the other light, beautiful and happy, and left this wretched and fleeting life. The sons of nations, men on the earth, everywhere in this country – those who have been rightly trained in computation – call the month in which the young man Edgar, dispenser of treasure to warriors, departed from life on the eighth day, the month of July. His son then succeeded to the kingdom, a child ungrown, a prince of nobles, whose name was Edward. And ten days before, there departed from Britain a famous man, the bishop, good from his innate virtue, whose name was Cyneweard. Then in Mercia, as I have heard tell, widely, almost everywhere, the praise of the Ruler was cast down to the ground; many of the wise servants of God were dispersed. That was a great cause of mourning for any who bore in

Unlike *The Coronation*, the association of *The Death of Edgar* with late tenth-century praise-poetry and Benedictinism is more difficult to demonstrate, since this text apparently lacks structural cohesion, as has been pointed out by some editors. Dobbie for example contrasts this poem with the other *Chronicle* panegyrics stating that *The Death* 'deals not with a single event of national significance, but with all the important happenings of the year 975'.[54] In his edition of *Brunanburh* Campbell likewise suggested that the first twelve lines of *The Death* might constitute a poem in itself. He also noted that, being of 'inferior quality', the remaining lines were possibly added by the chronicler.[55]

The Death certainly presents two parts that can be clearly distinguished. On the one hand, the first section (lines 1–12) is close to traditional obituary poetry, as the major topic is the king's death with minimum reference to the subsequent accession of his son Edward. On the other, a second section (lines 13 to the end) offers an account of apparently disparate events: the exile of Cyneweard, bishop of Wells; the scattering of the monks in Mercia; the banishment of Oslac, earl of Northumbria; the allusion to the ominous comet; a subsequent great famine; and, finally, God's providential re-establishment of prosperity. A separate analysis of these two parts may however prove that they work as a harmoniously unified poem that not only adheres to the encomiastic format but also functions as a poetic sequel to *The Coronation*. In addition to this, the study will also demonstrate that *The Death* exhibits several features which suggest that, like the preceding poem, this is a further piece that was probably created in the Benedictine orbit.

The first section of *The Death* presents some aspects that have been associated with the traditional genre of the obit, which could be regarded as a sub-type of the panegyric.[56] Thomas D. Hill has cited the first four lines of this poem as an example of what he calls the 'variegated obit', a topos which presents

his breast and mind an ardent love for the Creator. Then the Author of glories, the Ruler of victories, the Governor of the heavens, was too greatly scorned, when his rights were violated. Then also the valiant man Oslac was driven from the country, over the tossing waves, the gannet's bath, the tumult of waters, the homeland of the whale; a grey-haired man, wise and skilled in speech, he was bereft of his lands. Then was also revealed up in the skies a star in the firmament, which men firm of spirit, wise in mind, skilled in science, wise orators, far and wide called 'comet' by name. The vengeance of the Ruler was manifested widely throughout the people, a famine over the earth, which the Guardian of the heavens, the Prince of the angels, afterwards amended. He gave back bliss to each of the islanders through the fruits of the earth.'

54 *The Anglo-Saxon Poetic Records*, vol. 6: *The Anglo-Saxon Minor Poems*, ed. Elliott van Kirk Dobbie (New York, 1942), p. xlii.

55 Campbell, *Brunanburh*, p. 36.

56 The first section of *The Death* complies with the two major characteristics of the eulogistic genre mentioned by Townend: a notable concern with naming and the use of heroic diction. Thus, *The Death* introduces the allusion to the king's name (2a) and that of his successor (12b). This first part also makes use of typically encomiastic style, as observed in the epithets employed for Edgar (*Engla cyning*, 2a, and *beorna beahgyfa*, 10a). As in *Brunanburh* with Æthelstan and his brother Edmund, *The Death* praises both the king and his successor Edward, the latter being referred to as *eorla ealdor* (12a). See Townend, 'Pre-Cnut Praise-Poetry', pp. 353–5.

the death of a particular character – often a biblical patriarch, apostle, saint or a remarkable churchman – in a specially elaborate pattern.[57] The motif is particularly frequent in late tenth-century literature in both Old English and Latin. Among the numerous instances recorded by Hill, some of the passages are interestingly close to the diction and imagery offered by *The Death*. For example, in *The Fates of the Apostles* the account of the deaths of the disciples, especially that of St Andrew, follows a similar formulaic pattern: '[Andreas] him ece geceas/ langsumre lif, leoht unhwilen ...' (19–20).[58] In Byrhtferth's *Northumbrian Chronicle*, a parallel formula is consistently employed for the deaths of outstanding ecclesiastics: 'Eodem anno Alberht archiepiscopus ex hoc luce migravit ad aeternae lucis perennitatem. ...'[59] Æthelweard's *Chronicon* likewise offers this formulaic reference to Edgar's decease:

> Postque spiramen reddit authori
> Telluris insultus, marcescens ab ea
> Lumina cernit altitonantis,
> Omissa tandem luce corrupta,
> Anglorum insignis rex Eadgarus.[60]

Accordingly, it is quite clear that at generating the account of the king's death the author of *The Death* was following a conventional obituary pattern that often applied to saints, bishops and other prominent characters. In this sense, this poem recalls the preceding coronation piece in which Edgar's characterization as a priestly figure was consciously elaborated. The formulaic presentation of Edgar's obit in *The Death* therefore connects with the Benedictine ideological conception of the king in his double role as *rex et sacerdos*. Furthermore, it suggests that this poem participated in the well-known genre of the obit and, by extension, of the panegyric.

At the end of the first section, the troublesome period immediately following the king's death is anticipated when the poet hints at the fact that this event was unexpected, as the adjective *geonga* (8b) – referring to Edgar – suggests; also, the poem states that Edward was too young to succeed his father (*cild unwaxen*, 11b). These lines therefore serve as a transitional passage connecting to the second section, an idea that supports the assumption that the two parts should be

---

57 Thomas D. Hill, 'The "Variegated Obit" as an Historiographic Motif in Old English Poetry and Anglo-Latin Historical Literature', *Traditio* 44 (1988), 101–24, esp. pp. 116–17.

58 Translation by Hill: '[Andreas] chose the eternal, long-lasting life, light that does not pass ...'.

59 My translation: 'In that same year archbishop Alberht departed from this light to the perpetuity of the eternal light ...'. Text from *Symeonis monachi opera omnia*, ed. T. Arnold, RS 75 (London, 1882–85), II.53. For further examples of this formula in Byrthferth's work, see Hill, *op. cit.*, p. 109.

60 'And afterwards Eadgar, the distinguished king of the English, gave back his spirit to the maker of the world, and fading away from it [i.e. from the world], and having at last left this corrupted light, he saw the light of him who thunders on high', Campbell, *Æthelweard*, p. 56. Note that Campbell does not translate *insultus* 'as its sense is obscure' in the passage.

read as a single composition. The second section thus opens with the account of Cyneweard's banishment. It is not surprising that the poet chose Cyneweard as a representative victim of the anti-monastic revolt. He is specifically mentioned in *ASC* A, s.a. 964, which narrates an episode that is no doubt particularly significant in the reform process, the driving of priests from minsters and replacing them with monks. Here, Cyneweard's promotion to the abbacy of Milton Abbas (later, to the bishopric of Wells) is clearly connected to the expulsion of the clerks from the Old and the New Minsters. The reference to his banishment in the poem is therefore probably viewed as a logical consequence of the political disturbances following Edgar's death. In diction typical of praise-poetry, Cyneweard is thus valued positively as *tirfæst hæleð* (13a) and as *bisceop se goda,/ ðurh gecyndne cræft* (14b–15a). By presenting him eulogistically, the poet characterizes Cyneweard as a heroic victim of the revolt and effectively portrays his exile as a great loss for the English nation.

The poem then offers a detailed account of the anti-monastic reaction in Mercia (16–23) with an allusion to the expulsion of the monks from their monasteries in retaliation for Edgar and the reformers' strict impositions in the preceding years.[61] The phrase *gleawra Godes þeowa* (19a) now clearly refers to monks that are described as fervent servers of the Lord – *þam þe on breostum wæg byrnende lufan / Metodes on mode* (19–21a) – and, as in *The Coronation*, are said to be numerous (*fela*, 18b). A probable member of the monastic clergy, the author of *The Death* thus mournfully regrets the convulsion occasioned in the reformed church and the abusing of his devout Mercian colleagues and, in a clearly disaproving tone, laments the ominous breaking of God's law (*his riht tobræc*, 23b). The idea of Oslac's overseas banishment is next introduced (24–28). Again the emphasis is on violent social turmoil, as the verb *dræfed* (24a) echoes *todræfed* (18b) referring to the monks in the preceding lines. As with Cyneweard and the Mercian monks, the poet resorts to eulogistic language so that Oslac is described as *gamolfeax hæleð* (26b) and *wis] wordsnotor* (27a). Oslac, earl of Northumbria, was presumably influential during Edgar's reign, especially from 968 onwards, as he consistently witnessed royal charters and diplomas.[62] From the poet's perspective, Oslac, like his ecclesiastical counterpart

---

[61] See D. J. V. Fisher, 'The Anti-Monastic Reaction in the Reign of Edward the Martyr', *Cambridge Historical Journal* 10.3 (1952), 254–70.

[62] He subscribes to S 712, 712a, 716, 732–4. Interestingly, Cyneweard and Oslac jointly sign as witnesses in S807. For this, see Rumble, *Property and Piety*, no. vi. In 'The Death of Edgar (and others)', *ANQ* 4 (1965), 52–5, N. D. Isaacs has pointed out that Oslac's departure might be a reference to his death instead of his exile. However, the use of the expressions *dræfed* (24a) and *hama bereafod* (18b) rather point to severe political measures of expropriation and banishment carried out after Edgar's reign. Besides, the verb *dræfed* parallels *dræfde* in the prose entry narrating the expulsion of secular canons at Edgar's behest (964A). Also, see D. Whitelock, 'The Dealings of the Kings of England with Northumbria in the Tenth and Eleventh Centuries', *The Anglo-Saxons: Studies in Some Aspects of their History and Culture Presented to Bruce Dickins*, ed. Peter Clemoes (London, 1959), pp. 70–88.

Cyneweard, therefore possibly deserved to appear as an honourable representative of the nobility affected by the crisis following Edgar's death.

By alluding to three major social ranks (priests, monks and noblemen) in the same order found in *The Coronation*, *The Death* resembles the first poem in that it shows a preoccupation with the social repercussions caused by the event in question, the difference being that in the second poem two of the ranks (priests and noblemen) are represented by individuals rather than groups. In clear contrast to *The Coronation*, *The Death* stresses the fragmentation of society with the three-fold reference to the exile of Bishop Cyneweard, a prominent representative of the priesthood, the scattering of the monks in Mercia, and the banishment of Oslac, an outstanding nobleman. In his *Vita S. Oswaldi*, Byrhtferth describes Edgar's death and the subsequent disturbances in a similar way to that of the *Chronicle* poem:

> Obiit tam inclytus rex viii. idus Julii; cujus obitu turbatus est status totius regni, commoti sunt episcopi, irati sunt principes, timore concussi sunt monachi, pavefacti populi, clerici læti effecti sunt quoniam tempus eorum advenit. Expelluntur abbates cum monachis suis, introducuntur clerici cum uxoribus suis, et erat *error pejor priore*. Expulsus est et abbas Germanus cum aliis, et apte, ut qui erat particeps iniquitatis, fieret particeps transmigrationis. Namque scimus quia sæpe perit justus cum impio, non spiritu sed a corpore. Hæc non sunt exotica quæ dico verba sed satis cognita, quia prius a nostratibus sunt sanctæ Dei ecclesiæ vastatæ, expulsis scilicet Domini servis, qui (non) diebus non noctibus cessabant a Divinis laudibus, licet aliqui non rite fecerunt, sed tamen plurimi bene egerunt.[63]

This exerpt likewise presents the aftermath of Edgar's death as a general state of chaos affecting both the nobility and the clergy (bishops, abbots and monks) – with clerics turning back to their licentious way of life. Also, like the author of *The Death*, Byrthferth personalizes his account and, naturally from a monk's viewpoint, mentions Abbot Germanus, as a distinguished victim of the disorder.[64] Interestingly, the final reference to the expulsion of the zealous monks is close to the phraseology found in *The Death* (lines 20–21a).

---

63 'The illustrious king died on 8 July, and by his death the state of the whole kingdom was thrown into confusion, the bishops were agitated, the noblemen stirred up, the monks shaken with fear, the people terrified; the clerics were made glad, for their time had come. Abbots, with their monks, were expelled; clerics, with their wives, were introduced; and the last error was worse than the first. Abbot Germanus also was expelled along with the others – and fittingly, that he who shared in the injustice, should share in the transmigration. For we know that the just man often perishes with the wicked, not in spirit, but in body. These words which I utter are not extravagant, but well known, that before the holy churches of God were laid waste by our countrymen, when the servants of the Lord, who ceased not day and night from the divine praises, were expelled, though some did not act rightly, yet many did well' (*EHD*, p. 912).

64 The prominence of Germanus in the Benedictine movement is well attested. Germanus was a disciple of Oswald and spent several years in Fleury. He later returned from Fleury and became abbot of Winchcombe until this community was dissolved as a consequence of the the the anti-monastic reaction. Germanus and his fellow monks were then relocated at

In this context of social fragmentation, the appearance of the comet is thus a fitting allusion in *The Death*, since it was traditionally considered as a sign foretelling 'pestilence, famine, war or change of king'.[65] Right after the comet, a great famine is interpreted as 'the Ruler's vengeance' (*Waldendes wracu*, 34a) and the result of the breaking of God's law in Mercia. Similarly, the New Minster Refoundation Charter alludes to the canons' depravity as provoking *iusti uindictam iudicis* ('the vengeance of the Just Judge').[66] This imagery is in turn reminiscent of the natural upheaval occurring after Christ's death in the biblical account (Matt. 27:51). In this sense, *The Death* recalls the reference to the completion of the first millennium in *The Coronation*, since the natural disasters in the first were probably intended to associate the aftermath of Edgar's death with the apocalyptic time.

With its resonances of the Second Coming and the Final Judgment, *The Death* thus dovetails with the preceding poem. The final reference to God's providential intervention in restoring prosperity (35b–37) is also significant, since it would perfectly fit a Benedictine author concerned with transmitting the idea of a re-establishment of law and order after the critical stage following Edgar's death.[67] As a whole, with its account of the king's obit and the subsequent social disorder, *The Death* can therefore be read as a poem which counterbalances the contents of *The Coronation*.

Conclusions

As this paper has suggested, the relationship between *The Coronation* and *The Death* goes beyond their merely sharing encomiastic features, since the two poems evince a consistent use of imagery and diction that parallels the propagandistic features found in contemporary pro-reform texts. To begin with, Edgar's sacerdotal and christological status is clearly hinted at in both, as observed in the ambivalent use of epithets alluding to Christ and Edgar in *The Coronation* and in the priestly characterization of the monarch with the formulaic reference to the obit and the allusion to God's revenge as a result of the failure to keep

---

Ramsey. He later became abbot of Cholsey where he died *c.* 1013. See Michael Lapidge, 'Abbot Germanus, Winchcombe, Ramsey and the Cambridge Psalter', *Words, Texts and Manuscripts: Studies in Anglo-Saxon Culture Presented to Helmut Gneuss on the Occasion of his Sixty-Fifth Birthday*, ed. M. Korhammer (Cambridge, 1992), pp. 99–129.

[65] Michael Swanton, *The Anglo-Saxon Chronicle* (London, 1996), p. 121. See also Byrhtferth's *Enchyridion* (*c.* 1010–12) in *Byrhtferth's Enchiridion*, ed. Peter S. Baker and Michael Lapidge, EETS ss 15 (Oxford, 1995), pp. 120–1.

[66] Here the charter paraphrases Gregory the Great's *Moralia in Job*. See Rumble, *Property and Piety*, iv, p. 81 and n. 48.

[67] Cf. 'The image of a land of plenty is a commonplace of insular political thought which equated good harvests and clement weather with the rule of a righteous king; conversely, famine and hard winters were associated with an unjust ruler or one who harboured sin', Joanna Story, *Carolingian Connections: Anglo-Saxon England and Carolingian Francia c. 750–870* (Aldershot, 2003), p. 219.

His law in *The Death*. In addition, the two poems exhibit a concern with the social impact caused by the event in question. *The Coronation* manifestly puts the emphasis on the solid concord of three social ranks witnessing the ceremony whereas *The Death* highlights the rupture of that ideal unity by illustrating the political disorder produced by Edgar's death.

Also, in the two poems eschatological resonances can be discerned. In *The Coronation* the presentation of the event is clearly associated with Christ's Second Coming and in *The Death* the social and natural disorders described are deliberately compared to Doomsday. Consequently, the two poems seem to function as a diptych offering, on one hand, a positive evaluation of Edgar's coronation as a climatic moment of the reform and, on other, its temporary decline with the king's death.[68] A further reason for reading *The Coronation* and *The Death* together is their existence in a blended version in Æthelweard's *Chronicon*, where the two poems effectively merge to produce a long, solemn panegyric that fittingly honours Edgar and serves as an appropriate coda to this chronicle.

The elaborate contents and the diptych-like structure of the *Chronicle* poems, which significantly differ from the surrounding prose entries, therefore do not suggest scribal improvisation to comply with the annalistic sequence but rather an independent circulation.[69] It is possible that chroniclers could have freely used eulogistic material at hand at particular places in the annals. Significantly, the two poems appear in *ASC* ABC versions, which convey (especially B) the chronologically closest accounts of the reported events. Their presence in what seems to be the authorized southern recensions suggests that they might have been officially sanctioned as royal panegyrics associated with the contemporary reform movement.[70] By inserting the poetic pair in the *Chronicle*, clerical compilers most likely intended to honour the reform's greatest benefactor who, as a quasi-saintly figure, was thus appropriately furnished with an apotheosis-like poem – exalting the king at the peak of his career –, and a fitting obituary piece,

---

68   A similar two-fold display is presented in the Exeter Book with the *Guthlac* poems, in which *Guthlac* A is about major events in the life of the saint and B is about his death. The possible influence of hagiography in the Edgar poems is thus to be taken into account, since, as Thormann states, they 'draw upon the formulas and themes of Christian narrative and elegy, appropriating the conventions of religious poetry for secular purposes', Thormann, 'The *Anglo-Saxon Chronicle* Poems', p. 65.

69   With regard to the panegyrics of the *Chronicle*, Campbell, *Brunanburh*, p. 37, has suggested that 'Such poems must have been a popular form of composition with certain poets of the age.' See also Townend, 'Pre-Cnut Praise-Poetry', p. 353, who states that the Edgar poems, together with *Brunanburh* and *The Capture*, 'were not composed specially for the *Anglo-Saxon Chronicle*, but rather enjoyed an anterior (and possibly subsequent) circulation'.

70   Even though David Dumville in *Wessex and England from Alfred to Edgar: Six Essays on Political, Cultural, and Ecclesiastical Revival* (Woodbridge, 1992), ch. 3, has challenged the Winchester ascription of A, most scholars still think these three versions of the *Chronicle* seem to be associated with centralized authority. For the contrary view, see Bately, *MS A*, pp. xc and xxxiii, where she argues that the block of annals from 924–75 contains 'material with Winchester connexions'.

equally enhancing the king's reign as a golden age with the description of the
desolate climate of the post-Edgarian period.[71]

Apart from the *Anglo-Saxon Chronicle* poems and Æthelweard's *Chronicon*, there are no extant panegyrics of Edgar or any other tenth-century king
to corroborate the existence of an independent royal eulogistic trend. In the
case of Æthelstan, however, there are fragments of two lost Latin poems – one
celebrating his coronation and another one praising his courageous participation at Brunanburh – that were incorporated by William of Malmesbury in his
De gestis regum.[72] In this light, it may be tentatively assumed that Malmesbury
rescued these poems from a eulogistic tradition associated with kings who were
well-known benefactors of ecclesiastical interests. Similarly, the reference to
some *Bella Athelstani regis* in a thirteenth-century book-list from Glastonbury
might point to the existence of a Latin version of *Brunanburh* outside of the
Chronicle.[73] On this basis, Lapidge suspects the possible use of a Latin poem
celebrating Æthelstan's victory at Brunanburh in the passage alluding to that
battle in Wulfstan Cantor's *Vita S. Æthelwoldi*.[74] Despite their fragmentariness,
these cases may point to the existence of a eulogistic trend that was known by
authors who, like Wulfstan Cantor or Malmesbury, made use of this material
for the composition of their works. Accordingly, we may conclude that the compilers of *ASC* could have equally employed pre-existing panegyrics like *The
Coronation* and *The Death* which might have been incorporated at particular
places of the annals.

It is also quite clear that Edgar's popularity did not wane after his death
and that a eulogistic trend might have continued well after that, since the later
ASC DE versions offer either revised renderings of the preceding poems or,
perhaps, different poetic adaptations recovered from either a contemporary or an
earlier eulogistic corpus that was available at that moment. Edgar poems in the
Northern *Chronicle* recensions offer significant divergences such as the substitution of the coronation poem for a laudatory piece celebrating Edgar's accession
(959DE), attributed to Wulfstan the Homilist, which interestingly conveys a
critical reference to Edgar's excessive toleration of pagan customs at the end.
These divergences were perhaps induced by the natural change of perspective
of early eleventh-century chroniclers, who were not fully in agreement with
Edgar's policy in the preceding period.[75] The 975DE entry also dramatically
departs from the contents and the format of the ABC poems[76] but, as Bredehoft

---

[71] Cf. Plummer, *Earle's Two Saxon Chronicles Parallel*, II.152: 'Across the troubles of the
intervening years later chroniclers looked back upon the reign of Edgar, "the peaceful,"
as on a golden age'.

[72] For the poem on Æthelstan's coronation, see Joseph Stevenson, *The Church Historians
of England*, vol. 3, part I (London, 1854), ch. 133. For the Latin poem on the battle of
Brunanburh, see Stevenson, *ibid.*, ch. 135.

[73] See T. Hearne, *Iohannis Glastoniensis Chronica*, 2 vols. (Oxford, 1726), II.438.

[74] Lapidge and Winterbottom, *WulfstW*, p. 17, nn. 6 and 7.

[75] Cf. Thomas Bredehoft, *Textual Histories: Readings in the Anglo-Saxon Chronicle* (Toronto,
2001), p. 108.

[76] For example, the reference to the 'anti-monastic reaction' is presented in a prose coda.

states, it 'clearly seems to have been composed by a poet who was aware of the traditional content of the earlier *Chronicle* verse, despite the fact that he composed in a less traditional verse form.'[77] It is possible, then, that the later versions of *ASC* were still reworking or adapting earlier panegyrics in order to comply with contemporary stylistic concerns and the new political situation.

The continuity of a tradition of Edgarian praise-poetry may be supported by the writings of Ælfric, a writer of the second generation of Benedictines and a disciple of Æthelwold. In the epilogue to the book of *Judges* from the Old English version of the *Heptateuch*, Ælfric has a well-known diggression in which Edgar is praised together with his predecessors Alfred and Æthelstan.[78] Resonances of praise-poetry devoted to Edgar seem to be in Ælfric's mid-Lent homily (*LS* XIII), in which a couple of passages apparently paraphrase the images of chaos and destruction offered in *The Death*.[79] These lines may thus point to the great influence that a surviving tradition of panegyrics devoted to Edgar may have exerted on works written by ecclesiastical authors.

Finally, *The Battle of Maldon* bears witness to the continuity of praise-poetry devoted to the benefactors of the Benedictine cause. Scragg has already pointed out that we possibly owe the survival of this poem to Byrhtnoth's well-attested support of ecclesiastical interests.[80] In this light, if Byrhtnoth's active contribution to the reform explains the preservation of a poem narrating the defeat and death of this ealdorman, it seems fairly reasonable to assume that *The Coronation* and *The Death* could stand for samples of praise-poetry celebrating King Edgar as the greatest exponent of the reform movement. Accordingly, it is therefore possible that the two Edgar poems in *ASC* illustrate an incipient tradition of royal panegyrics, the development of which was probably truncated by the unfavourable political circumstances after the king's death.[81]

---

77 Bredehoft, *Textual Histories*, pp. 105–6.
78 For the text, see *The Old English Version of the Heptateuch*, ed. S. J. Crawford, EETS 160 (London, 1922; repr. with additions by N. R. Ker 1969), pp. 416–17, with a translation in *EHD*.
79 *LS* XIII, lines 12–54, pp. 294–95. Note parallelism in a preceding passage from the same work, lines 139–46.
80 *The Battle of Maldon*, ed. D. G. Scragg (Manchester, 1981), p. 18. See also *The Battle of Maldon, AD 991*, ed. Donald Scragg (Oxford, 1991), p. xii.
81 My thanks to Donald Scragg, Frederick M. Biggs, John D. Niles, Shashi Jayakumar, Michael D. C. Drout, Maria J. Mora and Rebecca Stephenson for their helpful comments on this essay.

Index

Ingram Content Group UK Ltd.
Milton Keynes UK
UKHW021913100523
421541UK00007B/261